GCSE EDITION

and

Nutrition

Anita Tull

B.Ed., M.Sc.

Oxford University Press

Oxford University Press, Walton Street, Oxford OX2 6DP
Oxford New York Toronto
Delhi Bombay Calcutta Madras Karachi
Kuala Lumpur Singapore Hong Kong Tokyo
Nairobi Dar es Salaam Cape Town
Melbourne Auckland Madrid
and associated companies in
Berlin Ibadan

First published 1983
Second edition 1987
Reprinted 1987 (twice), 1989, 1990, 1991 (twice), 1992, 1993, 1994
ISBN 0 19 832748 X

Acknowledgements

Illustrations are by Patricia Capon, Deborah Cook, Karen Daws, Illustra Design and Colin Mier.
The cover illustration is by Norman Messenger.

The publishers would like to thank the following for permission to reproduce photographs:
Paul Barnard, pp.158 and 233; Bedfordshire Area Health Authority, p.10; Belling & Co. Ltd, p.253; Birds Eye, p.147; British Egg Information Service, pp.91 (bottom left and right) and 93; British Friesian Cattle Society, p.78; British Meat, p.97; Camera Press, p.67 (right); Camera Talks/'Vitamin Deficiencies', p.26 (right); J. Allan Cash, p.72; Central Office of Information, p.162; Roger Charlesson, pp.66 (top), 109, 110, 121, 123, 131, 143, 144 and 153 (bottom); Chubb, p.276; Electrolux, pp.156 and 168; H. Fereday & Sons Ltd, p.266; Flour Advisory Bureau, pp.66 (bottom) and 67 (left); Food and Agricultural Organization, pp.27, 34 and 68; Fullwood and Bland Ltd, p.79 (top left); Richard and Sally Greenhill, p.49; Habitat, p.159; Sue Heap, p.239; H. J. Heinz Co. Ltd, p.141; Hermes Sweeteners, p.76; ICI Plastics, p.250; Raymond Irons, p.105; Lakeland Plastics, p.171; Milk Marketing Board, pp.71, 79 (top right), 80, 81 (bottom), 86 and 87; Moulinex, p.262; Oxfam, pp.6, 7; Pifco, p.154; Phillips, pp. 261 and 264; Photographs And All That, pp.136 (top right), 221 and 222; Prestige, p.153 (top); Ross Poultry, p.102; Sainsbury's, p.138; Alison Souster, pp.62, 63 and 136 (top left); Sun Alliance Insurance Group, p.18; Syndication International p.9 (left); Tefal, p.265; Tesco Stores Ltd, p. 11; Tetra Pak, p.81 (top); Thorn EMI, pp.164 and 261 (right); John Topham, p.106; Tower, p.161; Anita Tull, pp.202, 203, 209, 210, 215, 216 and 222 (right); C. James Webb, pp.23, 24, 26 (left), and 29; Thomas Wilkie, p.91 (top left).

The author and publishers would like to thank Mrs Guida Wong and Miss Ann Brown for their help in checking the manuscript. Special thanks to Judith Christian-Carter for her advice on the questions and activities for GCSE.

The charts of recommended daily intakes of nutrients in Chapter 1 are taken from: *Recommended Intakes of Nutrients in the UK*, DHSS Report no. 120 (HMSO)

Phototypeset by Tradespools Limited, Frome, Somerset
Printed in Great Britain at the University Press, Cambridge

Contents

Preface

This book is designed to provide a comprehensive text for students working towards GCSE examinations, where the main area of study is food and nutrition. The text has been revised to include information on diet and related health disorders, and on recommended dietary goals and their implications for health.

It has been written with an emphasis on the scientific aspects of the subject to enable students to understand the value of food, and the principles behind its production, storage, preparation, and use. Meal planning, practical food preparation, hygiene and safety, kitchen equipment, and the protection of the consumer are also covered.

The book is divided into five main chapters. At the end of each section within a chapter there are short revision questions for use in class or private study, and each chapter ends with a series of more structured questions and activities that require investigation and individual or group study. The unifying common themes of Home Economics, and where relevant the other major aspects of the subject (family, home, and textiles), are included in these.

Numerous diagrams and photographs are used to help explain and emphasize points. Experimental work which can be conducted in a home economics room or science laboratory is also included, to form a link between the practical and theoretical aspects of food science.

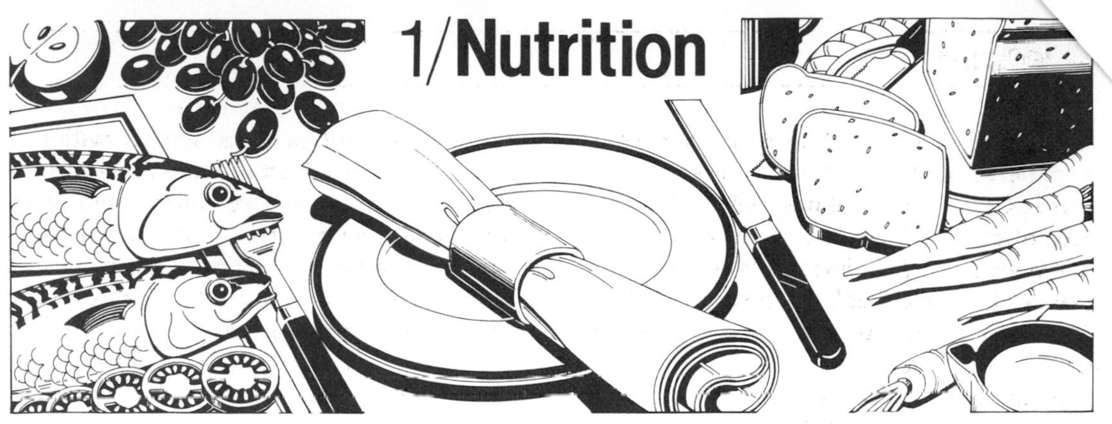

1/Nutrition

Diet and health

Food is vital to life. It can be defined as any solid or liquid substance which, when taken by the body, provides it with the necessary materials to enable it to grow, to replace worn-out and damaged parts, and to function normally.

The human body is like a complex piece of machinery in that it is prone to faults and weaknesses if it is poorly maintained. This can happen if too little or too much food is eaten, or if the daily food intake is in any way unbalanced.

Choice of food

Those people who are fortunate enough to have a choice of food to eat (i.e. people in most affluent countries), have the opportunity to choose a healthy and varied food intake, and to control their eating habits. How that choice is made, however, depends on several different factors (listed below), some of which may be more influential than health considerations.

Factors which influence food choice:

1. Personal likes and dislikes.
2. Religious and moral beliefs, social custom and tradition.
3. Food availability and variety on sale.
4. Cost.
5. Physical needs of the body.
6. Time available to shop for and prepare food.
7. Storage, preparation, and cooking facilities.
8. Our perception of food, i.e. what our senses tell us about it.
9. Food science and technology.
10. Advertising.

One way of ensuring that health and fitness are maintained, when food is plentiful, is to have an understanding of food and its effects on the body and to use this knowledge wisely.

What is nutrition?

Food, like other substances, is composed of different chemical elements, arranged in a variety of ways to form **molecules**. These molecules collectively give individual foods their flavour, colour, and texture, and affect their reaction to heat and their digestion.

In addition, there are molecules in food which the body uses in order to function correctly and to stay healthy. These are the **nutrients**. There are many different nutrients, and each has its own function in the body. Each nutrient is vital to life, and the health of an individual will suffer if any one nutrient is in short supply.

The study of nutrients and their relationship with food and living things is called **nutrition**. Most foods contain more than one nutrient, and are therefore of use to the body in several ways. Some foods, such as sugar, contain only one nutrient, and are of limited use to the body. However, no single food provides *all* the nutrients required by the body in sufficient quantities, so a variety of foods must be eaten.

The terms used in the study of nutrition include the following:

Diet means the food that a person normally eats every day. There are also special diets, e.g. slimming diets, low-fat diets.

Malnutrition means an incorrect or unbalanced intake of nutrients.

Under-nutrition means an insufficient total intake of nutrients.

Balanced diet means a diet that provides the correct amount of nutrients for the needs of an individual.

Metabolism

The human body is a complex living structure composed of millions of individual units called **cells**. Cells are grouped into systems containing various **tissues** and **organs**, each performing special functions.

Within the body, chemical reactions and changes are continually taking place. These enable the body to carry out all the necessary functions and processes, as well as to grow and to replace damaged and worn-out body cells. This complex collection of chemical reactions is called **metabolism.**

Energy is required for all metabolic reactions, and the body must remain healthy if it is to be efficient. This is mainly achieved by the intake of nutrients in food, and humans, like all living things, must have a regular supply.

Nutritional disorders owing to food shortages

It is a tragic fact that today, in an age of advanced technology and scientific knowledge, there are still many people in the world (see p. 60) whose health and quality of life suffer through lack of food, as a result of poverty, war, disaster, pollution, or other social and political factors.

When the choice of food is severely limited, as during a famine, illness and death on a large scale are the usual results. The recent and ongoing famines in countries including Ethiopia and The Sudan have been brought to the public's attention, but they are by no means the only examples of famine.

Many people in such countries receive little and often no food for long periods of time for a variety of reasons (see p. 60), and as a result suffer from malnutrition and the effects of long-term starvation.

Children in particular suffer badly, as their requirements for nutrients are high. In such a situation, they may develop one of the following conditions:

Marasmus

This name comes from the Greek word meaning 'wasting', and it mainly affects babies under one year old. The body adapts to the shortage of food by the wasting of muscles and the depletion of fat stores, so that energy is only supplied to vital organs, e.g. brain, heart. The child therefore becomes very thin and weak and the condition often results in death.

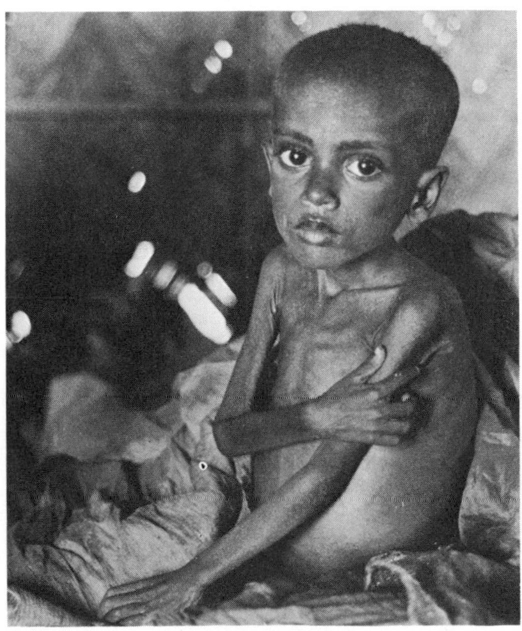

This child is suffering from marasmus.

Kwashiorkor

At one time it was thought that this condition resulted from a lack of protein in the diet. It is now known to be a poor adaptation to famine (where total food intake is reduced) and results in these symptoms:

retarded growth
chronic diarrhoea and infections
deterioration of hair, skin, and nails
retention of fluid under the skin, causing swelling (called **oedema**)
poor digestion of food

In adults, starvation results in a variety of symptoms, including:

1 Wasting of body tissue, especially adipose tissue (see p. 15).
2 Wasting of muscles and organs, such as the heart and intestines, to a size where they are too small and weak to function properly.
3 Dryness of hair and skin.
4 Oedema in the limbs and on the face.
5 Personality changes, causing restlessness, indifference, hysteria, and severe moodiness.

The treatment of starving people is difficult, not only due to lack of money and political reasons. Infections such as gastroenteritis, cholera, and pneumonia often aggravate the plight of the starving and are the final cause of many deaths.

When digestion (see p. 41) is poor, due to changes in the intestines, small, frequent feeds of specially formulated food have to be given, and recovery may be very slow. Large numbers of volunteer helpers are needed to distribute food and assist medical teams, often in very difficult situations where roads are bad and transport is scarce.

Nutritional disorders due to unwise food choice

It is an unfortunate and disturbing fact that many people in affluent societies (such as Britain), who have enough to eat, suffer from health disorders which are the result of overindulgence in food, or unwise choices of diet. An unbalanced diet, e.g. one containing too

A feeding centre in Ethiopia.

much fat or sugar, can result in a variety of nutritional disorders, including:

heart disease
obesity
tooth decay and gum disease
intestinal diseases (see p. 35)
anorexia nervosa

Heart disease

Heart disease is a major cause of death in the UK and in other countries such as the USA, Finland, and Norway. There are different types of heart disease, **coronary heart disease** (CHD) being the most common. This can eventually lead to **heart attacks.**

What happens in heart disease

To work normally, the heart needs a supply of oxygen from blood in the coronary arteries so that it can pump blood through vessels to all parts of the body.

If the coronary arteries become blocked with fatty deposits (called *atheroma*), then the blood carrying oxygen cannot reach the heart so easily, and may be prevented from doing so altogether, as the drawings on the next page show:

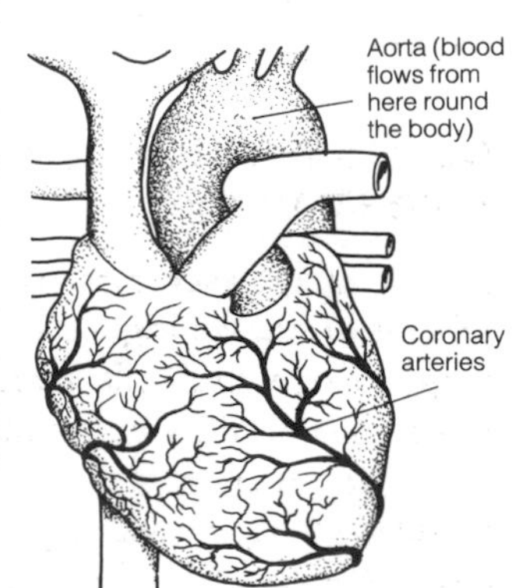

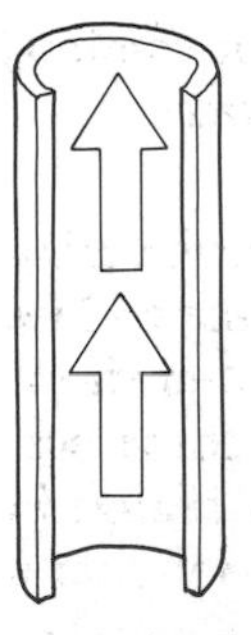

Normal artery: blood can flow through normally.

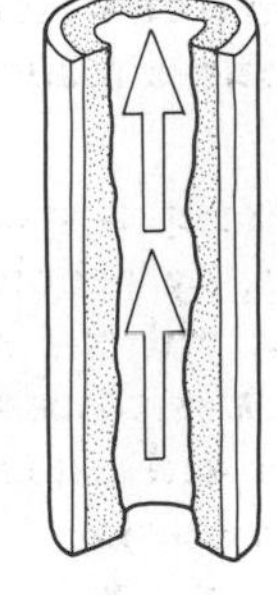

Partly blocked artery: blood flow is restricted.

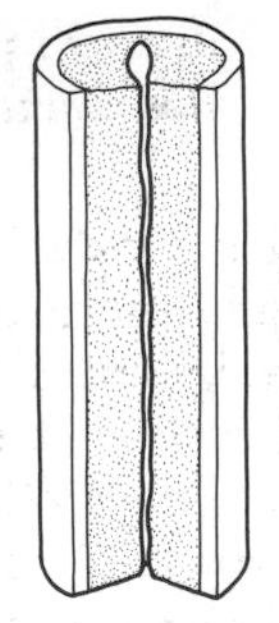

Badly blocked artery: blood cannot flow through.

As a result, the heart has to work harder to pump blood through the arteries, and it becomes partially starved of oxygen. This causes a temporary, severe, cramp-like pain across the chest, down the arm and around the neck. This is called **angina**. If there is a sudden and complete blockage in the arteries, no blood will get through, and the person will suffer a **heart attack**. The severe pain described above is worse and lasts for several hours, and the person will feel sick and faint. In the process the heart is badly damaged and afterwards will be weaker.

If the heart stops beating during the attack, this is known as a **cardiac arrest**, and unless emergency first aid is at hand, the patient will die.

Causes of heart disease

Because heart disease is such a major concern, there has been much research into its causes and ways of preventing it.

It has become clear that there is no single cause of heart disease, and it may be brought about by one or more of the following factors:

smoking
stress
high blood pressure
choice of food
lack of exercise
overweight
age
heredity

For the purposes of this book, choice of food as a factor in the cause of heart disease will be covered, but it should be emphasized that all factors have importance in this disease.

Choice of food and heart disease

It is well known that if a person eats too much food, they are likely to become overweight, which puts extra strain on the heart.

Research also shows that certain types of food, especially those containing fat, can increase the risk of heart disease in some people. Diets which contain a large proportion of saturated fatty acids (see p. 16), may lead to an increase in the blood of a substance called **cholesterol**. Cholesterol occurs naturally in the blood, but high blood cholesterol levels have been associated with an increase in the number of people suffering from CHD.

Cholesterol is known to speed up the blocking of the arteries in the heart, so treatment for heart disease usually involves reducing the number and amount of fat containing foods in the diet, as well as increasing exercise, losing weight, and giving up smoking.

Prevention of heart disease should begin in childhood, as blocking of the arteries has been found in some children. This means choosing a diet that contains only a moderate amount of foods containing fats and preventing an excessive gain in weight. A reduction in the amount of sugar eaten is also important, as excess sugar is converted into fat in the body, causing weight gain and therefore strain on the heart.

Obesity

Obesity (excessive weight gain) is a very common nutritional disorder in affluent countries, including Britain. In some cases it may be caused by hormonal disorders, but the major cause is the consumption of more food than the body needs. The excess is stored as fat in the body.

Years ago, to be overweight was considered desirable, because it indicated that a person was wealthy and could afford to live richly. This idea has now changed, and not just for fashion reasons. Obesity is undesirable and unhealthy for the following reasons:

1 Extra weight puts a strain on the heart and blood circulation.
2 Obese people are more prone to heart disease, chest infections, varicose veins, hernias, high blood pressure, diabetes, gall stones, and skin infections.
3 Extra body fat can cause complications during operations.
4 Unhappiness about being obese, and comments made by other people, may make an obese person turn to food for comfort, thus making their condition worse.

A great deal of money is spent on slimming aids and products, by people trying to lose weight quickly but with the minimum effort. However, weight loss takes time to be permanently effective and requires a change in eating habits and behaviour. Will-power and determination are needed, and an understanding of how food affects the body. An increase in exercise is also beneficial.

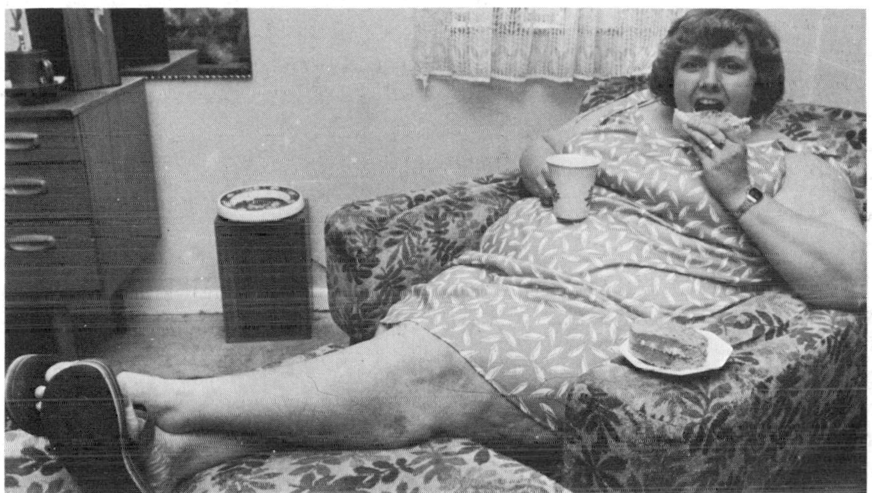

Obesity.

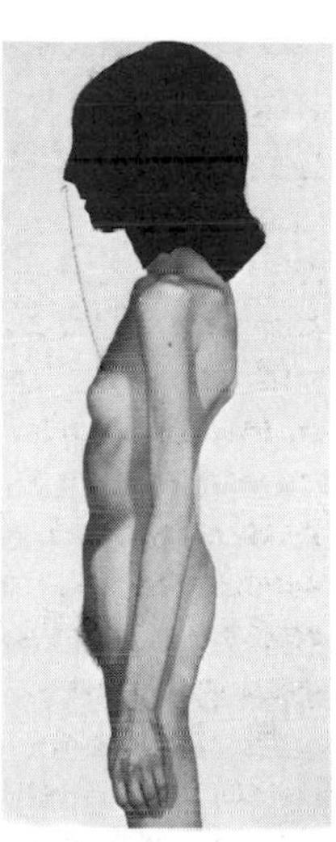

Anorexia.

Anorexia nervosa

This is sometimes called the 'slimming disease', and is the result of either excessive dieting or an eating disorder, leading to drastic weight loss, which often reaches a dangerous level. It is common in adolescent girls in countries where food is plentiful.

It may be sparked off by:

1 Emotional shock or trauma, e.g. grief.
2 Stress.
3 Unhappiness about body weight and size.
4 A need to have control over one's life by strict dieting.
5 Fear of growing up.

Often, the shape of the body is distorted in the eyes of the anorexic patient and they see themselves as much larger than they actually are. This results in them following a very strict and often misguided slimming plan, which can become obsessive. Death can occur in severe cases, and treatment is long and involves a lot of patience and perseverance by all concerned.

Tooth decay and gum disease

Most people in affluent countries will at some time have a tooth filled by the dentist because it has started to decay. Many people, even children, will lose some or all of their teeth for the same reason and will need false ones; in 1978 in England and Wales, about 30% of all adults had no natural teeth.

Dental caries is the name given to the condition where the teeth decay, usually as a result of insufficient care. Decay starts when food, in particular sweet, sticky food, is left as deposits on the teeth after eating. Bacteria

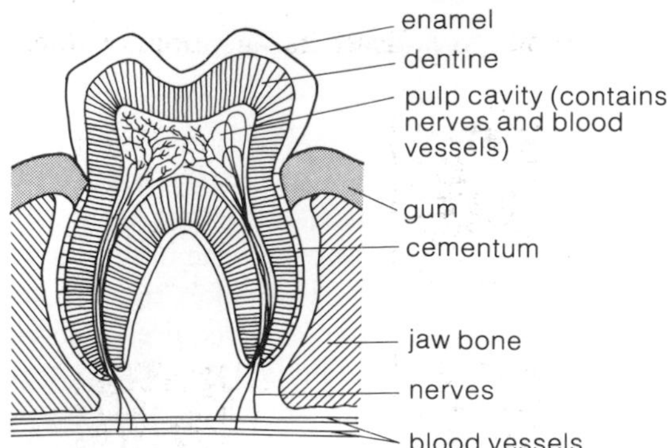

1 Decay starts in enamel.

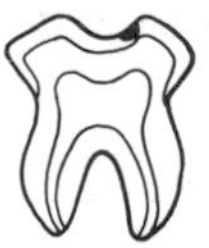

2 Decay affects dentine.

3 Decay reaches nerves.

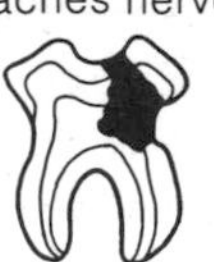

4 Infection may cause abscess.

normally present in the mouth combine with these deposits to form a film called **plaque**. The bacteria then change the sugars in the food to acids, which dissolve the protective enamel coating of the teeth, forming a hole. If unchecked, decay will continue until the whole tooth is affected and has to be removed.

Gum disease is very common, and is caused by irritating substances produced by the bacteria present in plaque, in the area where the teeth join the gums. The gums become sore and infected as a result, and in some cases the teeth may become loose. Bad breath is another symptom of this disease.

Both conditions can be prevented by:

1 Regular and thorough cleaning of the teeth.
2 Reduced consumption of sweet, sticky foods.
3 Regular dental check-ups.

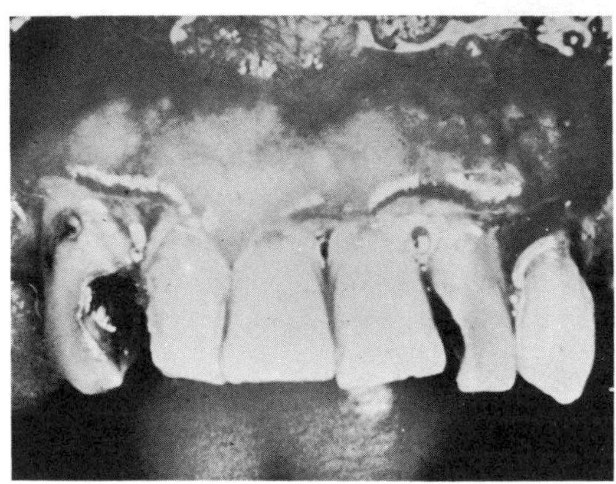

Tooth decay and gum disease.

Dietary goals

In recent years, there has been much concern about, and research into, the disorders described above. A committee of dietitians, health education officers, teachers, and relevant government bodies, known as the National Advisory Committee on Nutrition Education (NACNE) was formed to draw up a list of recommendations, or dietary 'goals', for the public to follow in order to encourage more healthy eating. These dietary goals were published in a report in 1983, and were highlighted in the Government's Green Paper on Health in 1991. They are as follows:

1 **Eat less sugar** It is recommended that the current average consumption of 38 kg (84 lbs) of sucrose (see p. 19) per person, per year should be reduced to 20 kg (44 lbs), and that only 10 kg (22 lbs) of this should be in the form of snack foods and drinks. This would help to reduce cases of dental caries and overweight, and would therefore be of benefit to health.
2 **Eat less fat** It is recommended that the amount of energy obtained from fat should be reduced from 38% to 30%. This would lower the level of cholesterol in the blood, and would therefore help to reduce the risk of heart disease.

It is suggested that only 10% of this energy should be obtained from saturated fatty acids (see p. 16), which would mean changing the types of fat eaten and used in cooking.

3 **Eat more dietary fibre** It is recommended that adults should aim to eat 30 g of dietary fibre per day, which could be obtained from foods such as fruit, vegetables, and wholegrain cereal products. This would help to prevent the development of intestinal disorders (see p. 35).

4 **Eat less salt** It is recommended that people should reduce the amount of salt they add to food, as in some cases it can cause high blood pressure, which increases the risk of heart disease.

5 **Drink less alcohol** It is recommended that the amount of energy obtained from alcohol should be no more than 4% per day, which for many people would mean substantially reducing the amount they drink every day. This would lower the risk of damage to the liver and heart, as well as lessening the social problems associated with alcohol consumption.

In order to benefit from following these dietary goals, people would need to be aware of the amounts of sugar, fat, salt, etc., that different foods contain. Many people would have to find the determination to alter their eating habits permanently.

Nutritional labelling

With dietary goals in mind, and increasing public awareness of food and its effects on health, many food manufacturers have taken steps to show the nutritional content of their products on the labels they use. Legislation is also being introduced to make it compulsory for manufacturers to list the nutritional content of a food product, as well as all the other ingredients and additives (see p. 121) it contains.

Some food retailers, such as Tesco, now publish leaflets on food and health and use symbols, like those shown below, on various foods to indicate its nutritional value:

For a nutritional label to be effective, it needs to be clearly set out so that it can be understood by the public, and help them to make an informed choice of food. This may involve the use of words, e.g. 'high in fat', 'low in sugar', and figures, e.g. 'contains 40% fat per 100 g'.

Following the dietary goals

To follow the dietary goals successfully, people firstly need to have some knowledge about which different nutrients foods contain. Food labels can help here, as well as leaflets and books containing information on food.

Ideally, healthy eating should begin in infancy, when a baby is weaned onto solid foods. This means encouraging the baby to choose low-sugar foods, and restricting the number and amount of fat containing foods it eats. This needs to be carried on into childhood, teaching the child about which foods to choose, and encouraging sound eating habits.

Further suggestions for following the dietary goals are listed below:

Reducing sugar consumption

1 Avoid adding sugar to drinks, and choose soft drinks that have a reduced sugar content or contain sugar substitutes (see p. 75).
2 Include more naturally sweet foods, e.g. fruits, into meals, without adding more sucrose to them.
3 Use sugar-reduced products, such as fruit

canned in fruit juice, jams, and other spreads, which are now available in many shops.

4 Gradually cut down on the amount of sugar normally added to items such as custard, breakfast cereals, cakes and biscuits, etc.

5 Restrict the consumption of sweets and other sugar-containing snacks, so that they become a treat rather than a habit.

Reducing fat consumption

1 Use low-fat dairy products, e.g. yogurt (can be used as a substitute for cream in many dishes), cheeses (e.g. cottage), skimmed and semi-skimmed milk in cooking and for normal consumption.

2 Make more use of poultry and white fish, both of which contain less fat than red meat.

3 Avoid fried foods, and grill or bake them instead.

4 Make more use of low-fat spreads as a substitute for margarine and butter.

5 Become aware of the many foods, such as sausages, cakes, biscuits, crisps, and pastries, which have a high 'hidden' fat content (i.e. fat which is not visibly obvious, but is included in their ingredients), and restrict the consumption of these.

6 Make more use of some of the fat-reduced products that are now available, e.g. canned fish in brine, low-fat salad dressings, etc.

Increasing dietary fibre consumption

1 Make more use of wholegrain cereal products in cooking, e.g. wholemeal flour instead of white, wholegrain rice, wholemeal pasta, etc.

2 Include more wheatmeal or wholemeal bread instead of only white bread in meals.

3 Eat more fresh fruit and vegetables.

4 Choose breakfast cereals and snacks which are rich in fibre and, preferably, low in sugar.

5 Add a little bran to soups and casseroles.

6 Make more use of pulses (see p. 115), many of which are rich in dietary fibre.

Reducing salt intake

1 Try alternative flavours to salt (e.g. spices and herbs) when cooking, or, if a salty flavour is required, make use of salt substitutes which contain less sodium (see p. 32).

2 Reduce the amount of salt added to cooked items, such as vegetables, soups, etc, and the amount added to meals at the table.

3 Cut down on salty snack foods (e.g. roasted peanuts and crisps).

4 Reduce the number and amount of foods eaten, that have salt added as part of their processing, e.g. bacon, cheese, sausages, cooked meats, smoked fish, canned vegetables in brine, etc.

Reducing alcohol consumption

1 Become aware of the alcohol content of different types of drinks.

2 Where possible, dilute alcoholic drinks with fruit juices, mineral waters, etc.

3 Make a positive effort to limit the number and amount of alcoholic drinks taken at any one time.

4 Try some of the alcohol-reduced beverages that are now available.

The nutrients

There are five main groups of nutrients:

protein
fat
carbohydrate
vitamins
minerals

Each group has several members, which each have their own chemical names.

Water can also be called a nutrient, as it is vital to life.

Some foods contain another substance, called **dietary fibre** (sometimes also called fibre, unavailable carbohydrate, or roughage), which is not strictly a nutrient, but is still of importance to the body. It will be discussed separately.

Protein

Functions

Our bodies are composed of millions of cells which are constantly being replaced and repaired. As the body grows, new cells are added to increase body size.

Each cell contains a substance called **protoplasm,** which amongst other things contains protein. Protein is vital for the **growth, repair,** and **maintenance** of the body.

Protein can also be used to provide the body with energy, once it has been used for its main functions of growth and repair.

Chemistry

There are many different proteins and they are all complex molecules which contain these elements:

oxygen (O)
carbon (C)
hydrogen (H)
nitrogen (N)

and sometimes:

sulphur (S)
phosphorus (P)

The protein molecules are arranged in the form of small units joined together like links in a chain. These units are called **amino-acids.**

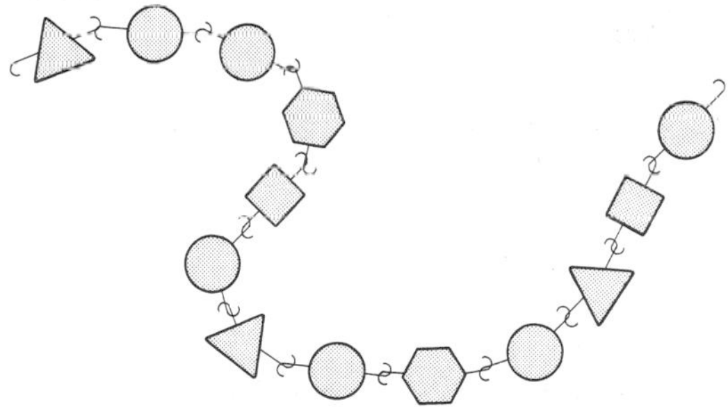

Each amino-acid has its own chemical name, and at least twenty-two different amino-acids are now known. Different proteins consist of a varying number and combination of these amino-acids, which means that a vast selection of proteins is possible. (Compare this to the number of words that can be made from the twenty-six letters of the alphabet.)

Sources

Of these twenty-two amino-acids,
ten are **essential** for growth and repair in **children.**
eight are **essential** for repair and maintenance in **adults.**

This means that they must be obtained from foods containing protein in the diet, as they cannot be made in the body.

Proteins that contain all the **essential amino-acids** in sufficient quantity are said to be of **high biological value** (HBV). They are sometimes also called **complete** proteins.

HBV proteins are found mainly in animal foods:

meat	cheese
fish	milk
eggs	

Proteins that lack one or more of the essential amino-acids are said to be of **low biological value** (LBV). They are sometimes also called **incomplete** proteins.

LBV proteins are found mainly in plant foods:

cereals, e.g. wheat, rice, oats
pulses, e.g. peas, beans, lentils
some nuts
vegetables (a little)

There are two exceptions to this:

Soya beans (plant protein) contain HBV protein.

Gelatine (animal protein) contains LBV protein.

This does not mean that LBV protein foods are inferior to HBV protein foods. Indeed, if a combination of LBV foods are eaten together, e.g. beans on toast (wheat), or lentil soup with bread, then the essential amino-acids which are limited in one are provided by the other. In this way they can compensate for each others' deficiencies to provide a sufficient supply of essential amino-acids.

Animal protein foods are expensive to produce, and recently there have been attempts to manufacture alternative protein-rich foods from e.g. soya beans. This is discussed in greater detail on pp. 108–9.

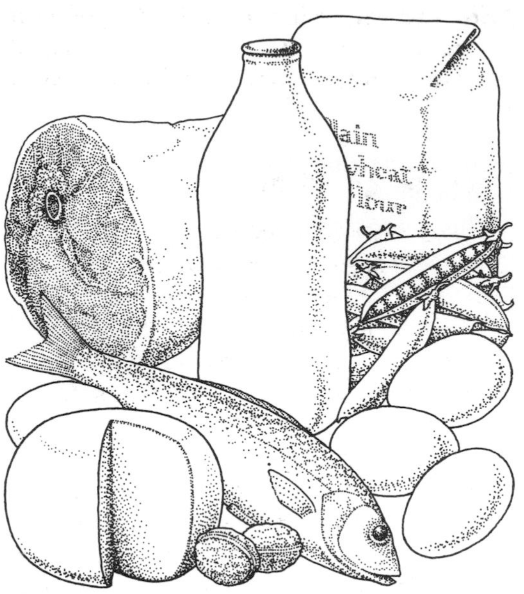

Protein names

Each protein has its own chemical name. Some examples are:

Protein name	Where found
collagen	meat, fish (connective tissue)
myosin	meat, fish (muscle tissue)
elastin	meat (muscle fibres)
caseinogen	milk, cheese
lactalbumin	milk
lactoglobulin	milk
ovalbumin	egg white
mucin	egg white
lipovitellin	egg yolk
gluten (glutenin)	wheat
gliadin	wheat
zein	maize
hordenin	barley

Protein requirements

Everyone needs some protein in their daily diet, even when they have stopped growing, but at certain times of our lives these needs vary. For example:

Babies and children require a lot of protein as they are growing rapidly.

Adolescents require protein for their rapid spurt of growth.

Pregnant women require more than normal to cater for the growing baby.

Nursing mothers require more than normal for milk production during breast-feeding (lactation).

Protein is required at all other times for body maintenance, repair, and the growth of hair, nails and skin.

The Department of Health and Social Security publishes lists of 'Recommended Daily Intakes of Nutrients'. These are based on research into the needs of people of different age groups and societies, and are intended to be used as guide-lines by doctors and dietitians in the assessment of diets.

In the case of protein, the Recommended Daily Intakes are as follows:

	grams per day
Children	
0–2 years	30
2–5 years	40
5–9 years	50
Adolescents	
Boys	70–75
Girls	58
Adults	
18–35 years (sedentary)	55–68
18–35 years (fairly active)	63–75
18–35 years (very active)	63–90
75 + years	48–53
women (pregnant)	60
women (lactating)	68

Deficiency

A deficiency of protein in Britain is rare, but in poor countries it may contribute to the symptoms associated with famine (see p. 6).

Effect of heat

When proteins are heated, their chemical structure is **denatured** (changed). This is a permanent alteration and cannot be reversed. As heating continues, proteins **coagulate** (set), and generally become less soluble.

If overheated, they become less digestible. The effect of heat on specific proteins is shown below.

Meat

Dry or moist heat
Collagen and elastin molecules start to coagulate at 60°C, contracting as they do so, and causing the meat to shrink. Under 100°C, coagulation is slow; over 100°C, coagulation is rapid and the protein becomes hard and less digestible. In the presence of moisture, collagen is converted into the protein gelatin which is soluble.

Milk

Boiling or baking
Lactalbumin and lactoglobulin coagulate gradually as milk is heated, and form a 'skin' on the surface.

Cheese

Dry heat
Protein coagulates rapidly to a rubbery texture and finally to a crisp and less digestible state.

Egg white

Dry or moist heat
At 60°C coagulation starts when ovalbumin denatures into a solid, and continues until the whole white is solid and opaque.

Egg yolk

Dry or moist heat
Proteins start to denature at 70°C, and continue to do so until the yolk becomes dry and hard.

Wheat

Dry heat
Gluten starts to coagulate at 80°C, and continues to do so until the heating ends. In this way it helps to form the structure of cakes, bread, and other baked wheat products, during baking. (See pp. 66–7.)

Denaturation of protein is also brought about by:
Mechanical agitation, as in the whipping of egg white, which causes ovalbumin to set partially.
Acids, alcohol, as in the marinading of meat in vinegar, wine, etc., and the clotting of caesinogen in the stomach which is aided by acid.

Revision questions

1. What are the functions of protein?
2. What are the elements of which proteins are composed?
3. What is an amino-acid?
4. What is an essential amino-acid?
5. How many essential amino-acids do
   a adults require?
   b children require?
6. What are high biological value proteins, and in which foods are they mainly found?
7. What are low biological value proteins, and in which foods are they mainly found?
8. How can LBV protein foods be made more valuable to the body?
9. Name two proteins found in
   a meat
   b milk
   c egg
   d cereals
10. Explain why the following have a high requirement for protein:
    a children
    b pregnant women
    c adolescents
11. Why are Recommended Daily Intakes lists published?
12. What is denaturation?
13. Describe the effect of heat on meat, egg, and milk protein.

Fat

Functions

1 Provides a convenient and concentrated source of energy, supplying more energy than the same weight of carbohydrate or protein. (See p. 37.)
2 Surrounds and protects certain vital organs, e.g. kidneys, glands.
3 Forms an insulating layer (adipose tissue) beneath the skin to help preserve body heat and protect the skeleton and organs.

4 Provides a source of the fat-soluble vitamins A, D, E, and K.
5 Provides a reserve of energy for long-term storage, which can be utilized if energy intake is restricted.
6 Provides texture and flavour in food and helps to make it palatable.
7 Foods containing fat provide a feeling of fullness (satiety) after a meal, as fat digestion is slow.

Chemistry

Fats and oils have the same basic chemical structure, but their physical appearance differs at normal room temperature:

Fats are **solid** at room temperature.
Oils are **liquid** at room temperature.

For the purposes of this section, the word 'fat' refers to both.

Fats are composed of the elements:
carbon
hydrogen
oxygen

These are formed into two types of substance, called **glycerol** and **fatty acids.**
These combine to form **fat molecules** in the following way:

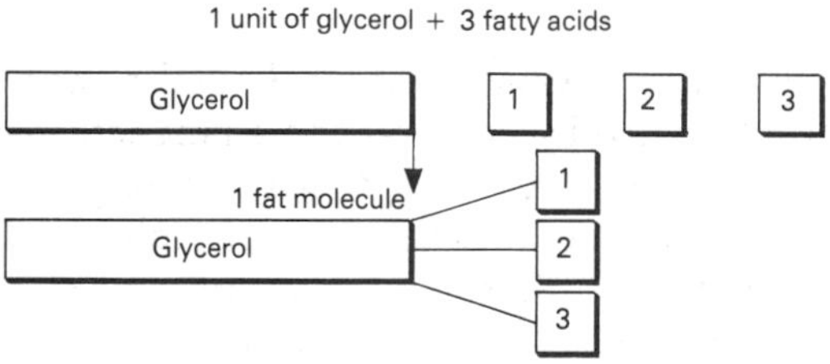

1 unit of glycerol + 3 fatty acids

Glycerol 1 2 3

1 fat molecule

Glycerol 1 2 3

At least forty different fatty acids are known, each with its own chemical name. They may be either **saturated** or **unsaturated,** according to the way in which their carbon and hydrogen atoms are arranged.

Saturated fatty acids

All the carbon atoms are **saturated** with hydrogen atoms and cannot accept any more:

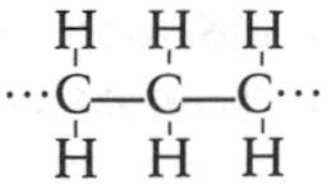

```
  H  H  H
  |  |  |
…C—C—C…
  |  |  |
  H  H  H
```

Examples:	*Found mainly in:*
butyric acid	milk, butter
palmitic acid	animal fats
lauric acid	dairy foods, coconut oil
stearic acid	beef fat

Saturated fatty acids are predominantly present in fats which are solid at room temperature.

Unsaturated fatty acids

Some of the carbon atoms are joined to others by a **double bond** and so are not completely saturated with hydrogen atoms. They could therefore accept more hydrogen atoms:

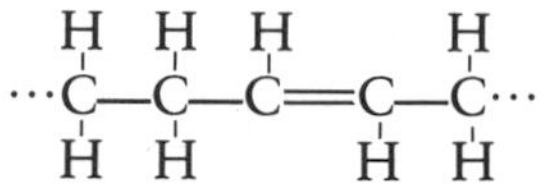

```
  H  H  H     H
  |  |  |     |
…C—C—C═C—C…
  |  |     |  |
  H  H     H  H
```

Monounsaturated fatty acids have one double bond in the molecule, e.g. oleic acid, found in most animal and plant fats and oils, especially olive oil.
Polyunsaturated fatty acids have more than one double bond in the molecule, e.g. linoleic acid, linolenic acid, both found mainly in vegetable oils. Unsaturated fatty acids occur mainly in oils.

Different combinations of fatty acids combine with glycerol to form a wide variety of fat molecules.

Sources

Most fats contain a mixture of saturated and unsaturated fatty acids, but in widely varying proportions. This affects the hardness of the fat. Fats and oils are obtained from both plants and animals.

Animal sources

Meat	solid fats,
lard, bacon fat (pigs)	containing
suet (cattle)	mostly saturated
visible and invisible fat	fatty acids
Dairy produce	
fat in milk and milk products (butter, cream, cheese)	a mixture of unsaturated and short chain
egg yolk	saturated fatty acids, as oils

Source	Type of fat
Fish	
fish-liver oils (cod, halibut) oily fish (tuna, herring, salmon, pilchard, etc.)	oils, containing mostly unsaturated fatty acids
Plant sources	
Seeds cotton, maize, sesame, olive, soya, sunflower, etc. *Nuts and pulses* brazil, peanut, etc. *Kernels* palm etc.	oils, containing mostly poly-unsaturated fatty acids
Fruits avocado pear (oil in flesh)	mostly mono-unsaturated fatty acids

Fat is present in food either as visible or invisible fat:

Visible fat
(easy to detect in food)
fat on meat
butter, margarine
lard, suet
cooking fats and oils

Invisible fat
(a constituent part of food, mixed with other ingredients and difficult to detect)
lean meat – fat within muscle (marbling)
egg yolk
flesh of oily fish
nuts, seeds, fruits
prepared foods, e.g. pastry, cakes, biscuits, chocolate, sauces
fried foods, e.g. fritters, croquettes

Low-fat foods.

Requirements

An intake of fat in the diet is essential as some fatty acids are required for important functions in the body, e.g. in cell membranes. These **essential fatty acids** must be provided by the diet as they cannot be made in the body.

Fat-soluble vitamins A, D, E, and K must also be provided by food containing fat.

A fat-free diet is not only difficult to prepare but is also very unpalatable. The amount of fat that people eat varies greatly according to individual taste and according to traditional methods of food preparation in different societies. In Britain, our total fat consumption has risen steadily since the beginning of this century (except during food rationing in the Second World War), and currently, fat provides an average of 35–45% of our total energy requirements. For total energy requirement figures, see p. 40.

There have also been major changes in the types of fat that we eat. We eat more invisible fat today, in the form of crisps, snacks, cakes, and biscuits, and more fat from plant sources is consumed, as oils and margarine.

This increase in fat consumption has led to concern for our health, as it has been linked to a variety of diseases including obesity (see pp. 8–9) and heart disease.

Effect of heat

When heated, solid fats melt to become liquid oils. As heating continues, the oil becomes thinner in consistency, and begins to bubble. At very high temperatures, the fat molecules begin to decompose into glycerol and fatty acids. A blue haze can be detected, then smoke, and soon after this, the fat ignites and burns rapidly.

Fried foods readily absorb fat and this increases their energy value (see pp. 37–8). Fat-soluble vitamins are not affected by heat.

When fat catches fire, it burns rapidly.

Revision questions

1 What are the functions of fat in the body?
2 What is the difference between fats and oils?
3 What are the elements of which fats are composed?
4 How are fat molecules composed?
5 Name three saturated and three unsaturated fatty acids.
6 Name four plant and four animal sources of fat.
7 What is the difference between visible and invisible fat?
8 Why is an excessive intake of fat undesirable?
9 What factors are associated with coronary heart disease?
10 Describe the effect of heat on fat.

Carbohydrate

Functions

The complex metabolism of the body requires a source of **energy** in order for it to function. Carbohydrate is a very important source of energy and it acts as a 'protein sparer', so that protein can be used for its primary functions (see p. 13.)

Chemistry

There are several types of carbohydrate, but they all contain three elements:

carbon oxygen hydrogen.

Oxygen and hydrogen are present in the same proportion as for water (H_2O), hence the term 'hydrate'.

H
> O
H

Sources

Carbohydrates are produced mainly by plants during the process of **photosynthesis**, in which the following reaction occurs:

carbon dioxide + water
(CO_2) ↓ (H_2O)
energy from sunlight
↓
carbohydrate + oxygen

The carbohydrate produced by the plant is stored for future use.

Classification of carbohydrates

Monosaccharides

These are sometimes called **simple sugars**, as they are the common base units of which other carbohydrates are built, and they are chemically sugars. They are soluble in water and of varying sweetness.

There are three main monosaccharides:

Fructose

Fructose is sometimes called 'fruit sugar', because it is found predominantly in fruits, plant juices, and honey.

Glucose
Glucose is the form of carbohydrate that the body uses for energy, and all other carbohydrates are converted into glucose during digestion. The glucose is then circulated around the blood stream to the body cells.

Glucose is found in ripe fruits and some vegetables, e.g. onions, beetroot. It is also available commercially in powdered, liquid, or tablet form. It provides a fast source of energy and is often taken by athletes for this reason.

Galactose
Galactose is found in the milk of mammals, where it forms part of the milk sugar, lactose.

Disaccharides

These are sometimes called **double sugars**, as they are composed of two monosaccharide units joined together. They are soluble in water.

There are three main disaccharides:

Sucrose
Sucrose is formed from one unit of **glucose** and one unit of **fructose**:

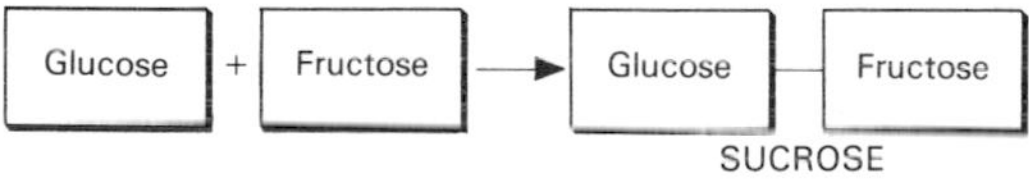

Sucrose is most commonly used in cookery, and is obtained by refining sugar cane or beet. It is also present in some fruits and vegetables.

Lactose
Lactose is formed from one unit of **glucose** and one unit of **galactose**:

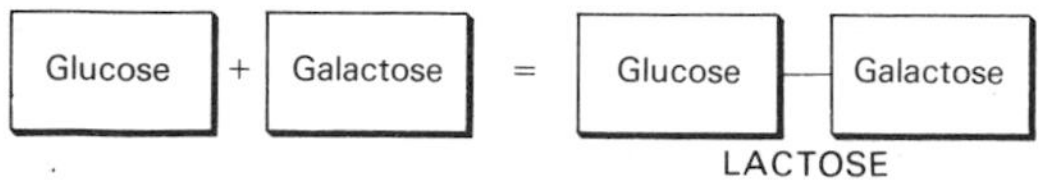

Lactose is found in the milk of mammals, to supply the infant with a source of energy. It is not as sweet as sucrose.

Maltose
Maltose is formed from two units of **glucose** joined together:

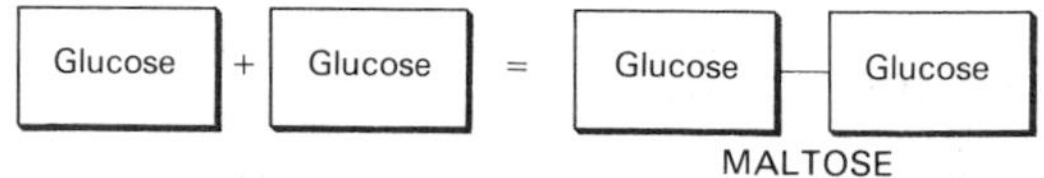

It is sometimes called 'malt sugar', and is found in cereals such as barley, where it is formed during germination.

During digestion, disaccharides are broken down to monosaccharides before being absorbed into the bloodstream.

Polysaccharides

These are formed from a varying number of monosaccharide units – the prefix 'poly' meaning 'many'. They are usually insoluble in cold water and are tasteless.

There are five main polysaccharides:

Starch
Starch is formed from many glucose units joined together like links in a chain:

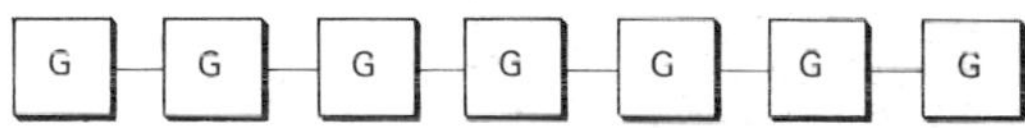

It is formed during photosynthesis in plants as a chief food reserve, in particular in root vegetables, cereals, and pulses.

During digestion, the chains of glucose units are broken down into smaller chains, then into disaccharides, and finally into single glucose units, which are absorbed into the blood.

Dextrin
Dextrin is formed when foods containing starch, e.g. bread, are baked or toasted. The dextrin forms part of the crust on such foods and is more soluble than starch.

Cellulose
Cellulose is formed by plants from glucose units joined together in such a way that a strong, structural material is produced. The plant uses this for support in stems, leaves, husks of seeds, and bark. It is found in

virtually all foods of plant origin. Despite being composed of glucose, it cannot be digested by man, but it is of great value to the body as dietary fibre (see p. 34).

Pectin

Pectin is formed by some plants, e.g. plums, apples, in their fruits and roots. It is a complex polysaccharide. It forms gels in water and is responsible for setting jam (see p. 233). It can be commercially extracted for this purpose.

Glycogen

Glycogen is formed after digestion in man and other animals. To ensure that the body has a reserve of energy that can be quickly utilized, some glucose is converted into glycogen for temporary storage in the liver and muscles. When energy is required, it is converted to glucose.

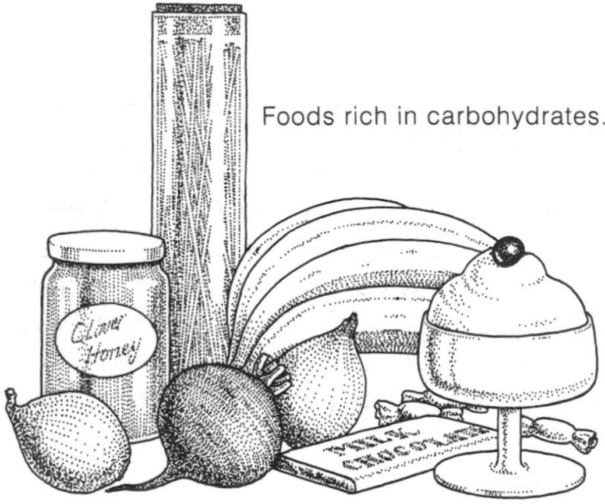

Foods rich in carbohydrates.

Carbohydrate requirements

Carbohydrate should be used in preference to protein as an energy supplier, so that protein can be used for body growth and repair. Protein- and carbohydrate-rich foods are usually eaten together for this reason, e.g. meat and potatoes, bread and cheese.

If more carbohydrate than the body requires is eaten, then the excess will be converted into fat and stored under the skin. This is one of the major causes of obesity (see pp. 8–9). The consumption of too many carbohydrate-based snack and convenience foods, e.g. sweets, chocolate, instant meals, and puddings, may lead to an excess intake of energy from carbohydrate. These foods should therefore be eaten in moderation.

For total energy requirement figures, see p. 40.

Diabetes mellitus

Glucose is carried in the blood to all body cells to supply them with energy. In order for glucose to enter the cells, a hormone, **insulin**, is required to act as a chemical 'key'.

Insulin is produced by the pancreas, and if insufficient is made, then the glucose will stay in the bloodstream and will eventually spill over into the urine where it will be detected. In the meantime the cells will have to obtain energy from the body fat stores, which will result in a loss of weight and general weakness.

This condition is called **diabetes mellitus** (diabetes for short), and the patient is said to be **diabetic**. It may be present at birth or may develop at any age.

Diabetes has to be kept under control as there is no real cure. In severe cases, insulin injections (given daily) and a special diet are prescribed, to ensure that the carbohydrate intake does not exceed the dose of insulin. In milder cases, a carbohydrate-controlled diet and tablets may be sufficient.

Effect of heat on carbohydrate

Sugar

Dry heat

Sugar first melts, then caramelizes and finally burns, leaving a black residue.

Wet heat

Sugar first dissolves, then becomes a syrup which caramelizes, and finally burns when the water has evaporated.

Starch

Dry heat

Starch changes to dextrin.

Wet heat

Starch grains first soften, then absorb water and swell, causing some to rupture. The starch then dissolves to form a paste.

Revision questions

1 Why does the body require carbohydrate?
2 What are the elements of which carbohydrates are composed?
3 What is photosynthesis and why is it important?
4 Name three monosaccharides and give their sources.
5 Name three disaccharides, describe their composition, and give their sources.
6 Name four polysaccharides, describe their composition, and give their sources.
7 What happens if too much carbohydrate is eaten?
8 What is diabetes mellitus and how can it be treated?
9 Describe the effects of heat on sugar and starch.

Food tests

It is possible to test different foods for the presence of protein, fat, and carbohydrate by using specially prepared chemical solutions. These should only be used in a science laboratory.

Test for protein

The **Biuret test** is used. The food to be tested should be made as liquid as possible (e.g. milk, egg white, cheese liquidized with water) and placed in a test tube. An equal volume of 2 molar sodium hydroxide plus 1 drop of 0·1 molar copper (II)sulphate solution is added. A mauve colour develops if protein is present.

Test for fat

Ethyl alcohol is used. The food to be tested, e.g. cooking oil, egg yolk, finely grated cheese, crushed nut, should be placed in a clean, dry test tube with some ethyl alcohol (2 drops of oil to 5 cm^3 of ethyl alcohol), and thoroughly shaken to dissolve the fat. The solution is then poured into another test tube containing a little water.

A cloudy white emulsion indicates the presence of fat.

Tests for carbohydrate

Test for starch

Iodine solution is used. The food to be tested, e.g. starch powder, potato, flour, ground rice, should be heated in water and boiled to cook the starch. When cool, a few drops of iodine solution should be added.

If the mixture turns dark blue, this indicates that starch is present.

Test for glucose

Benedict's solution is used. The food to be tested, e.g. glucose syrup, banana, etc., should be boiled in a test tube with a little of the Benedict's solution.

It will change from clear blue to opaque green, then yellow, and then to a brick red colour. This indicates the presence of glucose. Care should be taken as this may boil out of the tube.

Vitamins

Vitamins are a group of different chemical substances, most of which have been identified during this century as vital to the body. At first, scientists labelled each with a letter, but once their chemical composition was ascertained, it was possible to give them all names. However, the letter classification is still in use.

The body requires only small amounts of each vitamin, but as it cannot make most of them itself, they must be supplied by food. In general, vitamins are required to regulate the maintenance and growth of the body, and to control metabolic reactions in cells.

A diet lacking in one or more vitamins will result in specific **deficiency diseases**. Many of these occur in poor countries.

Vitamins can be classified according to the substances in which they dissolve. There are two groups:

1 **Fat-soluble vitamins**: vitamins A, D, E, and K.
2 **Water-soluble vitamins**: vitamin C and the vitamin-B complex.

Fat-soluble vitamins

Retinol (Vitamin A)

Functions

1 Required to make a substance called **visual purple**, which is formed in the retina of the eye to enable it to see in dim light.
2 Required to keep the **mucous membranes** in the throat and the digestive, bronchial, and excretory systems moist and free from infection.
3 Required for the maintenance and health of the skin.
4 Required for the normal growth of children, particularly the bones and teeth.

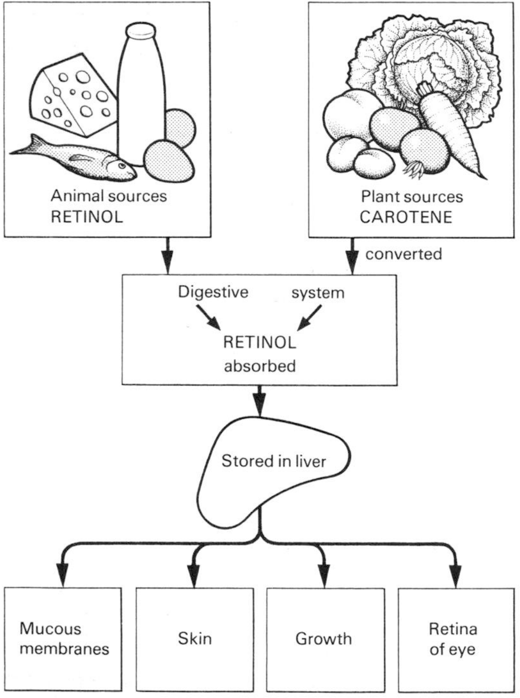

Functions of vitamin A.

Sources

Vitamin A is found as **retinol** in animal foods, particularly:

milk, cheese, eggs (yolk), butter
oily fish, e.g. herring, pilchard, sardine
liver, kidney, cod- and halibut-liver oil

Vitamin A is found as **carotene** in plant foods, particularly:

carrots, spinach, watercress, parsley, cabbage, prunes, apricots, tomatoes

Carotenes form the yellow/orange pigments in plants, and during digestion they are converted into retinol. Two parts of carotene are required to form one part of retinol.

Grass contains carotenes, and during the summer when more carotene is present, milk from cows will contain more vitamin A than in winter.

Vitamin A is added by law to margarine to ensure that people obtain enough.

Requirements

As vitamin A is fat-soluble, it can be stored in the body, mainly in the liver, so a daily supply is not always necessary.

The recommended daily intakes are:

Children	µg*/day
0–2 years	350
2–5 years	300
5–9 years	350
Adolescents	
Boys and girls	725
Adults	
18–35 years	750
35+ years	750
women (pregnant)	750
women (lactating)	1200

Special requirements

Children need plenty for growth and development.

Expectant and nursing mothers Extra vitamin A is needed for the development of the baby and the maintenance of the mother.

People who cannot digest and absorb fat well Vitamin A may have to be adminstered as an injection to overcome this.

Deficiency

1 The retina ceases to make visual purple, and vision in dim light is impaired, leading to **night blindness**. In severe cases the structure of the eye deteriorates and eventually ruptures, causing total blindness.

*µg = microgram

This occurs frequently in poor countries, such as India, where the diet is deficient in vitamin A. Consequently the liver does not build up a store of the vitamin. During pregnancy, many women develop a deficiency, as the growing baby is provided with any vitamin A that is available. Many babies develop a deficiency soon after birth as they do not receive an adequate supply from food. Every year, many children go blind as a result.

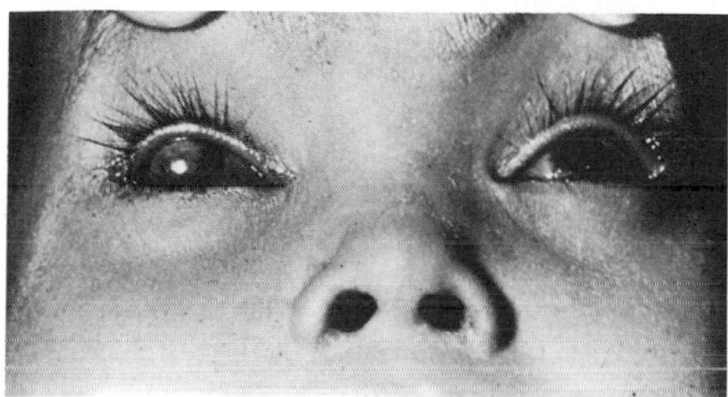

Blindness caused by vitamin A deficiency.

2 The skin and mucous membranes become dry and infected, and resistance to disease is reduced.
3 Growth of children is retarded.

NB Too much vitamin A in the diet is poisonous to the body as it is stored, and this can affect the skin and joints, especially in children.

Stability in food preparation

Retinol and carotene are both insoluble in water, and are unaffected by normal temperatures and methods of food preparation.

Cholecalciferol (Vitamin D)

Functions

Required for the proper formation of bones and teeth, which contain large amounts of the minerals **calcium** and **phosphorus**. Vitamin D helps to promote the absorption of these minerals. After digestion, they are absorbed from the small intestine into the blood, which takes them to the bones and teeth to be deposited.

Sources

Cholecalciferol is found in good supply in the following foods:

liver
fish-liver oils
oily fish, e.g. herring, pilchard, sardine

It is also found in smaller amounts in:

egg yolk
margarine (added by law)
milk and dairy products (variable supply)

Sunlight is also an important source of vitamin D. When the body is exposed to the ultra-violet rays of the sun, a substance

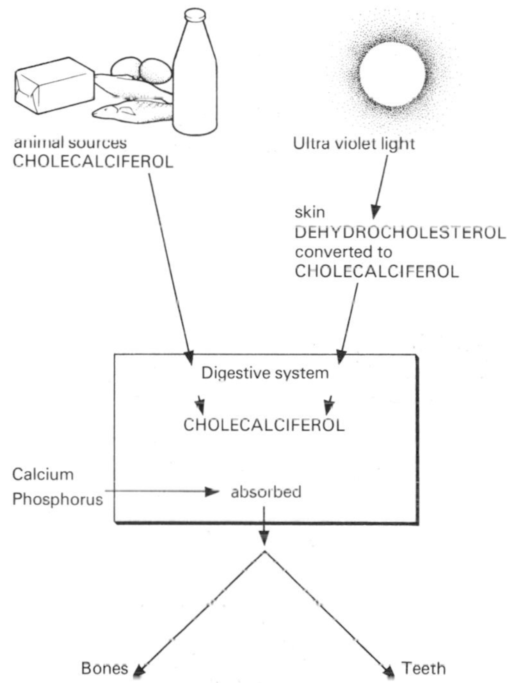

Functions of vitamin D.

under the skin (dehydrocholesterol) is converted to cholecalciferol, which is sent for storage in the liver, to be used as required. This accounts for the variable supply of vitamin D in dairy foods, as it depends on the exposure to the sun that the dairy animal has.

Requirements

Vitamin D is fat soluble, and can be stored in the body. In addition, some is made under the skin by the action of sunlight.

The recommended daily intakes from food are:

Children	μg/day
0–2 years	10
2–5 years	10
5–9 years	2·5
Adolescents	
Boys and girls	2·5
Adults	
18–35 years	2·5
35+ years	2·5
women (pregnant)	10
women (lactating)	10

Deficiency

1 Absorption of calcium and phosphorus from the small intestine is reduced, so that there is insufficient to maintain the strength of the teeth and bones. These become weak, and the bones of the legs may bend under the weight of the body. The ends of the limb bones become enlarged and the skull becomes fragile. This disease is called **rickets**, and mainly affects children.

2 An adult form of rickets known as **osteomalacia** may occur, particularly in the elderly, and can result in serious fractures after even a minor fall.

3 Growth of children is retarded.

Young children with rickets.

Stability in food preparation

Vitamin D is unaffected by normal cooking temperatures and processes, and does not dissolve in water.

NB Too much vitamin D in the diet can be dangerous as it results in an excess absorption of calcium into the blood. The extra calcium is deposited in the lungs and kidneys and can cause death.

Tocopherol (Vitamin E)

Functions

Vitamin E is found in all cell membranes, but its exact functions in the body are not clear. It is thought to have some effect upon the fertility of rats, but this has not been shown in humans.

Sources

Vitamin E is widely distributed in small quantities in many plants, especially:

lettuce, grasses
peanuts, seeds
wheatgerm oil

It is also found in milk and milk products and in egg yolk.

Deficiency

A deficiency of this vitamin has not been seen in humans, probably because it is so widely available in food.

Vitamin K

Several substances with similar functions are known to exist in this group, so that there is more than one vitamin K.

Functions

Along with other substances, vitamin K assists in the production of coagulation factors in the blood, to enable it to clot properly after an injury.

Sources

Vitamin K is widely distributed in foods, especially in leafy vegetables such as spinach. Bacteria which are normally present in the intestinal tract also produce a useful supply of the vitamin, which the body is able to use.

Deficiency

A deficiency is rarely seen, but sometimes new born babies may not have sufficient, so that their blood will not clot properly if they suffer injury during birth.

Revision questions

1 List the functions of vitamins A and D.
2 List the sources of retinol.
3 List the sources of carotene.
4 Why is milk produced in summer richer in vitamins A and D than winter milk?
5 Why is margarine a good source of vitamins A and D?
6 What are the symptoms of a deficiency of vitamins A and D?
7 Why are babies prone to vitamin-A deficiency in poor countries?
8 What is the link between vitamin D and the minerals calcium and phosphorus?
9 List the food sources of vitamin D.
10 How does ultra-violet light help the body to make vitamin D?
11 Why is too much vitamin D dangerous?
12 What are the functions of vitamins E and K?
13 List the main sources of vitamins E and K.

Water-soluble vitamins

Vitamin-B complex

At one time it was thought that there was only one vitamin B, but further research revealed that at least thirteen substances exist which make up this group, which is why it is called the vitamin-B complex. The main vitamins in the complex are described here.

Sources

The main food sources of the vitamin-B complex are:

- cereals – especially wholegrain cereals
- cereal products – e.g. bread, flour
- yeast and yeast extracts, beer
- wheatgerm
- all meat – especially pork, ham, bacon, liver, kidney, heart
- eggs
- fish roe
- milk

Thiamin (Vitamin B_1)

Functions

1 Involved in the complex series of metabolic reactions which release **energy** from carbohydrate.
2 Required for the normal **growth** of children and the maintenance of general health.
3 Required for the function and maintenance of the **nerves**.

Requirements

Thiamin cannot be stored by the body, so a daily supply is necessary for all age groups. (See p. 27.)

Requirements are increased during pregnancy and lactation, and during periods of increased metabolism, e.g. muscular activity, and some illnesses. People in very active jobs are therefore likely to need more thiamin.

Bacteria which are normally present in the intestinal tract are able to make some thiamin in man and other mammals. However, this is only a small contribution to the daily intake, and depends on how much is taken in food.

Deficiency

A deficiency of thiamin may occur for several reasons, including:

alcoholism
some digestive disorders
pregnancy – loss of appetite, vomiting

A deficiency may result in the following symptoms:

1 Depression, irritability, difficulty in concentration, defective memory, anxiety.
2 Growth retarded in children.
3 Nerves become inflamed and painful (neuritis), muscles become weak, reflexes are reduced.
4 Severe deficiency leads to the disease **beri-beri,** where a patient becomes exhausted and loses weight, muscles become weak especially in the legs, ankles and wrists drop. Fluid may be retained in the tissues, causing swelling.

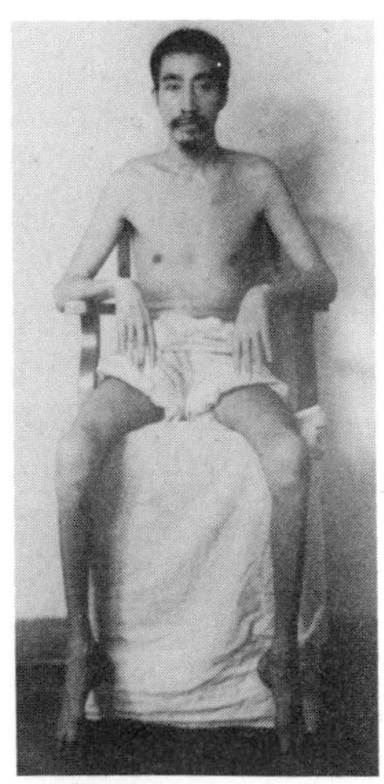

Beri-beri is caused by a deficiency of thiamin.

Stability in food preparation

Thiamin is very soluble in water, and some is destroyed by high temperatures used in cooking.

Riboflavin (Vitamin B_2)

Functions

1 Essential for normal growth.
2 Required for the release of energy from food, especially amino-acids and fat, by **oxidation.**

Requirements

Riboflavin can be stored in small amounts in the liver, spleen, and kidneys, but a daily supply is required by all age groups.

Bacteria normally present in the intestine can produce some riboflavin, but not enough to meet all the body's needs.

Deficiency

A deficiency of riboflavin can result in:

1 Failure to grow.
2 Skin lesions, dermatitis (skin disorder), and conjunctivitis (disorder of the outer membrane of the eye).
3 Tongue may swell, mouth and lips become sore.

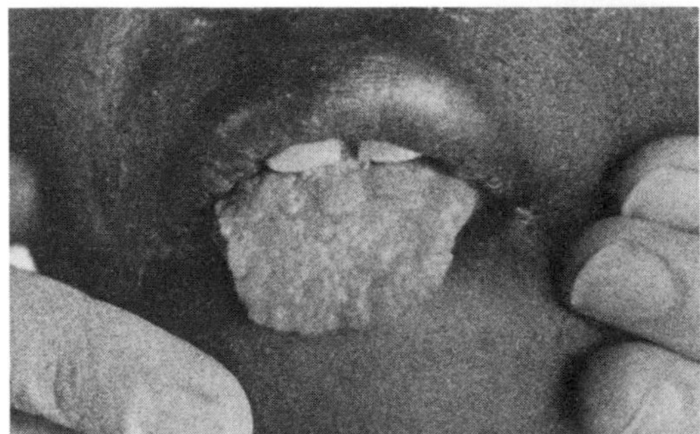

Stability in food preparation

Riboflavin is soluble in water, and is destroyed if heated in the presence of an alkali (e.g. bicarbonate of soda). Exposure to light also destroys the vitamin. This is why foods such as milk should be stored in the dark.

Nicotinic acid

Functions

Like the other B vitamins described earlier, nicotinic acid is also an important factor in the release of **energy** from food, especially carbohydrate, by oxidation.

Sources

Apart from the food sources listed on p. 25, nicotinic acid can be made in the body from the amino-acid **tryptophan** (in protein). Foods such as egg and milk, which are poor sources of nicotinic acid, contain tryptophan and are therefore useful to the body in this way.

Some foods contain nicotinic acid in a form that is unavailable to the body. This is true of the cereal **maize**, and in areas of the world where maize is the staple food, nicotinic acid deficiency is a major problem. However, in Mexico, where maize is the staple food, it is the custom to treat it with limewater before making the maize into tortillas. The limewater releases the nicotinic acid from the maize, so that a deficiency is unlikely.

Requirements

A supply of nicotinic acid is required every day, and more is needed during pregnancy and lactation.

Deficiency

A deficiency of nicotinic acid results in the disease **pellagra**, which is characterized by the following symptoms:

1 **Dermatitis**, especially on the skin around the neck which is exposed to the sun.

2 **Dementia** – loss of memory, confusion, depression.

3 **Diarrhoea**, abdominal discomfort, loss of appetite, loose and frequent stools.

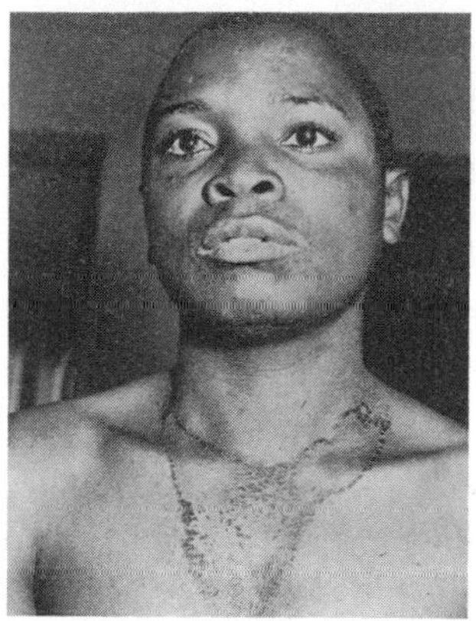

Dermatitis caused by pellegra.

Stability in food preparation

Nicotinic acid is readily soluble in water, but is resistant to heat, oxidation, and alkali. It is the most stable vitamin in the B complex, in normal cooking processes.

Recommended daily intakes of the vitamin B complex

	Thiamin	Riboflavin	Nicotinic acid
Children	mg/day	mg/day	mg/day
0–2 years	0·5	0·6	7·0
2–5 years	0·6	0·8	9·0
5–9 years	0·8	1·0	11·0
Adolescents			
Boys	1·1	1·7	19·0
Girls	0·9	1·4	16.0
Adults			
18–35 years (sedentary)	1·0	1·3–1·7	15–18
18–35 years (fairly active)	1·2	1·3–1·7	15–18
18–35 years (very active)	1·4	1·3–1·7	15–18
35+ years	0·8	1·3–1·7	15-18
women (pregnant)	1·0	1·6	18·0
women (lactating)	1·1	1·8	21·0

Vitamin B_{12} (Cobalamin)

Functions

Vitamin B_{12} is required for the metabolism of amino-acids as well as other enzyme systems throughout the body.

Requirements

Vitamin B_{12} is produced in the intestines by bacteria, and is only found in useful amounts in animal foods. Therefore vegans, who eat no animal foods, may have an insufficient intake. Requirements are higher in pregnancy and lactation.

Deficiency

A deficiency of vitamin B_{12} results in a special type of anaemia in which the red blood cells (erythrocytes) become enlarged. This may occur in patients with dietary disorders or in old age.

Ascorbic acid (Vitamin C)

Functions

1 Required to make **connective tissue** which binds the body cells together.
2 Assists the absorption of the mineral **iron** from the small intestine during digestion.
3 Assists in the building of strong bones and teeth.
4 Required for the production of blood and the walls of blood vessels.
5 Required for the building and maintenance of the skin and linings of the digestive system.

Sources

Vitamin C is found mainly in fresh fruits and vegetables.

Rich sources
rosehips, blackcurrants, green peppers

Good sources
citrus fruits – oranges, grapefruits, lemons
strawberries
cabbage, spinach
Brussels sprouts, broccoli

Reasonable sources
bean sprouts, peas
potatoes – these make a real contribution to our supplies of vitamin C because we eat potatoes in large quantities.

The amount present in food varies according to the time of year, stage and place of growth, variety of plant and degree of ripeness.

Requirements

Although it is a water-soluble vitamin, ascorbic acid has been shown to be stored in the body, mainly in the liver and adrenal glands, and throughout the body fluids and tissues. A healthy man has up to 1·5 g of ascorbic acid stored in this way, of which about 45 mg are used per day. Symptoms of scurvy (see below) appear when this store drops to below 300 mg, which takes about three months on a diet completely devoid of vitamin C. A daily supply of vitamin C is required to keep the store 'topped up', but it is not a vital requirement every day.

The recommended daily intakes are:

Children	mg/day
0–2 years	15
2–5 years	20
5–9 years	20
Adolescents	
Boys and girls	25
Adults	
18–35 years	30
35+ years	30
women (pregnant and lactating)	60

Deficiency

Prolonged deficiency may lead to:
1 Connective tissue not made or maintained correctly.
2 Walls of blood vessels weaken and break in places. Blood escapes and appears as small red spots (haemorrhages) under the skin.
3 General weakness, irritability, pain in muscles and joints, loss of weight, fatigue.
4 Gums bleed, teeth loosen.

A severe deficiency leads to the disease **scurvy**, which was common years ago among sailors on long sea voyages, where fresh fruit and vegetables were not available. The symptoms, in addition to the above, include:

5 Cuts and wounds fail to heal properly.
6 Scar tissue may weaken and break open.
7 Anaemia – because iron is not absorbed properly without vitamin C.

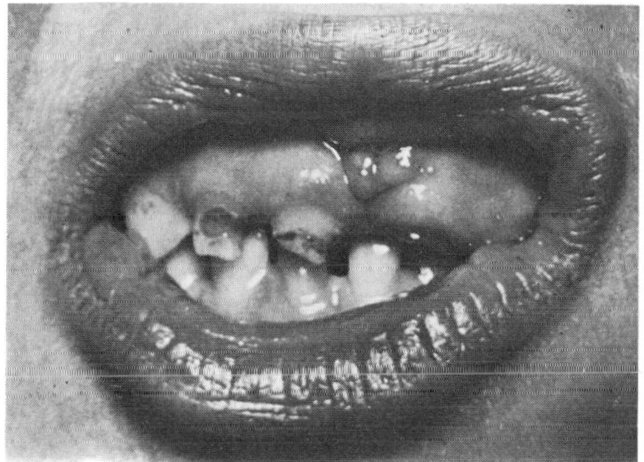

Scurvy causes swollen gums and loose teeth.

It is rare to see true cases of scurvy in Britain, but some elderly people or people on low incomes are known to be slightly deficient and may show some of the symptoms.

Stability in food preparation

Vitamin C is very quickly and easily destroyed by the following conditions:

1 Heat – dry or moist.
2 Exposure to air – this leads to the **oxidation** of ascorbic acid into a form which is useless to the body.
3 The presence of an alkali, such as bicarbonate of soda, which causes vitamin C to be oxidized.
4 Water – vitamin C dissolves in water, therefore cooking methods which use the minimum amount of water should be chosen.

To prevent the loss of vitamin C, foods should be cooked and served as quickly as possible.

Revision questions

1 How many vitamins are there in the B complex?
2 List the functions and food sources of the three main B-complex vitamins.
3 Why do people who have very active jobs require plenty of thiamin?
4 What are the symptoms of beri-beri and how is it caused?
5 What are the symptoms of a deficiency of riboflavin?
6 What are the symptoms of pellagra, and how is it caused?
7 What effects do cooking processes have on the main B vitamins?
8 What are the functions of vitamin C?
9 What is the connection between vitamin C and iron?
10 List the main sources of vitamin C.
11 How is the amount of vitamin C present in food affected?
12 What are the symptoms of a deficiency of vitamin C, and what is the name of the disease associated with it?
13 What is the effect of cooking processes on vitamin C?

Mineral elements

Apart from carbon, hydrogen, and oxygen, the main elements of which protein, fat, and carbohydrate are composed, the body also requires at least twenty other elements for a variety of reasons. These are called **mineral elements**, and they are required for:

1 Body building.
2 Control of body processes, e.g. transmission of nerve impulses.
3 Essential parts of body fluids.

Some mineral elements are required in relatively large amounts. These include:

calcium (Ca)
iron (Fe)
phosphorus (P)
potassium (K)
sulphur (S)
chlorine (Cl)

sodium (Na)
magnesium (Mg)

Others are required in minute amounts and are known as **trace elements**:

iodine (I)
copper (Cu)
manganese (Mn)
fluoride (F)
cobalt (Co)
nickel (Ni)
zinc (Zn)
chromium (Cr)

Most trace elements are supplied by a wide variety of foods, and are unlikely to be deficient in the body. The mineral elements of greatest importance are included here.

Calcium

Functions

1 With phosphorus, it combines to make **calcium phosphate**, which is the chief material that gives hardness and strength to **bones** and **teeth**.
2 Required for part of the complex mechanism which causes **blood** to **clot** after an injury.
3 Required for the correct functioning of **muscles and nerves**.
4 Required for maintenance of bones and teeth once formed.

Sources

Calcium is found in good supply in:

milk
cheese
bread (added to white flour by law)
bones of canned fish
hard water

It is also found in green vegetables, but it may be unavailable to the body, as cellulose, which the body cannot digest, affects calcium absorption. Similarly, it is found in whole grain cereals, but it may combine with a substance called **phytic acid** which makes it unavailable to the body.

Requirements

The absorption of calcium (and phosphorus) and the mineralization of bones and teeth is controlled by vitamin D. The body must have a sufficient supply of all three in order for it to function properly.

The recommended daily intakes of calcium are:

Children	mg/day
0–2 years	600
2–5 years	500
5–9 years	500
Adolescents	
Boys and girls	700
Adults	
18–35 years	500
35+ years	500
women (in last 3 months of pregnancy)	1200
women (lactating)	1200

Special requirements

Children need calcium for growth of bones and teeth.
Pregnant women need extra calcium for the growth of the baby and for the maintenance of their own bones and teeth.
Senior citizens With increasing age, the skeleton becomes weaker, and bone breakages occur easily. Calcium is required to maintain the strength of the bones for as long as possible.
After a bone breakage Calcium and phosphorus are both required to mend a fracture.

Deficiency

1 Children – bones and teeth are not mineralized properly, and are improperly formed. The leg bones may bend under the weight of the body as in rickets (see p. 24) (this is not due to a deficiency of calcium alone).
2 Adults – strength of bones and teeth is not maintained, possibly resulting in **osteomalacia** (adult rickets).
3 Muscles and nerves do not function correctly, which may result in a condition

called **tetany**, where the muscles contract rigidly and the patient has convulsions.

N.B. Too much calcium in the body is dangerous, as it will be deposited in various organs of the body, e.g. the kidneys, and this can be fatal. The effects of this were demonstrated after the Second World War, when extra vitamin D was given in cod-liver oil, to safeguard against rickets. As a result of mothers giving extra vitamin D, calcium was absorbed in excessive amounts, and this resulted in several deaths.

Phosphorus

Functions

Phosphorus works in conjunction with calcium and therefore has the same functions. In addition, it is important because it is a vital component for the production of energy in the body.

Sources

Phosphorus is present as **phosphate** in all plant and animal cells, and is therefore present in all natural foods. It forms part of many proteins, and is often used as an additive in manufactured foods.

Requirements

A normal diet will supply sufficient phosphorus for all age groups.

Deficiency

A deficiency of phosphorus is not known to occur in man.

Iron

Functions

Iron is a component of **haemoglobin**, the substance which gives red blood cells their colour. Haemoglobin is required to transport **oxygen** around the body to every cell, for the production of **energy** and the maintenance of all cell functions.

Sources

Good sources
Liver, kidney, corned beef, cocoa, plain chocolate.

Reasonable sources
White bread (added by law), curry powder, treacle, dried fruit, pulses.
Wholemeal grains: these contain iron, but it may be unavailable to the body due to the presence of phytic acid.
Green leafy vegetables: these contain some iron, but it may be unavailable to the body.

NB **Egg yolk** is known to be a good source of iron, but it has been shown in experiments that the iron is poorly absorbed by humans. The reason for this is not entirely clear, but it is known that ascorbic acid (vitamin C) helps to increase the amount of iron that can be absorbed. Egg yolk should therefore not be relied on as the main source of iron in the diet, and foods containing vitamin C should be eaten with it whenever possible.

Requirements

Red blood cells die every six weeks, and must be replaced. This process is continually occurring in the body. As the blood cells are removed from the body, some of the iron is saved. However, some iron is lost, and must be replaced by a daily food supply.

The recommended daily intakes are:

Children	mg/day
0–2 years	6
2–5 years	7
5–9 years	10
Adolescents	
girls	15
boys	15
Adults	
18–35 years	10 (men) 12 (women)
35+ years	10 (men) 12 (women)
women (pregnant)	15
women (lactating)	15

Special requirements

Babies are born with a supply of iron to last them about three months, as milk contains very little iron. After this time they need to be given iron in the form of solid food or mineral drops.

Pregnant women Iron requirements are increased in pregnancy to allow for the development of the growing baby's blood supply. Iron tablets are usually given to allow for this.

Girls and women The regular menstrual loss of blood means that iron is lost and must be replaced. After the birth of a baby, iron supplies must be replaced.

Injuries and operations result in loss of blood and the iron must be replaced.

Deficiency

1 Haemoglobin is not made properly, so that insufficient oxygen is carried around the body. This leads to fatigue, weakness, and a pale complexion. In severe cases this leads to the condition known as **iron deficiency anaemia.**

2 General health is affected, as cells cannot function properly.

NB Too much iron is toxic to the body, and therefore its absorption has to be controlled in the small intestine. Normally, only a small percentage of the iron in the diet is absorbed, but if more is required (e.g. in pregnancy), then more will be absorbed to meet these demands.

To ensure that iron is properly absorbed, foods containing iron should be eaten with foods containing Vitamin C.

Sodium, chloride, and potassium

Functions

These are all required to maintain the correct concentration of the body fluids. Chloride is also required for the production of **hydrochloric acid** in the gastric juice of the stomach.

Sources

All three are usually eaten as ordinary salt (sodium chloride) or as potassium chloride in food.

They are also added as salt to foods, e.g.:
yeast extract
cheese
bacon
fish

They are found naturally in fish, meat, and many other foods.

Requirements

Everyone requires these elements. Sodium and chloride are especially necessary in hot climates where they are lost in sweat. Workers in heavy industry need them for the same reason. Excess intakes are excreted in the urine and sweat.

It is sometimes necessary to place a person on a **salt-restricted diet**, for certain medical conditions, e.g.:
heart, kidney, or liver disease
high blood pressure

This means that low-salt foods (e.g. natural cereals, fruit, unsalted butter, etc.) must be eaten, with small amounts of fresh meat and fish, and root vegetables, and no salt may be added to food. Alternative flavourings, e.g. herbs, spices, can be used as a substitute for salt.

Deficiency

Salt tablets are issued to some workers in hot climates (e.g. in civil engineering) where they may be unused to long periods in such heat.

Fluoride

Functions

Fluoride has been shown to be an important factor in the strengthening of teeth against decay. It is thought that it combines with the protective enamel coating of the teeth, thus making them more resistant to attack by the acid produced by bacteria in the mouth.

Sources

Fluoride is found naturally in tea, sea-water fish, and in some parts of the country in water supplies.

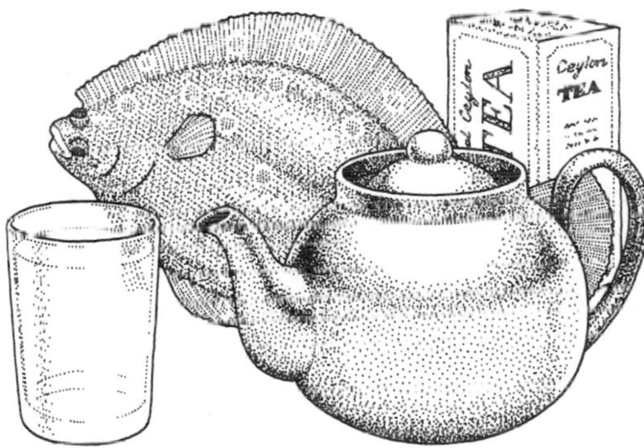

Fluoridation of water supplies
In areas of the country where fluoride occurs naturally in the water supply, the number of children who require treatment for tooth decay is known to be significantly lower than in other areas. Because of this, it has been recommended that all water supplies should have fluoride added to them at a strength of 1 mg per litre, to reduce the number of children requiring dental treatment. There have, however, been problems in putting this into practice as many people object to having their water supply interfered with. As a result, only 10% of the population have water supplies with added fluoride in them.

Requirements

The strengthening effect that fluoride has on the teeth is only of value when the teeth are developing in children. Only minute quantities are required for this.

An excess intake of fluoride can be harmful, as it causes the teeth to become 'mottled' with dark brown spots.

Iodine

Functions

Iodine is required to make the hormone **thyroxine**, which is produced by the **thyroid gland** in the neck.

Thyroxine, along with other hormones, helps to control the rate of metabolism in the body.

Sources

Iodine is widely distributed in foods, but is found in good supply in:

- sea foods
- milk
- green vegetables, especially spinach
- fresh water (depending on area)
- iodized salt (added commercially)

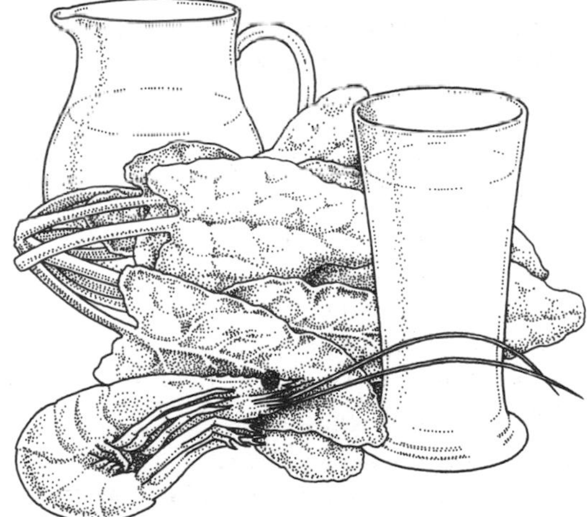

Requirements

A minute quantity is required every day, and in our whole life, only one tenth of an ounce (2·8 g) is needed by the body.

Deficiency

A deficiency of iodine leads to a reduction in the amount of thyroxine produced by the thyroid gland. As a result the metabolism slows down, and the gland swells up. This swelling can be seen in the neck and is called a **goitre.**

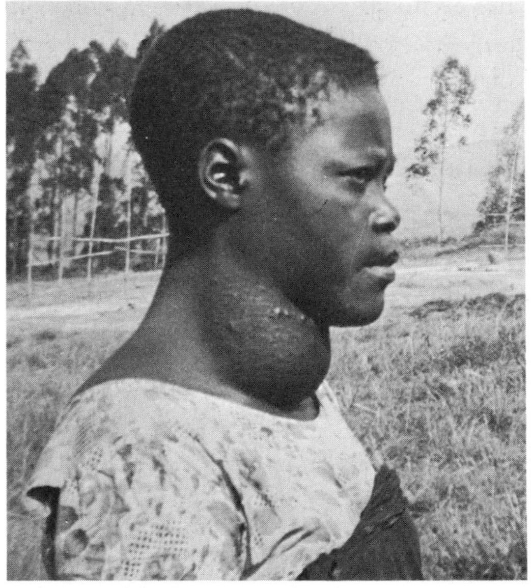

Revision questions

1 List five mineral elements and five trace elements.
2 List the functions and main sources of calcium, iron, sodium and chloride, iodine, and fluoride.
3 What is rickets, and what is its connection with vitamin D?
4 What is phytic acid, and what effect does it have on certain mineral elements?
5 What is tetany, and what causes it?
6 What is the function of haemoglobin, and which mineral element is connected with it?
7 Why do women, babies, and people recovering from injuries require extra iron?
8 Why is it necessary to take salt tablets in hot climates?
9 Why is it recommended that water supplies should be fluoridated?
10 What is a goitre and how is it caused?

Water

Functions

1 Water is vital to life. 70% of the human body is water.
2 Required for all body fluids, e.g. digestive juices, mucus, saliva, blood, lymph, sweat, and urine.
3 Required as part of many metabolic reactions.
4 Keeps linings of mucous membranes, digestive tract, and bronchial tubes moist.
5 Some nutrients dissolve in water for proper absorption.
6 Lubricates joints and membranes.

Sources

Many foods contain water, and some, such as fruits and vegetables, are composed mainly of water. In addition to the water that is taken in food and as liquids, some water is produced during the many metabolic reactions of the body.

Requirements

Water should be drunk every day, especially in hot weather when much is lost through sweating. Water is constantly lost in this way through the skin, and also from the lungs, kidneys, and bowels. A minimum of two to three litres per day is recommended.

Extra water is required:

1 During illness where a raised temperature results in increased sweating.
2 If vomiting or diarrhoea has occurred, both of which can cause **dehydration** rapidly, especially in babies.
3 In lactation, when extra water is required for milk production.

Dietary fibre

After food has been digested, absorbed, and metabolized, waste products are removed from the body by the process of **excretion.**

Liquid waste is processed by the **kidneys** and excreted as **urine**, and solid waste as faeces, from the large intestine.

The removal of waste products is vital as they are potentially harmful (toxic) to the body. Normally, the excretion of urine occurs regularly throughout the day, and the excretion of the faeces every day or so according to individual variation (which is quite normal).

The faeces are formed in the large intestine after the nutrients and some of the water have been absorbed following digestion. The solid residues pass along the intestine by the process of **peristalsis**, which involves regular muscular contractions of the intestinal wall. These push the residues along.

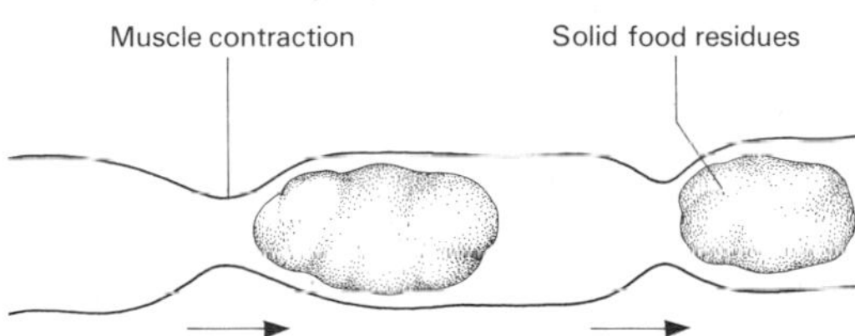

The **faeces** finally collect in the **rectum** and are passed out through the **anus** (see p. 42). Usually the whole process takes place with minimum effort, providing the faeces are **bulky** and **soft**.

Dietary fibre (sometimes called **fibre**, **unavailable carbohydrate**, or **roughage**), is the name given to the indigestible parts of food (usually the carbohydrate **cellulose**; see p. 19), which remain in the large intestine after digestion. The main sources of dietary fibre are:

Wholegrain cereals (as **bran**), e.g. wheat, rice, oats, wholemeal bread, breakfast cereals. Bran can also be purchased separately.
There is also some present in:
Fruits, especially skins, apples, plums.
Vegetables, especially leafy vegetables, celery, potato skins.

Functions

Even though it is not digested, dietary fibre is of great importance as it absorbs a lot of water, and binds other food residues to itself, thus ensuring that the faeces are soft and bulky and pass easily out of the body in the minimum time.

If the faeces are not removed quickly and regularly, several problems can arise, including:

Constipation

Many people suffer from constipation. The faeces become very hard and move slowly through the intestine, and a lot of effort is required to remove them. In addition, abdominal discomfort and a general feeling of ill health accompany this condition.

Diverticular disease

The extra strain put on the muscular walls of the intestine through constipation may lead to **diverticular disease**, which is the development of small, blown-out pouches in the wall of the large intestine. If the faeces are small and hard (due to a lack of dietary fibre and insufficient water), the muscular walls of the intestine have to work harder to move them along. This causes increased pressure in the intestine and leads to pouches of the bowel lining being forced out through the intestine wall. If the pouches (called diverticula) become inflamed, this causes discomfort. Part of the treatment for this is to put the patient on a high-fibre diet.

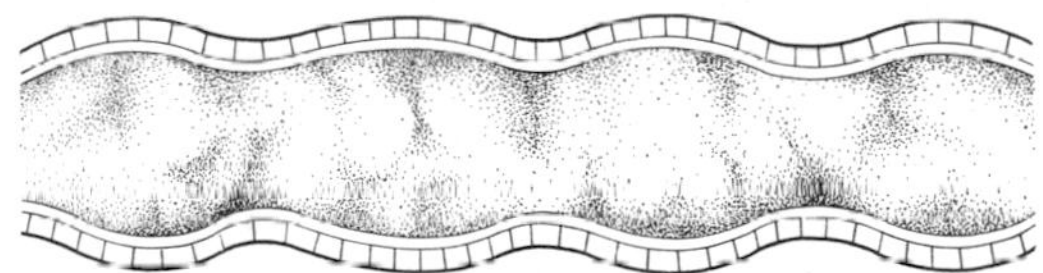

(a) High-fibre diet – the soft, large faeces are moved along the intestine easily.

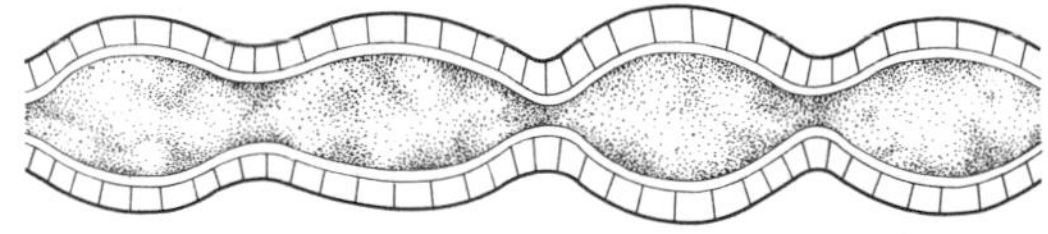

(b) Low-fibre diet – the small, hard faeces cannot be moved so easily, and extra effort is required to push them.

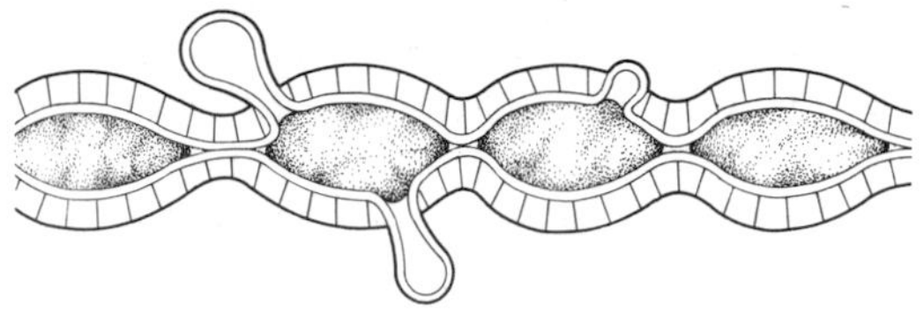

(c) This leads to the development of diverticula.

Varicose veins and hernias

These may be caused by the increased effort required to remove hard faeces in constipation sufferers.

Refined foods

It is often suggested that people today do not eat enough dietary fibre in their food, and that this is a major cause of many disorders of the intestinal tract, including those described above.

Many foods eaten today are **refined.** This means that they are processed in food factories into a variety of products, during which much of their dietary fibre content is removed.

Refined foods include:
white flour, white bread
instant puddings and desserts
white sugar
white (polished) rice
instant potato

Such foods are often blamed for the reduction in the amount of dietary fibre eaten, as they are convenient to prepare, highly palatable, and relatively inexpensive.

Lack of exercise is also a major factor in causing intestinal disorders, as exercise helps to keep the intestines active.

People who suffer from constipation often resort to using laxatives, which irritate the intestine and cause it to expel the faeces unnaturally fast. This is unwise as it can lead to total dependence on laxatives, as the normal process will be stopped.

It is advisable that everyone should eat plenty of dietary fibre in their food, to avoid any problems of constipation and its accompanying disorders. The regular consumption of wholegrain cereals, wholemeal bread, fruit, and vegetables, and an increase in exercise should be sufficient to prevent such problems. A reduction in the amount of refined foods eaten is also advisable, though they need not be avoided altogether.

Foods containing dietary fibre.

Revision questions

1. Why is water vital to life?
2. Name five foods that have a high water content.
3. Apart from water taken in foods, how else does the body obtain it?
4. How is water lost from the body?
5. What is the recommended daily requirement for water?
6. When does the body require extra water?
7. Why are vomiting and diarrhoea dangerous to babies and young children?
8. Why does the body have to remove waste products?
9. What is peristalsis?
10. Why is dietary fibre important to the body?
11. List the main sources of dietary fibre.
12. Why is constipation undesirable?
13. What is diverticular disease?
14. How do refined foods affect the removal of waste products?
15. Why is the continued use of laxatives undesirable?

Energy

Every function and process in the body requires a source of **energy**, and without it there would be no life on the earth.

Energy is used in various forms in the body:

Mechanical energy for the movement of muscles (voluntarily and involuntarily).
Chemical energy for all chemical and metabolic reactions.
Heat energy to maintain the body temperature.
Electrical energy for the transmission of nervous impulses.

One form of energy can be converted into another form in the body, but all energy must be supplied initially by food, and released for use in the body after digestion and absorption.

Foods which supply energy

The three main nutrients, protein, fat, and carbohydrate, all supply energy. Of the three, fat provides the most concentrated source of energy, weight for weight. Thus, the main energy-supplying foods are:

- fats (lard, butter, margarine, suet)
- oils (vegetable, nut, animal)
- fatty foods, e.g. egg yolk, cheese, cream, meat
- sugar, cereals, cereal products, starchy vegetables

Measurement of energy

Energy is measured in **kilocalories** (kcal) or **kilojoules** (kJ), just as weight is measured in pounds or kilograms, and liquids in pints or litres.

A kilocalorie* is defined as:

The amount of **heat energy** that is required to raise the temperature of 1 kilogram of pure water by 1°C.

1kcal = 4·2 kJ (the joule is the metric unit of measurement for heat and energy.)

*sometimes written as Calorie

The three main nutrients, protein, fat, and carbohydrate, can all supply the body with energy, and are therefore said to have a **calorific value** or **energy value**.

1 gram of pure **protein** has an energy value of 4 kcals or 17 kJ.
1 gram of pure **fat** has an energy value of 9 kcals or 38 kJ.
1 gram of pure **carbohydrate** has an energy value of 3·75 kcals or 16 kJ.

Fat supplies over twice as much energy as the same weight of protein or carbohydrate. Protein is normally only used as an energy supply once it has performed its primary functions of growth and repair, or if the diet is deficient in fat or carbohydrate.

Most foods are a mixture of these nutrients and so their energy values vary greatly. Energy value can be assessed by burning a carefully weighed portion of a particular food in a special piece of equipment called a **calorimeter**. The amount of heat energy produced is measured in kcal or kJ.

Energy values of various foods

Food	kcals/25 g (1 oz)	kJ/25 g (1 oz)
White bread	68	286
Wholemeal bread	65	273
White flour	100	420
Boiled rice	35	147
Plain chocolate	155	651
Honey	80	336
Jam	74	310
Sugar (white)	112	470
Sugar (brown)	112	470
Butter	226	949
Margarine	226	949
Lard	262	1100
Cheese (Cheddar)	120	504
Cheese (cream)	232	975
Milk	19	80
Egg	46	193
Double cream	131	550
Roast beef	109	458
Roast pork	90	378
Roast lamb	83	347
Cod (steamed)	23	97
Cod (fried)	40	168
Herring	54	227
Apples	13	55
Bananas	22	92
Oranges	10	42
Dried fruit	70	294
Baked beans	26	109
Peas (fresh)	14	59
Cabbage, spinach	5	21
Potatoes (boiled)	23	97
Potatoes (fried)	68	286
Potato crisps	159	668
Peanuts	171	718
Sweet biscuits (plain)	158	664

Figures are based on averages of various samples.
(From: *The Composition of Foods*, McCance and Widdowson)

Energy release in the body

Energy from food is released in all body cells by **oxidation.**

Oxidation is the reaction of a substance with oxygen to produce energy. In the body, oxygen is inhaled from the air and carried to the bloodstream, where it is attached to haemoglobin in the red blood cells. (**Iron** is a vital component of haemoglobin, and is therefore an important nutrient in energy release. If the body is deficient in iron, the patient becomes tired and lethargic due to a lack of energy.)

Glucose, which is the main source of energy from food, is released into the bloodstream after digestion and is carried to the cells where it reacts with oxygen (oxidation) to produce energy, with **carbon dioxide** and **water** as by-products:

Glucose + oxygen → Energy + CO_2 + water

The carbon dioxide is exhaled and the water is excreted through the skin or kidneys, or it is used for other reactions.

The **vitamin-B** complex and **phosphorus** are vital factors in energy release as they are actually involved in the series of reactions that produce energy. **Iodine** is also important as it helps to control the rate of energy release in the hormone thyroxine.

It is often stated that food is 'burnt' in the body to produce energy, and to some extent this is true, as oxidation results in some energy loss as **heat**. This is used to maintain the body temperature. The rest of the energy is used for **muscle movement.**

Oxidation is a **continual process**, so that the body has a constant supply of energy for all its processes. The body is able to store small amounts of energy as **glycogen** (carbohydrate) in the liver and muscles, and this can be released very quickly when a sudden supply is required, e.g. to run a race. Energy can also be stored as **fat** in the **adipose tissue** under the skin. In times of famine this can be slowly released to maintain life.

Energy requirements

The amount of energy used by the body is the **energy expenditure**, and this varies widely from individual to individual, according to:

age
sex
occupation
physical activity
state of body, e.g. pregnancy, illness

Age

Young children require more energy for their size than adults as they are growing rapidly and tend to be very active most of the time.

With increasing age, the need for energy decreases, partly due to a slowing down of the body and partly because of reduced physical activity.

Sex

Men tend to be larger overall in body size than women, and therefore use more energy. This does not really apply to children.

Occupation and physical activity

The amount of energy people use in physical activity varies according to their occupation and their recreational activities. Occupations are classified according to how active they are as follows:

Sedentary: Office workers, clerical tasks, drivers, pilots, teachers, journalists, clergy, doctors, lawyers, architects, shop workers.
Moderately active: Light industry and assembly plants, railway workers, postmen, joiners, plumbers, bus conductors, farm workers, builders' labourers.
Very active: Coal miners, steel workers, dockers, forestry workers, army recruits, some farm workers, builders' labourers, unskilled labourers.

State of body

Pregnancy: Energy requirements are increased to allow for the growth of the baby, and the adjustment of the mother's body to pregnancy.
Lactation: Extra energy is required for the production of milk, and some of this is laid down as fat stores during the pregnancy.
Illness: The metabolism of the body may be raised at times during an illness or fever, but at other times may be decreased due to a reduction in physical activity.

At least half of the energy released in the body is used for **basal metabolism** (resting metabolism). This is the amount of energy that is required to keep the body alive when it is at complete rest and warm. It is used to keep the heart, lungs, and digestive system moving, to maintain the nerve impulses to and from the brain, and for all the necessary chemical reactions in the body.

The rest of the energy is used by the **muscles** for physical work and to maintain **posture**. Energy expenditure for these purposes varies widely from person to person, but for an average-sized man aged about thirty, energy expenditure for different activities is as follows:

Activity	kcals used per hour	kJ used per hour
Sleeping	70	294
Sitting	85	357
Standing	90	378
Playing tennis	350	1470
Playing football	480	2000
Cycling	400	1680
Walking slowly	185	777
Swimming	575	2415
Housework	200	840
Walking upstairs	1000	4200

If the energy intake in food exceeds the amount of energy expended by an individual, then the excess will be stored in the body as fat. This is one of the major causes of obesity, but it does not account for those people who appear to be able to eat what they like without putting on weight. It is likely that differences in **metabolic rate** (i.e. the rate at which oxidation occurs), and the amount of heat produced during oxidation, account for this variation.

Foods which have high energy values should be eaten in moderation by people who lead sedentary lives, as they can increase the daily intake considerably. Some foods, such as chocolates, sweets, crisps, and similar snacks, are particularly bad in this respect as they are **energy dense**, but contain very little else in the way of nutrients. Such foods are sometimes referred to as providing 'empty calories', because they are of little value to the body.

The recommended daily intakes of energy are:

Children		kcals/day	kJ
0–1 year		800	3360
1–2 years		1200	5040
2–3 years		1400	5880
3–5 years		1600	6720
5–7 years		1800	7560
7–9 years		2100	8820
Adolescents			
Boys		2800	11760
Girls		2300	9660
Men			
18–35 years:	sedentary	2700	11340
	moderately active	3000	12600
	very active	3600	15120
35–65 years:	sedentary	2600	10920
	moderately active	2900	12180
	very active	3600	15100
Women			
18–35 years:	sedentary	1900	7980
	moderately active	2200	9240
	very active	2500	10500
35–55 years:	most occupations	2050	8610
Men and women 75+ years		2000	8400
Women:	pregnant	2400	10080
	lactating	2700	11340

Weight reduction

In order to lose weight, it is necessary to reduce the energy intake from food, so that the reserves of energy in body fat are utilized and weight is consequently lost. An increase in physical activity is also beneficial.

A weight-reducing diet involves calculating the day's energy intake and reducing it to a level at which energy reserves will be used up. Usually, an intake of 1000 kcal (4200 kJ) per day for women and 1500 kcal (6300 kJ) per day for men is prescribed. A reduction of 3500 kcal will cause about 1 lb of body fat to be lost. On 1000 kcals a day a woman could lose 2–3 lb a week. Charts showing the energy values of different foods are produced which assist in calculating this. It is however important to gain the advice of a doctor before attempting to lose weight as some diet sheets can be misguided and nutritionally unsound.

Weight reduction is a gradual and fairly long-term process. The aim should be to change one's eating habits in order to prevent future weight gain.

Effect of cooking on energy values

The energy values of some foods can be increased considerably by the addition of fat, as in frying; for example, a fried egg has an energy value of almost double that of a boiled egg. (A boiled egg yields 80 kcal; a fried egg yields 150 kcal.) This is because most foods absorb a substantial amount of fat during frying. They absorb even more if they are placed in the fat before it has reached the correct cooking temperature.

The addition of fat to a food, e.g. butter added to mashed potato, or butter on sweetcorn, also increases the energy value.

This should be taken into account when planning meals, especially for someone who is on a weight-reducing diet.

Grilling foods such as chops and sausages is preferable to frying them, as some of the fat content inherent in the food will melt away, and reduce the energy value accordingly.

The use of sugar substitutes such as saccharine, which are very sweet but have little energy value, helps to reduce the energy value of drinks and other dishes, e.g. custard, which are traditionally sweet.

Foods which contain a high proportion of water, e.g. fruits and vegetables, are low in energy value as water yields no energy. Such foods are useful in weight-reducing diets.

Many special foods and meal substitutes are produced with the intention of helping people on weight-reducing diets, but they are often very expensive, and do not necessarily help to re-educate people's eating habits. It is better just to follow a diet that contains plenty of fruit and vegetables and a balanced amount of protein, fat, and carbohydrate.

A weight-reducing diet.

Revision questions

1. Why does the body require energy?
2. What forms of energy does the body use?
3. Define a kilocalorie.
4. How many kilocalories do one gram of pure fat, protein, and carbohydrate each produce?
5. Why do the energy values of foods differ?
6. What is oxidatio[illegible] occur?
7. Which nutrients a[illegible] release in the bod[illegible]
8. How does the boc[illegible]
9. Why do people h[illegible] ments for energy?
10. Why is it unwise t[illegible] requirements?
11. What is basal metabolism?
12. What is the best way to lose weight?
13. What effect does frying have on the energy value of foods?
14. How are sugar substitutes useful in weight-reducing diets?
15. Give the energy values for five different foods and say why they are different.

Digestion and absorption

When food has been eaten, it must be broken down in the body by the process of **digestion**, so that the molecules of which it is composed (in particular the nutrients) can be **absorbed** into the bloodstream. The whole process takes place in the **digestive system** (sometimes called the **alimentary canal**), which begins at the mouth and ends at the anus (see p. 42. It consists of various organs and tissues, each with special functions.

Digestion and absorption occur by both **physical** and **chemical** means.

Physical breakdown of food

Food must be small enough to swallow, and is first broken up (masticated) in the mouth by the action of the teeth and jaws. The muscular action of the stomach also results in the reduction in size of the food particles.

Chemical breakdown of food

During digestion, a variety of chemicals or 'digestive juices' are produced. These contain numerous substances known collectively as **enzymes**.

Enzymes are able to speed up chemical reactions, and are found in all living matter. Each chemical reaction which occurs in and animals has a **specific** act upon it and speed it up. This hat a particular enzyme can only on one type of reaction and no other. nsequently there are many enzymes.

The enzymes in digestion speed up the breakdown of food and the release of nutrients, and without them the whole process would be impossible. In the following equation, A stands for a food and B for a nutrient it contains.

In order to enable food to move around the digestive system, **mucus** is produced. This lubricates the food and the membranes of the system, which enables the food to move easily. The muscular walls of the various parts of the system push the food along by means of regular contractions. This process is known as **peristalsis** (see p. 35).

Digestion at each stage of the digestive system

The physical and chemical breakdown of food at each stage will be discussed here, and the *enzymes* involved are shown in *italic*.

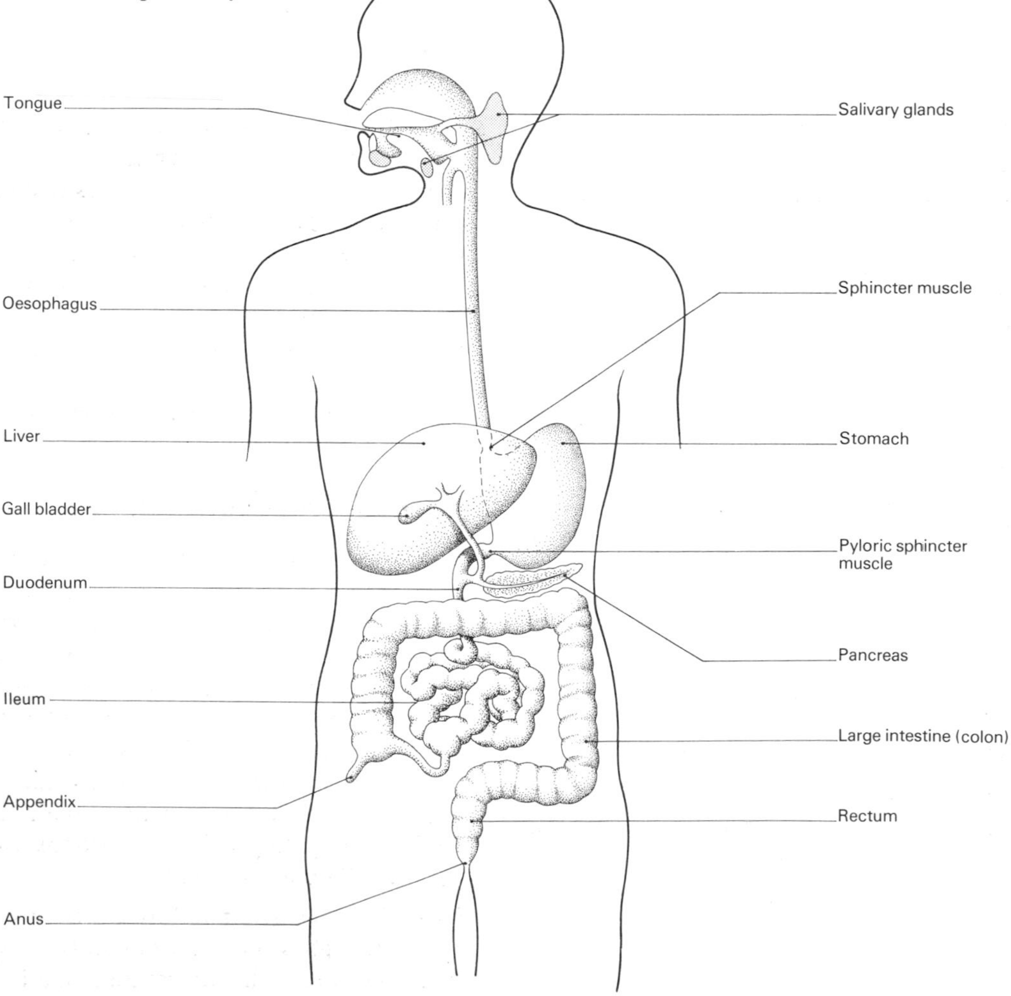

The human digestive system.

Mouth

Physical breakdown

Teeth: tear, rip, and grind the food into pieces small enough to swallow.
Tongue: pushes the food round the mouth and down the throat.
Salivary glands: produce saliva to moisten food and make it easy to swallow.

Chemical breakdown

Protein None.
Fat None.
Carbohydrate *Salivary amylase* produced by the salivary glands converts some starch to maltose. Cooked starch is acted on more quickly than raw starch.

Oesophagus

Food is transported down to the stomach by peristalsis.

There is no physical or chemical breakdown here.

Stomach

Physical breakdown

Food enters the stomach via the muscle at the top. Strong muscular waves move the food around and help to break it down and mix it with gastric juices and mucus produced in the stomach. The broken-down food is referred to as **chyme**.

Chemical breakdown

Protein *Pepsin* starts the breakdown of protein into smaller chains of amino-acids called peptones.

Rennin clots milk so that *pepsin* can act upon it more efficiently. More rennin is produced in young mammals whose diet consists solely of milk.
Fat None.
Carbohydrate Hydrochloric acid produced by the stomach stops the action of salivary amylase, and helps pepsin to work.

Food stays in the stomach for about four to five hours, and leaves in small amounts via the pyloric sphincter muscle.

Duodenum

Physical breakdown

None.

Chemical breakdown

The chyme is mixed with bile from the gall bladder and pancreatic juice from the pancreas. Bile neutralizes the acid and stops the action of pepsin.
Protein *Trypsinogen* (an inactive enzyme) produced by the pancreas mixes with *enterokinase* which activates trypsinogen to form *trypsin. Trypsin* continues the breakdown of proteins to peptones.
Fat Bile emulsifies fats to disperse them in the liquid in small droplets, and *pancreatic lipase* breaks fat into soluble glycerol and insoluble fatty acids. The fatty acids react with the bile to become soluble.
Carbohydrate *Pancreatic amylase* breaks down undigested starch to maltose.

Ileum

Physical breakdown

None.

Chemical breakdown

The glands produce intestinal juice which contains a variety of enzymes.
Protein *Erepsin* converts peptones to amino-acids to complete protein digestion.
Fat Further broken down by *lipase*.
Carbohydrate *Maltase* breaks down maltose to glucose.
Invertase breaks down sucrose to glucose and fructose.
Lactase breaks down lactose to glucose and galactose.

Absorption of nutrients

The absorption of nutrients occurs in the small intestine, along its whole length. Alcohol is the only substance that can be absorbed elsewhere, usually in the stomach.

Food is passed along the small intestine slowly, taking about two to three hours to reach the large intestine. This allows plenty of time for absorption to take place. The walls of the intestine are lined with thousands of tiny finger-like projections called **villi** (see diagram overleaf).

Each villus is surrounded by a wall of single cells, through which the nutrients pass, to reach the centre. In the centre is the **lacteal**

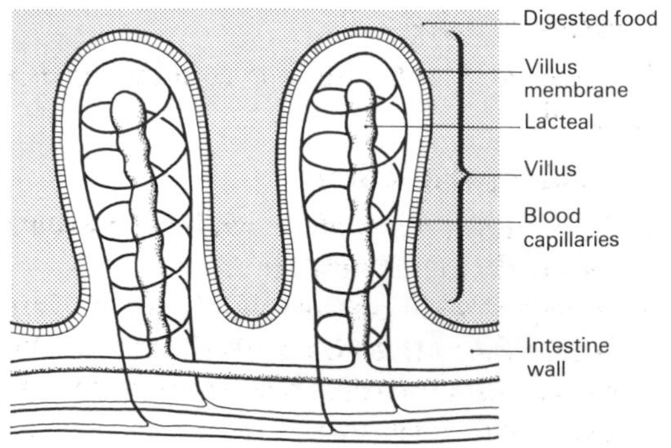

which is connected to the lymphatic system. The lacteal is surrounded by tiny **blood capillaries**, which are connected to larger blood vessels. Absorption of the various nutrients occurs as follows:

Glucose, amino-acids, water-soluble vitamins and **minerals** are all absorbed into the blood capillaries, where they dissolve in the blood, and are carried away to other parts of the body.

Glycerol and **fatty acids** are absorbed into the lacteal where they recombine to form fats, which mix with the lymphatic fluid. They then pass round the body in the lymphatic system, and join the blood circulation as insoluble fat. They are converted to soluble fat in the liver.

The **fat-soluble vitamins** are absorbed with the fats, and are taken to the liver as well.

Large intestine (colon)

After the nutrients have been absorbed, the waste products and food residues pass into the large intestine, still in a liquid state. Water is absorbed along the large intestine, thus making the food residues (faeces) more solid. This may take up to twelve hours, and the faeces finally collect in the rectum, ready for excretion. The whole process is assisted by dietary fibre in food (see pp. 34–6).

Digestion and cooking

Digestion is assisted by the pre-cooking of foods to soften or tenderize them:
e.g. meat – cooking breaks down tough connective tissue and renders the meat more digestible (see p. 98).

Cooking also renders some foods more solid so that the enzymes are able to act upon them more efficiently:
e.g. eggs – cooking them lightly coagulates the protein, thus making them set so that they stay in the stomach for longer.

Revision questions

1 What is the purpose of digestion?
2 Draw and label the various organs of the digestive system.
3 What do enzymes do?
4 Why is mucus produced throughout the digestive system?
5 Copy out and complete the chart below, showing the digestion of the various nutrients:

Organ	Protein	Fat	Carbohydrate	Vitamins Minerals
Mouth Oesophagus Stomach Duodenum Ileum Colon				

Indicate which enzymes are involved in each case.

The nutrient content of foods

It is difficult to measure accurately the amounts of the different nutrients that people eat every day, and the amounts that are present in the food they consume.

The nutritional value of different foods is affected by:

1 The species or type of plant or animal.
2 Where and how they are grown or reared.
3 The effect of harvesting and slaughter.
4 The time taken to transport food to various countries.
5 The effect of processing the food in a factory.
6 The amount of wastage when preparing a food.

7 The effect of various processes and cooking practices in the kitchen.

The way in which food is prepared for consumption in the kitchen does have an important effect on the nutritional content. Some processes and practices lead to a **loss** of nutrients, whilst others **conserve** or **enhance** the nutritional value of food.

Practices which lead to a loss of nutrients

Heating

1 Destroys some vitamin C, thiamin, and riboflavin.
2 With an alkali (as in the addition of bicarbonate of soda to green vegetables to preserve their colour), heating leads to the destruction of vitamin C and riboflavin.
3 Overheating protein leads to hardening and reduced digestibility.
4 Keeping food hot further destroys vitamin C, thiamin, and riboflavin.

Soaking

Leads to loss of vitamin C, thiamin, riboflavin, and nicotinic acid into the liquid.

Exposure to air

1 Leads to the oxidation of vitamin C in vegetables, fruit, and fruit juices.
2 Leads to the gradual deterioration of fat due to **rancidity** (see p. 71).

Exposure to light

Leads to the destruction of riboflavin and vitamin A.

Practices which conserve nutrients

Steaming

Water-soluble vitamins are retained more effectively as food does not come into direct contact with water.

Stews and gravy

Preparation of gravy from vegetable cooking water retains some water-soluble vitamins. Water-soluble vitamins are retained in liquid used in a stew.

Pressure cooking

Less destruction by heat as cooking time is reduced.

Vegetable preparation

1 Preparation just before cooking prevents the oxidation of vitamin C.
2 If vegetables are prepared some time before they are to be cooked, they can be stored in a plastic bag to prevent the oxidation of vitamin C.
3 Placing green vegetables into boiling water, for cooking without pre-soaking, reduces the loss of water-soluble vitamins by leaching.
4 Minimum cooking time reduces heat destruction of vitamin C, thiamin, and riboflavin.

Practices which enhance nutritional value

Combining foods

1 The combination of low biological value protein foods (e.g. bread with lentil soup, baked beans on toast) ensures the inclusion of essential amino acids which are lacking in one food, and can be provided by the other.
2 The combination of vitamin C with foods containing iron enhances the absorption of iron from the small intestine.

Preparing food

1 The preparation of curry spices in iron pots leads to iron passing into the spices.
2 Grating cheese enables the fat content to be more easily digested.
3 Homogenizing milk (see p. 80) reduces the size of the fat droplets, which enables them to be digested more easily.

Revision questions

1 Explain how
a heating, **b** soaking, **c** exposure to air affect the nutrient content of foods.
2 Which cooking methods help to conserve water-soluble vitamins?
3 How should vegetables be stored, prepared, and cooked to retain vitamins?

Nutrients per 100 g of various foods

	Bread (white)	Bread (wholemeal)	Rice (polished, boiled)	Cheese (Cheddar)	Eggs (whole, raw)	Meat (lean beef, raw)	Beef-roast (lean and fat)	Fish (white steamed)	Milk (whole, fresh)	Sugar (white)	Beans (butter, boiled)	Cabbage (spring, boiled)	Oranges
Protein	7·8	8·8	2·2	26·0	12·3	20·3	22·4	18·6	3·3	Tr	7·1	1·1	0·8
Fat g	1·7	2·7	0·3	33·5	10·9	4·6	28·8	0·9	3·8	0	0·3	Tr	Tr
Carbohydrate g	49·7	41·8	29·6	Tr	Tr	0	0	0	4·7	105	17·1	0·8	8·5
Fibre g	2·7	8·5	0	0	0	0	0	0	0	0	5·1	2.2	2.0
Sugars g	1·8	2·1	Tr	Tr	0	0	0	0	4·7	105	1·5	0·8	8·5
Starch & dextrin g	47·9	39·7	29·6	0	0	0	0	0	0	0	15·6	Tr	0
Calcium mg	100	23	1	800	52	7	14	15	120	Tr	19	30	41
Iron mg	1·7	2·5	0·2	0·4	2·0	2·1	1·9	0·5	0·05	Tr	1·7	0·5	0·3
Phosphorus mg	97	230	34	520	220	180	150	240	95	Tr	87	32	24
Sodium mg	540	540	2	160	140	61	51	100	50	Tr	16	12	3
Magnesium mg	26	93	4	25	12	20	18	21	12	Tr	33	6	13
kCal	233	216	123	406	147	123	349	83	65	394	95	7	35
kJ	991	918	522	1682	612	517	1446	350	272	1680	405	32	150
Water g	39·0	40·0	69·9	37·0	74·8	74·0	48·4	79·2	87·6	Tr	70·5	96·6	86·1
Retinol (Vit A) µg	0	0	0	310	140	Tr	Tr	Tr	35	0	0	0	0
Thiamin (Vit B) mg	0·18	0·26	0·01	0·04	0·09	0·07	0·05	0·09	0·04	Tr	–	0·03	0·1
Riboflavin (Vit B) mg	0·03	0·08	0·01	0·5	0·47	0·24	0·24	0·09	0·19	Tr	–	0·03	0·03
Nicotinic acid (Vit B) mg	1·4	3·9	0·3	0·1	0·07	5·2	3·9	2·1	0·08	Tr	–	0·2	0·2
Ascorbic acid (Vit C) mg	0	0	0	0	0	0	0	Tr	1·5*	0	0	25	50
Cholecalciferol (Vit D) µg	0	0	0	0·26	1·75	Tr	Tr	Tr	0·03	0	0	0	0
Carotene µg	0	0	0	205	Tr	Tr	Tr	Tr	22	0	Tr	500	50

g = gram
mg = milligram
µg = microgram

* falls to 0·5 after 24 hours
– = no information available
Tr = Trace

Meal planning

Food is a vital part of our lives and much of our time is spent in its preparation.

Everyone has different needs and requirements for food, according to:

their age and sex
their health condition
their daily activity
the climate in which they live
their likes, dislikes, food customs and taboos

The preparation and consumption of food is also influenced by:

1 The interest and motivation of the person who is preparing the food.
2 The culinary abilities and skills of the food preparer.
3 The time and the facilities that are available for preparing food.
4 The foods that are available.
5 The income available to be spent on food.

Appetite and the desire to eat food are also affected by:

1 The colour, appearance, and presentation of the food.
2 The taste, smell, and texture of the food.
3 The surroundings and atmosphere in which the food is eaten.

Until fairly recently, meals were a very time-consuming part of family life. Long and elaborate preparation was often involved, and the whole family would sit down together to eat in a leisurely manner.

Food habits have changed to fit in with rapidly changing lifestyles. The increase in shift-working, more women going out to work, and television viewing at mealtimes, have all contributed towards a general reduction in the time spent in preparing food and eating meals, and often one or more members of the family will be absent at mealtimes.

Advances in kitchen technology, such as the introduction of freezers and microwave cookers, have helped to reduce the time spent on food preparation. Convenience foods and 'instant' meals are also important factors in this change.

There is now a great variety of foods to choose from in the shops, due to advances in food production, technology, transport, and storage. A vast number of foods are imported from overseas, and foreign restaurants and 'take-away' food shops have also contributed significantly to the change in people's eating habits.

Meals still have to be planned, however, and individual needs have to be considered. Few people work out a detailed weekly plan for their meals, and buy their food strictly according to that plan. But in some cases this long-term meal planning is necessary; in catering establishments such as canteens, hospital kitchens, restaurants, and hotels, it is of vital importance.

Terminology associated with meal planning

Balanced meal

A balanced meal is one which provides all the nutrients an individual needs in suitable amounts throughout the day. It should also provide a balance of texture, flavour, colour, and variety of foods in order to be appetizing.

Diet

The word 'diet' refers to the food eaten by an individual every day. There are also special diets, e.g. low-fat diets, low-salt diets, diabetic diets, etc.

Meals

Breakfast

The word means to break a fast, i.e. a period of time when food is not eaten (during sleep).

Lunch/dinner

There is often regional confusion as to the application of these two words. Some people refer to the meal eaten at midday as dinner, while others call it lunch; others refer to the meal eaten in the evening as dinner. For the purposes of this section, the following words will be used to denote the main meals of the day:

breakfast
midday meal
evening meal

Tea
Tea used to be served in many homes at about four o'clock in the afternoon, and usually consisted of a drink of tea with some form of cake or biscuit. It is less common now, but often children will have tea when they arrive home from school.

High tea
The meal eaten at about six o'clock in the evening is sometimes referred to as high tea. It usually consists of a cooked dish, with a drink and some form of cake or biscuit.

Supper
The last meal eaten before bedtime is usually referred to as supper. This might be a full evening meal, or it might be a hot drink and biscuits.

Courses

The word 'courses' refers to how a meal is divided up. A three-course meal consists of:

1st course – starter/appetizer
2nd course – main part of meal
3rd course – sweet, or cheese and biscuits

Individual requirements for food

Pregnant women

It is important that the diet of a pregnant woman should be nutritionally sound, so that she produces a healthy baby, and at the same time maintains her own health.

Even before pregnancy, it is vital that a woman of child-bearing age has a balanced diet so that she is able to cope with the demands of pregnancy, once this occurs.

There used to be a popular saying that a pregnant woman should 'eat for two'. In one sense this is true, but what it does *not* mean is that she should eat double her normal amount of food. This is not necessary, and it could lead to obesity. What it *does* mean, however, is that her diet should provide sufficient nutrients to cope with the demands of the growing baby (foetus) as well as the needs of her own body. The increased requirements for individual nutrients in pregnancy are shown in the tables of Recommended Intakes.

The foetus receives nutrients from the mother. The nutrients are carried from the mother's blood stream through the **placenta** (afterbirth) and **umbilical cord** into the baby's blood stream.

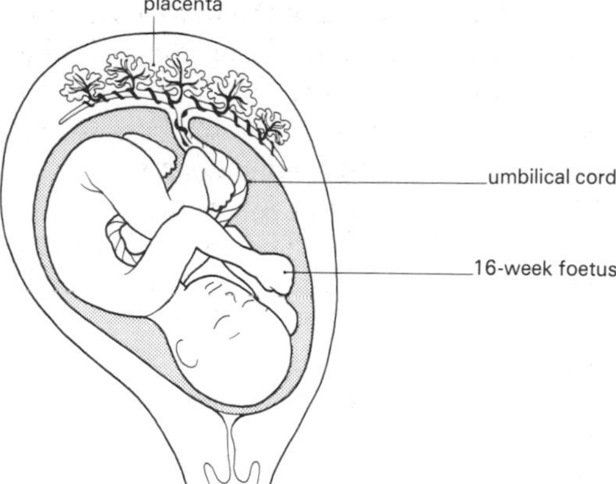

The mother's blood enters the placenta, carrying nutrients, and the blood from the foetus leaves, carrying waste products.

Nature ensures that if a particular nutrient is in short supply, it is the foetus who receives that nutrient, not the mother. In countries where food supplies are scarce and diets are consequently poor, this may affect the health of the mother quite drastically. For example, she may suffer from:

Lack of calcium
If the diet is deficient in calcium or vitamin D, then some of the calcium from the mother's bones and teeth will be removed and passed on to the foetus. This will weaken the mother's bones and teeth, and she may even develop adult rickets (osteomalacia).

Lack of vitamin A
If the diet is deficient in vitamin A, then any that is stored in the mother's liver will go to the foetus. This may result in the symptoms of vitamin A deficiency (see pp. 22–3). Often, the foetus' store of vitamin A does not build up sufficiently. Once born, many babies develop vitamin A deficiency symptoms, and every year, many thousands go blind. In the UK, however, vitamin A deficiency is rare.

Lack of iron

A deficiency of iron can lead to anaemia in the mother and a failure to build up a store of iron in the foetus. This store is important because both breast milk and cow's milk are poor sources of iron, and the new-born baby has to rely on the store of iron that it builds up as a foetus, for the first two to three months of its life. In the UK, to prevent anaemia in pregnancy, iron tablets are prescribed to most pregnant women.

In the UK, a careful check is made on the health of the mother and the progress of the foetus at ante-natal clinics. The mother is given advice about diet during pregnancy by the doctor or dietitian. On the whole, healthy babies are born here.

During pregnancy it is advisable that the intake of the following nutrients should be increased in the daily diet:

vitamin D

minerals, especially iron and calcium, particularly in the last three months

It may also be necessary to increase the intake of fibre to prevent constipation which may be a problem during pregnancy.

It is important *not* to increase the energy intake in the form of carbohydrates and fats too much as this could lead to an excess of body fat being laid down which might not be easy to lose afterwards. It is normal for about 4 kg (8·8 lb) of extra body fat to be laid down as a store of energy for breast-feeding and increased activity by the mother after the birth. The body weight is also increased due to the weight of the baby and the fluid by which it is surrounded.

Post-natal (after the birth of the baby)

After the birth, the mother's nutrient requirements increase, to enable the body to cope with the demands of breast-feeding and the increased activity and work associated with rearing a baby.

Her liquid consumption needs to be increased if she is breast-feeding.

Infancy (up to one year)

An infant's diet for the first few weeks of life consists solely of milk. Human breast milk is specifically designed to feed human babies and it therefore follows that it is more suitable than other milks for a number of reasons:

1 The correct composition and proportions of nutrients are provided.
2 The milk is at the correct temperature and consistency.
3 Virtually all the milk is digested by the baby.
4 The baby takes only what he needs, and is therefore less likely to become overweight.
5 Immunity from certain diseases is passed to the baby from the mother to help build up his resistance.
6 No preparation is required and there is little chance of gastric infections occurring as the milk is sterile.

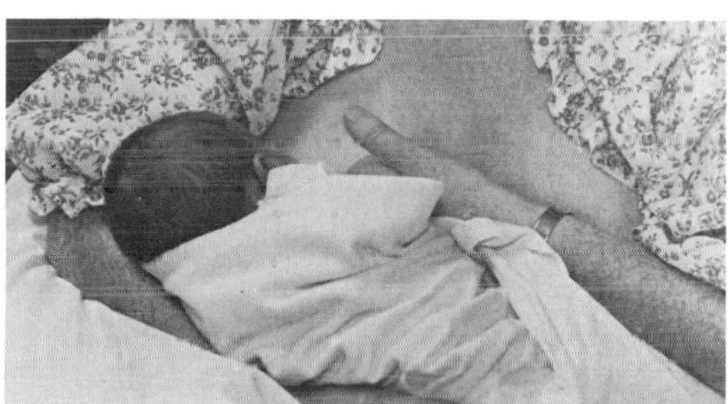

Human breast milk is ideal for babies.

This does not mean, however, that bottle-fed babies are at a disadvantage, providing that the milk they are given is prepared exactly as instructed. Problems arise if too much powdered milk is used to make up a feed, as this can lead to obesity and a strain on the kidneys caused by increased concentration of the milk.

Powdered milk preparations are usually made from cow's milk which is specially modified to make it similar to human milk.

Baby (2–3 months)

Extra iron and vitamin C to supplement the milk diet can be provided in the form of special syrups, juices, or drops. It is, however, dangerous to put syrups on to a dummy for the baby to suck, as the sugar in them can cause tooth decay even before the teeth are fully formed. The syrup should be diluted with water and given as a drink.

Weaning

Weaning means the gradual introduction of solid foods into the diet of a baby, to supplement the milk, which is still provided.

Weaning is normally started after three to four months as the milk no longer provides enough nutrients on its own to cope with the baby's rapid body growth. It is inadvisable to start weaning any earlier, as the baby's kidneys and digestive system may not be developed sufficiently to cope with the extra food.

Different foods should be introduced gradually, a little at a time, and should be sieved or puréed so that the baby can swallow them without choking. Suggested introductory foods:

rusks or ground cereals in milk
puréed vegetables, meat, fish, fruit
sieved cooked egg or egg custard

It is not necessary nor advisable to add sugar to these foods as this will encourage the baby to want sweet foods when he is older, and this can have undesirable consequences. Nor should extra salt be added, as this will put a strain on the kidneys.

As the baby becomes used to solid foods and his teeth start to develop, coarser foods like the types listed above can be introduced, which are less finely puréed. Foods to encourage chewing and to help teething can be given, e.g.:

dry rusks
toasted bread
pieces of fruit, e.g. apple (skinned)

Foods for a baby can be prepared from family meals by using a liquidizer, sieve, or special baby-food grinder. Commercially-produced baby foods can also be purchased. These can be quickly prepared, and contain the right amounts of nutrients to provide a balanced diet.

Toddlers and young children (up to 5 years)

Different foods in various forms should continue to be introduced, so that the child does not become too limited in his food choice. At this age, growth and activity are greatly increased, and meals should provide plenty of the following nutrients to cope with this:

protein – for body growth
calcium – for bones and teeth
fluoride – for teeth
iron – for red blood cells

The diet should be well balanced in all other respects.

Children should be discouraged from eating in between meals, especially sweets and snacks such as crisps, as this may lead to a poor appetite at mealtimes and therefore an unbalanced diet. Tooth decay and obesity may also occur.

Good food habits and table manners should be encouraged at this age, and mealtimes should become regular, enjoyable occasions.

Children of this age often have small appetites, and sometimes a child may not want to eat. This is unlikely to be harmful, and it is unwise to try and force the child to eat if he does not want to. It is probably best to give a child small portions with the option of eating a little more if desired.

To encourage children to eat, food should be served attractively, and strongly spiced or flavoured foods should be introduced only gradually. Suggested meals for this age group are given below.

Breakfast

wholegrain, unsweetened cereal with milk, and perhaps fruit or yogurt

eggs – boiled, poached, or scrambled
or a small piece of fish, poached
or a small rasher of bacon and a tomato

toast (preferably wholemeal bread)
butter or margarine
yeast extract or a little jam or marmalade

milk or fruit juice

Midday meal

a small piece of baked or poached fish
or a small portion of meat or bean stew
or a cheese and vegetable omelette
or a salad
with any of the above:
green vegetables, carrots, potatoes, rice, or pasta

fresh fruit, mousse, fool, or yogurt
egg custard, rice or other milk pudding
drink – e.g. fruit juice, milk

Evening meal
egg – boiled, poached, or scrambled
or fish cakes, lentil burger
or small salad with meat, egg, or cheese
wholemeal bread, butter or margarine

small piece of cake or fruit
or yogurt
milk or fruit juice

a drink before bedtime – milk, fruit juice

School-age children

Activity and body growth continue to increase at this period of life. Meals must therefore provide ample energy, and nutrients for body growth and maintenance. New foods will continue to be introduced, and by this stage mealtimes should be well established.

School meals may supply about one third of the child's total daily requirements for nutrients. If a child takes a packed lunch, care should be taken to ensure that this is well balanced. (See pp. 52–3.)

Adolescents

Adolescence is a period of rapid growth and body development, and consequently nutrient requirements increase at this stage of development.

The hormones for adulthood are produced at this stage and may cause skin disturbances. It is important for adolescents to eat plenty of fresh fruit and vegetables and to avoid eating too many fatty foods which may aggravate these conditions. The diet should provide sufficient protein, and particularly for girls, sufficient iron to avoid the symptoms of anaemia which may develop at the onset of menstruation.

Snacks for school-age children and adolescents

It is likely at this age that snacks between meals will be eaten, as the appetite is often large. It is important to discourage the consumption of too much 'junk food', i.e. food that provides very little else except fat or sugar, which adds to the total energy intake but not to body building or maintenance. Fatty foods, such as potato chips, fall into this category, and whilst they provide more than sugar, their high fat content and satiety value is likely to affect the appetite, so that other, more nutritious foods are not eaten at mealtimes.

The following foods are preferable as snacks between meals:

fresh fruit
raw vegetables, e.g. carrots, celery
yogurt
crispbreads with a little butter/margarine
soup

A large consumption of carbonated drinks and squashes should also be discouraged as the sugar content of such drinks is often very high. Fruit juice, milk, or water are preferable.

The snacks industry is a very large one and many of its customers are young people to whom it advertises snack products in many ways. It is therefore difficult to impose sensible eating habits on this age group. However, if sound eating habits are established when children are very young, they are less likely to break them at this age.

Adults

Once body growth has declined in adulthood, food is required to maintain and repair the body and to keep it healthy.

Nutrient requirements will to some extent be determined by body size and the amount of daily activity (see pp. 39–40). On the whole, women need a smaller amount of food than men, but their requirement for iron is greater because of menstruation. Nutrient requirements for women will also differ during pregnancy and after the birth of a baby.

The type of job and amount of daily activity will affect the amount of energy and nutrients that are required, and meals should be planned according to these needs. Energy requirements for different occupations were discussed on pp. 39–40, and suggested menus for these are given overleaf.

Very active jobs

It is important that meals for this type of worker provide sufficient energy, and it is advisable to supply about one third of the energy in the form of fat, as carbohydrate foods tend to be bulky and would therefore be difficult to digest while working actively. Extra water and sodium chloride should be taken if the work is carried out in a hot atmosphere. Suitable foods include:

Breakfast
wholegrain cereal and/or fresh fruit salad

grilled bacon, egg, sausage, tomato
or omelette with cheese, mushrooms, or meat
or poached fish with eggs

toast, butter, marmalade or jam

coffee or tea

Midday meal (packed)
vegetable or meat pasties, pulse-based soup
or sandwiches or rolls with various fillings (eggs, cheese, meat, etc.)

fresh fruit
yogurt
a piece of cake or biscuit

soup, coffee, tea, or other drink

Evening meal (or midday cooked meal)
soup, e.g. lentil, onion, potato, vegetable

meat or poultry: in stews or pies, or roasted
or pasta with a meat sauce
or nut or pulse roast with savoury sauce
or grilled or fried fish

fresh vegetables or salad

fresh fruit
or steamed pudding, fruit pie, mousse, milk pudding, custard or other sauce
drink

It is important to try and spread the energy intake throughout the day.

Sedentary jobs

Careful attention should be paid to the energy intake of meals for this type of worker, as it could easily exceed energy output and therefore lead to weight increase. Energy-dense snack foods, such as chocolate, pastries, cakes, biscuits, and crisps, should be eaten in moderation as they are highly palatable and convenient, and can increase the energy intake quite markedly.

Meals should also not be too bulky as they may take longer to digest in an inactive job. Suggested foods include:

Breakfast
fresh fruit or fruit juice

a small amount of cereal or yogurt
or grilled bacon and tomatoes
or poached fish or egg

toast, butter, marmalade

tea or coffee

Midday meal (packed)
a round of sandwiches or rolls with various fillings, e.g. egg, canned fish, cottage cheese

fresh fruit
yogurt
a small piece of cake

drink

Evening meal (or cooked midday meal)
soup or fruit juice

meat or fish (as a stew, grilled, etc.)
or egg and cheese dish
or pulse- or nut-based dish e.g. lentil curry

fresh vegetables

mousse, yogurt, fresh fruit, or small portion of steamed or baked pudding

drink

The daily intake of **alcohol** increases the energy intake, as alcohol yields 29·3 kJ (7 kcal) per gram. Many people have a drink with a meal and add to their energy intake considerably in this way.

Packed meals

Many people take a packed midday meal to work or school, or as a picnic in preference to a bought meal in a canteen or restaurant. Such meals are therefore an important part of the daily food supply, and as such, should be well planned and prepared. The following list of rules for packed meals should be considered:

1 The meal should be substantial and should supply one third of the daily intake of nutrients and energy.
2 It is important to provide a balanced meal. Foods that supply mainly energy and little else should be kept to a minimum.
3 The food should be easy to eat, with the minimum of cutlery and the minimum of waste, bearing in mind that it may have to be consumed in an awkward place, such as a building site.
4 The food should be carefully packed, so that it does not become crushed or damaged in transit. Delicate items should be packed above more robust foods. A sturdy package, e.g. a plastic box with a lid, is ideal for transporting the food. Items inside the box should be individually wrapped.
5 If the food is to be left in a warm place before being consumed, e.g. in a car, then foods such as cooked meats should not be included to avoid the possibility of bacterial growth.
6 A variety of textures and flavours should be included, and there should also be a drink. Drinks and soups can be kept hot in vacuum flasks.

Suggested foods for packed meals include:
- soups
- sandwiches or rolls, with any of these fillings: egg/cress; cheese/tomato; tuna fish/tomato; cold meat; tuna fish/cucumber; peanut butter/cucumber
- pasties (meat or vegetable)
- egg and cheese flan
- fresh fruit
- cake or biscuit
- fruit juice, milk, or hot drink

Senior citizens

As age increases, activity slows down, especially after retirement from an active job. Food is required to maintain the health and state of the body as in younger age groups, but there may be an increased requirement for:

Calcium and vitamin D – to help prevent **decalcification** (the gradual removal of calcium) from the bones and teeth so that they do not become brittle and weak.
Iron to prevent anaemia.

The size of meals should decrease with less activity, but the quality should not. There is no need for the elderly to eat soft or smooth foods only, unless they have a digestive disorder which makes this necessary; crisp, crunchy, and hard foods can still be enjoyed, even with dentures, providing that they fit properly.

It may be necessary to increase the intake of fibre to avoid constipation, which is a common disorder in this age group. Many elderly people resort to using laxatives to prevent or ease constipation. This is undesirable and usually unnecessary if the diet contains sufficient fibre.

A reduced income may mean that it is not possible to buy much meat or other protein foods, and this poses problems to many senior citizens. Pulses and cereals can be eaten as cheaper alternatives to meat and other animal protein foods, or to supplement them. Decreased mobility may also influence where food is purchased and how often, and the elderly may require help from the social services department or from willing neighbours. The loss of a partner may also affect the motivation to cook and eat well, and this often leads to poor health among the elderly.

Meal planning during illness and convalescence

When someone is ill or recovering from an illness, accident, or operation, it may be necessary to adjust their normal diet to compensate for body weakness, poor appetite, or poor digestion.

If the illness is serious or complicated, it may be necessary for the doctor to prescribe a strict diet, which should be followed carefully.

When the patient is convalescing (recovering) from an illness or operation, it is necessary to provide food which will compensate for the loss of nutrients and strength which have occurred, e.g. loss of calcium and protein from a bone fracture, or loss of iron as a result of losing blood.

Feeding a patient during illness

In the initial stages of an illness, the body temperature may rise while an infection is being fought. This will lead to an increase in body water loss through sweating, and will need to be compensated for by an increase in liquid consumption. Often the appetite at this stage is poor, therefore liquids taken should provide energy, vitamins, and protein to make up for the reduced food intake. Suggested liquids include:

soups and broths
fruit juice (for vitamin C)
glucose-based drinks (for energy)
milk
water

There should always be a supply of fresh water by the patient's bed, as it may be required often.

As the patient gradually recovers, the appetite slowly returns, and solid foods can be given, but the following points should be remembered:

1 As the appetite is likely to be poor, the food provided must contain a good balance of nutrients so that it is useful to the body.
2 Small portions should be served with the option of extra should the patient want it.
3 The food should be easy to eat and digest.
4 Greasy foods should be avoided as they may be indigestible. Strong flavours may be unpalatable.
5 The patient will generally be using less energy while in bed, so the energy value of the food should be lower than normal.
6 The food should tempt the patients' appetite, and this can be achieved by attractive serving, variety of colour and texture, and food which is well cooked and well presented.
7 Particular likes and dislikes for food should be taken into account.
8 Careful attention to hygiene in the preparation and serving of the food is most important, and the food must be very fresh.
9 Left-over food should not be served to avoid the possibility of contamination.
10 Food preparation should be carried out away from the patient as the smell of cooking may affect the appetite.

Suitable foods to serve include:

Breakfast
wholegrain cereal with milk or fresh fruit salad
egg, poached, boiled, scrambled (garnish with toast, tomato, parsley)
or fish, poached (white fish is more digestible than oily fish)
toasted wholemeal bread, lightly buttered
a drink, e.g. milk, fruit juice, malted milk

Midday meal
minced beef in a savoury sauce
or fish, steamed and served in a sauce
or casseroled or grilled chicken with salad
or omelette with cheese, mushrooms, or meat
or soup, containing meat or pulses
fresh vegetables or salad in each case
fresh fruit salad or stewed fruit
or mousse or fruit fool
or individual steamed pudding with a sauce
or egg custard or crème caramel
or milk pudding (rice, tapioca, semolina)
or jelly made with milk and fresh fruit

Evening meal or tea
a small piece of cake
plain biscuits, made with wholemeal flour
bread, butter, jam or honey
fresh fruit
yogurt
a drink, e.g. milk, fruit juice, malted milk

The consumption of some or all of the following foods should be reduced or omitted during most illnesses:

1 Oily or fatty foods, e.g. oily fish, pork, lamb, fried foods, as these may be indigestible.
2 Heavy, stodgy foods, e.g. suet puddings, rich cakes, pasta.
3 Highly spiced or strongly flavoured foods.
4 Rich pastries and biscuits.

Feeding a patient during convalescence

The guidelines for feeding convalescents are similar to those for feeding patients who are ill, except that the appetite is likely to be better and the patient may be able to eat at a normal table instead of in bed, so that serving is easier.

If a patient has a broken limb, foods that contain good supplies of calcium should be eaten (e.g. cheese, milk), so that the bone heals strongly. Extra protein and vitamin D will also be needed for this purpose.

If the patient is recovering from an accident or operation, extra protein for body repair, and iron to replace that lost in blood, should be taken.

Vegetarian meals

Vegetarians are people who will not consume animal food, for which an animal has had to be slaughtered or has suffered in any way. There are several reasons why a person may become a vegetarian, including:

1 Religious belief.
2 Objection to the slaughter of animals, because it is considered to be cruel, or economically wasteful (it is expensive to rear animals and a lot of land is used, which could produce far more food if it were used for growing cereal crops).
3 Dislike of animal flesh.
4 Dietary reasons.
5 Belief that a vegetarian diet is more healthy than a carnivorous (meat-eating) diet.

There are two types of vegetarian:
lacto-vegetarians
vegans (strict vegetarians)

Lacto-vegetarians

Lacto-vegetarians will *not* eat:
meat, fish, lard, suet, fish oils

To produce these, the animal or fish has had to be slaughtered. However, they *will* eat food products from animals, e.g.:
free-range eggs, milk, cheese, butter, cream, yogurt

To produce these does not involve suffering for the animal. Special vegetarian cheese can be purchased, which is made with vegetable rennet rather than animal rennet (see p. 43), which comes from the stomach of the calf.

There are no real problems associated with providing a lacto-vegetarian diet, and the majority of nutrients are easy to obtain. There may be a slight problem with iron, however, as it is known to be made unavailable to the body in certain plant foods (see p. 31) and may be unavailable from egg yolk (see p. 31).

It may be beneficial to limit the number of dairy foods, e.g. cheese, butter, and whole milk, to avoid a large intake of saturated fatty acids (see p. 16). Reduced-fat versions of these foods could be used instead, e.g. cottage cheese, skimmed milk.

Suggested foods for a lacto-vegetarian include:
savoury flans, e.g. eggs, cheese, onion, and mushroom
vegetable pies with cheese shortcrust pastry
cheese Scotch eggs
salads with pulses, cheese and eggs
nuts and beans used to provide extra protein

Vegans (strict vegetarians)

Vegans will not eat any food that is made directly or indirectly from an animal, even if the animal has not been slaughtered for that purpose. They also refuse to use products such as soaps, cosmetics, and polishes, which involve the use of animal oils, fats, etc.

With careful planning, vegan meals can be made appetizing and good to eat; and with a knowledge of the value of foods, they can be nutritionally well balanced. There are several important points that must be taken into consideration when planning vegan diets:

1 **Protein** is found in relatively small amounts in plant foods, therefore a large bulk may have to be eaten in order to provide enough. The richest sources are:
soya beans
other beans
pulses
cereals
nuts

As many plant proteins are of low biological value (see p. 13), it is necessary to eat a mixture of plant protein foods to make up for the deficiencies of essential amino-acids in each.

The extra bulk from carbohydrates, cellulose, and water in these foods may

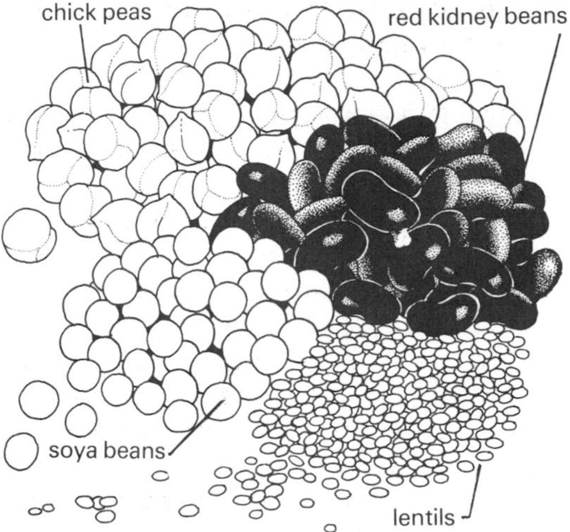

lead to indigestion and fullness after a meal, so it may be necessary to spread out the intake of food through the day.

2 **Vitamin D** is found in very few plant foods in useful amounts, so the action of sunlight on the skin is an important source. Vitamin D is added to margarine, but if there are animal products in the margarine vegans will not eat it.
3 **Vitamin A** is present in plants as carotene (see p. 22).
4 **Calcium** can be provided by pulses, cereals, nuts, fruit, and vegetables, but some may be unavailable to the body, due to the presence of phytic acid (see p. 30). This may pose problems for young children whose bones are still developing, and who may not be able to eat large quantities of such foods in order to obtain sufficient calcium.
5 **Vitamins B and C** can be provided by fruit and vegetables, and vitamin B is also found in wholegrain cereals, yeast extract, and bread.
6 **Fat** is provided by vegetable oils and is also found naturally in nuts.

Extra vitamins and minerals can be taken in the form of tablets and drops, providing that they are made synthetically (man-made) and do not come from animals originally. Vitamin B_{12} is only found in animal foods, and vegans may be at risk of developing a deficiency anaemia. It may be necessary for them to take it in tablet form to avoid this.

There are many varieties of nuts, pulses, and cereals which can be used to produce satisfying and interesting meals for vegans. The use of spices, herbs, unusual vegetables and fruits adds variety and flavour, and there is no need for the diet to become monotonous. Many recipe books have been published, giving ideas for vegan meals, and there are several restaurants and eating houses which cater solely for vegetarians.

Suggested meals for vegans include:

- bean and vegetable stews (made with vegetable stock)
- salads with nuts and cooked pulses
- nut roasts with vegetables
- soups with cereal (e.g. barley, rice)
- vegetable curry and rice

Food customs among minority groups

Food customs and habits vary between different countries and within individual countries according to tradition, religious belief, climate, food supply, and facilities. In the UK, there are now numerous ethnic minority groups, all of which have different needs and customs related to food.

It is not possible here to go into great detail about each, as they are very complex, but some basic information is useful to anyone involved in catering for such groups. Three of the largest ethnic groups are considered here.

Jews

Jewish food customs and dietary laws are based on the ancient Jewish law in the Old Testament of the Bible (Leviticus, chapter 11). Only foods that are considered fit for human consumption, according to these laws, are permitted, and are collectively known as 'kosher' foods. These include:

beef, veal, mutton, lamb
all salt and freshwater fish, except for shellfish and eels
duck, chicken, turkey, goose

Foods that are considered to be unfit for human consumption are called 'trefah' or non-kosher foods, and include:

rabbit, hare
pork, bacon, ham
shellfish
eels
eggs with blood spots
gelatine

Meat and poultry has to be slaughtered by an approved ecclesiastical representative, according to a special ritual.

Orthodox Jews are not allowed to mix milk and meat in any way. This means that:

1 Milk and meat may not be cooked or prepared together, and separate utensils and pans are required.
2 Milk and meat may not be served together, and must have separate cutlery and serving dishes.
3 Milk may not be eaten after meat, until three to six hours have elapsed. Milk can only be eaten before meat if the hands are washed and the mouth is rinsed in between.

Hindus

Hindus regard the cow as sacred and therefore will not kill it for food. However, products from the cow which do not involve slaughter are eaten, e.g. milk, butter which has been pasteurized (ghee), and curds. Cheese is not often eaten.

Orthodox Hindus will not eat any animal food which has been killed. In all cases, the pig is regarded as unclean and is not eaten.

Muslims

The food customs of Muslims were originally the same as those of the Jews. The pig is regarded as unclean, and is therefore not eaten. Other meat has to be ritually slaughtered, and many special Pakistani butcher's shops (Halal) have been opened in areas of the UK with high Muslim populations.

Some fish is eaten, and the Jewish rules on milk are not so closely followed.

Revision questions

1 Why do people vary in their needs for food?
2 How is the appetite affected?
3 Why have peoples' food habits altered in recent years?
4 Why is the diet of a pregnant woman important, and how can the mother-to-be ensure that she produces a healthy baby?
5 What is the function of the placenta as far as food is concerned?
6 Give four reasons why breast milk is best for a baby.
7 What is weaning, when should it be started, and what foods are suitable?
8 Why is it inadvisable for children to eat between meals?
9 Why is it important that adolescents have a well-balanced diet?
10 What are the dangers and disadvantages of eating too many sweet and fried foods?
11 Why is it important that a very active worker has a satisfying and nutritious meal at midday?
12 What are the important points to remember when preparing packed meals?
13 What important points should be remembered when preparing foods for people who are:
a ill in bed
b recovering from a bone fracture?
14 What is the difference between a lacto-vegetarian and a vegan? Suggest suitable meals for each.
15 Briefly describe the food customs of Jews, Muslims, and Hindus.

Questions and activities

1 Collect a variety of (e.g. 6) packets or cans of food such as breakfast cereals, fruit, cake mixes, baby foods.
Study the ingredients lists and other information on the labels.
   - **a** Which of your examples give nutritional information? (e.g. low fat, vitamin content, etc.)
   - **b** How easy is this information to understand? Could it be made any clearer, and if so, how?
   - **c** Why do food manufacturers print nutritional information on food labels? Which particular groups of people might benefit from such information?
   - **d** How else do the manufacturers in your examples try to promote the nutritional value of their product? (e.g. pictures, advertisements, etc.)
   - **e** Giving examples, write about the importance of clear labelling on household products, medicines, and clothing, with regard to safety, efficient use, and care of such items.

2 Make a list of the priorities the following people might have when choosing their food:
   - **a** a mother of two school age children
   - **b** a widowed man, living on a pension
   - **c** a student living on a grant
   - **d** a pregnant woman

Choose one of the above and write about the other priorities they would have with regard to their weekly income, and the various benefits that are available to help people in certain circumstances.

3 Plan a day's meals, giving detailed reasons for your choice, for the following situation:
A young couple have decided to try as far as possible to follow the dietary goals (see p. 10) recommended by various nutrition reports. They both work, take a packed lunch, and enjoy cooking and food in general. They live in a large town, with a large population of young couples. What other ways, besides dietary ones, could the couple keep fit and healthy? What facilities in the town might they use to help them?

4 What effect(s) do the following have in each case on the nutrients in the foods listed? How could the nutrients be preserved?
   - **a** leaving milk in a bottle outside in sunlight for several hours
   - **b** boiling cabbage for 20 minutes in a pan full of water
   - **c** grilling a lamb chop until it is dry and hard
   - **d** leaving a carton of fresh orange juice open for several days

Which groups of people in Britain today might need to take extra nutrients to maintain their health? Give reasons why this may be necessary.

5 Good health is important even before a baby is born.
   - **a** Find out and write an account about the information that is available for a pregnant woman from the various health and welfare services.
   - **b** What is the role of the Health Visitor once the baby is born?
   - **c** What is wrong with the following situation? A mother makes up her baby's bottle of milk, and adds an extra scoop of milk powder and some sugar. She then props the baby up in his carrycot with the bottle while she makes dinner. The baby frets and tries to drink the milk.
   - **d** Apart from food, what other factors influence the growth of children?

6 Compare the two meals listed below, which were chosen by two school children from the canteen at lunchtime:

choice 1	*choice 2*
cheese and egg salad	sausage roll
wholemeal bread roll	chips
butter	doughnut
banana	apple
fresh orange juice	orange squash

a Which choice of meal is closer to following the dietary goals? Why?

b What are the main nutrients supplied by each choice of meal? Which meal has a greater variety of nutrients?

c Which meal is more suitable for helping a child to grow? Give reasons for your answers.

One reason many schools offer a choice, instead of a set meal, is to avoid food wastage. Find out how food waste and other household rubbish is dealt with in your area, i.e. where it goes, what it costs to deal with it, etc. Why is it important to cut down on food wastage?

7 Obesity is a major health hazard and affects many people. Make a study of the help that is available in the media (TV, radio, magazines, etc.) for people who are trying to reduce their weight. Investigate a variety of products (foods, drinks, exercise machines, etc.) that are sold to encourage people to slim. How are such products promoted? Criticize (constructively) such products, and suggest how they could be improved or what alternatives could be used by people trying to lose weight.

8 Using information collected from newspapers, magazines, TV, etc., compare and contrast the lives of two school-age children – one living in Britain, the other in the Sudan or Ethiopia – in terms of their health and family life. What conclusions can you draw from your findings?

9 Which nutrients are required for the following? In each case, explain how and why they work:

a prevention of anaemia

b strength of bones and teeth

c production of energy in the body

What forms of energy are used in the home for the comfort of people and efficient running of a household?

10 Health food shops are becoming more abundant in shopping centres and towns. If possible, visit a health food shop, and collect some information about the products sold there.

What kind of image or message do such shops try to promote to the public?

Why are such shops becoming more popular?

Compare the prices of some of the products with their equivalents in ordinary supermarkets. Comment on any differences.

2/Foods and food science

Food production, processing, and retail

World food production

Approximately 14% of the world's population (about 400 million people) do not get enough food to eat, and suffer from undernutrition, while many of the rest eat too much. The rich parts of the world (including the UK) produce and consume the most food and have the smallest populations, while the poor parts have the least food and the highest populations.

In poor countries, many people farm their land in order to provide food for themselves, and often have to sell a large proportion of their produce to pay for the rent of the land. The amount of food that they produce is often very small for a variety of reasons, including:

1 **Poverty:** being unable to buy fertilizers, farm machinery, better seeds, etc.

2 **Crop failures:** due to infestation by pests (e.g. locusts), disease, infertile ground, lack of water, etc.

3 **Bad climate:** e.g. drought, flood, high winds.

4 **Limited agricultural technology:** lack of knowledge and finance to improve their farming methods.

5 **War:** damage to land and belongings.

In richer countries, farming and food production are highly mechanized, and technological advances have enabled high yields of food to be produced from crops, and many crop diseases to be eliminated.

A large proportion of the plant foods consumed in rich countries are used for feeding animals which are being reared to produce meat and dairy foods. In poorer countries plant foods are the main (staple) food of the people, as meat is far too expensive.

Poor countries often use large areas of their valuable growing land to grow 'cash crops', e.g. sugar or bananas, for export to rich countries, rather than for growing much needed food for their own people. Often the money earned from the exports goes into the hands of the few rich people in those countries and is not used for buying food.

Because of the increase in world population numbers, especially in poor countries, much research has been carried out to find ways of producing larger crops and alternative sources of protein (see pp. 108–9). The problem is by no means solved, however, and the distribution of world food supplies remains very unfair.

Food production in the UK

Most of the spare land in the UK is devoted to agriculture, and it has to be intensively farmed to cater for the dense population. About half of the UK's food supplies are imported from various parts of the world, and since 1972 Britain has belonged to the European Economic Community (EEC) or Common Market. The EEC directly influences food supply and production in Europe, by means of the Common Agricultural Policy (CAP).

Common Agricultural Policy

The EEC established the CAP in 1957 for all its member countries. Its aims were:

1 To increase the productivity and efficiency of farming.
2 To increase and maintain farmers' incomes.
3 To secure supplies of food, and to increase self sufficiency in food and prevent price fluctuations.
4 To provide food at reasonable prices.

Foods from the rest of the world are still imported, as not all foods can be grown within the EEC, and some foods are exported. Some farmers who are considered to have a good production potential are given subsidies to improve their farming facilities.

The EEC enforces its own regulations for various aspects of food production and retail, such as hygiene, weights and measures, labelling, and food additives.

Food manufacture and technology

Food manufacture and technology have developed rapidly over the last hundred years. Before then, food was manufactured and sold locally to a small area, and processing and technology were very limited.

Today, a relatively small number of large companies in the UK each produce several kinds of food products. These companies often own large areas of farm land and the farmer grows food specifically for the company to process, e.g. vegetables for freezing or canning. They also import foods from various parts of the world.

Food technology influences people's food habits in several ways:

1 78% of the population of the UK live in urban districts, away from the areas where food is produced. Food manufacturers have enabled a wide choice of food to be brought to these people, in good condition, all year round.
2 New foods and food inventions, such as imitation cream, TVP (see pp. 108–9), and instant foods, have been developed and the number of different types of processed foods available has increased from about 1,500 in 1950 to about 10,000 today. This has also widened people's food choice.
3 Food technology also affects the nutritional value of people's diets. In many processing methods nutrients are lost (e.g. milling of wheat to make white bread), and may or may not be replaced. Food additives are also used which may in the long term affect people's health (see pp. 121–2).

Food retailing

Before the advent of the supermarket in the late 1940s, different types of food were sold in specialist shops (greengrocer's, butcher's, fishmonger's, etc.).

Today, over 60% of foods are sold through supermarkets, many of which now belong to large 'chain' companies (i.e. a company which owns a number of supermarkets in different parts of the country). In 1973, four major retail chain companies accounted for a quarter of the total retail grocery sales in the UK. Chain companies generally buy their food direct from manufacturers rather than from a wholesaler, and they often sell some products under their own brand name, at a lower price than the manufacturing companies' equivalents.

Hypermarkets are a development of the supermarket, and are often situated in out-of-town areas. They are usually very large shops which sell not only food, but a wide range of other goods for the home.

The chart on the next page lists the main types of food retail outlets, and the advantages and disadvantages of each type.

Type of outlet	Advantages	Disadvantages
Supermarket or hypermarket	1 A wide range of goods available. 2 Prices generally cheaper for many items. 3 Food is usually good quality and fresh. 4 Food is selected by the customer – even fruit and vegetables. 5 Car parking is usually easy and convenient. 6 The standard of hygiene is usually very high. 7 Unusual foods may be stocked.	1 Supermarkets do not usually deliver food to the home. 2 The service may be impersonal. 3 It may be hard to get advice. 4 Self service may result in the customer spending more money than intended, and goods are often attractively presented to encourage this 'impulse buying'. 5 There may be long queues at the checkouts, which can increase shopping time considerably.
Small independent grocer	1 The personalized service is helpful to the customer. 2 The shop may deliver the goods. 3 These shops are often near to residential areas, and therefore handy.	1 The food may be expensive. 2 There may be a limited selection of food. 3 Food may not be very fresh as turnover may be slow.
Specialist shop	1 Advice on the food being sold is usually good. 2 Food is usually of good quality. 3 The selection of food within the range is normally good.	1 Food may be expensive. 2 The food may not be very fresh in some cases as turnover may be slow.
Open market	1 The food may be considerably cheaper. 2 There is normally a rapid turnover of food, so it is fresh.	1 The food actually sold may be of inferior quality to that on display. 2 The food may be open to flies and the standards of hygiene may not be very high. If the market is near the road, the food may be exposed to dust and car fumes. 3 It may not be possible to tell how fresh certain foods are, e.g. canned foods, cold meats, etc.

Points to look for in food shops

1 A high standard of hygiene.
2 Rotation of goods, so that old stocks are sold first.
3 Efficient, helpful, knowledgeable service.
4 A good selection of goods, in both range and sizes of products available.
5 Competitive prices.

Budgeting for food

When shopping for food, it is important to take economy into account as food is an expensive item in a family budget. The following guidelines should be followed:

1 Plan the weekly shopping before going out, and aim to stick to the plan as far as possible.
2 Look for competitive prices.
3 Look for good quality food that is good value for money.
4 Buy only the amounts that are required for particular meals, unless the extra food is to be used up on another occasion.

Bulk buying

Many people buy food in bulk once a month or less. This has the following advantages:

1 It saves time and petrol.
2 It leaves more time for leisure activities.
3 It may save money.

In order to be able to bulk buy, the following factors have to be considered:

1 There must be sufficient storage space in the home for the food.
2 The initial outlay of money must be available.
3 Transport to and from the shop must be available.

Many large supermarkets and hypermarkets cater for people who wish to buy food in bulk, and often sell large packs of goods at a lower price per unit than smaller packs. There are also many farms and small-holdings which sell produce that can be picked by the consumer in bulk, e.g. fruit and vegetables. Some farms also sell bulk quantities of meat for storage in the freezer as do many butchers' shops.

Bulk buying can be very useful, but care should be taken to ensure that unnecessary items are not bought and that there is not a tendency to eat more food just because it happens to be in the house.

Revision questions

1 What are the main reasons for famine in poor countries?
2 Why are countries such as the UK and the USA able to have more than enough to eat?
3 What is the Common Agricultural Policy?
4 How has food technology influenced people's food habits?
5 Compare the advantages and disadvantages of shopping for food in supermarkets, hypermarkets, independent grocers, specialist shops, and open markets.
6 What points should you look for in food shops?
7 What are hypermarkets?
8 How can the consumer shop wisely for food?

Cereals

Cereals are the seeds of cultivated grasses, which originally grew wild. About 10,000 years ago, ancient man continually moved about in tribes, searching for food, hunting animals, fishing, and gathering fruits. When it was discovered that certain types of grasses could be cultivated and used for food, tribes gradually settled in one area and concentrated on growing cereals and rearing animals to provide their food.

Cereals are the most important single food in nearly every country of the world. Even when a country becomes wealthy and eats more animal foods, cereals are still eaten in large amounts. In most countries, cereals are the staple foods for the majority of the population, because they are relatively easy to grow and are cheap in comparison to meat.

Types

Name	Areas grown
Wheat	USA, Canada, Argentina, Europe, Russia, Egypt, Northern India.
Maize	Southern USA, Italy, India, Yugoslavia, Egypt.
Rice	Damp tropical areas, e.g. India, China.
Oats 	Cold temperate climates, e.g. Scotland.
Barley 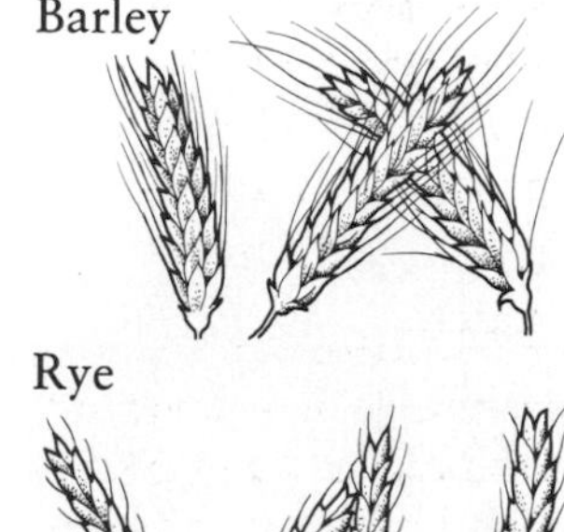	Temperate climates, e.g. UK.
Rye 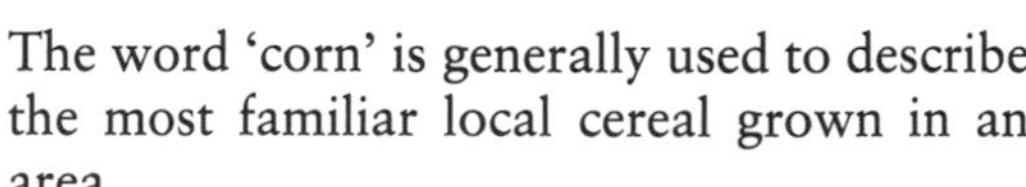	Cold climates, e.g. Scandinavia, Russia, Poland.

The word 'corn' is generally used to describe the most familiar local cereal grown in an area.

Wheat

Wheat is a main cereal food in many countries.

Wheat grains are divided into different layers. Each has a different function in the plant and contains different amounts and types of nutrients.

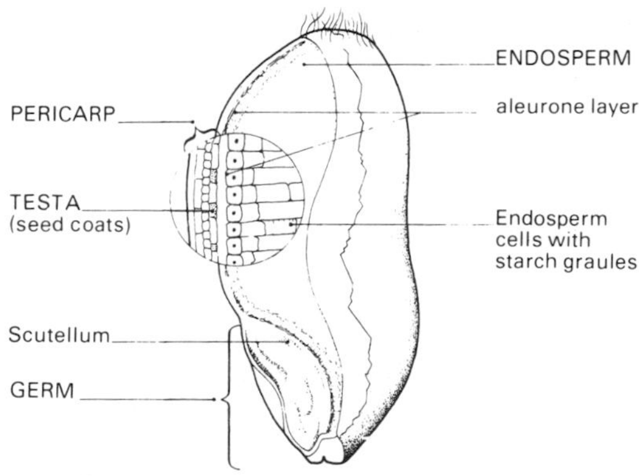

Distribution of nutrients in wheat

Part of grain	Nutrients
Pericarp, testa and aleurone layer	B vitamins (especially nicotinic acid); mineral elements (50% of total grain): iron*, phosphorus, calcium*; protein (concentrated source). Also contains cellulose, in the form of bran.

Scutellum	B vitamins (especially thiamin); protein.
Germ	B vitamins; vitamin E; protein; fat; iron.
Endosperm	B vitamins; protein; starch.

*Phytic acid is also present in these layers of the wheat and binds with calcium and iron in an insoluble form which limits their absorption in the body.

Types of wheat

Several varieties of wheat are grown, to produce different types of flour. The most common are:

Winter wheat, which is grown in the UK and Europe, and is sown in autumn and harvested the following summer. It produces **soft, weak** flour with less than 10% protein.

Spring wheat, which is grown in Canada, and is sown in early spring and harvested during the same year. It produces **hard, strong** flour with more than 10% protein.

Milling and flour production

Wheat is usually ground into flour before it is used as a food. This is achieved by **milling.** Modern milling is carried out using a series of **steel rollers**. The object of milling is to separate the endosperm from the rest of the grain, and to reduce the grain down to fine flour particles. The process is carried out in the following stages:

1 **Blending** of different varieties of wheat grain.

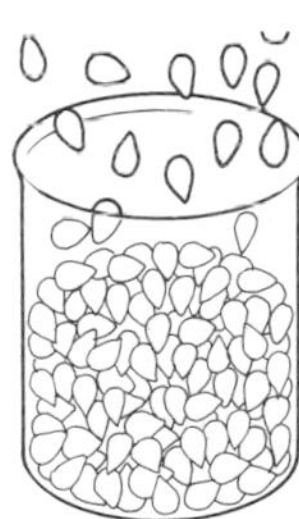

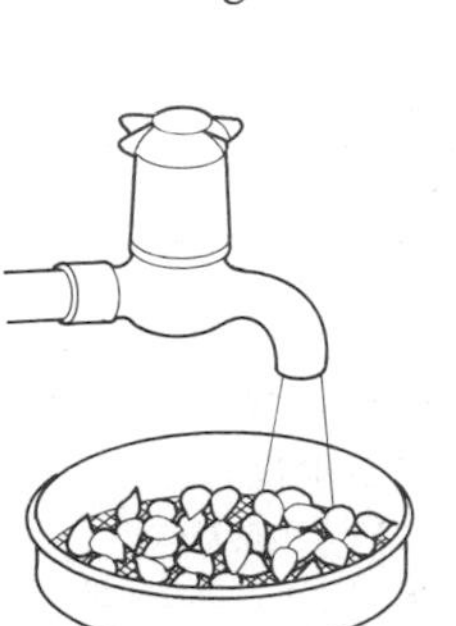

2 **Removing** dirt and stones by washing.

3 **Breaking** the grains between rollers rotating at different speeds.

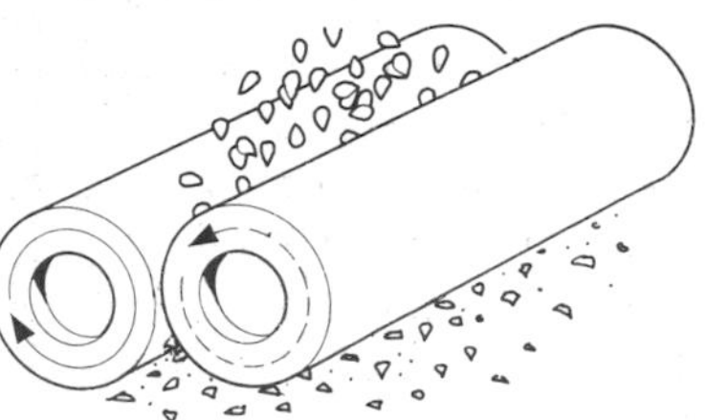

4 **Sieving** the crushed grain into

a a small amount of flour

b particles of endosperm (semolina)

c particles of bran with endosperm attached

5 **Removing the bran** by further rolling. The bran is used for animal feeds.

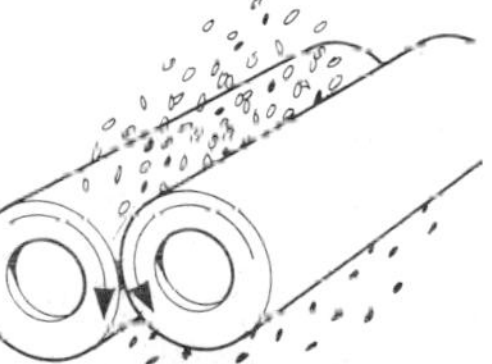

6 **Converting the endosperm into flour** by passing it through the next series of rollers, each set closer together than the last in order to produce a fine flour with the minimum damage to the starch granules. (Damaged starch granules produce poor quality flour.)

7 **Sieving** to remove the **germ** as a powder.

The milling process can be adjusted according to the amount and type of flour required from the original grain. The percentage of the whole grain used in the flour is called the **extraction rate** of the flour:

Type of flour	Extraction rate
Wholemeal (Contains all the components of the original grain, and is brown due to the bran.)	100%
Wheatmeal (Contains 85% of the original grain, with 15% discarded as bran, but is still brown due to the remaining bran.)	85%
White (Contains 70% of the original grain, with most of the bran, germ, fat, and minerals removed.)	70%

Advantages of wholemeal flour

1 The nutrient content of the grain is retained.
2 The bran provides a valuable source of fibre (see pp. 30–2).
3 The flour gives a pleasant 'nutty' flavour to baked items.

Disadvantages of wholemeal flour

1 It does not keep for as long as white flour due to the fat content which can become rancid relatively quickly.
2 The presence of phytic acid (see p. 30) may affect the absorption of calcium and iron.
3 It does not have such good baking qualities as white flour for items such as pastry and cakes.

Advantages of white flour

1 It has good baking qualities, producing a fine texture in cakes, bread, and pastry.
2 It contains less phytic acid.
3 It contains less fat and is therefore less likely to become rancid.

Disadvantages of white flour

1 It contain less fibre.
2 It contains less calcium and iron, although by law these are added to flour used for making bread.
3 It contains less protein and vitamins.

Loaves made from wholemeal and white flour.

Protein content and baking quality of flour

Wheat flours which have a protein content of more than 10% (hard, strong flours made from spring wheat) are normally used for bread making; flours with a protein content of less than 10% (soft, weak flours made from winter wheat) are normally used for cake, pastry, and biscuit making. The reason for the difference is the amount of **gluten** formed from the protein in the flour when it is mixed with water. However, not all flours of high protein content produce sufficient or strong enough gluten; **durum wheat**, which is used to make pasta, has a high protein content, but is unsuitable for baking as its gluten is tough and does not stretch.

The gluten of flours used for bread making has the ability to stretch and hold pockets of gas produced by yeast during rising and baking. When baked in the oven, the gluten stretches and eventually coagulates, forming a framework in the baked item. The dough should be kneaded thoroughly to develop the gluten and increase its elasticity. The addition of salt helps to strengthen the gluten, whereas sugar softens it. In commercially-produced bread, **dough improvers** such as vitamin C are added to help develop the gluten.

The gluten in flour helps the dough to stretch.

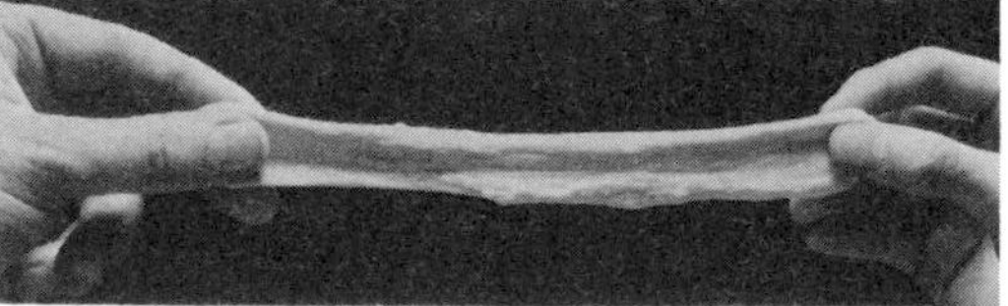

The loaf on the left was made from strong plain flour, the loaf on the right from weak flour.

The gluten of flours used for cake, pastry, and biscuit making is weaker and less elastic than that in strong, hard wheat flour, and is damaged by over-handling. It can be used to make bread, providing that it is handled less and more yeast is used to raise the dough. However, the volume of bread produced is usually less. When used in cake, pastry, or biscuit making, the gluten stretches and holds pockets of gas produced from raising agents. It sets to form a framework in the baked item, with a finer texture than the texture of bread.

Plain cake flour has no raising agent added to it, whereas self-raising flour has baking powder added commercially. Flour with an extraction rate of 80% can also be used for cakes, and may have baking powder added.

Rice

The structure of rice is similar to that of wheat grains.

Types

Patna: the grains of this type are long and thin, and it is traditionally served in savoury dishes.
Carolina: the grains of this type are round, and it is traditionally used in puddings with milk.
Flaked: the grains are flaked by machine, and it is usually made into puddings.
Ground: the grains are crushed into a powder, and it is used in cakes, puddings, soups, and biscuits.

Importance in the diet

Rice forms the main component of the diet in many countries, particularly China, Japan, and India.

Whole grain rice is a good source of thiamin, 79% of which is found in the pericarp, aleurone layer and scutellum. The endosperm contains only 9% of the thiamin. Most rice is milled (polished) to remove the outer layers of the grain and thus make the rice easier and quicker to cook. This results in a large loss of thiamin from the grain, and is the cause of many cases of beri-beri (see p. 26) in poor countries where rice is the main food.

Rice also contains other B vitamins, which are often lost when the rice is washed before and after cooking, and during boiling.

Rice growing in a paddy-field in Thailand.

Preparation

Rice should be cooked in the minimum amount of water, for the shortest time possible, until the grains are just tender. If overcooked, the starch gelatinizes and the grains stick together instead of remaining separate.

Maize

Maize is generally more resistant to drought and gives a higher yield than wheat or rice. It is grown in many countries and there are many varieties.

Sweetcorn (corn on the cob) The freshly picked grains on the cob are usually boiled and served as a vegetable. The grains can also be removed from the cob and boiled for use as a vegetable.
Whole maize meal The grains are crushed into meal and used as a type of flour in some countries, such as Mexico. Some of the germ and pericarp can be removed by sieving if required.

A maize plantation in East Africa.

Importance in the diet

The nutrient content of maize is similar to that of other cereals, except that the yellow varieties contain a good supply of carotene, which is converted in the body to vitamin A.

The nicotinic acid in maize is present in a bound form and cannot be efficiently absorbed by the body. This is mostly overcome in the preparation of tortillas in Mexico (see p. 27).

Oats

Oats were at one time the staple cereal food of Scotland, and grew very well in the cold climate. Their consumption has fallen however, due to the introduction of breakfast cereals. These have largely replaced porridge, which is made from oats.

Oats are usually rolled rather than crushed, and are partially cooked during the process. Coarse, medium, and fine grades are sold. They can be treated to make them quick to cook, and are used mainly in the preparation of breakfast cereals such as muesli and porridge, and in baking cakes and biscuits. Oats have a relatively high fat, protein, and fibre content compared to other cereals.

Barley

Barley is widely grown, and is a hardy cereal plant. At one time it was eaten in quite large amounts, but now it is mainly used as cattle food and in the brewing and whisky industries. It is sold as **pearl barley**, which is the grain with the husk removed, and is still used to thicken soups and stews.

Rye

Rye is grown mainly in the north and east of Europe, because it is resistant to the cold. It is made into rye bread, which is very dark brown in colour, and also into crispbreads, which are traditionally produced in Scandinavian countries.

Rye crops are prone to attack by a mould called **ergot**, which if eaten is toxic to the body and causes 'ergotism', one of the symptoms of which is a burning sensation in the feet.

Cereal products

Breakfast cereals have become very popular, and are an easy-to-prepare food for breakfast. They are made from various cereals, including wheat, rice, maize, and bran from wheat, by roasting and baking. They may be shredded, rolled, 'puffed' or flaked, and mixed with a number of ingredients such as dried fruit, honey, sugar or coconut. Breakfast cereals are often fortified with vitamins and minerals to increase their food value.

Several popular breakfast cereals have sugar added during processing, or are coated with a sugar layer. They therefore have a higher energy value which should be taken into account.
Cornflour is made from maize, and is virtually 100% starch. It is used as a thickening agent and is the basis of custard powder.
Pasta is made from **durum wheat** flour, water, and sometimes egg, which are mixed to a paste, then shaped and partly baked,

resulting in a dried product with good keeping qualities. It is also possible to buy pasta made from wholegrain wheat. The various shapes have names and are traditionally served with different ingredients.

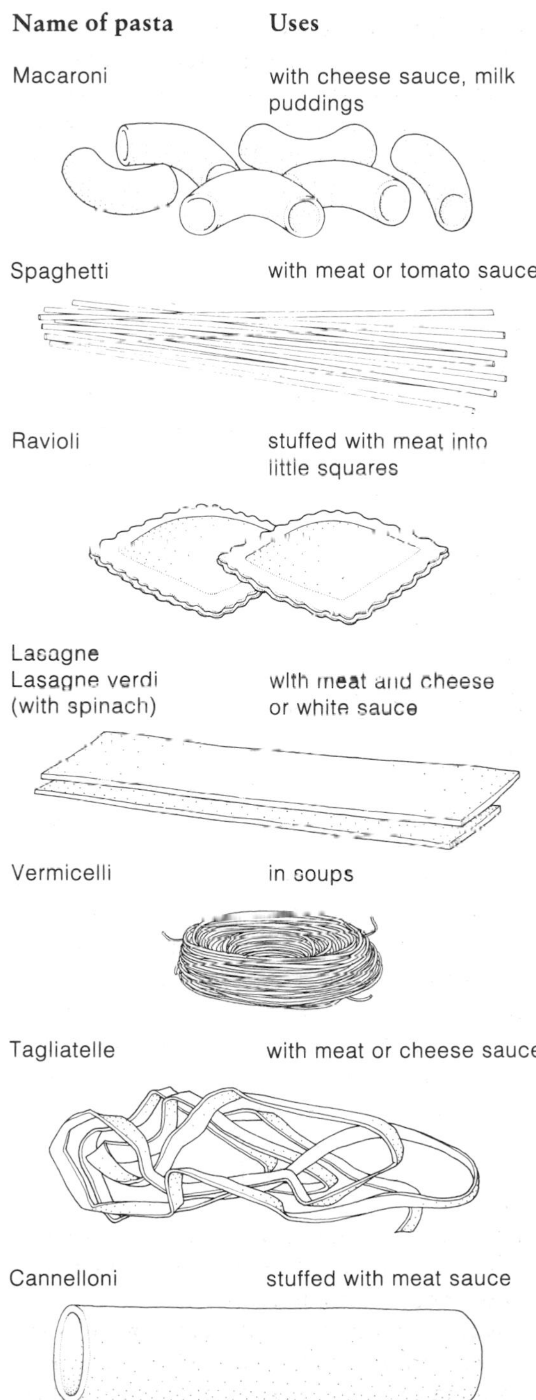

Name of pasta	Uses
Macaroni	with cheese sauce, milk puddings
Spaghetti	with meat or tomato sauce
Ravioli	stuffed with meat into little squares
Lasagne Lasagne verdi (with spinach)	with meat and cheese or white sauce
Vermicelli	in soups
Tagliatelle	with meat or cheese sauce
Cannelloni	stuffed with meat sauce

Storage of cereals

Cereals should be stored in cool, dry conditions, to prevent them from becoming mouldy. Wholegrain cereals keep for a shorter time than refined cereals because of the fat content of the germ. Cereals are prone to attack by insects and should be regularly inspected if stored for long periods of time.

The following foods are often called cereals but strictly they are not:

Tapioca is made from a tuber vegetable called the cassava, and is used in puddings and as a thickener in soups and stews. It is almost 100% starch.

Arrowroot is made from the maranta plant, which has underground stems from which the arrowroot is obtained. It is a white powder and is used as a thickener. It is also used as a glaze for fruit, because when boiled with water, it becomes clear.

Sago is made from the sago plant, and is used in milk puddings.

Revision questions

1 What are cereals, and what was their importance in the life of early man?
2 Name the six main cereal plants and say where each is grown.
3 Which nutrients are found in the following parts of the wheat grain?
 a scutellum
 b aleurone layer
 c endosperm
 d germ
4 What is winter wheat used for in baking and why? What is spring wheat used for and why?
5 How is wheat milled?
6 What is the 'extraction rate' of flour?
7 Why are wholemeal cereals nutritionally preferable to refined ones?
8 How does the protein content of flour affect its baking qualities?
9 How can gluten be developed in a bread dough?
10 Name the two main types of rice and give their uses.

11 Why is beri-beri a common disorder in poor countries where rice is the staple food?
12 How should rice be cooked, and why?
13 What are the main uses of barley, oats, and rye?
14 How should cereals be stored?

Further work with cereals

1 To examine the gluten content of flour:
Mix 50 g (2 oz) of:
   a strong plain flour
   b ordinary plain flour
   c self-raising flour
with enough water to form a dough.
Place each in a piece of muslin and rinse out the starch under a gentle stream of water, squeezing the bag to help. Continue until no more starch is washed out and a small ball of gluten is left.
Weigh the gluten samples and work out the percentage of gluten in the different flours. Explain why there are differences.

2 Observe wheat grains under a magnifying glass and sketch one. Carefully cut a wheat grain lengthways and observe again, looking for the outer layers, germ, and endosperm.

3 Compare the wheat grain to rice, barley, and maize grains under the magnifying glass.

4 Boil 50 g (2 oz) of white patna rice and 50 g (2 oz) of whole grain patna rice, and compare the time it takes for each to become tender. How do you account for the difference?

5 Measure the length and width of rice grains before cooking, and compare these with cooked rice. How do you account for the difference?

6 Observe starch granules (in water) from rice, flour, maize (cornflour), and potato under the microscope. Sketch your observations.

Fats and oils

Fats and oils have many uses in food preparation and are important sources of energy in the diet. The functions, composition, and chemistry of fats and oils are discussed in Chapter 1, pp. 15–18.

Uses

Fats and oils have many uses, including:
- **spreading** on bread, etc. (butter, margarine)
- **creaming** for cakes (see p. 194) (butter, margarine)
- **shortening** for pastry (see p. 211) (lard, vegetable fat)
- **frying:** deep and shallow (see pp. 160–1) (lard, vegetable oil for deep frying; also butter, margarine for shallow frying)
- **oiling** baking tins (any melted fat)
- **salad dressings** (see p. 226) (vegetable oils)
- **ice cream manufacture** (vegetable oils)

Properties

Fats are solid at room temperature and oils are liquid. This is because they have different **melting points** due to the type of fatty acids they contain. In general, the more **saturated** fatty acids a fat contains, the more **solid** it will be, and the more **unsaturated** fatty acids it contains, the more **liquid** it will be at room temperature.

Effect of heat

When a fat is heated, it melts to an oil, then gradually heats up until eventually it ignites. Some fats can be heated to higher temperatures than others, and are therefore more suitable for frying.

Vegetable oils can generally be heated to higher temperatures because of their fatty acid content and their purity. Fats such as butter and margarine cannot be used for frying at high temperatures as they contain other substances such as water and emulsifiers which make them burn easily.

When a fat is heated, at a certain temperature a thin, bluish haze of smoke will be given off which will give food an unpleasant flavour. The temperature at which this happens is the **smoke point**, and at this temperature the fat molecules start to split up which reduces the keeping qualities of the fat. Soon after this, the fat will ignite and burn fiercely. The temperature at which this occurs is called the **flash point**.

Fat	**Smoke point** (**when fresh**)
vegetable oil	227–232°C
lard	183–205°C
vegetable fat	180–188°C

Rancidity

Fats and oils and foods containing them can develop 'off' flavours and odours due to the fat becoming **rancid**.

Rancidity is caused by the action of the enzyme **lipase**, or by **oxidation**. **Lipase** causes the fat molecules to be broken down, and the 'off' flavours and odours develop because of the free fatty acids in the food. Heat can destroy lipase and the micro-organisms in the food that may produce lipase.

In **oxidation**, oxygen is absorbed by the fat and reacts with the fat molecules, causing substances to be produced which give the fat an unpleasant flavour and odour. Oxidation is accelerated by light, impurities in fat, enzymes, and the presence of many polyunsaturated fatty acids. **Antioxidants** are added to foods containing fats, and they may be packed in foil-lined containers to prevent light from reaching them.

Rancidity can occur in fat-containing foods that are kept in cold storage or frozen.

Types of fats and oils

Edible fats and oils are obtained from both animals and plants.

The main animal sources are:

- **milk fat:** butter, ghee (clarified butter), cream
- **meat:** dripping, lard, suet, fat under the skin and in muscles
- **marine:** liver oils, oily flesh, whale oil

Butter

Butter is made from cream (see pp. 84–5) which has to be separated from milk. By law, butter must contain at least 82% fat. Cream contains 35–40% fat.

After being separated from the milk, the cream is first pasteurized. Undesirable flavours and air are removed, then it is held at 4·5°C (40°F) to harden the fat globules. It is then held at 15–18°C (59–64°F) for three to four hours to develop the acidity (for flavour) and to prepare it for churning. It is then cooled to 7°C (50°F) and churned.

Traditional butter churns are gradually being replaced by butter-making machines which carry out the complete butter-making process. Churning breaks up the seal of milk solids around the fat globules so that they **coalesce**, i.e. stick together. The non-fat milk solids then mix with the liquid in the cream to form **buttermilk**, which is drained off and used for cattle feeds or sold as a drink. The fat is then chilled, washed, and hardened, and salt is added, depending on the flavour required. Salt helps to preserve the butter. Usually 1·5% salt is added, but some butter is sold unsalted. After this, the butter is worked until smooth, and then packed.

This continuous buttermaker produces and packs five tons of butter an hour.

Composition

Butter contains the following:

- 82% fat: the fatty acid, **butyric acid**, gives butter its characteristic flavour
- 15% water
- 0·4% protein
- 2·3% minerals
- vitamins A and D: according to the time of year

The colour of butter varies according to the breed of cow, the quality of grass, and the carotenes present. Additional colouring may be added.

Salt and extra flavouring may be added as well as preservative and antioxidant.

Uses in food preparation

Butter is popular because of its flavour. It is used for spreading on bread and biscuits and it is sometimes served with vegetables.

In cookery, butter can be used for cakes, although it takes longer to cream than margarine. It can be used for pastry, together with lard or vegetable shortening, and for shallow frying at relatively low temperatures. Unsalted butter can be used for butter icing, home-made cream, brandy butter, and sauces.

Suet

Suet is obtained from the fat around vital organs, e.g. kidneys, usually from the ox. The fat content varies from 70% to 99%, and it is a very solid, hard fat, composed of mainly saturated fatty acids.

Suet is either sold in cartons, or is shredded and mixed with flour to prevent it from sticking together. It is used in making pastry, puddings, dumplings, and sweet mincemeat.

Dripping

Dripping is the fat that is released during the roasting of a joint of meat (usually beef). On cooling, it separates into a layer of fat and a layer of meat extractives in a jelly. The fat can be used for roasting other joints or vegetables, or for shallow frying. Some people eat dripping spread on bread or toast.

Lard

Lard is produced from pigs that are specially bred for this purpose. The fat is obtained from the fatty tissues under the skin. They are cut into small pieces and heated to remove the lard. This is called **rendering**.

The quality of lard depends on where it is on the body. Antioxidants are added to it to prevent rancidity, and it may be modified to improve its baking qualities.

The taste of lard is bland. It is used as a shortener for pastry, but it is mixed with margarine for added flavour. It is not generally used in cake making as it has poor creaming properties.

Lard is also used for deep and shallow frying. It must be pure for this purpose so that it can be heated to high temperatures.

Marine oils

Fish-liver oils (e.g. cod, halibut) are rich sources of vitamins A and D, and used to be given to children on a regular basis to supplement their diet. It is now realized that a well-balanced diet can provide all the required fat-soluble vitamins. If too many are given, they are stored in the body and may cause poisoning.

Whale and fish oils contain many polyunsaturated fatty acids and must be refined, as they deteriorate rapidly after being extracted. Whale oil was at one time used for margarine manufacture, but in recent years mainly plant and fish oils have been used.

Plant oils

Plant oils are mostly obtained from the **seeds** of plants such as:

- soya bean
- cottonseed
- sunflower
- groundnut
- coconut
- palm
- linseed
- olive
- sesame
- maize

A soya bean plant.

Apart from their uses in the food industry, plant oils are also used in the manufacture of paints, varnishes, and plastics.

Refining

The plants that produce oil seeds are grown in many parts of the world. All oils that are used for food have to be **refined** first.

Oil is contained in the cells of the seeds. It is **extracted** from them either by squeezing or by dissolving the oil in a solvent, e.g. trichloroethylene.

The cell walls of the seeds are hard to penetrate, therefore expensive machinery has to be used in order to extract the oil.

The process involves the following stages:

1 Cleaning the seeds.

2 Breaking by rollers.

3 Cooking the seeds in steam.

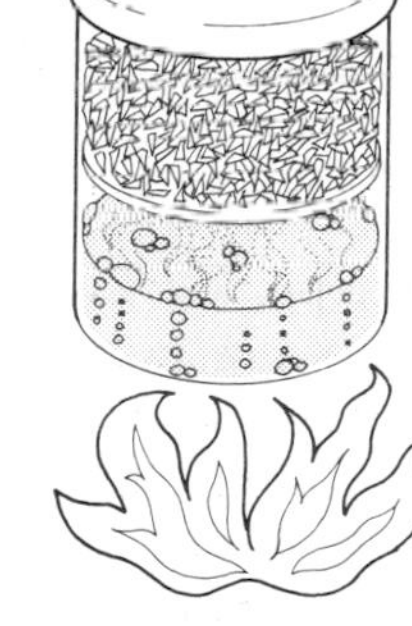

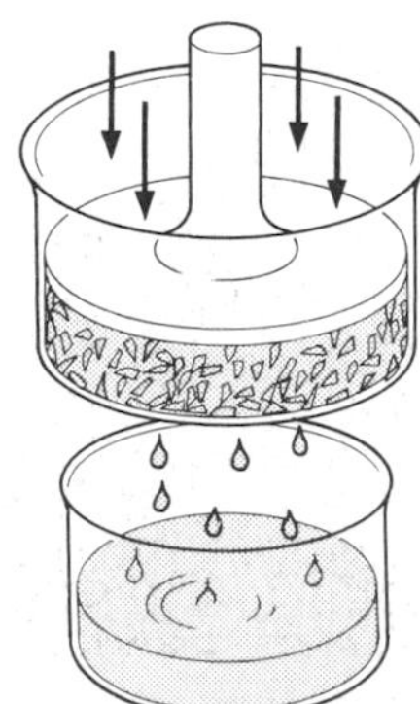

4 Expelling the oil by squeezing.

or
by extracting the oil with a solvent.

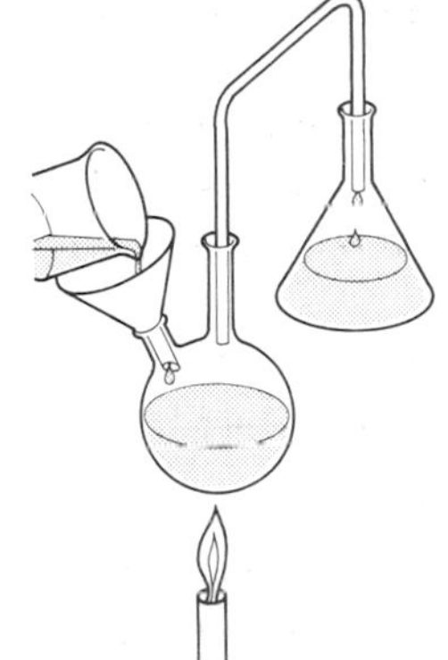

5 Removal of natural acids.

6 Bleaching to lighten the colour.

7 Deodorizing and improving the taste and smell.

The oils are either sold separately or they may be blended. Some oils, e.g. olive oil, are more expensive than others.

Oils that are exported to colder countries such as the UK have to be treated to stop them forming fat crystals in cold weather. This is called **winterization**.

Oils are used for:
margarine manufacture
frying
salad dressings

They are also used in the baking industry.

Margarine manufacture

It is possible to produce solid fats from liquid oils by a process called **hydrogenation**. This process is used in the manufacture of margarine.

Unsaturated fatty acids have the capacity to take up more hydrogen atoms (see p. 16), and if they do, they become more solid. If oils have hydrogen bubbled through them under carefully controlled conditions, their fatty acids take up the hydrogen atoms and they become solid. This is what is meant by hydrogenation. The process can be stopped when the required hardness has been reached.

Margarines which are made from mainly vegetable oils, such as sunflower or soya oil, will have a higher polyunsaturated fatty acid content (see p. 16), than margarines which are made from mainly animal fats and oils. This information is normally displayed on the labels of margarine cartons, to enable the consumer to choose a product high in polyunsaturated fat, as recommended for following the dietary goals (see p. 10).

The manufacture of margarine from plant and marine oils is carried out in this way, as follows:

1 The oils are refined.

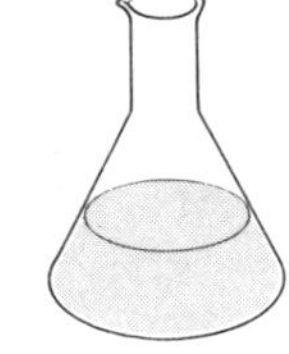

2 The oils are hydrogenated, then deodorized.

3 Flavours, preservatives, salt, colour, and by law, vitamins A and D are added.

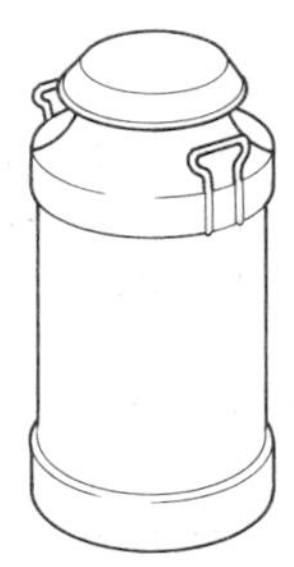

4 Cultured, pasteurized milk is blended in.

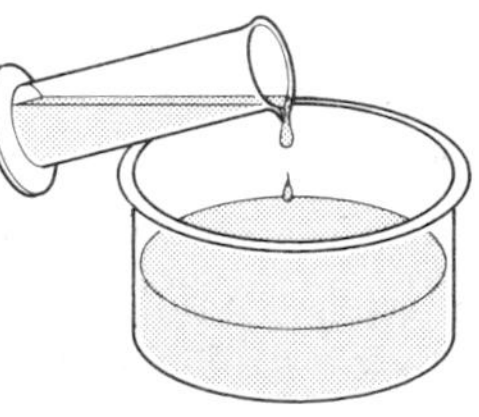

5 The mixture is emulsified and stabilized.

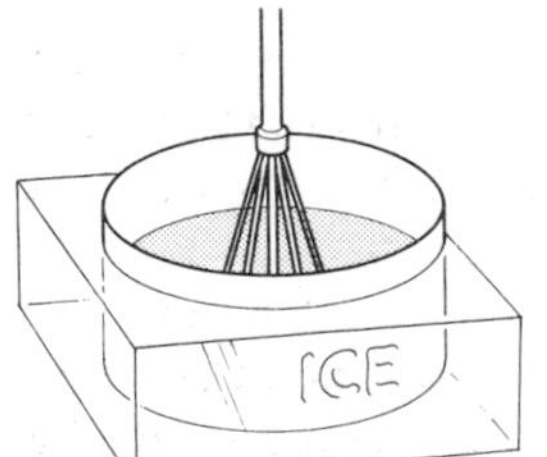

6 The margarine is chilled and textured (e.g. whipped for cake making, or blended with other oils).

7 It is finally packed either in paper or plastic tubs.

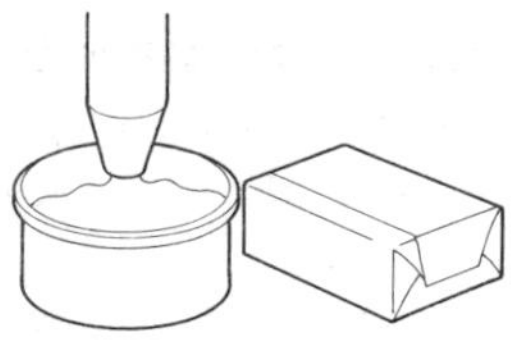

Block margarine is of a similar hardness to butter, and is sold in paper wrapping. It is suitable for pastry making, and if softened, can be used for creaming.

Soft margarine is not hydrogenated as much as block margarine and is therefore softer and very suitable for creaming. It can be spread and used straight from the refrigerator, but is not suitable for pastry making as it is too soft for rubbing in.

Some margarines are sold as butter substitutes, and may have up to 10% butter added. Others are rich in polyunsaturated fatty acids (see p. 16).

Cooking fats

White cooking fats, suitable for making pastry and other dishes, are produced in a similar way to margarine, except that they are nearly 100% fat. They can be used for creaming in cake making, and may be made softer by being whipped with a harmless gas. They can also be used for frying.

Low energy value spreads

Low-fat spreads with a low energy value (compared to normal fats) are useful for energy-reduced diets. They contain a large percentage of water which has to be thoroughly blended with the fat and emulsified to prevent separation. They are not suitable for frying as the high water content causes them to spatter when heated.

Storage of fats and oils

Fats should be stored in a cool place, covered, and away from strong odours which they could absorb.

Oils that have been used for frying should be strained to remove any impurities and food particles which may cause them to become rancid. They should not be used over and over again, as the molecules split up when heated and this may cause rancidity.

Revision questions

1 What are the uses of the following fats and oils in cookery?
a margarine (soft and hard) **b** butter
c lard **d** suet **e** vegetable oil
2 How do the fatty acids affect the characteristics of the fat?
3 Why is it important not to overheat oil used for frying repeatedly?
4 Why do fats become rancid? How can this be prevented?
5 What are the main sources of fats?
6 How is butter produced?
7 Where is suet found, and what is its function in the animal's body?
8 How is lard produced?
9 What are the main sources of plant oils?
10 How are plant oils obtained?
11 How is margarine produced?
12 What is hydrogenation?
13 What is the difference between soft margarine and block margarine?

Further work with fats and oils

1 Compare the length of time taken to cream 50 g (2 oz) caster sugar with 50 g (2 oz) of the following until soft and light:
a soft margarine
b butter
c block margarine
d lard
} all taken directly from the refrigerator
Account for the differences. Which fat creamed the most easily?

2 Repeat the above but cream each for only three minutes. Add one egg gradually and 50 g (2 oz) flour. Float small samples of each in vegetable oil.
If the mixture has been sufficiently creamed and there is enough air in the mixture it will float on the surface of the oil. If not, it will sink.

3 Leave samples of butter, margarine, and lard **a** at room temperature and **b** in the refrigerator. Check every few days to see how long it takes for them to become rancid.
How does refrigeration help to prevent fats becoming rancid quickly?

4 Compare samples of shortcrust pastry made with:
a lard
b oil (mix with the flour)
c soft margarine
d block margarine
e margarine plus lard
f butter
Compare the doughs before baking for texture and ease of preparation. Compare the baked pastries for flavour, texture, colour, and shortness.

Sugar and sweeteners

Sweet foods are highly palatable and very popular. Many processed foods have sweeteners added and much of their success depends upon obtaining the right degree of sweetness to attract the consumer.

Foods have been sweetened for thousands of years. The early sweeteners were natural ones such as honey. Sugar (sucrose) has been used for many centuries in some parts of the world, such as India, as a preservative and flavouring but was not used in Europe until about the thirteenth century. At that time, it was an expensive commodity and did not become a major item of the diet in Europe until the late nineteenth century. Since then, consumption has risen dramatically and it now stands at about 1 kg (2·2 lb) per person per week in the UK.

Research into artificial sweeteners has been going on for many years. Initially, the aim was to find a suitable, cheaper alternative to sucrose, and later, to find a low energy value substitute for sucrose for use in energy-reduced diets. **Saccharin** was discovered in 1879, and in recent years it has been used in the manufacture of many foods. It is 300 times sweeter than sucrose. It has recently been a cause of controversy amongst medical experts in the USA and other countries. Some experts have claimed that it can adversely affect health, but their research has also come under criticism. The use of saccharin in food has been banned in the USA, but it is still used in other countries, including the UK.

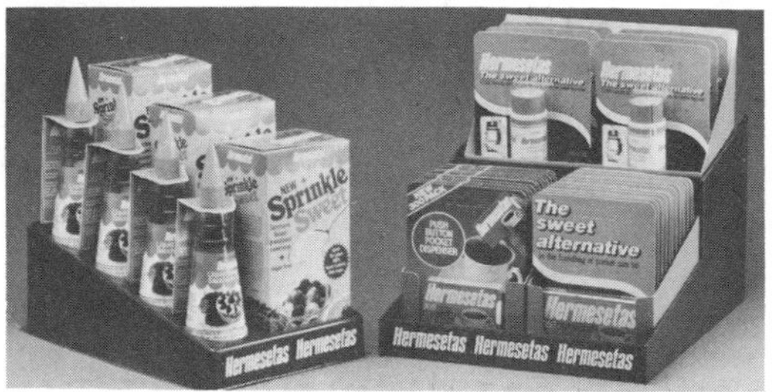

Artificial sweeteners are produced in tablet, liquid, and crystal form.

Another sweetener, **cyclamate**, was discovered in the late 1930s. This is about 30 times as sweet as sucrose. It too has caused concern about its use in food, and it was banned from use in the USA, the UK and several other countries in the late 1960s.

Sugar (sucrose)

Types

Sugar is made from either sugar **cane**, which is grown in tropical countries, or sugar **beet**, which is grown in temperate climates, such as the UK.

Sugar beet. Sugar cane.

Production

Sugar cane The sugar is found in the soft fibres in the centre of the cane. To extract the sugar, the canes are first crushed, then sprayed with water. This makes a solution containing 13% sugar (sucrose), 3% impurities and 84% water. The impurities are removed by boiling, adding calcium oxide (lime), and filtering.

A clear, brown solution (molasses) is left. This contains a mixture of sugar crystals and liquid. The liquid is spun off, and raw sugar (brown in colour) is left.

Sugar beet The sugar is stored in the root of the sugar beet. The beets are shredded and the sugar extracted by soaking them in hot water. The solution obtained contains about 14% sugar (sucrose), 4% impurities, and 82% water. The impurities are removed and the water is evaporated off to leave raw brown sugar, as for cane sugar.

Sugar refining

Raw sugar, from either cane or beet, contains about 96% sucrose, as sugar crystals and molasses. The raw sugar is mixed with sugar syrup, and the syrup is then forced out in a centrifuge, leaving crystals which are then washed in water. Next the crystals are dissolved in water and the impurities are removed as before. The liquid is then allowed to filter though a deep layer of bone charcoal to remove all the coloured impurities. A clear liquid is left.

The liquid is then evaporated to produce sugar crystals of the desired shape and size. The crystals are washed again, and centrifuged. The syrup that is spun off is used for the manufacture of golden syrup or soft brown sugar.

Granulated sugar is made as described above.
Caster sugar is made in the same way as granulated sugar, but the process is modified so that very small crystals are obtained.

Icing sugar is obtained by pulverizing granulated sugar to a very fine powder in a special mill.

Brown sugar is made by crystallizing the syrup obtained at the end of the refining process. It is moister than white sugar. There are several types of brown sugar, including:

soft brown sugar (dark or light)

demerara sugar, which has larger crystals and is traditionally served with coffee and used in cake making.

Coffee crystals are large sugar crystals, sometimes made in different colours. They take longer to dissolve than other sugars.

Lump sugar is made in the same way as granulated sugar, but two crystal sizes are used, the larger to provide the traditional sparkle of the lump sugar and the smaller to bind the two together. The crystals in liquid form are poured into special moulds and cooled until solid, then cut into cubes or lumps.

Honey

Honey is produced by bees from the nectar obtained from various flowers. Bees collect the nectar, which is a solution in water of various sugars – sucrose, glucose, and fructose. During its passage through the bee's body, enzymes convert these sugars into mainly glucose and fructose. The resulting honey is deposited in honeycombs, and consists of about 75% sugars (glucose, fructose, and some sucrose), 20% water and 5% extracted flavours peculiar to the flower from which the nectar was obtained.

Honey is sold in both liquid and granulated forms. Honeys are supersaturated solutions, and they tend to granulate because the sugars gradually crystallize out of solution. Honey to be sold liquid is processed by flash heating to 60–71°C (140–160°F).

Importance in the diet

Sugars are an important source of energy to the body, and are relatively quickly digested and absorbed. Artificial sweeteners such as saccharin provide the body with very little energy.

An excess of sugar in the diet is undesirable because it can lead to obesity and tooth decay. It is therefore sensible to limit the amount of sweet foods eaten, particularly between meals.

Revision questions

1. Why is sugar added to so many foods?
2. Why is saccharin used to sweeten foods?
3. How is sucrose obtained from sugar cane and sugar beet?
4. How and why is sugar refined?
5. Describe the different sugar products and what they are used for in food preparation.
6. What is honey and how is it produced?
7. What is the importance of sugar in the diet? Why is it inadvisable to consume too much?

Further work with sugar

N.B. Sugar solutions boil at very high temperatures, therefore care must be taken when conducting these experiments.

1. Mix 1 tablespoon water with 1 tablespoon granulated sugar in an evaporating dish. Heat gently until the sugar has dissolved and boil without stirring. Observe the changes in colour, consistency, and smell of the sugar solution, as the water evaporates. The change in colour is due to the sugar being **caramelized** (a change in molecular structure due to the removal of water). Continue heating and observe the changes in colour, smell, and appearance and how rapidly these occur. What is left in the dish when all the water has gone?

   Which recipes involve caramelization of sugar? Why is it important not to overcook the solution?
2. Repeat experiment 1 but stir the solution while it is boiling, and observe the changes in texture and appearance. Why does this happen?
3. Repeat experiment 1 but add a pinch of potassium hydrogen tartrate (cream of tartar). Observe the difference in time taken for the sugar to caramelize.
4. Repeat experiment 1 but use 100 g (4 oz) sugar and 50 ml (2 fl oz) water. Using a sugar thermometer, drop small samples of the solution into a jug of cold water at 10°C intervals from 110°C to 180°C. Squeeze the samples and observe their textures and flavour. Why is temperature important in sweet making?

Milk

Milk and its products are known as **dairy foods.** The main milk products are:

- butter
- cream
- cheese
- yogurt

Butter is discussed in the section on fats and oils as its main component is fat (see pp. 67–8). Cream, cheese, and yogurt are discussed in this chapter

History of milk production

Today, it is taken for granted that milk supplies are always available and that they are clean and safe to drink. Such a situation was unknown before the 1850s, as there was no legislation to prevent the sale of unhygienic or untreated milk. Then, milk supplies were on a very small scale and the milk that was available was often contaminated with bacteria from diseased cows and dirty utensils.

In the 1860s, the demand for milk increased as the population of the UK grew. Dairy farmers increased their production accordingly; but the continuous outbreaks of diseases such as cattle plague and foot and mouth disease caused serious problems. In 1866, the Government took steps to control the situation, by introducing the Cattle Diseases Prevention Act. Also at this time, the transportation of milk by railway became increasingly common, so that towns were able to receive more regular supplies.

In 1870, the first dairy foods manufacturing factory was opened in Derby, and by 1900, a whole system of factories was in operation throughout the country.

It was not until 1884 that the first milk was sold in bottles. In 1894, the heat treatment of milk by sterilization was tried, but the results were not popular. Louis Pasteur's experiments on heating milk to destroy harmful bacteria (see pp. 132–34) in the late 19th century paved the way for the hygienic production and distribution of milk and dairy products.

Production

In the UK, most of the milk we buy comes from cows, although goat's milk can also be obtained in some areas.

Milk is made from water plus the nutrients in the grass and other foodstuffs which make up the cow's diet. Some of the nutrients eaten are used for the growth and maintenance of the cow's body and the rest are used for milk production. A cow can eat up to 70 kg (150 lb) of grass a day, and extra nutrients in the form of supplements can also be given.

The nutrient content of the grass may vary according to:

1 The time of year – more vitamin A (as carotene) is found in summer grass.
2 Soil fertility.
3 The variety of grass.

The amount and quality of milk produced by a cow depends on:

1 The quality and amount of food eaten.
2 The breed of cow; Friesians as a breed are high producers of milk.
3 The health of the cow.

Friesian cows are the most popular breed for milk production.

Cows are usually milked twice a day, in the early morning and late afternoon. Most milk is produced after calving, and the production gradually decreases until it stops about ten months after calving. Over 20 litres (44 pints) a day can be obtained from one cow at the height of milking.

Milk is collected . . .

. . . and transported quickly and hygienically.

Treatment and processing

Milk produced by a healthy cow contains very few harmful bacteria, but cows can catch a variety of diseases which could be passed on to humans, e.g. tuberculosis, brucellosis. All dairy herds have to be inspected by a vet to ensure that they are healthy before they are used for milk sales, and at regular intervals thereafter.

Rules of hygiene must be strictly followed at all stages from production to retail to the consumer.

Hygiene rules

These rules are laid down by the Government and Health Authorities in the form of Acts and Regulations. The EEC also enforces hygiene rules. There are rules for each stage of processing.

Milking premises Rooms for cooling, storage, and milking should be airy and light, with good drainage and easily cleaned surfaces. They must be supplied with adequate water, and must be cleaned every day.

Cows must be clean and free from disease. Their teats and udder must be washed before milking.

Equipment and containers The milk must be covered and all equipment and containers must be thoroughly cleaned after use.

Farm workers must have proper washing facilities. They must cover cuts on their skin, and they must not spit or smoke.

Milk collection

Milking machines for the hygienic and efficient collection of milk are in use on nearly all dairy farms. A record is kept of the milk yield from each cow, and samples are taken to check the fat and protein content of the milk. This helps the farmer to assess the food intake of the cow.

Once collected, the milk is cooled to 4·5°C (40°F) and put into a large vat. A road tanker collects the milk from several farms and transports it rapidly to a depot or manufacturing creamery. Each batch is checked for quality, quantity, and hygiene. If it fails the tests, the batch is rejected. The tanker is cleaned after use.

Processing

Milk can be made safer to drink and will keep a little longer if it is heat treated. 96% of milk sold in the UK is subjected to heat treatment. The farmer must obtain a special licence to sell untreated ('raw') milk.

There are various methods of heat treatment and milk is sold according to the following colour codes:

Types of milk and treatment	Colour of cap/ carton
Pasteurized	silver
Pasteurized homogenized	red
Pasteurized Channel Island or South Devon	gold
Untreated	green
Untreated Channel Island or South Devon	green with gold stripe
Sterilized	blue
Ultra heat treated	pink

Pasteurized milk

Louis Pasteur believed that milk soured because of the presence of bacteria. He showed by experiment that if heated, the souring process could be delayed, and the milk could be made safer to drink due to the destruction of harmful bacteria.

It took several years for legislation to be brought in and for the process to be perfected before pasteurization of milk became standard practice.

The aim of pasteurization is to destroy harmful (pathogenic) bacteria without adversely affecting the flavour and quality of the milk.

Pasteurization is usually carried out by heating the milk in a **heat exchanger**. There are two main methods:

1 The milk is heated to not less than 72°C (162°F) for at least 15 seconds, then cooled rapidly to not more than 10°C (50°F). This is called the Flash Process.

2 The milk is heated to 63°C (145°F) for half an hour, then cooled rapidly as above. This is called the Holder method, and is less commonly used.

The milk must be cooled rapidly, otherwise the nutritional value is affected, and bacterial growth is encouraged.

After cooling, the milk is put into insulated stainless steel tanks and bottled as soon as possible.

Bottle filling and capping: these machines work at 300 bottles a minute.

Homogenized milk

To **homogenize** is to produce a substance which is of a uniform consistency. When milk is homogenized, the cream does not rise to the surface as it does in pasteurized milk, but remains evenly distributed throughout the milk in tiny droplets.

The milk is first pasteurized, and then forced through a tiny mesh under pressure. This breaks up the fat globules in the milk into very small droplets. It is then cooled and bottled.

Channel Island or South Devon milk

Jersey, Guernsey, and South Devon breeds of cow produce very creamy milk, with a minimum fat content of 4% (other breeds have a fat content of about 3%). It is heat-treated, cooled and bottled in the same way as pasteurized milk.

Sterilized milk

Sterilization kills harmful and souring bacteria more completely than pasteurization and the milk will therefore keep for several weeks if unopened.

The milk is first homogenized, put into glass bottles with long necks, and sealed with a metal cap. It is then sterilized inside the bottles in one of the following ways:

1 In a **batch process**, where the milk is heated in bottles in an autoclave (a large industrial pressure cooker) at up to 113°C (235°F) for 15–40 minutes.

2 In a **continuous process**, where the bottles pass on a conveyor belt through hot water tanks, into a steam chamber (under pressure) at 113°C (235°F) for 15–40 minutes, then into cooling tanks.

Ultra heat treated milk

Ultra heat treatment (UHT) is a relatively new method of heat-treating milk, and the milk can be kept in sealed packs for several months. The milk is heated in a heat exchanger at 132°C (270°F) for not more than one second. It is then rapidly cooled and packed into foil-lined containers which are sealed. The rapid treatment does not adversely affect the colour or nutritional value of the milk. It can be stored at room temperature when unopened.

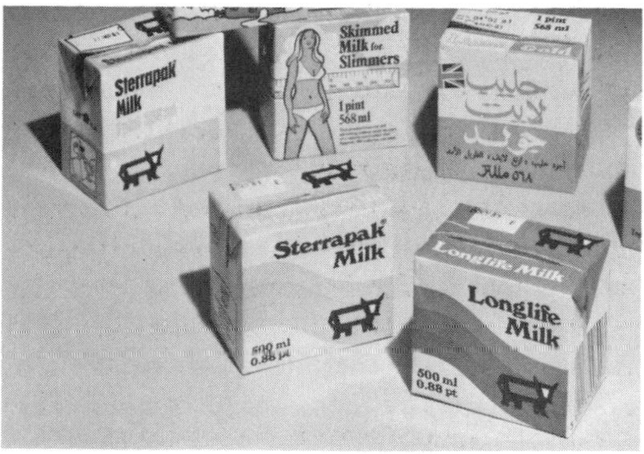

Dried milk

Milk can be preserved by removing water so that the resulting powder contains 5% or less moisture. There are two main methods of drying milk, spray drying and roller drying.

Before drying, the milk is homogenized and heat treated. It may be **skimmed** (i.e. most of the fat content may be removed) or left as whole milk.

Spray drying

The milk is sprayed through a very fine jet into a chamber in which hot air is circulating. The water is quickly evaporated and the drops of milk fall to the bottom as a powder. The milk reconstitutes easily with water if in a fine powdered form. Most dried milk is prepared in this way.

A spray-drying chamber.

Roller drying

The milk is spread onto rollers which are heated. As the rollers revolve, the water evaporates and a thin film of milk is left which is scraped off. Milk dried in this way does not reconstitute with water as easily as spray dried milk, and this method is little used now.

Dried milk which contains less than 26% fat should not be given to babies, and manufacturers are required to state this on the label.

The dried milk is packed into foil-lined cardboard drums or tins, which are made air-tight to prevent any fat present from becoming rancid (see p. 71).

Condensed milk

Milk can be preserved by the addition of sugar and the removal of water. Condensed milk is made with either whole, partly skimmed (some fat removed), or skimmed milk. The milk is homogenized and heated to 80°C (176°F) for 15 minutes. Sugar is then added and it is heated under a vacuum to evaporate some of the water until the milk is approximately 2½ times more concentrated than fresh milk. It is then cooled and put into sealed cans.

Evaporated milk

Evaporated milk is prepared in a similar way to condensed milk, but no sugar is added. It is approximately twice as concentrated as fresh milk. It is put into sealed cans and sterilized for 20 minutes at 115·5°C (240°F).

Skimmed milk

The fat content of milk can be skimmed off, thus reducing the energy value of the milk. Skimmed milk is available in cartons or bottles, or in a dried form, and is useful in low-fat or energy-reduced diets.

Frozen milk

Pasteurized homogenized milk can be frozen in polythene bags for up to a year. Ordinary pasteurized milk is not suitable as it tends to separate on thawing.

Dried milk substitutes

It is possible to buy dried milk substitutes where skimmed milk and **non-milk fats** (e.g. from plants) are combined, and used in the same way as dried milk.

Dried artificial cream for coffee

Artificial creams have been developed using vegetable fat, glucose syrup, and sodium caseinate. These are dried into granules or powder and are used in coffee drinks instead of milk or cream.

Storage of milk in the home

Fresh milk should be stored in a cool, dark place, preferably a refrigerator, and covered over to prevent exposure to dust, bacteria in the air, and contamination by strong flavours from other foods. It should be used within two to three days, if pasteurized or homogenized. Sterilized, canned, and UHT milks should be treated as fresh once opened.

Dried milk should be stored in a cool, dry place with the lid firmly in place to prevent absorption of moisture. Once opened, it should be used up within the time stated by the manufacturer, and when reconstituted with water, should be treated as fresh milk.

The importance of milk in the diet

Milk is the single most complete food known to exist naturally. It is specifically designed by nature to feed the offspring of mammals, (cows, goats, sheep, man, etc.), and it therefore contains sufficient nutrients in the right proportions for the animal it was designed to feed. Milk is, however, deficient in ascorbic acid (vitamin C) and iron, containing only traces of these. Babies are born with a supply of these in the body to last them for the first few weeks of life, until they can be provided by food.

The nutrients in milk are in a readily digestible form, and little is wasted during digestion. Milk is a valuable food not only for babies, but for people of all ages.

Nutrients in milk

Protein

Milk proteins are of a high biological value (see p. 9), and the chief ones are:

caseinogen
lactalbumin
lactoglobulin

Caseinogen accounts for about 80% of the protein in milk, and in fresh milk it is combined with calcium and phosphorus as **calcium caseinate.** If an acid is added to the milk, or if it is soured naturally by lactic acid bacteria, the casein coagulates and separates from the calcium and phosphorus. This happens in cheese making. During digestion, it is coagulated by rennin to form a clot. (See p. 39.)

Lactalbumin accounts for about 8% of the protein in milk, and **lactoglobulin** for about 3·5%. When milk is heated, they both coagulate and form a 'skin' on the surface of the milk. They are not coagulated by rennin in the stomach during digestion, or by acid.

Fat

The fat content of milk is often used as a guide to the quality of the milk, and may affect its price. By law, whole milk must contain a minimum of 3% fat and that produced by Channel Island and South Devon cows must contain a minimum of 4% fat.

The fat is present in the form of tiny globules or droplets, which being lighter than water, rise to the surface to form a cream layer (except in homogenized milk).

Milk fat contains both saturated and unsaturated fatty acids, the proportions of which vary, according to the feed given to the cow.

Milk fat is used in the production of butter (see p. 71), and cream (see p. 84).

Carbohydrate

The only carbohydrate in milk is the disaccharide, **lactose** (see p. 15). Cow's milk contains about 5% lactose, whereas human milk contains just over 7%. Lactose is less sweet than sucrose, and is therefore not easy to detect. Lactic acid bacteria readily ferment lactose to lactic acid, thus causing the milk to go sour, and curdle.

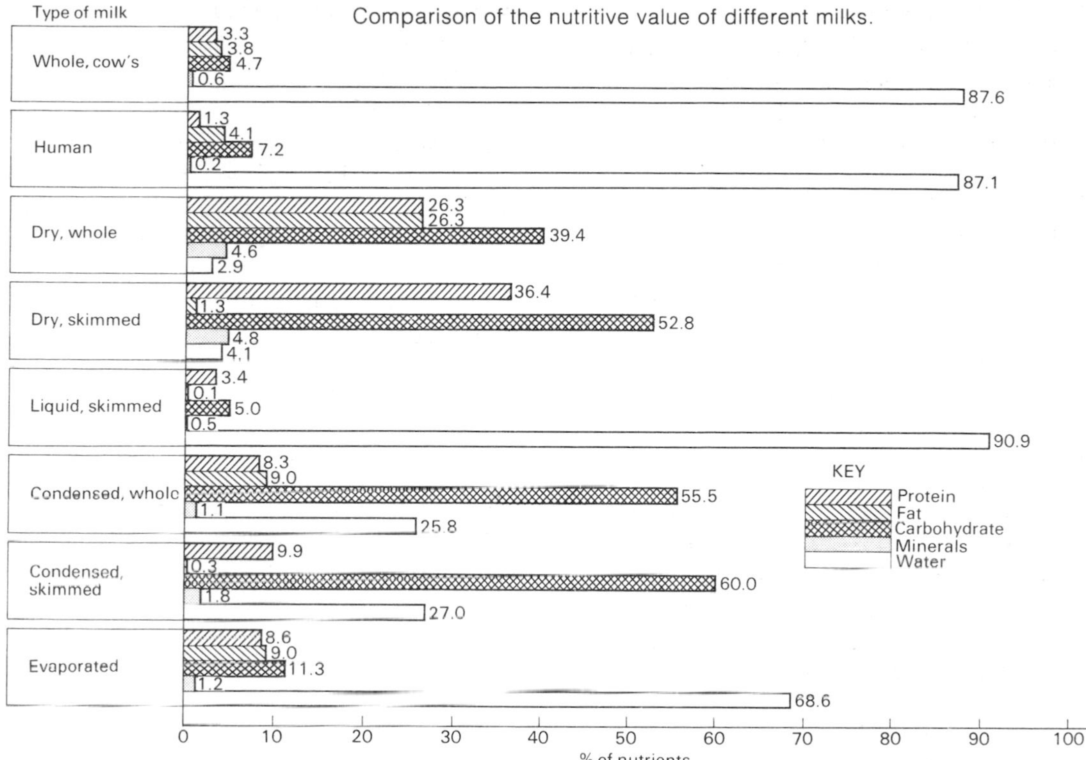

Vitamins

Fat soluble Milk contains a relatively good supply of retinol (vitamin A). The amount varies according to the time of year. In the summer, when cows can graze on fresh grass, milk contains more vitamin A and carotene than in the winter. Skimmed milk contains less vitamin A as it is associated with the milk fat which is removed.

Milk contains more vitamin D in the summer, when the cows are exposed to sunlight for longer periods. It is not a rich source of this vitamin.

Water soluble Milk is an important source of riboflavin, but this will be reduced if the milk is left exposed to sunlight, which will destroy the riboflavin. Milk is a relatively good source of thiamin.

Milk is a poor source of ascorbic acid (vitamin C), and this is usually destroyed when the milk is heat treated.

Minerals

Milk is an excellent source of **calcium**, and milk and milk products are important suppliers of this mineral in the diet. Milk also contains a good supply of **phosphorus**, plus smaller amounts of **sodium**, **chlorine**, and **potassium**. Milk is a poor source of **iron**.

Two thirds of the minerals in milk are combined with milk solids (e.g. calcium and phosphorus with caseinogen), and the rest are dissolved in water.

The effect of heat on the nutritional value of milk

Pasteurization of milk causes a slight loss (up to 10%) of the thiamin, and a 25% loss of the vitamin C.

UHT and dried milk The nutrient losses are similar to those of pasteurized milk.

Sterilization of milk leads to a loss of 20% of the thiamin and 60% of the vitamin C. The sugar, lactose, is partially caramelized and this accounts for some of the flavour and colour change.

Condensed milk The nutrient losses are similar to those of pasteurized milk.

Evaporated milk About 40% of the thiamin and 60% of the vitamin C are lost.

Uses of milk in food preparation

Milk is a cheap and versatile ingredient for a variety of recipes, including:

- sauces
- beverages
- soups
- milk puddings
- custards (egg or cornflour)
- batters
- cold sweets, e.g. fruit fool, blancmange
- scones

Revision questions

1. Why was milk often unsafe to drink before the 1860s?
2. How was this situation changed?
3. How is milk produced by the cow?
4. Why does the nutrient content of milk vary slightly throughout the year?
5. What does the amount and quality of milk produced depend on?
6. Why is milk heat treated?
7. What hygiene rules do milk producers have to abide by?
8. List the various heat treatments given to milk.
9. Describe the principle behind and the process involved in the various heat treatments given to milk.
10. How else can milk be preserved? Describe each method and give the advantages and disadvantages of each.
11. How should fresh milk be stored in the home?
12. Why is milk such a valuable food?
13. Describe the proteins found in milk and their reactions to heat and acids.
14. How is the fat in milk distributed, and how is this different in homogenized milk?
15. What is lactose?
16. Why does the retinol content of milk vary throughout the year?
17. Why is it inadvisable to leave milk standing on the doorstep for too long?
18. List the minerals found in milk.
19. How does heat affect the nutritional value of milk?
20. Why is milk so useful in food preparation?

Cream

Cream contains all the main components of milk but in different proportions; i.e. the fat content is higher, and the quantity of non-fat solids and water is lower.

The greatest amounts of cream are produced by Channel Island and South Devon cows.

Types of cream

The Cream Regulations of 1970 lay down the legal definitions of different creams, according to the fat content. These are the minimum percentages of fat which the different types of cream must contain:

clotted cream	55%
double cream	48%
whipping cream	35%
single cream	18%
half cream	12%
sterilized cream	23%

Production

Milk is left to stand for 24 hours. During this time, the cream forms a layer on the surface, and can be skimmed off by mechanical separators, at a temperature of 35–54°C (95–104°F). The cream is then cooled to 4·5°C (40°F) and stored until processed.

The cream is then pasteurized in a similar way to milk, to improve its storage qualities as well as make it safe to eat.

Single and **half** cream are homogenized to prevent separation, due to their relatively low fat content.

Sterilized cream is heated either in bottles or cans, at 116°C (240°F) for 20 minutes. It has a different flavour to fresh cream.

Ultra heat treated cream is treated in a similar way to UHT milk, and can be kept unopened in foil-lined cartons for several months. Once opened it should be treated as fresh cream.

Long-life cream is sold in jars, in which it is pasteurized at 65·5°C (150°F) for 30 minutes, then cooled to 4·5°C (40°F) for storage. This will keep longer than fresh cream but for less time than sterilized cream.

Cultured (soured) cream is prepared in a similar way to yogurt, and has a nutrient content similar to that of normal cream except that the lactose has been converted by special bacteria to lactic acid. It is used in both sweet and savoury dishes.

Uses of cream in food preparation

Cream that has a fat content of 35–42% can be whipped up until stiff and used for decorating cakes and flans, for serving with scones and fruit, and for incorporating into dishes such as mousses, soufflés and cheese-cakes. The cream should be kept in a cold place (4·5°C, 40°F) for several hours before use. It should be gently whipped until stiff, and care should be taken not to overwhip it, as it will separate into large fat globules and liquid whey. This separation is irreversible.

Single cream will not whip, but can be used for pouring over fruit or in coffee, and for adding to casseroles and soups.

Storage of cream in the home

Fresh cream should be stored in a cool, dark place, away from strong odours, and covered up. It should be used within the time recommended by the manufacturer.

Single cream should not be frozen, as it separates when thawed. Whipping and double cream should only be frozen if they are lightly whipped until stiff first. Rosettes of whipped cream can be frozen on greaseproof paper, for use on trifles, cakes, and cold sweets.

Revision questions

1. Why is the nutrient content of cream different to that of milk?
2. List the different types of cream and their fat contents.
3. How is cream produced commercially?
4. Why is cream used in food preparation?
5. How should cream be stored in the home?

Cheese

Cheese making is a method of preserving the nutrients of milk when it is in plentiful supply. Cheese has been made for centuries throughout the world.

At least 400 varieties of cheese are known, and they are now made on a large scale in creameries. In the past, they would have been made in farmhouses, but increased demand for cheese has led to large-scale production, and import and export all over the world.

Types of cheese

English cheeses are classified according to how they are manufactured and the ingredients used:

1. Hard-pressed cheeses, e.g. Cheddar, Derby, Cheshire, Double Gloucester, Leicester.
2. Lightly-pressed cheeses, e.g. Caerphilly, Lancashire, Wensleydale.
3. Blue-veined cheeses, e.g. Blue Stilton, Blue Wensleydale.
4. Acid curd cheeses, e.g. curd cheese, cottage cheese.
5. Processed cheeses
6. Cream cheeses

Production

The production of Cheddar cheese is described here, but the process is basically the same for most cheeses, with slight variations in temperatures, ingredients, and processes used.

1. Pasteurized fresh milk is used, and is pumped into large vats at 30°C (86°F).
2. **Ripening.** A special bacteria culture is added to the milk, to convert the lactose in it to lactic acid. The lactic acid helps to preserve the cheese.
3. After half an hour, the milk is reheated to 30°C (86°F), and the enzyme rennin, in the form of **rennet**, is added, to make the milk **clot** (set). The caseinogen coagulates with the acid and rennet.

Adding the starter culture to the milk.

4 The rennet is left to react for 30–45 minutes, during which time a solid **curd** and liquid **whey** are formed.
The curd consists of the coagulated caseinogen, plus about 80% of the calcium in the milk, plus fat and fat-soluble vitamins and some thiamin.
The whey consists of most of the water, water-soluble vitamins, lactose, some minerals, and the proteins lactalbumin and lactoglobulin.

5 The curd is cut with special knives to release the whey, which is drained off.

Draining the whey from the curd.

6 The curd is then scalded to 30°C (86°F) for 40–45 minutes, while being stirred, to help to expel the whey and gain the correct consistency. Lightly-pressed cheeses do not have such a solid curd, and less whey is drained off.

7 Drainage of the curd continues as the curd settles, and it is cut into blocks. The blocks are piled on top of each other and repiled at regular intervals to complete the draining – this is known as **cheddaring**. The acidity of the cheese at this stage has increased.

8 The curd may then be cut in a mill into small chips, and 2% of **salt** is added for flavour and to preserve the cheese.

9 The salted curd is then packed into metal moulds, lined with cheesecloth. Traditional moulds are cylindrical, but for large-scale production, square and rectangular moulds are used.

10 The curd is pressed hard for 24 hours, and the moulds are sprayed with hot water to form a rind on the cheese for protection.

11 The cheese is then removed, date stamped, and left to **ripen** at 10°C (50°F) for about four months, during which time the characteristic flavour, smell, and texture of the cheese develop as a result of enzyme and bacterial activity. Mature Cheddar is left to ripen for about twelve months.

12 At the end of the ripening period, the cheese is graded according to its flavour, texture, appearance, and colour.

Testing and grading the cheese.

Cottage cheese

Cottage cheese is made from skimmed milk (pasteurized), and a special starter is added to develop the texture and flavour – brought about by the natural souring of the milk by lactic acid bacteria. The curd is cut into small pieces and slowly heated. The whey is drained off, and the curd is washed and cooled.

Cream may be added and blended in. Additional ingredients such as pineapple, chives, or peppers can also be added.

Cottage cheese has a short shelf-life, and must be kept in a cold place. It is useful in energy-reduced and low-fat diets, and is a good source of protein, riboflavin, calcium, and phosphorus.

Processed cheese

Processed cheese is made by thoroughly mixing Cheddar and other cheeses. Sometimes colouring and flavouring are added. It is packed in foil.

Cream cheeses

Cream cheeses are not true cheeses, but are made from cream with a fat content of 30–60%. They have a similar composition to cream, but contain less water and more fat.

Storage of cheese in the home

Hard cheeses should be wrapped in foil or plastic to prevent them from drying out, and then stored in a cool place.

Lightly-pressed cheeses have a shorter storage life than hard cheese. They should be stored in a similar way.

Acid curd cheeses and cream cheeses should be eaten within a few days of purchase and stored in a cold place.

Hard cheeses can be frozen quite well if wrapped in foil. They may become rather crumbly on thawing.

Blue-veined cheeses

Blue-veined cheeses, e.g. Stilton, are produced by inoculating the curd with a harmless mould which grows in the air spaces in the curd. The mould produces the characteristic flavour of the cheese.

Stainless steel needles are used to inoculate the cheese.

Importance of cheese in the diet

Cheese is a relatively concentrated source of protein, and an important source of calcium, retinol (vitamin A), and riboflavin. Over 90% of the cheese is digested, so there is little wastage. Cheese can be included in most meals for all age groups, and is a useful food for snacks and packed meals.

Nutritive value

	Cheddar cheese %	Cottage cheese %
protein	26·0	13·6
fat	33·5	4·0
carbohydrate	trace	1·4
minerals	3·4	1·4
water	37·0	78·8

Effect of heat on cheese

When hard cheeses are heated, the fat first melts, and the protein (caseinogen) continues to coagulate. Overheating causes the protein to toughen and become stringy, thus reducing its digestibility, and eventually the cheese will burn.

Uses of cheese in food preparation

Apart from its use in salads and snacks, cheese is used in the following ways:

as a **garnish** for soups, meat sauces, cauliflower cheese, etc.
grated on salads, meat dishes, etc.
in **sauces**
in **savoury flans**, e.g. quiche lorraine
in **cheesecakes**
in **shortcrust pastry**

Revision questions

1 List the main types of English cheese and give examples of each.
2 How is Cheddar cheese produced?
3 What is whey?
4 What are curds?
5 Why is salt added to cheese?
6 What happens during the ripening stage of cheese making?
7 Why is cottage cheese different from Cheddar cheese?
8 What is processed cheese?
9 How should cheese be stored in the home?
10 Why is cheese an important food in the diet?
11 What happens when cheese is heated?
12 How is cheese used in food preparation?

Yogurt

Yogurt is a cultured milk product, which in the UK is usually made from cow's milk, but goat's or ewe's milk can also be used. Yogurt is eaten all over the world, and originates from West Asia and Eastern Europe.

Yogurt sales in the UK have significantly increased since the 1960s, when fruit-flavoured varieties were introduced. Sales almost quadrupled between 1970 and 1980, and in 1980, 100,000 tonnes (98,420 tons) were sold. The most popular varieties containing fruit are (in order of popularity):

strawberry
black cherry
raspberry
peach melba
pear

Types of yogurt

Yogurt is divided into two categories according to its consistency and method of manufacture:

set yogurt
stirred yogurt (either thick or pouring consistency)

In the UK the stirred variety is the most popular.

Composition

Yogurt can be made from milk in any of the following forms:

whole milk; minimum fat content 3·5%*
partially skimmed milk: minimum fat content 1–2%*
skimmed milk (concentrated or normal): minimum fat content 0·3%*
evaporated milk
dried milk

or any combination of these.

*as recommended by the Food Standards Committee in 1975.

Concentrated skimmed milk is most frequently used in commercial yogurt manufacture.

The Food Standards Committee also recommend that yogurt should contain not less than 8·5% **non-fat solids**, which consist of casein and whey proteins. The more solids there are, the firmer the yogurt will be and the less likely it is to separate.

The milk used must conform to the same high standards of hygiene and composition as required for liquid milk, and it must also be free from the antibiotics which are given to cows to treat udder infections. These antibiotics affect the bacteria used in yogurt production.

Bacteria culture

The taste and texture of yogurt are brought about by the carefully controlled addition of a special harmless bacteria culture. The bacteria used belong to the **lactic acid** bacteria group which are capable of fermenting the disaccharide sugar **lactose** in milk, to produce lactic acid under the right conditions of temperature, moisture, and food.

The two bacteria used are:

lactobacillus bulgaricus
streptococcus thermophillus

During fermentation, the milk proteins coagulate and the yogurt sets. **Acetaldehyde** (CH_3CHO), which is a colourless, volatile liquid (i.e. it evaporates rapidly), is also produced. It is acetaldehyde which is mainly responsible for the characteristic flavour of yogurt.

Commercial manufacture

The process outlined below is a general one, and it may vary according to the manufacturer.

1 The milk is homogenized (see p. 80) to give the finished yogurt a smooth, creamy texture. This also helps to prevent the final product from separating.
2 The milk is then pasteurized at 85–95°C (185–203°F) for 15–30 minutes. This helps to stabilize the proteins and results in a nearly sterile product.
3 The milk is then cooled to 40–43°C (104–109°F), which is suitable for the fermentation process to take place.
4 The two bacteria (the 'starter' culture) are added to the milk in equal proportions, usually as 0·5–2% of the total finished product.
5 The culture is then incubated at 37–44°C (98·4–111°F) for four to six hours, during which time fermentation takes place, the product becomes acidic, the flavours develop, and the proteins coagulate.
6 Once the level of acid reaches 0·8–1·8%, the bacteria growth stops. The bacteria remain alive, although their activity is retarded.
7 The yogurt is then cooled to 4·5°C (40°F), and held at this temperature during storage and distribution to shops.
8 Certain additives may be included in the yogurt:
   vitamins A and D
   stabilizers, e.g. gelatine, agar, pectin, to prevent the yogurt from separating into curds and whey
   sucrose as a sweetener in fruit-flavoured yogurt
   colour
   preservatives
   flavourings, e.g. lemon, chocolate

   All additives are strictly controlled by legislation.

The manufacture of set and stirred yogurt is slightly different.

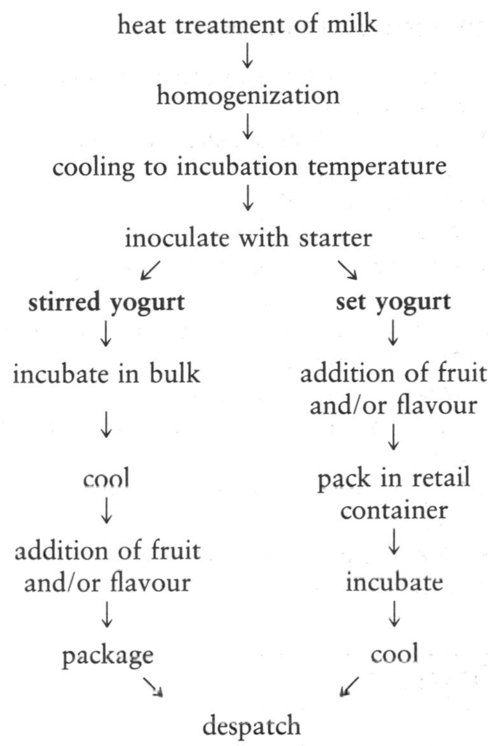

Storage of yogurt

Yogurt should be stored at 4·5°C (40°F). At this temperature the bacteria remain alive, but grow and multiply very slowly. After about ten days, they multiply sufficiently to raise the acid content to a point at which the yogurt becomes unpalatable, and to cause separation.

Faults in yogurt

Separation into curds and whey

Causes

1 Wrong incubation temperatue.
2 Poor starter culture.

Fermentation of sucrose by yeast

Cause

Yeast cells from the skins of fruit added to the yogurt ferment the sucrose and produce CO_2 gas and alcohol. This causes the yogurt to 'blow' or become gassy.

Too much acid

Cause

1 Faulty starter culture.
2 Incorrect proportion of the two bacteria.
3 Incorrect cooling of the yogurt.

Preparation of yogurt at home

Yogurt can be made in the home with either a yogurt-making machine or a vacuum flask. If using a yogurt machine, the manufacturer's instructions should be carefully followed to achieve satisfactory results.

The following method can be used for making yogurt at home, in a vacuum flask. All equipment used must be sterilized with boiling water.

575 ml (1 pint) sterilized or UHT milk
50 g (2 oz) dried skimmed milk
1 tbsp natural yogurt

1 Heat the milk to 43°C (110°F), and blend in the skimmed milk and yogurt.
2 Warm a flask with hot water, empty, and pour in the milk mixture and seal. Leave for seven hours to incubate.
3 Cool rapidly, refrigerate for four hours.
4 Flavour and sweeten as required.
5 Use within five days, storing in the refrigerator.

The importance of yogurt in the diet

Yogurt contains all the nutrients found in the milk from which it is made, plus any that are added in the form of fruit, sucrose, vitamins A and D, etc.

Low-fat yogurt contains the following nutrients (with approximate percentages):

	Type of yogurt		
Nutrient	Fruit	Flavoured	Plain
Water	75%	80%	86%
Protein	4·8%	5%	5%
Fat	1·0%	0·9%	1·0%
Minerals	0·8%	0·8%	0·8%
Lactose	3·3%	4·8%	4·6%
Other sugars	14·6%	9·2%	1·6%
	(mostly sucrose)		(galactose)

Yogurt is useful in the diet for:
1 Energy-reduced diets.
2 Weaning babies on to solid foods.
3 Convalescents.
4 Alternatives to puddings.

Uses of yogurt in cooking

1 As a substitute for double cream in cheesecakes, soufflés (cold), mousses, etc.
2 Salad dressings, as a substitute for mayonnaise.
3 For certain meat dishes, e.g. goulash.
4 For cold drinks with fruit.

Revision questions

1 What is yogurt?
2 What is the difference between a set yogurt and a stirred yogurt?
3 How are the taste and texture of yogurt brought about?
4 Describe the manufacture of yogurt.
5 What additives are put into yogurt?
6 How should yogurt be stored?
7 How can the manufacture of yogurt go wrong?
8 What is the value of yogurt in the diet, and why is it so popular?
9 How can yogurt be used in food preparation?

Further work with dairy foods

1 Test some fresh pasteurized milk with universal indicator paper to measure the pH. Leave some in the refrigerator and some in a warm room. Test the pH daily and observe the changes in the appearance and smell of the milk. Comment on the time taken for each sample to sour and the reason for the changes in pH. Discard the milk afterwards.

2 Add two teaspoons of lemon juice to four tablespoons of fresh milk and observe the reaction. Comment on this, and compare it with adding tomato juice, water, and bicarbonate of soda.

3 Place a small amount of grated Cheddar and processed cheeses in separate test tubes. Heat gently and observe the changes that take place. Allow the cheese to bubble, then cool it and observe the texture. Account for the change in texture after heating.

4 Collect samples of different cheeses and compare them for flavour, appearance, cost, smell, and colour. Set up a tasting panel to establish the most popular types.

Eggs

Eggs have been used as a food for centuries. It is known that as long ago as 1400 BC, natives in South-East Asia kept poultry, and that throughout history eggs have not only been eaten, but have been involved in rituals and used as currency all over the world.

Production

Traditionally, eggs were produced by **free range** farming. This meant that hens were allowed to roam loose in the farmyard, eating grain and other food from the ground. The eggs were laid in a hen house. Free range hens are still kept, but usually on a small scale.

Free-range farming.

As the demand for eggs grew, large scale production in the form of **battery farms** was developed. Thousands of hens are kept in cages in large hen houses which are artificially lit and heated. The hens remain in the cages at all times and the eggs they lay are collected, usually on a conveyor belt, graded, and checked for quality.

Battery farming.

Deep-litter farming.

Another form of large-scale egg production involves keeping large numbers of hens together in huge heated sheds, but not in cages. The hens lay their eggs in nest boxes. This is called **deep-litter** farming.

Types

Most eggs eaten in this country are hens' eggs, but duck and goose eggs can be eaten, providing that they are very fresh.

Eggs are graded according to size, and since 1973 eggs have had to be classified according to the EEC regulations on eggs:

Size of egg	Weight
1	70 g+
2	65–70 g
3	60–65 g
4	55–60 g
5	50–55 g
6	45–50 g
7	45 g or less

Eggs are also graded according to quality:

Extra The eggs have been packed in the previous seven days and are of high quality.

Class A are good quality and are the usual grade sold to the consumer.

Class B are of lower quality and may have dirty shells.

Class C are usually sold to cake manufacturers as they have weak or damaged shells.

All egg cartons should state the week in which they were packed during the year, and the supplier.

Structure and composition

Eggs are composed of three main parts:
- the shell
- egg white
- egg yolk

88·5% of an egg is edible.

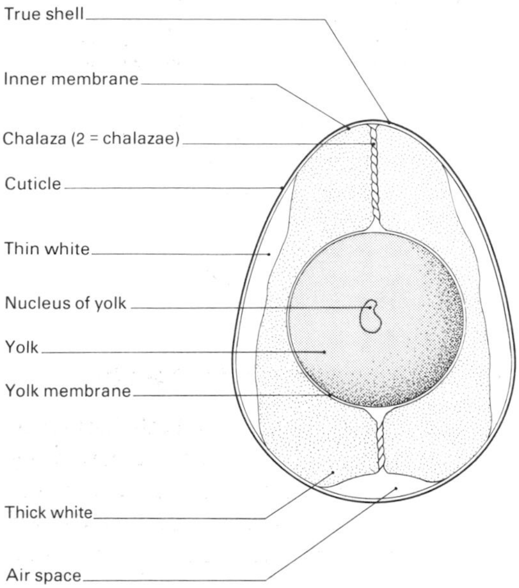

True shell
Inner membrane
Chalaza (2 = chalazae)
Cuticle
Thin white
Nucleus of yolk
Yolk
Yolk membrane
Thick white
Air space

The structure of a hen's egg.

Shell

The shell consists of an outer **cuticle**, a **true shell**, and **inner membranes**. The true shell forms 11·5% of the whole egg. It consists of:
- 97% calcium carbonate ($CaCO_3$)
- 3% protein

The shell is **porous** (pores are tiny holes), and therefore allows the developing chick to obtain oxygen. The pores also allow bacteria and odours to enter, and water and carbon dioxide to escape. The membranes that line the shell inside act as chemical filters to bacteria to protect the inside.

At one end of the egg, the membranes separate into an **air space**, to supply the chick with oxygen.

The colour of the shell varies according to the breed of bird and does not influence the nutritional value of the egg in any way. The shell is relatively strong, but older birds tend to produce weaker shells.

White

Egg white has two visible layers:
- the **thick white** (nearest to the yolk)
- the **thin white** (nearest to the shell)

The white forms 58·5% of the whole egg, and consists of:
- 88·5% water
- 10·5% protein
- riboflavin and other B vitamins
- a trace of fat

The main proteins in egg white are **ovalbumin** and **mucin**.

Yolk

The yolk is covered by a membrane to separate it from the white, and support it. The yolk forms about 30% of the whole egg. It consists of:
- 16·5% protein
- 33% fat
- 50% water
- fat-soluble vitamins A, D, E, and K
- mineral elements, including iron (see p. 31)
- lecithin (an emulsifier)

The colour of the egg yolk is related to the diet of the hen and is due to the presence of **carotenes** (see p. 22). The nutritional value of the egg is not affected by the colour of the yolk.

The yolk is supported by the **chalazae** which are attached to the egg white, and help to keep the yolk away from the shell where it could pick up bacteria. The yolk is more vulnerable to bacterial attack when it is older as the yolk membranes weaken.

Testing an egg for freshness

Before eggs are packed they are checked for defects by being passed over a strong light. This process is known as **candling** because wax candles were originally used for this purpose.

Candling at an egg-packing factory.

As an egg gets older, several changes take place:

1 Water moves from the white into the yolk.
2 The yolk membrane weakens.
3 The thick white becomes thinner.
4 The size of the air space increases.
5 Moisture is lost through the shell.
6 Bacteria enter through the shell.
7 The bad smell of hydrogen sulphide is produced by the reaction of sulphur from the egg white and phosphoric acid in the yolk.
8 The egg eventually decomposes as bacteria contaminate the contents.

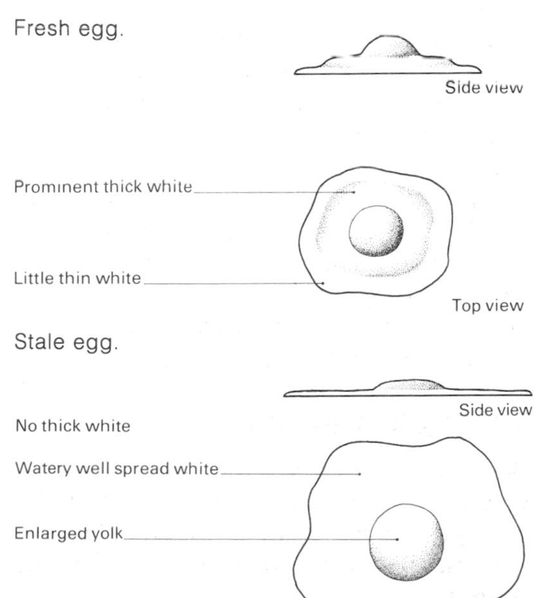

Eggs can be checked for freshness in the home, by placing them in a jug of brine (salt and water). If the egg sinks, then it is fresh. If it floats on the surface, it is stale, because the air space has enlarged and water has evaporated from the egg, making it lighter.

Importance of eggs in the diet

Eggs are a good source of high biological value protein, and are easily digested by most people, especially when lightly cooked. As they are used in so many different ways in food preparation, they make a valuable contribution to the diet.

There is no carbohydrate in eggs, and the iron in the yolk may be unavailable to the body (see p. 31). As most of the calcium is concentrated in the egg shell which is not eaten, eggs are not a very useful source of this mineral.

The effect of heat on eggs

Ovalbumin in the egg white starts to coagulate at 60°C (140°F), until the whole white is solid and opaque. The proteins of the egg yolk start to coagulate at 70°C (158°F) and continue until the yolk is dry and hard. If overcooked, the protein becomes tough and difficult to digest.

If an egg is boiled for some time, a green/black ring of **iron sulphide** forms around the yolk. This is due to the reaction of sulphur in the egg white with iron in the egg yolk, particularly in eggs which are not very fresh. This reaction can be prevented to a certain extent by cooling the egg rapidly as soon as it has been cooked.

If eggs are heated too quickly, the proteins will coagulate and shrink rapidly, causing any liquid that the egg contains to be squeezed out, and the protein to become tough. This is called **syneresis**.

Uses of eggs in food preparation

Eggs are used for a variety of processes in food preparation, and are very versatile in this respect. Their uses include:

1 **Trapping air** Both egg white and the whole egg are capable of trapping air, due to the ability of ovalbumin to stretch (see p. 178).
The ability of eggs to do this is utilized in:
Cake making Eggs are used to trap air as a raising agent.
Lightening mousses, soufflés, etc., as meringue or whole egg.

2 **Thickening** Eggs are used to thicken custards, sauces, soups, etc., because of the coagulation of the egg proteins.

3 **Emulsifying** Egg yolk contains **lecithin** which is an emulsifier and enables oil and water to be mixed to an emulsion without separating. This is made use of in:
Mayonnaise (see p. 226).
Cake making, when eggs are added to the fat and sugar in a creamed mixture (see p. 194).

4 **Binding** Ingredients for rissoles, croquettes, and meat or fish cakes can be bound together with egg, which when heated will coagulate and hold the ingredients together.

5 **Coating** Eggs are used as a coating for fried food, either on their own, or combined with flour or breadcrumbs. This forms a protective layer on the outside of the food which sets and holds it together and prevents it from overcooking.

6 **Glazing** Egg yolk, egg white, or whole egg can be brushed over pastries, bread, etc., to produce a golden brown shiny glaze during baking.

7 **Enriching** Eggs can be added to sauces, milk puddings, soups, etc., as a way of including extra protein.

8 **Garnishing** Hard-boiled egg white and yolk can be used to garnish salads, etc.

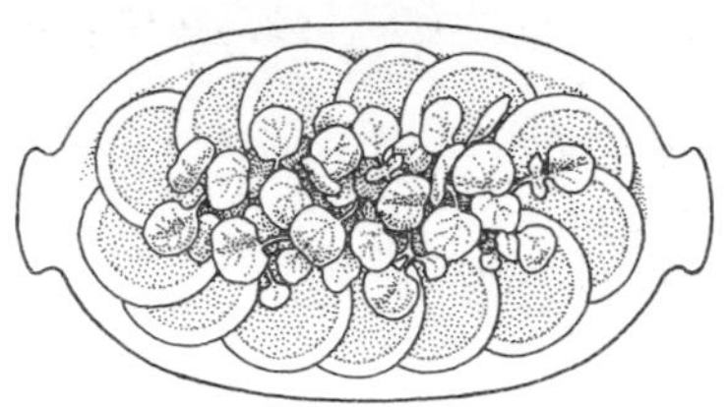

Eggs are also used as a main ingredient in a variety of dishes, thus providing an important supply of protein in the diet. Eggs can be cooked by the following methods:

baking – in small dishes or with vegetables in custards and flans
frying – normally shallow fried
boiling
poaching
scrambling – over a gentle heat with a small amount of fat and milk

As they are easily digested, they are a valuable food for convalescents if lightly scrambled or boiled. Raw egg is not as easily digested as cooked egg, but it is sometimes put into drinks.

Storing eggs

Eggs should be stored in a cool place, e.g. a refrigerator or cold larder that is not too dry. They should be kept away from strong-smelling foods. If stored in the refrigerator, they should be removed an hour or so before use if they are to be whisked. If they are too cold, they will not whisk well.

Eggs should not be washed as this destroys the protective cuticle. They will normally stay in good condition if stored correctly for two to three weeks.

Eggs cannot be frozen whole, but the whites and yolks can be frozen separately.

Eggs are commercially stored in rooms of high humidity and low temperature (just above −2°C, 28°F) to prevent moisture loss and deterioration. They can be kept for up to six months.

Eggs can be preserved by pickling.

Revision questions

1 What is the difference between free range, deep litter, and battery egg production?
2 What sizes of egg are sold?
3 What function do the following parts of an egg have?
   a chalazae
   b cuticle
   c yolk membrane
   d air space
   e yolk
4 Why does the shell have pores in it? How do the pores affect the keeping qualities of the egg?
5 What is the food value of the egg white?
6 What is the food value of the yolk?
7 What changes take place in an egg when it gets older?
8 How are eggs checked for defects?
9 How can an egg be tested for freshness?
10 What is the importance of eggs in the diet?
11 How does heat affect eggs?
12 Why are eggs used in food preparation?
13 How should eggs be stored in the home?

Further work with eggs

1 Place three clear glass lids over squared paper and break an egg on to each. Use:
   a a six-week-old egg
   b a two-week-old egg
   c a very fresh egg
   Measure the area covered by each and observe the height of each egg. Comment on these observations.

2 To test the stability of egg whites:
   Whisk four separate 25 g (1 oz) quantities of egg white until stiff. To the four samples add:
   a $\frac{1}{8}$ tsp cream of tartar
   b $\frac{1}{8}$ tsp salt
   c 1 tsp sugar
   d nothing
   Set up four funnels with filter papers into 100 ml graduated cylinders. Put each sample of egg white into a funnel and measure the amount of liquid lost from each at ten minute intervals for one hour. Which addition gives the most stable foam? Why is this?
   Try the test with egg whites from stale eggs and record the amount of liquid lost at regular intervals.

3 Boil three fresh eggs in water in the following ways:
   a Boil for 10 minutes then plunge directly into cold water; leave until cold.
   b Boil for 10 minutes, then leave to cool in the hot water.
   c Boil for 10 minutes, remove from the water and leave to cool.
   Repeat **a**, **b**, and **c**, using eggs that are at least four weeks old.
   Repeat **a**, **b**, and **c** using fresh eggs, but boiling for half an hour each time.
   Observe the formation of the green/black ferrous sulphide ring between the white and yolk in each case. Account for the differences.

4 Prepare five egg custard mixtures as follows:
   200 ml ($\frac{1}{3}$ pint) fresh milk
   1 egg
   25 g (1 oz) sugar
   Warm the milk to 60°C (140°F). Do not boil. Beat the egg and sugar and add the warm milk. Pour into a small ovenproof dish and bake as follows:
   a Stand the dish in a tray of hot water and bake at gas 3, 160°C (325°F) for approximately 40 minutes or until set.
   b Repeat **a**, but do not use a tray of water.
   c Repeat **a**, but bake at gas 9, 240°C (475°F).
   d Repeat **c**, but do not use a tray of water.
   e Repeat **a**, but boil the milk before adding it to the egg.
   Compare the cooked custards for texture, appearance, and flavour. Account for the differences. What difference does the tray of water make to the finished result?

Meat

Meat has been a principal food in the diet for centuries, and is still in great demand, despite its expense.

The main reason for the high price of meat is the amount of time, effort, and feed it takes to rear animals for meat. Large amounts of food, e.g. pulses, cereal grains, nuts, vegetables, fish meal, and grass have to be provided, and the conversion of these into meat is very inefficient. Some people feel that this is a waste of food that could be used to feed humans, particularly in poor countries.

At a predetermined age, animals are slaughtered in abattoirs, and the cleaned and gutted carcases are hung in cold store, inspected and graded, ready for sale to a butcher.

The butcher cuts the meat into joints or cuts, according to the amount and position of bones, lean meat, and fat in the various parts of the body. Lean, tender joints are more popular and difficult to produce and therefore cost more, so the butcher must separate these accurately.

Meat is sold in either specialist butchers' shops, supermarkets, or direct from farm shops. It can be bought in bulk for freezing (e.g. as a half or whole animal) and many butchers joint it for the customer. Pre-frozen meat joints can also be bought in bulk from freezer centres. A good butcher should have a sound knowledge of what he is selling and should be able to advise the customer as to the suitability of different joints for cooking.

Types of meat

The main meats eaten in the U.K. are:

beef
veal (calf)
lamb
mutton
pork
bacon

Rabbit and hare are also eaten, but less often.

Structure and composition

Lean meat is composed of the **muscles** that move the body in an animal. Muscles are composed of **cells** in the form of long, slender **fibres**. These muscle fibres are made of two proteins, myosin and actin.

The size of muscle fibres is related to the **tenderness** of cooked meat:

slender, small fibres are associated with tender meat;
large, long fibres are associated with tougher meat.

Muscle fibres increase in size as the animal gets older, therefore the older the animal, the tougher the meat from it.

Those parts of the animal's body which do the most physical work, e.g. neck, shin, forearm, have the largest muscle fibres, and therefore make tougher meat.

Individual muscle fibres are formed into **bundles**, surrounded by a substance called **connective tissue**. The bundles are then formed into groups which are also surrounded by connective tissue. Whole muscles are attached to bones by means of **tendons**:

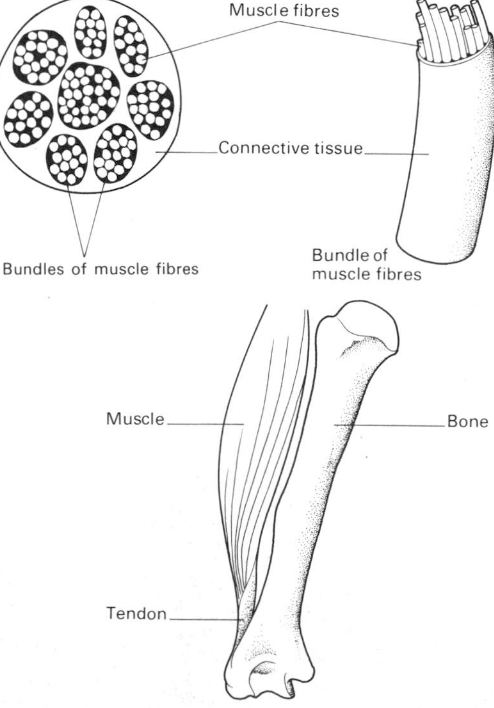

Connective tissue is made of two proteins, collagen and elastin.

Collagen is the main component of tendons, and the connective tissue surrounding muscles, particularly those which do the most work. Collagen is less flexible than elastin, and when heated in the presence of moisture, it is converted into soluble **gelatine**, which greatly increases the tenderness of connective tissue and therefore of the meat. Traditionally, tough cuts of meat were cooked by slow, moist methods such as stewing, to allow this conversion to gelatine to take place. However, it has been shown that if tough cuts of meat are roasted **slowly** at Gas 3, 160°C (325°F), there is sufficient moisture within the meat to convert the collagen and make the meat tender.

Elastin is a main component of ligaments (in between bones), and has the ability to stretch and return to its original shape. It is an insoluble and tough protein, but there is less elastin than collagen in muscles, so it does not have a major influence on the toughness of meat.

Fat

In meat, fat is found in the following places:
- under the skin in **adipose tissue**
- around vital organs, e.g. kidneys (suet)
- between bundles of muscle fibres (invisible fat)

The fat under the skin may be yellowish in colour, due to the presence of **carotenes** from plants, depending on what the animal was fed on. The fat in between the bundles of muscle fibres gives the meat a **'marbled'** effect. Marbling in lean meat is an important requirement when the meat is graded, and large amounts of feed are required to produce it. This is one of the reasons why lean meat is so expensive.

Marbling of fat in meat.

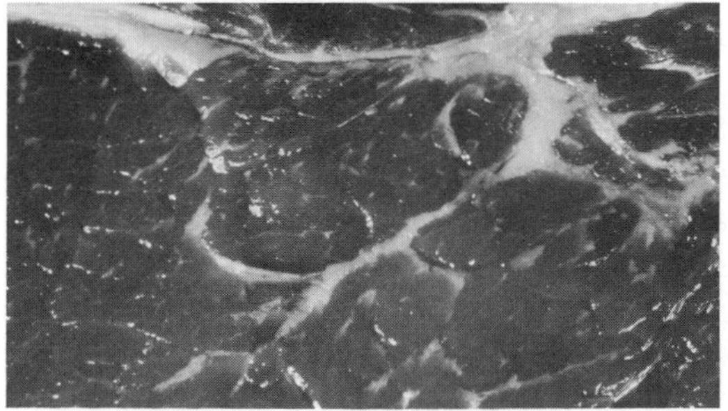

The fat content of meat helps to provide flavour, moisture, and texture to the cooked meat.

Colour of meat

The colour of meat is mainly due to the presence of **myoglobin**, which is a purple/red tissue pigment, and **haemoglobin** from the blood, some of which is left in the meat after slaughter.

In a living animal, haemoglobin takes oxygen to the muscles, and myoglobin holds it there, so that the muscle can work. There is therefore more myoglobin in well-used muscles such as the heart and shin, and in older animals, and the colour of the meat is darker in both cases.

When oxygen is taken to the tissues, the myoglobin is converted to **oxymyoglobin** which is bright red. After slaughter, the meat remains dark red until it is cut and exposed to the oxygen in the air, when it becomes bright red.

When fresh meat is stored for a few days, its colour changes to a brown/red, due to the formation of **metmyoglobin**. This does not seriously affect its palatability when cooked. If storage is continued, the meat may become green/brown due to the effect of enzymes and bacteria. In this case the palatability will be spoiled.

Choosing meat

As meat is an expensive food, it is wise to choose it carefully, considering the following factors:

Value for money

1 There should not be too much bone in a joint as this reduces its value for money. However, some is needed to produce flavour when cooking.
2 Cheaper cuts of meat, which are generally tougher, are just as nutritious as more expensive, leaner cuts. If cooked well, they

can be made into appetizing and nutritious meals.

3 There should not be too much visible fat on the joint, although this is a matter of personal preference.

Appearance

Meat should have the following physical characteristics:

1 **Colour**

Meat	Colour of lean	Colour of fat
lamb	pink/brown	cream/white
mutton	dark pink/brown	white
beef	red/brown	cream/pale yellow
pork	pink	white
veal	pink	white

2 It should be moist but not dripping.
3 It should have a fresh smell.
4 Lean meat should have a marbled appearance.
5 It should be slightly springy to the touch.

Intended use

1 Possible shrinkage should be allowed for during cooking when choosing a joint.
2 It is uneconomic to use expensive, lean joints of meat for stewing or casseroling.
3 As a general guide, about 100 g (4 oz) of meat should be allowed per person, unless it is included in a dish such as risotto where vegetables, cereal grains, or pulses form a main part of it.

The effect of heat and changes during cooking

Texture and tenderness

The proteins of meat denature at temperatures of 40°C (104°F) to 65°C (149°F). As the proteins denature, the structure of the meat tightens and the meat becomes firmer.

The protein of muscle fibres (actin and myosin) may toughen during some cooking methods.

The connective tissue is tenderized during cooking. It becomes shorter and thicker so that the meat shrinks in size. The collagen is converted to gelatine in the presence of moisture which greatly increases the tenderness. The elastin is only softened slightly.

Meat can be partially tenderized before cooking by:

1 Mechanically pounding, scoring, and cutting across the muscle fibres to reduce their length.
2 The use of enzymes, such as **papain** (from the pawpaw plant) which partially digest the protein.
3 Marinading in vinegar or alcohol.

Fat

The adipose tissue becomes more tender when cooked. The fat melts, and penetrates the lean meat during cooking, thus increasing the energy value of the lean meat. The fat content may also make the meat appear to be more juicy. On the skin of roasted meat, the fat becomes crisp and brown.

Colour

During cooking, the colour of meat changes from red to brown, due to the oxymyoglobin being converted to **haemochrome**.

Flavour

Cooking meat improves its palatability. In dry cooking methods, **extractives** containing flavour are squeezed out of the meat onto the surface as the protein denatures and shrinks. These extractives give meat its characteristic taste. The fat melts and this gives a crisp surface to the meat.

In moist methods of cooking, the extractives are leached into the cooking liquid, which should be served with the meat to give it flavour.

Nutritive value

Protein The nutritive value of proteins in meat is little affected in normal methods of cooking, but if overcooked, they become less digestible.

Vitamins The fat-soluble vitamins remain stable, but the vitamin-B group which are soluble in water may be leached into the cooking liquid in moist methods of cooking. Thiamin is particularly heat sensitive and may be destroyed in dry methods of cooking.

Minerals There may be some leaching of minerals into the cooking liquid in moist methods of cooking. The liquid should be served with the meat.

The importance of meat in the diet

Meat is an important food as it is a main source of high biological value protein for many people. The nutritional value of lean meat of most types is on average:

protein	20%
fat	5%
minerals	1%
water	74%

Meat joints normally have additional fat (up to 50%), which increases the energy value. The minerals found in meat include:

- iron
- phosphorus
- calcium (a little)

Meat also contains nicotinic acid, riboflavin, and thiamin in useful quantities. Pork is a particularly good source of thiamin. There is little retinol (vitamin A) or ascorbic acid (vitamin C) in lean meat.

Both the protein and fat in meat are readily digested and absorbed in the body, and there is little wastage.

Uses of meat in food preparation

Meat is used in a vast range of recipes all over the world. The various cuts of meat are used for different purposes, according to their suitability for each cooking method (see notes on tenderness, p. 98). As a general rule, lean, tender cuts are suitable for dry methods of cooking, e.g. grilling, roasting, and frying; whereas tough cuts of meat require long, slow, moist methods of cooking to tenderize them (see pp. 154–5).

Lamb and mutton

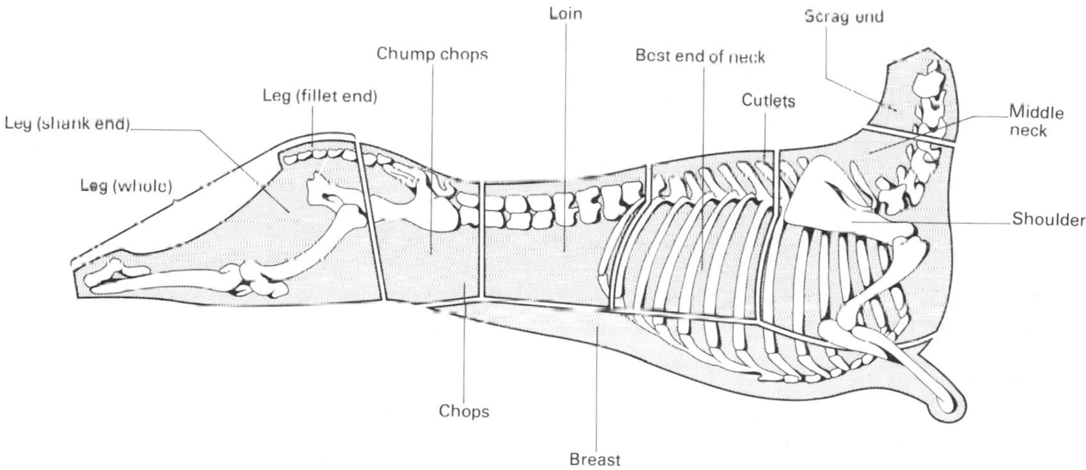

Joint	Method of cooking
Scrag end	Stew, braise
Middle neck	Stew, braise
Shoulder	Roast, braise
Cutlets	Grill, fry
Best end of neck	Roast, braise
Loin	Fry, grill, roast
Chump chops	Grill, fry, roast
Leg (fillet end)	Braise, pot-roast
Leg (shank end)	Roast, boil
Leg (whole)	Roast, braise
Chops	Grill, fry, roast
Breast	Stew, roast, braise

Pork

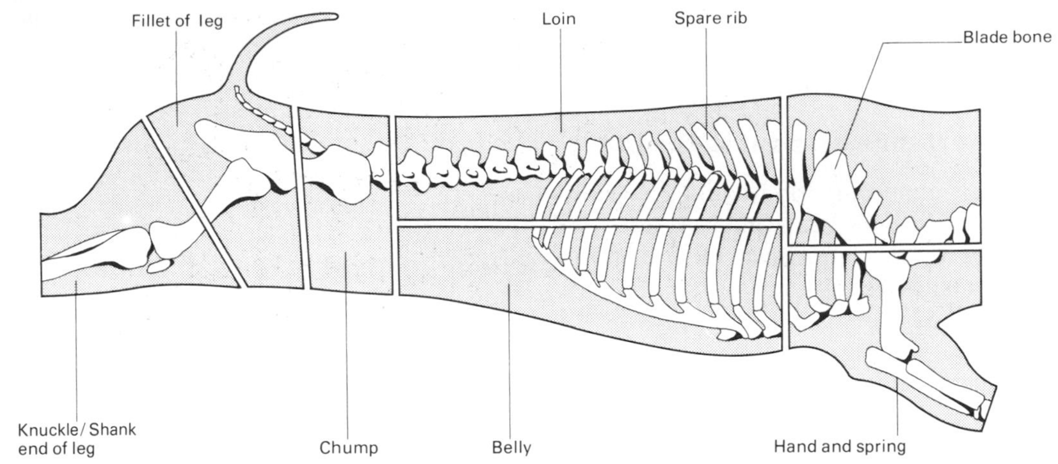

Joint	Method of cooking	Joint	Method of cooking
Blade bone	Pot-roast, braise	Chump	Fry or grill
Spare rib	As chops – fry or grill Roast	Knuckle/ Shank end of leg	Roast Salt and boil
Loin	As chops – fry or grill Roast	Belly	Pot-roast, boil, braise As slices – fry or grill
Fillet of leg	Roast – slice and salt skin Salt and boil	Hand and spring	Roast, braise Salt and boil

Bacon and ham

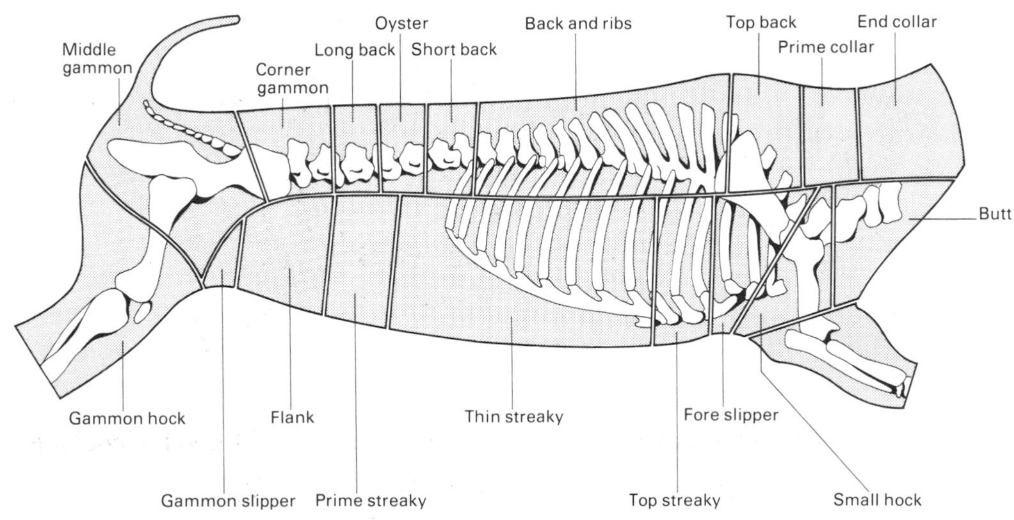

N.B. Bacon rashers are normally fried or grilled, and whole joints are roasted or boiled.

Beef

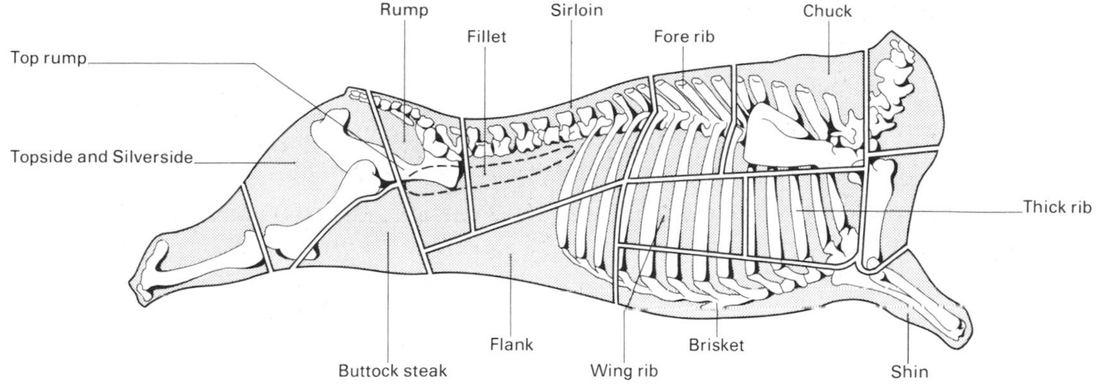

Joint	Method of cooking	Joint	Method of cooking
Chuck	Braise, stew	Buttock steak	Braise, pot-roast, stew
Fore rib	Roast	Top rump	Pot-roast, braise
Sirloin	Roast As steak – grill or fry	Flank	Salt and boil, stew
Fillet	Grill or fry	Wing rib	Roast
Rump	Grill or fry	Brisket	Braise, pot-roast Salt and boil
Topside	Roast, pot-roast, braise	Thick rib	Roast
Silverside	Roast, pot-roast, braise Boil, salt and boil	Shin	Stew, braise

Veal

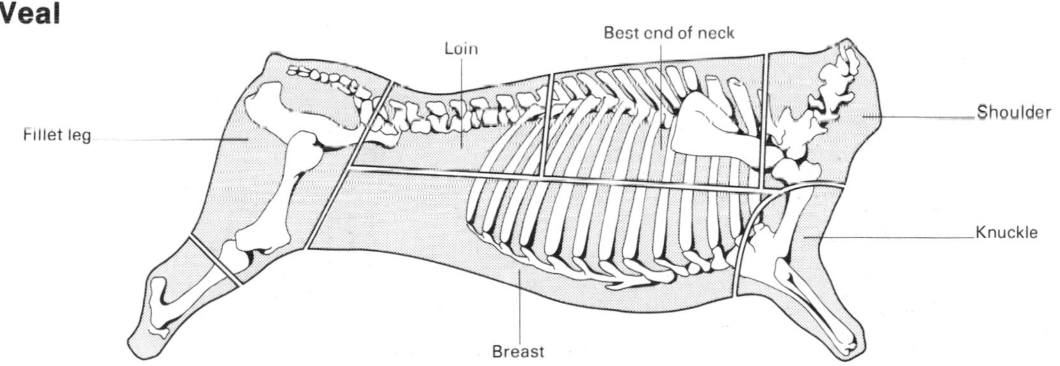

Joint	Method of cooking	Joint	Method of cooking
Shoulder	Roast, braise	Fillet leg	Roast
Best end of neck	Roast, stew As cutlets – grill or fry	Veal escalopes	
Loin	Roast As chops – grill or fry	Breast	Roast, stew
		Knuckle	Stew, braise

Poultry

Poultry is the name given to birds eaten for food and includes:

chicken goose
turkey pigeon
duck

At one time, chicken and turkey were a rare treat, but intensive rearing has made them more readily available. Chicken is now generally less expensive than other meat.

Structure and composition

Poultry meat has the same basic structure as other meat, except that there is less connective tissue, and consequently the meat is more tender. The legs and wing muscles which do the most work are generally tougher and darker in colour, due to the presence of myoglobin.

With the exception of goose and duck, there is less fat in the meat of poultry, and consequently it is drier in texture when cooked.

The flavour of poultry is generally not strong, and develops during cooking in a similar way to that of other meat.

Choosing poultry

Poultry should be chosen according to the following factors:

Appearance
Poultry flesh should have the following physical characteristics:

1 Poultry meat (except for pigeon which is darker) should be pink/white, with darker meat on the wings and legs.
2 It should be plump and springy to the touch.
3 It should have a fresh smell.

Intended use
Poultry for boiling (e.g. chickens) is generally tougher and less expensive than poultry for roasting.

Poussins are very young birds that are cooked and served whole or in half.

Turkeys are available in a range of sizes, particularly at Christmas and other festive occasions. Medium-sized birds tend to be more tender than larger ones.

Nutritive value

The protein of poultry is easily digested and of high biological value. With the exception of goose and duck, poultry contains less fat than red meat does. There is also less iron, thiamin, riboflavin, and nicotinic acid than in red meat.

Uses of poultry in food preparation

Chicken
Whole or joints: roast, braise, boil, casserole.
Joints: coat in egg and breadcrumbs and fry; grill, casserole.
Cooked chicken can be eaten cold, in salads, snacks, and picnic meals.

Turkey
Turkey can be cooked in a similar way to chicken. It is possible to buy boneless turkey rolls that can be roasted to provide three to four servings.

Inside a chicken-processing factory.

Duck and goose

Duck and goose are usually roasted. To reduce the fattiness of the meat, they can be placed on a rack during cooking and pricked with a knife at regular intervals to release the fat. They are often served with a sharp, acidic sauce, e.g. orange, to counteract the greasiness.

Bones can be boiled to produce stock for use in soups, stews, and sauces.

Storage of poultry

Freshly killed birds should be hung in a cool, dry place, with all the internal organs in place. This is to ensure that the meat becomes tender before it is cooked. Chickens are normally hung for one day, turkeys for up to five days, and geese and ducks for up to two days.

Fresh poultry should be kept in a cold place after the giblets (internal organs – neck, gizzard, and liver) and other organs have been removed. It should be eaten soon after purchase (two to three days if kept in the refrigerator).

Frozen poultry should be allowed to thaw completely before being cooked, and then thoroughly cooked to avoid salmonella food poisoning (see pp. 132–34).

Offal

Offal is defined as:

> 'Any part of a dead animal removed from the carcase in the process of dressing it, but does not include the hide or skin.'
> (Meat Regulations 1963)

The term is derived from the two words 'off fall', because the parts are removed from the carcase. In America, offal is now being called 'variety meats' to make it sound more appetizing.

The following internal organs count as offal:

liver
kidney
heart
brain
sweetbreads (pancreas and thymus glands)
tongue
tripe (the dressed stomach of an ox or sheep)
chitterlings (pig's intestines – often used as sausage casings)
lungs (these are not usually sold for human consumption)

The following parts of the body are also offal:

tail (e.g. oxtail)
feet (e.g. pig's trotters)
ears
head
eyes

Choosing offal

All offal, particularly the kidneys, liver, and heart, should be very fresh when it is bought. It should be eaten within twenty-four hours of purchase, and carefully washed and prepared before eating. Thorough cooking is necessary to prevent food poisoning and to tenderize the offal.

Some types, e.g. tripe and tongue, are prepared by the butcher before purchase. Tripe is cleaned and boiled for twelve hours and tongue is soaked and salted (except lamb and calf tongue).

Importance of offal in the diet

Protein The protein of offal is of high biological value, and if well cooked is readily digested.

Fat There is less fat in offal than in muscle meat in general.

Carbohydrate Liver may contain a little glycogen, but this is not an important source.

Vitamins As retinol (vitamin A) is stored in the liver, liver is a very good source of this vitamin. Kidney and heart contain some retinol.
Heart and liver contain useful amounts of thiamin.
There is some vitamin C in the liver, but it is not a valuable source.

Minerals Tripe contains a useful amount of calcium. Liver, and to a lesser extent kidney, are important sources of iron.

Uses in food preparation

Offal	Cooking method	Uses
liver	**Lamb's:** grill or fry. **Pig's:** fry, braise or stew. **Ox:** stew or braise gently.	Pâtés, casseroles, pastes.
kidney	Remove central core. **Lamb:** fry or grill. **Pig or ox:** stew or braise.	Steak and kidney pie, casseroles, breakfast.
heart	Stew or braise with a stuffing.	
brain	Grill or fry gently, or braise.	
sweetbreads	Stew, grill, fry, or steam.	
tongue	Boil gently until tender, then press until cold.	Salads, sandwiches.
tripe	Stew or braise.	Serve with onions.
tail	Stew or braise.	Soups, stews.

Storage

Offal should be kept in a cold place and used as soon as possible after purchase. It can be frozen for long term storage.

Meat products

A variety of meat products are available and are very popular. These include:

pâtés
sausages
faggots
meat extractives
cold cooked meats
pastes and spreads.

Sausages

Sausages have been made for many years, originally as a method of preserving and packaging meat.

There are many different types of sausage, but the basic ingredients are a mixture of meat and cereal, such as bread. Flavourings, herbs, and spices are also added, and the mixture is encased in specially prepared intestines or edible synthetic casings.

Meat extractives

These are sold as thick pastes, cubes, or powders, for use as drinks or in gravies, soups, and stews. They contain flavouring from meat, plus salt and spices. They have little nutritional value and are mainly used for their flavour.

Cold cooked meats

A large variety of cold meats can be bought. They are useful in packed lunches and picnics, as well as with salads, etc. Corned beef is a popular cold meat which contains a useful supply of iron. Cold meats are usually prepared from meat, cereal, flavourings, and spices.

Cooked cold meats should be sold separately from uncooked meat to prevent possible cross-contamination by bacteria. They should be stored in a cold place and eaten within a few days of purchase.

Sausages and cooked meats normally have preservatives added to them, and some cold meats are sold in cans for long-term storage.

Revision questions

1. What are the main types of meat eaten in this country?
2. What is lean meat?
3. What are myosin and actin, and where are they found?
4. How do muscle fibres affect the tenderness of meat?
5. How does the age of the animal affect the tenderness of meat?
6. What is connective tissue, and what is its connection with the tenderness of meat?
7. What is collagen?
8. What is the effect of moist heat on collagen?
9. What is elastin?
10. Where is the fat in meat found?
11. How is the colour of meat produced and how is it affected by heat?
12. What points should influence your choice of meat when shopping?
13. Describe the changes that take place when meat is cooked.
14. How can meat be tenderized?

15 How is the flavour of meat developed during cooking?
16 What is the nutritive value of meat, and how is this affected by heat?
17 Which methods of cooking are suitable for **a** lean and **b** tough cuts of meat?
18 Give three examples of poultry birds.
19 Why is poultry meat more tender than red meat?
20 What points should influence your choice of poultry?
21 How should meat and poultry be stored?
22 What is offal? Give five examples.
23 Why is it important that offal is very fresh when purchased?
24 What is the food value of offal?
25 Describe some meat products and give their uses in food preparation.

Further work with meat

1 Compare the cost per pound of different cuts of meat from one animal and comment on the differences.

2 Observe some different meat cuts with a magnifying glass and find the muscle fibre bundles, fat marbling, and connective tissue. Comment on the differences between each cut.

3 Using a small amount of shin of beef, cut it into cubes and boil one piece, grill another, bake another in the oven, and pressure cook the last. Compare each for flavour, colour, texture, and tenderness.

To compare differences in shrinkage during cooking, measure each piece before and after cooking, and comment on the differences.

4 Observe the changes that occur in fresh meat stored in the refrigerator for a few days in a glass dish (covered), on a plate (uncovered), and closely wrapped in polythene. What are the reasons for the changes?

Fish

There are a great many varieties of fish, and at one time they were profusely available. However, since the Second World War, there has been a great increase in fishing (partly to feed humans directly and partly to feed animals reared for food), and this has given rise to much concern about the dwindling of supplies of some varieties. Some countries have imposed fishing limits around their shores to regulate the amount of fish being caught (particularly young fish), but the problem still exists.

At sea, fish is gutted, cleaned, and frozen on board special boats, before it reaches the shore, as it deteriorates very rapidly once caught.

Types

Fish are classified in two ways:

1 According to their origin, i.e.:
Freshwater fish, e.g. salmon, trout.
Seawater fish, which are further divided into:
pelagic fish (which swim near the surface), e.g. herring, pilchard, mackerel.
demersal fish (which swim near the bottom), e.g. plaice, cod, hake.

Deep-sea fishing: a catch of cod.

2 According to their fat content and type, i.e.:
Oily fish have more than 5% fat in their flesh, which is therefore quite dark. Examples: mackerel, herring, pilchard, sprat, sardine, salmon.
White fish have less than 5% fat in their flesh, which is therefore white. They have oil in their liver. Examples: halibut, cod, whiting, coley, plaice, haddock, sole.
Shellfish, which are divided into:
molluscs (small, soft-bodied sea animals which live inside a hard shell), e.g. cockles, mussels, winkles.
crustaceans (soft-bodied, jointed sea animals which are covered by a hard protective 'crust' or external skeleton), e.g. lobster, crab, shrimp.

Shellfish should be eaten while very fresh.

Structure and composition

Fish has a muscle composition similar to that of meat, but there is far less connective tissue, therefore it is much easier to tenderize and quicker to cook. It is important not to overcook fish as the protein easily becomes tough and the flesh dry. The muscle is formed into flakes which separate on cooking.

Unlike meat, there is a lot of wastage with fish, i.e. the bones, head, fins, and often the skin. The only internal organ to be eaten is the roe of some species, where the eggs are found. Cod and herring roe are often eaten, and the roe of the sturgeon fish (caviare) is a prized delicacy and is very expensive.

Choosing fish

As fresh fish deteriorates rapidly after being caught, it is important to choose it carefully. Fresh fish should have the following characteristics:

1 Bright eyes, not sunken.
2 Plump, firm flesh.
3 Plenty of bright scales, firmly attached to the skin.
4 Moist skin.
5 A fresh, sea smell.
6 Bright red gills, not sunken.

Shellfish is normally sold cooked. As several species are scavenger feeders (i.e. they feed from sediment on rocks and pipes, often near sewage outlets), they may harbour food-poisoning bacteria and must be eaten as soon as possible after purchase.

Fish are sold in various ways:
Large fish, e.g. cod, coley, haddock, are cut into fillets, steaks, or cutlets:

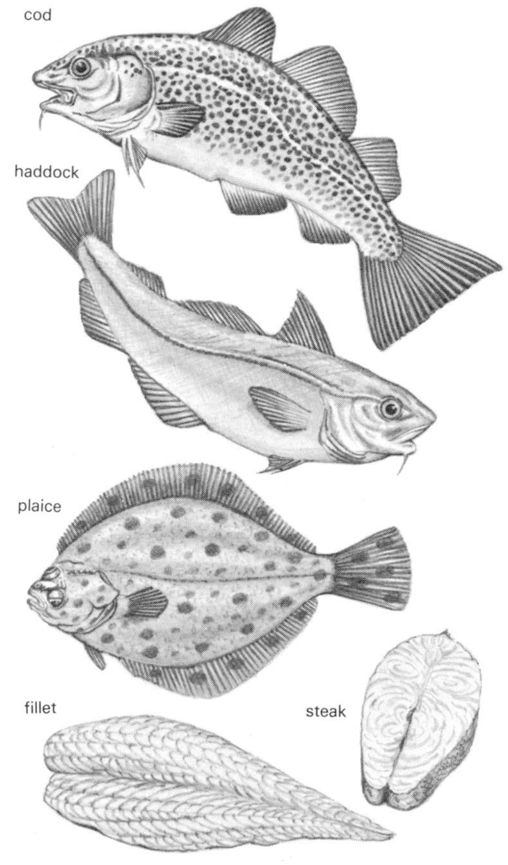

Small and medium fish, e.g. herrings, mackerel, rainbow trout, are usually sold whole, and can be filleted by removing the backbone, tail, head, and fins.

Very small fish, e.g. sprats and whitebait, can be fried and eaten whole.

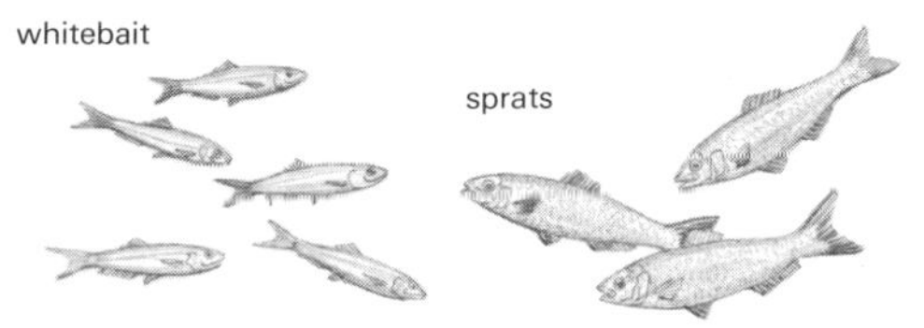

Importance of fish in the diet

For many people, e.g. Eskimos, Japanese, fish is a major source of protein. Like meat, the protein is of high biological value, and is readily digested and absorbed with little waste. White fish in particular is more easily digested than meat and is a useful food for people with digestive disorders.

Unlike meat, the fat in fish consists mostly of oils containing unsaturated fatty acids, which is of benefit to those following the dietary goals (see p. 10).

Nutritive value

The approximate nutritive value of fish is:

	Oily fish	White fish	Shellfish (edible part)
protein	19·0%	17·5%	15%
fat	15·0%	0·9%	4%
water	67·5%	80·0%	8·5%
carbohydrate	none	none	trace
minerals	2·5%	1·2%	1·4%

Vitamins

Fat soluble Oily fish contain useful amounts of vitamins A and D in their flesh. Canned oily fish contains the most vitamin D.
White fish contain vitamins A and D in their liver oils, not in their flesh.
Shellfish are not good sources of these vitamins, as they have a low fat content.
Water soluble Fish does not contain any vitamin C. Most fish contain small amounts of the B-group vitamins.

Mineral elements

Calcium Most calcium in fish is found in the bones. If the bones of canned fish, which have been softened, are eaten, they provide a useful source of calcium.

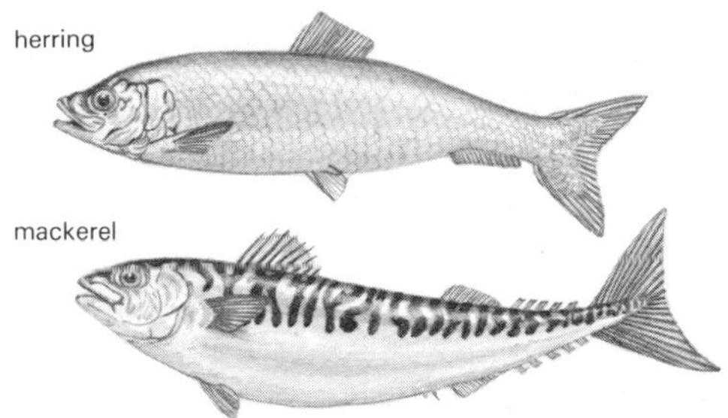

Iodine Seawater fish are good sources.
Iron Fish are not good sources of iron.
Fluoride Seawater fish are good sources.
Sodium and chlorine are found in all fish.
Potassium and phosphorus are found in all fish.

Methods of preparation and cooking

Fish can be used in many dishes, but is most popular in the UK fried in batter and served with potato chips. Overcooking tends to lead to dryness and breaking up of the flesh.

Fish	Uses
White	Steamed, poached, grilled, fried, baked. Serve in a roux sauce, or in pastry (e.g. Russian fish pie), curry, with sweet and sour sauce, etc.
Oily	Bake, fry, grill, poach. Serve with a sharp sauce, e.g. tartare, fry in oatmeal, stuff with breadcrumbs, herbs, orange, etc., and bake.
Shell	Serve as a starter, e.g. prawn cocktail, or in soups, salads, fried in batter, with rice, etc.

Storage

Fish should be eaten as soon as possible after purchase, and should be stored in the coldest part of the refrigerator (but not the ice box), well wrapped, to prevent the strong odours from contaminating other foods.

It is not advisable to freeze fresh fish bought from a shop as it must be frozen while very fresh.

Preserving fish

Apart from being frozen, fish is also preserved in other ways:

Curing

Fish is either smoked or salted.

Smoking is carried out over wood smoke in carefully controlled conditions. The smoke develops flavours in the fish and has a preservative action. The fish may either be cooked and smoked (e.g. smoked mackerel), or just smoked and left raw.

Examples of smoked fish:

Haddock is sold as golden cutlets, finnan haddock, or fillets. It is yellow in colour.

Salmon Smoked salmon is ready to eat, and is very expensive to buy.

Herrings are prepared in different ways to produce:

- **kippers:** herrings are split open and soaked in brine, then smoked.
- **bucklings:** the heads are removed, and the fish is salted, then smoked and cooked at the same time.
- **bloaters:** the fish are salted whole, then smoked.
- **roll mops:** the filleted fish are marinaded in vinegar and brine for ten days, then rolled with pickling spice, and pickled.

Salting Some varieties of fish are salted and dried, e.g. cod.

Canning

Several varieties of oily fish are canned, e.g. tuna, sardine, pilchard, herring, and may be served with oil or tomato sauce. The bones are softened and can be eaten, providing a good source of calcium.

Revision questions

1. How are fish classified? Give examples under each classification.
2. Why does fish take less time to cook than meat, and how does its structure differ?
3. What points should influence your choice of fresh fish?
4. Why is fish an important food in the diet?
5. How can fish be prepared and cooked?
6. How should fresh fish be stored in the home?
7. How is fish preserved?

Further work with fish

1. Weigh out four equal portions of the same fish and cook as follows:
   a grill
   b steam
   c fry
   d wrap in foil and bake
   Note the changes in appearance, size, and texture in each case. How do you account for the differences?
2. Grill a piece of meat and a piece of fish of equal weight together. How long does each take to cook? Why is this?
   Continue cooking the fish. What happens to it?

Alternative protein foods

There have been many attempts to manufacture foods which are rich in protein as alternatives to meat, for the following reasons:

1. Meat is expensive to produce, and has risen in price over recent years due to:
   a a shortage of good pasture land on which to rear animals;
   b increases in the price of feeds for animals.
2. In countries where there is a shortage of food (particularly protein-rich food), there is an urgent need for new protein foods to be manufactured, especially for babies and young children who suffer most under conditions of famine.
3. Cheaper feeds for animals are required, as meat is in high demand in many countries.

Several different raw materials have been used for the preparation of new protein foods. These include:

micro-organisms: bacteria, yeast, algae, plankton
plants: seeds, legumes, cereals, seaweed

Micro-organisms

Micro-organisms can be made to grow on industrial or agricultural waste materials, e.g. paper, wood, cotton, sugar-refining waste, and the production of protein is fast and efficient. Bacteria can double their weight in thirty minutes, and 80% of this is protein (yeast, algae, and plankton are slightly less efficient).

The protein products from micro-organisms are normally only used for animal feeds.

Plants

Seeds and legumes (pulses) can be used to produce protein-rich food. The main types used are soya bean, sunflower seed, groundnut, and sesame seed.

Soya has been the most important source of plant protein for this purpose, and is discussed here. The soya plant comes from the Far East, but different varieties have been successfully grown in different climates.

Soya beans were originally grown for the oil industry, but it was discovered that once the oil was extracted, the residues contained up to 50% protein, and could be made into flours or flakes for various uses. The flakes can be further refined and concentrated so that they contain up to 70% protein.

The extracted protein can be textured and flavoured to resemble meat. This is known as **textured vegetable protein** (TVP). The TVP can be shaped into 'meat' cubes or minced granules and used as a meat substitute in a variety of dishes. Usually other nutrients are added, e.g. iron, thiamin and riboflavin, according to the recommendation of the Food Standards Committee of the DHSS (Department of Health and Social Security), to bring the nutritive value close to that of meat.

TVP products have been available for some time and are used in commercially-prepared meat pies, stews, etc., and in canteen meals and vegetarian meals. They are a cheaper alternative to meat but are unlikely to replace it because of the popularity of meat and the reluctance of people to change their eating habits.

Pulses are a rich source of protein and other nutrients (see p. 116) and are therefore a valuable food in their own right.

Research into alternative protein foods is ongoing, particularly for use in poor countries. With a growing world population and less land on which to rear animals, they are likely to become more important as foods in the future.

TVP can be used to make meat go further.

Revision questions

1 Why have there been attempts in the recent past to find alternative sources of protein to meat, fish, and dairy foods?
2 What raw materials have been used for the preparation of new protein foods?
3 Why is soya a useful food for this purpose?
4 What is TVP? How is it used in meal preparation?

Further work with alternative protein foods

1 Prepare a variety of main course dishes, e.g. spaghetti bolognese, goulash, beef stew, meat pie, using **a** meat and **b** TVP meat substitutes. Compare the results according to these criteria:
   - texture before and after cooking
   - flavour
   - colour
   - cost
   - consistency of dish

2 Using the dishes made above, set up a tasting panel, asking participants to assess each dish according to the criteria set out in number 1. Draw up a chart to show the results, concluding which dishes were most popular and why.

Gelatine

Gelatine is a protein which is extracted from the collagen present in the skin, tendons, bones, and connective tissue of cattle that have been slaughtered for meat.

Properties

Gelatine is a tasteless, transparent, odourless, brittle solid which is faint yellow in colour. When mixed with water, the gelatine absorbs it and swells, due to the protein molecules in it forming a three-dimensional network which entangles the water and immobilizes it:

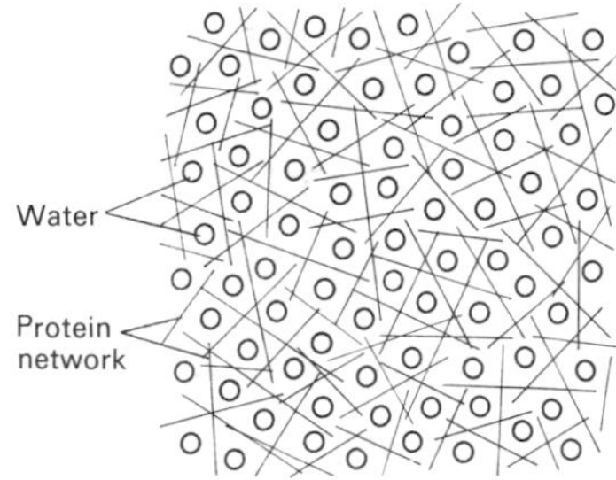

When the water is trapped in this way, it forms a **'gel'**. If the gel is then heated above 35°C (95°F), it becomes a liquid and is called a **'sol'**. When cooled, the sol becomes solid, and this process is called **gelation.**

The ability of gelatine to cause liquids to set in this way is used in food preparation for several purposes:

Domestic uses

1 Jellies: clear or plain, sweet or savoury.
2 Whips: made by beating plain jelly into a froth until it thickens.
3 Sponges: made by adding whipped egg whites to a plain jelly, to form a spongy-textured sweet.
4 Bavarian: made by folding in whipped cream to a plain jelly.
5 Creams: made with gelatine, milk or cream and eggs.
6 Soufflés: cold.
7 Sweets: marshmallows, Turkish delight, etc.
8 Aspic: for setting meat, fish, and vegetables in a savoury jelly.

Industrial uses

1 Ice cream: as a stabilizer, to ensure a smooth texture.
2 Meats: for canned hams and pressed meat, meat loaves, pâtés, pies, sausages, and brawn.
3 Thickening agent: for soup, cream.
4 Crystallized fruits: e.g. cherries.
5 Medicines: as a coating for pills and capsules.
6 Yogurt: as a stabilizer to stop separation.

Manufacture of gelatine

Gelatine is manufactured in the following way:

1 The selected raw materials are cut into small pieces and thoroughly washed.
2 The tissues are then placed into large tanks with calcium carbonate and water, and are thoroughly mixed for two to three months.
3 The calcium carbonate is then washed out and the tissues are put into large vats for carefully controlled cooking to extract the gelatine.
4 The resulting solution is filtered and concentrated, and impurities are removed.
5 The concentrated solution is then cooled and dried, and ground into a powder.
6 It is sold either as a powder, crystals, or in thin transparent sheets (leaf gelatine).

Gelatine in powder form.

Using gelatine in food preparation

Proportions to use:

12·5 g (½ oz) or 3 tsp gelatine (rounded tsp)
575 ml (1 pint) water or other liquid

To dissolve gelatine:

1 Sprinkle the gelatine into the liquid in a jug.
2 Stand the jug in a pan of hot water, stir and leave to dissolve.
3 The gelatine is ready for use when it is clear and transparent.
4 Do not boil the gelatine liquid.

Adding gelatine to a mixture

The dissolved gelatine should be poured slowly into the mixture, stirring all the time, to incorporate the gelatine completely. The mixture should not be icy cold as the hot gelatine liquid will not mix well and will form globules. This will prevent it from setting properly.

NB Fresh pineapple should be cooked first if used in a dish that is to be set with gelatine. This is because pineapple contains an enzyme called **bromelain** which prevents gelatine from setting. Heating will inactivate the enzyme.

Gelatine should not be added to very hot milk as it will cause it to curdle.

Gelatine can be used to help jam to set, but it will not keep for very long if this is done.

Storing gelatine

Gelatine absorbs moisture readily and should therefore be stored in a cool, dry place. It will also absorb odours from other foods, and so should be kept in an air-tight container.

The importance of gelatine in the diet

Gelatine is a protein, but although it is an animal protein, it has a low biological value (see p. 13). It is not, therefore, as useful in the diet as was once thought.

Gelatine can be used to set jam for people suffering from diabetes, where sugar intake has to be limited.

Revision questions

1 What is gelatine?
2 What are the properties of gelatine?
3 How does gelatine set liquids?
4 What is a gel?
5 What is a sol?
6 What is gelatine used for in food preparation?
7 What is gelatine used for in food manufacture?
8 How is gelatine produced?
9 How should gelatine be added to a mixture?
10 What effect does fresh pineapple have on the setting of gelatine?
11 How should gelatine be stored?
12 What is the food value of gelatine?

Further work with gelatine

Dissolve 12·5 g (½ oz) gelatine in 575 ml (1 pint) water. Divide equally into five beakers, with the following additions:

a no addition (control)
b 25 g (1 oz) fresh crushed pineapple
c 25 g (1 oz) fresh crushed pineapple that has been boiled for 10 minutes
d 25 g (1 oz) canned crushed pineapple
e 25 ml (1 tablespoon) canned pineapple juice

Leave in a cold place for at least 1 hour, then observe the differences in the way they have set.

Account for the difference between samples **b** and **c**, and **b**, **d** and **e**.

Vegetables

A wide variety of fresh vegetables can now be purchased. Many of them are imported and have only been available in the UK for a relatively short time. Vegetables are also available in a preserved state, frozen, canned, or dried. Many types can be grown in domestic gardens.

Vegetables are usually served as accompaniments to main meals, but with imagination and good cooking, they can be used as the main part of a meal in a variety of interesting ways.

Types

Vegetables can be classified according to the part of the plant from which they come, as described below. Some people distinguish vegetables from fruit by their inclusion in savoury parts of a meal, while fruits are eaten with sweet parts of a meal. However, some foods which are called vegetables, e.g. tomatoes, are really fruits.

If vegetables are grown out of doors in the UK, they are only available or are at their best and cheapest at certain times of the year. They are then said to be 'in season'. Many vegetables are grown in hot houses and are available for longer periods through the year.

Types	Season
Leaves	
cabbage – green, red, white	all year
spring greens	early spring
kale	winter to spring
Brussels sprouts	autumn to spring
spinach	all year
cress and watercress	all year
chicory	autumn to spring
endive	summer
Fruit	
tomatoes	summer to autumn
cucumber	spring to autumn
marrows	summer to autumn
corn on the cob (strictly a cereal but eaten as a vegetable)	late summer
capsicum (sweet red, green, yellow, or white pepper)	most of the year
aubergine	autumn
courgettes (sometimes called zucchinis)	summer, early autumn
Seeds and pods	
peas	summer
runner beans	late summer
broad beans	spring or summer
French beans	spring or summer
Stems	
celery	autumn and winter
Flowers	
cauliflower	all year but best in early summer and autumn
purple or green broccoli	as above
Roots	
carrot, beetroot	all year (new in early summer)
swede, parsnip, turnip	autumn to spring
radish	spring to autumn
Bulbs	
onions	all year
pickling onions	late summer
spring onions	spring to summer
shallots	summer
leeks	autumn to spring
Tubers	
potatoes	all year, but new in spring and summer
Jerusalem artichokes	autumn to spring

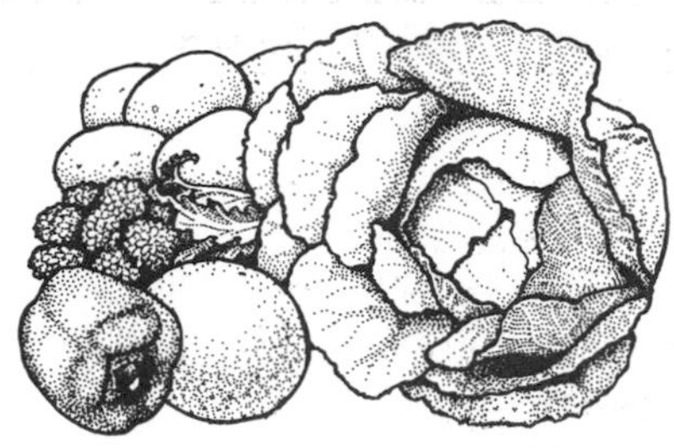

Colour of vegetables and fruit

The green colour of leafy vegetables is due to the presence of the green pigment **chlorophyll.** Chlorophyll is affected by pH. In **acid** conditions it changes to olive green, and in **alkali** conditions it becomes bright green. Some of the acids are released in steam when vegetables are cooking, particularly if they are cooked without a cover.

The yellow/orange colour of fruits and vegetables are due to the presence of **carotenoids**, which are not affected by normal cooking processes or changes in pH.

The red/blue colour of some fruits and vegetables (e.g. blackberries and red cabbage) are due to **anthocyanins**, which are sensitive to changes in pH. At neutral pH they are purple, at acid pH they are red, and at alkali pH they are blue. They are very soluble in water.

Preparation and choice

Vegetables should be chosen carefully. The following points should be considered:

1 Damaged, wilted, and bruised vegetables should be avoided, as there is likely to be waste and loss of nutrients.
2 Leaf vegetables should be crisp, firm, and of a good colour, and root vegetables should be firm and free of spade marks.
3 Insect- or mould-infected vegetables should be avoided.

In order to preserve the vitamin and mineral content, vegetables should be prepared as follows:

1 If the vegetable requires peeling, peel it very thinly, as there are vitamins and minerals under the skin which could easily be removed. Young vegetables, e.g. potatoes, carrots, often do not require peeling and can be served with their skins on.
2 Prepare vegetables just before cooking to prevent the destruction of vitamins by enzymes. They can be placed in a plastic bag in a cool place to prevent the oxidation of vitamins.
3 Wash the vegetables but do not soak them in water, as this will cause water-soluble vitamins and minerals to be lost.
4 Cook the vegetables in the minimum amount of boiling water. Placing them in boiling water destroys enzymes, and therefore helps to preserve the vitamins. They should be cooked for the minimum time, with a lid on the pan.
5 When the vegetables are just tender, they should be drained and served immediately. If kept hot, there will be further losses of vitamin C.

Conservative method of cooking vegetables

Vegetables, except for leaf types, can be chopped and sautéed in fat, then placed in a covered casserole with a little liquid in the oven, and cooked until tender. The juices should be used for gravy. This conserves most of the flavour, colour, and shape of the vegetables.

Effect of heat

Vegetables are cooked to reduce their bulk and make them more digestible by cooking the starch they contain. Some vegetables, e.g. potatoes, actually increase in bulk when cooked as they absorb water. Vitamins and minerals, particularly vitamin C, are destroyed by heat and vegetables should be cooked carefully to keep such losses to a minimum.

Importance in the diet

Vegetables are eaten in a variety of ways as part of main meals and as snacks. The nutrient content of different types varies considerably. With the exception of pulses, vegetables provide little protein and fat.

Vitamins

Water soluble

Vitamin B group Most vegetables contain some riboflavin and nicotinic acid, and pulses provide a good supply of thiamin.

Vitamin C The richest sources are Brussels sprouts, kale, cabbage, green peppers, watercress, spinach, cauliflower, tomato, and asparagus (in that order). Potatoes contain a reasonable amount, and as they are eaten in large amounts, are a useful source.

Fat soluble

Vitamin A as **carotene** Carrots and dark green vegetables contain the most, whereas potatoes, onions, and cauliflower contain none.

Vitamin D Vegetables do not contain vitamin D.

Green vegetables and peas contain a little vitamin E and vitamin K.

Carbohydrate

Plants produce starch during photosynthesis (see p. 18). The starch is stored in various parts of the plant, notably the roots and tubers. Some of the starch is converted into sugar in vegetables such as beetroot, onion, peas, leeks, tomatoes, and parsnips.

Minerals

Calcium and iron are found in various vegetables including watercress, cabbage, lentils, and spinach, but the presence of cellulose and **oxalic acid** reduces their availability to the body.

Storage of vegetables

Potatoes should be stored in a dark, cool, and dry place to prevent them from becoming mouldy and green (due to a reaction to light), and to stop them sprouting in warmth. Root vegetables should be stored in a similar way.

Leaf vegetables lose vitamin C and water rapidly during storage and should therefore be stored for the minimum time in a cool place, in a plastic bag.

All vegetables should be used as soon as possible.

Revision questions

1. How can vegetables be used in a meal to add interest and variety?
2. How are vegetables classified? Give three examples for each main group.
3. Why is it best to buy vegetables in season?
4. How should vegetables be chosen?
5. How should vegetables be prepared in order to preserve their nutrient content?
6. What is the conservative method of cooking vegetables?
7. What effect does heat have on vegetables?
8. Why are vegetables an important food in the diet?
9. How should vegetables be stored?

Further work with vegetables

1. Weigh out five 50 g (2 oz) samples of a leafy green vegetable. Place each into a small pan of boiling water (approx. 150 ml/ $\frac{1}{4}$ pint), with the following variations:
   a no addition (control)
   b $\frac{1}{4}$ tsp salt
   c 1 tsp vinegar
   d pinch of bicarbonate of soda
   e no addition
   Simmer samples **a** to **d** for 10 minutes. Plunge sample **e** into the water for a few seconds only, then remove. Drain the water from each into a beaker and observe the colour of the water and the vegetable. Account for the changes in colour. Why is it bad practice to add bicarbonate of soda to green vegetables?
2. Repeat the above experiment with sample **a** only, and boil rapidly for half an hour, observing the changes in colour, smell, and texture of the cooked vegetable at 5 minute intervals.
3. Repeat experiments 1 and 2 with carrots (simmer for 15 minutes) and observe the colour and texture changes.
4. Peel four old potatoes of similar size. Leave one whole, chop one into two, chop the third into four, and the fourth into small dice.

Cook each in boiling water for 5 minutes and then test with a skewer or fork. Which sample is the softest? Why?
Continue cooking the potatoes for a further 20 minutes. Observe the textures of each and account for the differences.
From the results of experiments 2, 3, and 4 write a short account of the importance of correct timing and cooking conditions for vegetables.

5 Repeat experiment 1 using red cabbage and observe the changes in colour and texture. Then add a pinch of bicarbonate of soda to the water from sample **c**, and observe the colour change. Add more bicarbonate of soda until a constant colour is maintained. Add a few drops of vinegar to the water from sample **d** and observe the colour change. Add more vinegar until a constant colour is maintained. Account for the changes in colour.

Pulses and nuts

Pulses

Pulses are the dried seeds of the legume plant family, which includes:

beans
peas
lentils

Many varieties are grown all over the world, in different climates.

Types

There are many types of pulse grown, but the most familiar ones in the UK are:

Beans:

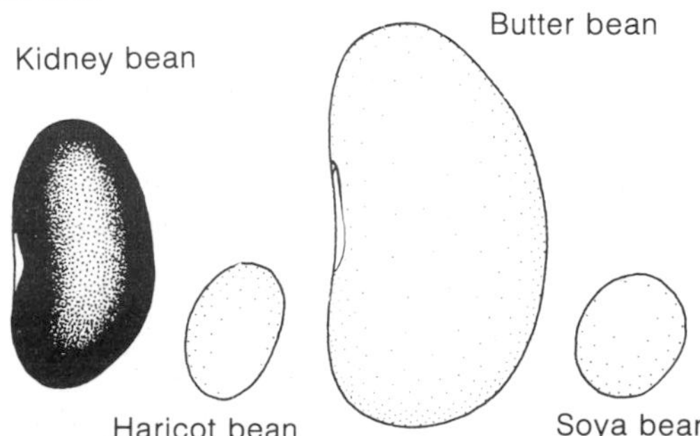

Seeds: lentils (orange and brown)

Peas: whole or split without skins (yellow or green)

Peanuts
Groundnuts (strictly pulses)

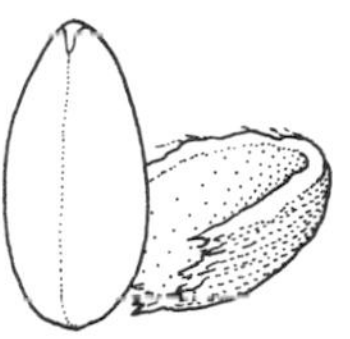
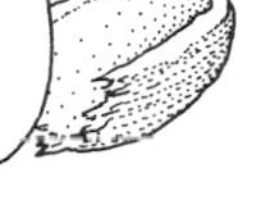
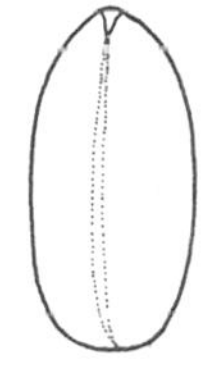

Preparation

All pulses, except for lentils, should be soaked in water for approximately eight hours before cooking, to allow water to be taken up by osmosis. This causes the pulse to swell and soften. The addition of bicarbonate of soda to the water hastens this process without significantly affecting the nutritional value.

It is inadvisable to use pulses which are more than one year old, as the skins tend to harden during storage and are difficult to soften.

Once softened, pulses should be boiled gently in the minimum amount of water until tender. Red kidney beans *must* be boiled for at least fifteen minutes, to destroy a natural toxin (poison) they contain. If eaten raw or partially cooked this toxin can cause food poisoning.

Uses

Pulses are included in meals in a variety of ways:

Soups and **stews** – to thicken and add extra protein.
Vegetable accompaniment – served in a sauce (e.g. parsley) with meat and other vegetables.
Salads Cooked pulses can be served cold in a dressing or with other salad vegetables.

Soya Soya beans are ground into flour or made into textured vegetable protein (see pp. 108–9).

Vegetarian meals Pulses are a main source of protein in vegetarian meals.

Importance in the diet

Pulses make an important contribution to the diet in many Eastern countries, where they may be the main source of protein and can be produced relatively easily. In Western countries such as the UK, where a greater variety of foods are available, pulses feature less importantly in the diet. However, in the UK approximately 300,000 tons of baked beans (haricot beans) in tomato sauce are consumed each year, which is a larger amount than in most other Western countries.

Nutritional value

Protein Most pulses contain approximately 20 g LBV protein per 100 g (dry weight). Soya beans contain up to 40 g per 100 g (dry weight) of HBV protein, and are therefore an exceptionally good source compared with other pulses.

Fat Soya beans and groundnuts contain up to 20% and 40% fat respectively, and are therefore a good source of fat compared to other pulses.

Carbohydrate Most pulses contain up to 20% carbohydrate.

Vitamins In general, pulses are a good source of the B group of vitamins, except for riboflavin. They have no vitamin C in their dry state, but on germination, they provide a rich source. Bean sprouts, which are easy to grow, provide a valuable source of vitamin C.

In view of the relative ease with which pulses can be grown and their nutritional value, it has often been suggested that more should be eaten, particularly in poor countries. However, it may be difficult to change people's food habits, and in poor countries there may not be the facilities to prepare pulses satisfactorily for consumption.

Nuts

In most people's diets, nuts are only eaten in small amounts because they are expensive, and therefore their contribution to the diet is small.

Types

coconut palm
brazil
walnut
hazelnut
almond
cashew
chestnut

Uses

Nuts are used in baking and confectionery, chiefly for their flavour and texture. They can also be used in poultry stuffings, served in salads, nut roasts, casseroles, and croquettes, and used as a garnish for vegetables.

Importance in the diet

Nuts are eaten in such small amounts by most people that they do not feature significantly in the nutrient content of the diet. However, they are a useful source of LBV protein and fat to vegetarians, as well as adding variety to their diet. They also supply some carbohydrate, calcium, and iron, plus a little thiamin.

Revision questions

1. What are pulses?
2. Give some examples of beans, seeds, and peas.
3. How should pulses be prepared?
4. How can bicarbonate of soda help in the preparation of pulses?
5. How are pulses used in meal preparation?
6. Why are pulses an important food in poor countries?
7. What is the food value of pulses?
8. Give some examples of nuts, and their uses in food preparation.
9. What is the importance in the diet of nuts?

Fruits

Fruits are a unique group of foods because there is such a wide variety of types, flavours, colours, and textures.

As far back as Roman times, apples and pears are known to have been grown, and in the sixteenth century, many types of fruit, including apricots, grapes, figs, plums, and peaches were introduced into the UK.

Relatively recent preservation techniques and modern transport facilities have contributed to the variety of fruit available.

Botanically, fruits are the part of the plant that carry the seeds for future generations of plants. They are often attractively 'packaged' by nature to encourage animals and birds to eat them and scatter the seeds.

Types

Hard fruits
apples (eating), e.g. Cox's Orange Pippin, Starking, Golden Delicious, Granny Smith, Worcester, Russet, Laxton Superb
apples (cooking), e.g. Bramley
pears, e.g. conference, William

Stone fruits
plums, e.g. Victoria, golden
damsons
apricots
greengages
peaches
cherries
grapes – black, green, red
nectarines

Citrus fruits
oranges
lemons
limes
grapefruits
tangerines
clementines
satsumas

Berry fruits
strawberries
raspberries
blackberries
gooseberries

Currants
black and red currants

Miscellaneous
melon – water melon, honeydew
bananas
rhubarb (strictly a stem, but eaten as a fruit)
pineapples

Dried fruit
sultanas
currants
raisins
dates
prunes

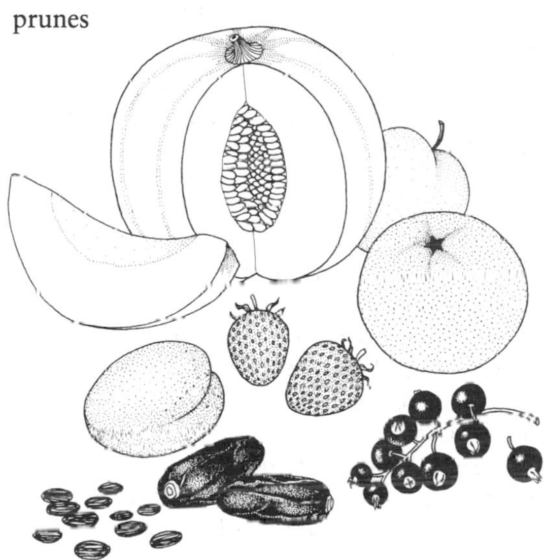

Preparation

Most fruits can be eaten raw when ripe, but they are cooked for various dishes, often by stewing them in a little water. Fruit should be cooked over a gentle heat for the minimum time. Very little water should be used as most fruits produce a fair amount of juice when cooked. This should be served with the fruit to conserve the nutrients.

Fruit should be chosen carefully, and the following points are useful as a guide:

1 Choose fruit that is just ripe, and has no bruising or blemishes.
2 Wash the fruit carefully, as it is likely to have been sprayed with pesticide and may be dusty.
3 Store the fruit carefully, taking care not to crush it as this will cause bruising.

Importance in the diet

Fruits are eaten mainly for their flavour, texture, and the variety they give to the diet. Their high water content makes them refreshing, particularly when eaten raw.

The nutrient content varies considerably between different varieties. In general, fruits are very low in protein and fat, their main contribution to the diet being vitamins, carbohydrate, and minerals.

Vitamins

Fruits are an important source of vitamin C (ascorbic acid). However, not all fruits are good sources. The richest sources are rose hips and blackcurrants. Citrus fruits (especially oranges, lemons, and grapefruits), gooseberries, strawberries, and raspberries provide a good source. Apples, damsons, peaches, apricots, and cherries provide some. This only applies to fresh or frozen fruit, not canned or stewed fruit as heat destroys much of the vitamin C content.

A reasonable amount of vitamin A is present as carotene in apricots, but there is very little in other fruits.

Fruits do not contain any vitamin D and very little of the vitamin B group.

Carbohydrate

Plants produce starch during photosynthesis, and in unripe fruits, most of the carbohydrate is present as starch. As the fruit ripens, the starch is converted to sucrose and then to glucose and fructose, and the fruit becomes sweeter in taste. Fruits are generally eaten before this conversion is complete, therefore a mixture of carbohydrate is provided.

Fruits are a useful source of dietary fibre, which is found on the skins, seeds, pith, and fibrous parts of the fruit. Pectin also helps to remove waste products from the body.

Minerals

Fruits supply a small amount of iron and calcium plus some of the trace elements.

Storage of fruit

Fresh fruit should be stored in a cool, ventilated place, and used as soon as possible. Soft fruits are best kept in the refrigerator, as they deteriorate rapidly in warm weather.

Revision questions

1 How are fruits classified? Give three examples of fruits in each category.
2 Why are fruits a valuable food in the diet?
3 Describe the food value of fruits.
4 How should fruits be prepared and chosen?
5 How should fruits be stored in the home?

Further work with fruits

1 Place samples of fresh fruits in the freezer for a few days, then remove and thaw. Observe the change in colour, texture, and overall appearance. Account for these changes.
Suggested fruits:

apple	raspberry
banana	tomato
orange	cucumber
strawberry	plum
melon	

2 Peel and chop five samples each of apple, banana, and orange.
- **a** Leave one sample of each exposed to the air.
- **b** Wrap one sample of each tightly in plastic cling wrap.
- **c** Sprinkle one sample of each with lemon juice.
- **d** Sprinkle one sample of each with bicarbonate of soda.
- **e** Plunge one sample of each into boiling water for a few seconds and then remove.

Account for the differences in appearance. What causes the browning in the apple and banana, and why is the orange not affected? What is the best substance to use to prevent browning in a fresh fruit salad, and why?

Herbs

Herbs have long been used as flavouring agents in food, and are believed by many people to possess medicinal properties.

Herb plants usually grow in temperate climates, and normally the leaves are used in food preparation, as they contain **aromatic oils.** When the leaves are crushed or chopped the oils release flavours and scents. Occasionally flowers, roots, or seeds are used.

Herbs can be easily grown in gardens or indoors in pots, and they can be dried or frozen for use all year round. Many recipes include herbs and the herbs can be used raw or cooked.

A **bouquet garni** is made from a variety of fresh or dried herbs (tarragon, mint, rosemary, sage, parsley, thyme) tied in muslin. It is added to soups, stews, etc., for flavouring, then removed before the dish is served.

Some commonly used herbs include:

Herb	**Uses**
Angelica 	The stems are candied (preserved in sugar) and then used for decoration on cakes, puddings, etc. The root is sometimes used to flavour drinks.
Basil 	The leaves are used for salads, tomato, egg, or mushroom dishes, and pasta dishes. It can also be used in sauces.
Bay	The leaves are used in meat and fish stews, soups, and marinades.
Chives	The leaves are used for salads, vegetable soup, omelettes, cream cheese, and meat broths.
Dill 	The leaves are used with fish, salads, and sandwich fillings made with cottage cheese. The seeds can be used in stews and bean soups.
Garlic 	The bulb is used and is divided into cloves. It has a very strong flavour and should be used sparingly. It can be used in stews, soups, salads, butter, mayonnaise, etc.
Marjoram 	The leaves are used for meat loaves, marrows, stuffed green peppers, pizzas, and pasta dishes.
Mint	The leaves are traditionally served chopped in vinegar with roast lamb. They can also be served with water ices, drinks, and fruit salads.
Parsley	The leaves are used for many dishes, e.g. stuffings, sauces, soups, and salads. It is a useful source of vitamin C if used in large quantities.
Rosemary	The leaves are served with roast lamb or chicken, fish, eggs, and cheese.
Sage 	The leaves are used for stuffings, sage and onion sauce, and it is put into sage Derby cheese.
Tarragon	The leaves are used to flavour vinegar, sauces, and mustards, or are cooked with chicken dishes.
Thyme	The leaves are used in stuffings, soups, stews, herb sauces, and with vegetables.

Spices

Spices have been used throughout history all over the world, and have for many centuries been an important trading commodity.

Spices are mostly grown in tropical countries, and tend to be derived from dried roots, seeds, or barks. They are used in food preparation either whole, crushed, or powdered. They generally have a strong aromatic flavour.

There are many spices in use. The more common ones are described below.

Spice	Uses
Allspice	Savoury sauces, marinades, Middle Eastern meat dishes, pickling.
Caraway	The seeds are used in bread, cakes and some cheeses, particularly in German and Jewish cooking.
Cayenne pepper	This is made from ground chillies and is a hot, fiery pepper, which should be used sparingly in cheese dishes, and with shellfish.
Chillies	Hot pickles, curries, and spicy West Indian and Mexican dishes. Also used in chilli and tabasco sauce. Chilli powder is used in chilli con carne.
Cinnamon	This comes from the bark of a tree. It is used in mulled wines, fruit cakes, apple pies, biscuits, etc.
Cloves	These are flower buds from the myrtle tree. Used for bread sauce, baked gammon, etc.
Coriander	The seeds are used in curries and other spicy dishes.
Curry powder	This is a mixture of several hot spices including turmeric. Used in mulligatawny soup and meat, fish, and vegetable dishes.
Ginger	The root of the plant is used either powdered, crystallized, or whole. Used for cakes, with melon, etc.
Mustard	The seeds are used to make mustard powder, or for pickling or chutney. Mustard is served with meat, cheese, ham, etc. It is used in oil and vinegar dressing.
Nutmeg	The seed is sold whole or powdered. It is used in egg custards, cheese sauce, milk puddings, moussaka.
Paprika	This is ground sweet red peppers, and is not usually very hot. Used in Hungarian cookery, e.g. goulash, and with egg, cheese, and shellfish as a garnish.
Peppercorns	These can be white or black and are served with most meals in powdered form.
Turmeric	This is made from the root of a plant and is used in curries, or for colouring rice yellow.
Vanilla	Vanilla plants are a type of orchid and the dried seed pods are used either whole or as an essence for cakes, puddings, etc.

Nutritional value

Spices are used in small quantities so they do not contribute significantly to the diet. However, curry powder contains a useful amount of iron, probably partly obtained from the iron pots in which it is prepared.

Food additives

Manufactured foods often contain certain food additives for the following reasons:

1 To preserve them from decay and spoilage (see pp. 132–5).
2 To improve the keeping qualities of the food during distribution.
3 To improve or enhance the flavour, colour, and texture of a food to make it more acceptable.
4 To produce a uniform food during large scale manufacture.
5 To provide easy-to-prepare convenience foods in a society that is busy and spends less time in the kitchen than in past years.

Additives, such as salt, alcohol, spices, and sugar have been in use for a long time, and there are now many synthetic additives used in a variety of ways.

Important requirements of food additives

For an additive to be acceptable for use in a food, it must conform to certain principles:

1 It must be safe to use.
2 It must be effective in its intended use.
3 It must only be used in the minimum quantity required for it to work.
4 It must not mislead the consumer about the quality or nature of a food.
5 It should, where possible, be of nutritional value to the body.

Natural versus synthetic additives

Much concern has been voiced by various groups of people about the use of synthetic additives in food. They are considered by some not to be as safe as natural additives (i.e. those produced by plants and animals). However, many of the most dangerous poisons occur naturally in plants and animal foods, and it is not possible to establish accurately what other chemicals they contain.

Synthetic additives, on the other hand, are generally pure and can be tested for their effects on the body by animal experiments. Also, the amount added to food can be strictly controlled.

Both natural and synthetic additives are used in foods, and their use is strictly controlled by law.

Ingredients:
Sugar, Starch, Vegetable oil, Emulsifier, Emulsifying salts, Sodium caseinate, Lactose, Whey powder, Sodium aluminosilicate, Lecithin, Flavourings, Colour, Antioxidant

The contents of a peach-flavour dessert whip . . .

INGREDIENTS WHEN RECONSTITUTED
NOODLES, ONION, CELERY, EDIBLE FAT, STARCH, MUSHROOM, SALT, SOYA FLOUR, PEAS, YEAST EXTRACT, SOUR CREAM SOLIDS, MONOSODIUM GLUTAMATE, HYDROLYSED VEGETABLE PROTEIN, EMULSIFIER, SOY SAUCE, FLAVOURING, COLOUR, HERBS AND SPICES, FRUIT ACIDS, GARLIC, SILICA, PRESERVATIVE, ANTIOXIDANTS.

. . . and of a dried stroganoff with noodles.

Types of additives and their uses

1 **Preservatives** and **antioxidants**, see pp. 144–5.
2 **Emulsifiers** and **stabilizers** are used to ensure that food products remain in a good stable condition for a certain period of time after they are manufactured (this may be several months).

Emulsifiers work in the following way:

Oil in water emulsion

Water
Oil

separates after a time.

Emulsifier molecules have a water-loving (hydrophilic) and a water-hating (hydrophobic) end.

Water hating
Water loving

The water-loving end is attracted to the water and the water-hating end to the oil.

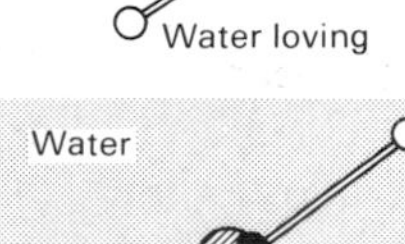

The emulsifier molecules therefore surround the oil droplets and prevent them from rising to the surface of the water.

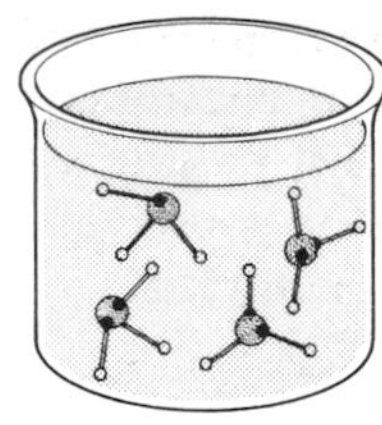

An example of an emulsifier is:

glyceryl	monostearate
(water-loving part of molecule)	(water-hating part of molecule)

Emulsifiers are used in products such as salad dressings, low-fat spreads, and ice cream.

3 **Acids** are used to develop an acid flavour in sweets, for setting jam, and in baking powder.
Types of acid used:
citric acid (from lemon juice)
tartaric acid (from grapes)
malic acid (from apples and grapes)
acetic acid (in vinegar)
lactic acid (from dairy foods)

4 **Non-stick agents** are used in powdery foods to prevent them from sticking together, e.g. magnesium carbonate is used in salt.

5 **Colourings** Natural food colours are chemicals produced by plants and animals.
When food is coloured during food manufacture, natural or synthetic colourings can be used. Colour in food is a very important aspect of consumer choice and the desire to eat. Firms spend a lot of time and money on research to get the right colour in their food. Some foods have to be coloured after processing as they lose their natural colour, e.g. canned peas go grey, as does blackcurrant cordial. There is a permitted list of food colours that may be used, and food manufacturers must abide by this legislation.

6 **Flavours and solvents** The flavour of a food product is an important factor in its success. The most widely used sources of food flavours are:

herbs	roots
fruits	seeds
berries	barks

Many flavours are extracted from oils, e.g. peppermint, clove, citrus oils, etc. The addition of a flavour enables the manufacturer to produce a consistent product.

Sweeteners such as saccharin are often added to foods instead of sucrose, as they are more concentrated and produce the desired degree of sweetness at a lower cost. Concern has recently been expressed in several countries about the use of these sweeteners, and some of them have been banned from use, although the evidence that they are harmful is still not clear (see p. 75).

7 **Nutrients** During the processing of some foods, e.g. cereals, nutrients are lost, and may be replaced by the manufacturer. This is called **restoration.** Nutrients may also be added to foods to **enrich** or **fortify** them. For example, vitamins A and D are added to margarine, and calcium is added to white bread by law. Fruit juices often have extra vitamin C added, and salt may have iodine added. The Food Standards Committee also recommends that TVP foods intended to replace meat should be fortified with nutrients to make them similar to meat in food value.

All manufactured food products in the UK have to bear a label stating exactly what is in the food, including any additives, which may be described by their chemical name or listed as e.g. 'permitted antioxidants', or by their 'E' number from a list prepared under EEC (see p. 61) regulations.

Strict controls and checks are made on the additives in food by various committees and government bodies in order to protect the public from having their food adulterated. These include:

The Food Standards Committee
The Food Additives and Contaminants Committee
Department of Health and Society Security (Chief Medical Officer's Department)

Revision questions

1. Why are additives put into foods?
2. What important principles must food additives conform to?
3. What is the difference between natural and synthetic additives? Give some examples of each.
4. What are emulsifiers and stabilizers, and how do they work?
5. Why are colourings added to food?
6. What are the most common flavours used in foods?
7. Why are nutrients added to foods?
8. How are additives controlled by law?

Convenience foods

Convenience foods are usually described as those foods which are processed and partly or totally prepared by a food manufacturer, so that they are either ready to eat, or require minimal preparation by the consumer.

These foods have gained in popularity in recent years, due to a number of factors, including:

1. Less leisure time being spent in food preparation.
2. Increased numbers of women going out to work and therefore having less time to prepare food.
3. Advances in food technology.
4. Increased freezer ownership and therefore convenient storage of ready-prepared foods.
5. The influence of advertising on people's food habits.

Years ago, most foods, including butter, cheese, and bread were prepared in the home, and many hours were spent in food preparation. Food technology at the time was limited, as were the means of preserving food and distributing it over a wide area.

Today, a wide range of convenience foods is available. They can be loosely classified as follows:

Type of food	Examples
Dehydrated	
1 'Instant foods' (quickly and easily prepared by reconstituting with water or other liquid)	mashed potato custard cold desserts soups coffee baby foods porridge snacks (pasta or rice based)
2 Foods requiring reconstituting and a short cooking time	soups main meals, e.g. curries, stews sauces custard pie fillings, e.g. lemon meringue TVP foods (see pp. 108–9)
3 Ingredients for main dishes requiring the addition of extra ingredients and liquid	cake mixes batter mixes scone mixes bread mixes crumble mixes cheesecake mixes icing mixes
Ready-to-eat	
1 Sweet	cakes biscuits fruit pies and tarts puddings and sweets
2 Savoury	meat pies, pasties cold meats pâtés salads, e.g. coleslaw pastes (fish and meat) cheese spreads preserves
Canned	
1 Foods requiring heating	pasta or pulses in sauce, e.g. beans baby foods stews puddings sausages soups milk puddings
2 Foods requiring no cooking	fish cold meats custard fruit
3 Foods requiring some cooking	vegetables pies and meat puddings
4 Foods used as part of a main dish	meat and fruit pie fillings special sauces, e.g. bolognese
Frozen	
1 Foods ready to eat on thawing	cold sweets, e.g. mousses, trifle ice cream fruit juice
2 Foods ready to cook	pastry yeast doughs sausage rolls mince pies beefburgers meat pies fish fingers
3 Foods cooked and ready to heat	fish in sauce casseroles pies

Advantages of convenience foods

1. Convenience foods are quick and easy to prepare and save time and fuel.
2. They are easy to store, especially dried foods, and are useful for taking on holiday.
3. They can be kept for emergencies.
4. A wide variety is available.
5. There is usually little waste.
6. They often have extra nutrients added.

Disadvantages of convenience foods

1 They may work out to be more expensive than fresh foods, but the time and fuel required to cook fresh foods and the wastage from them must be taken into consideration.
2 Too many processed and refined foods in the diet may limit the intake of fibre.
3 Servings in convenience meals may not be adequate, making it necessary to buy extra, which defeats the object.
4 Nutrients may be lost during processing and not replaced.

Using convenience foods

In theory, it is possible to live entirely on the convenience foods described, without necessarily suffering from any nutritional deficiences. However, in practice, most people would not be able to tolerate such a diet and it would become monotonous. In terms of flavour, texture, and appeal, there is no substitute for fresh foods.

In a broad sense, most foods in the shops are convenience foods, as they have been made and prepared by a manufacturer to save the consumer time.

Some people object to processed and refined convenience foods on the grounds that they are not as nutritious as fresh foods and contain many additives which are not naturally found in foods. A logical, sensible approach is to use both fresh and convenience foods in proportions that suit the individual in terms of money, time, likes, and dislikes.

There is no doubt that convenience foods have a firm place in modern-day eating habits and are likely to continue to be developed in the future.

Revision questions

1 What are convenience foods?
2 Why are they so popular?
3 Describe some different types of convenience food and give examples of each.
4 What are the advantages of convenience foods?
5 What are the disadvantages of convenience foods?
6 Why do some people object to convenience foods?

Further work with convenience foods

To assess the value of convenience foods to the consumer, prepare and cook a variety of convenience foods plus their home-made equivalents, e.g.:

bread mix
cake mix
scones
batters
soups
meat dishes, e.g. spaghetti bolognese
canned sauces
dried sauces
cold puddings

Compare the convenience foods and the home-made equivalents according to the following criteria:

cost of total ingredients
length of preparation and cooking time
processes required during preparation, e.g. whisking, creaming, beating
consistency and appearance before baking or cooking
appearance after cooking, e.g. size, volume, texture
flavour after cooking
additives used, e.g. preservatives
total amounts of ingredients used
keeping qualities before and after preparation
number of servings
versatility of mixture

Make constructive criticisms of the results and decide which foods are best value for money, most appetizing, and most useful to the consumer.

Questions and activities

1 Conduct a price survey over a specified period of time, e.g. every half term for three terms, on a list of 20 foods and household items (e.g. five fresh fruit and vegetables; five canned, packaged, or frozen goods; five household cleaners; five fresh meat, cheese, or fish items). Select two different types of shop if possible, e.g. a large supermarket chain and a small local grocery shop. At the end of the survey, evaluate your findings as follows: (You may wish to plot the prices on a graph.)

a Which group of foods had the greatest number of price increases or variations?

b List the possible reasons for these changes in price.

c Which of the two shops in your survey (or compared to someone else's survey), was overall more expensive to shop in? Give reasons why this may be so.

d How does each shop encourage customers (including disabled customers) to purchase goods there? (e.g. special offers)

e What factors, apart from cheaper prices, might encourage a customer to shop at one place rather than another?

f How does the law protect customers with regard to the price of food?

2 a What are 'E' numbers, and why are they printed on food labels?

b Select labels from three different food items. List the E numbers on them and find out what they stand for.

c Make a list of foods which contain no additives.

d Why are increasing numbers of food manufacturers and retailers selling foods with fewer or no additives in them?

e Design an attractive poster to explain, clearly and graphically, why the following additives are put into foods:

emulsifiers
flavour enhancers
colours
preservatives

3 In Britain, we are now able to buy a larger variety of foods such as fruits, vegetables, and cheeses, than was possible a few years ago.

a What are the reasons for this increase in consumer choice?

b Choose two examples of more unusual foods and write about the following aspects of each:

country of origin
price
uses
contribution to health

c Many other consumer goods for the home are imported from abroad. What problems could arise with regard to safety and guarantees, and how does the law aim to protect the consumer with regard to such goods?

4 Food technology is an important part of the food industry.
Give some examples of how technology has benefited the consumer in the production and retailing of food. In what ways are some aspects of food technology and politics not beneficial to the consumer? (e.g. surplus supplies of foods, pollution)

3/Practical food preparation

Principles behind the cooking of food

Heat

Heat is a form of energy, and is continually used in the home to:

cook food   heat water   heat rooms

In the body, some of the energy released from food during digestion is converted into heat to maintain body temperature.

Heat is produced when the **molecules** in a substance **vibrate** and **move rapidly**. The faster the movement, the more heat energy is produced.

Measurement of heat

The amount of heat energy produced is measured on a **temperature scale**, using a **thermometer**, which indicates the degree of heat.

The two temperature scales in common use are the Celsius (or centigrade) and Fahrenheit scales.

Heat transfer

Heat energy can be transferred from one point to another. This is the underlying principle in the cooking of food: heat must pass from the cooker to the food at a suitable rate.

Heat flows from a **high** temperature to a **lower** one, until a **constant** temperature is reached (this process is reversible). Heat can be transferred in three ways, by:

1 conduction   2 convection   3 radiation

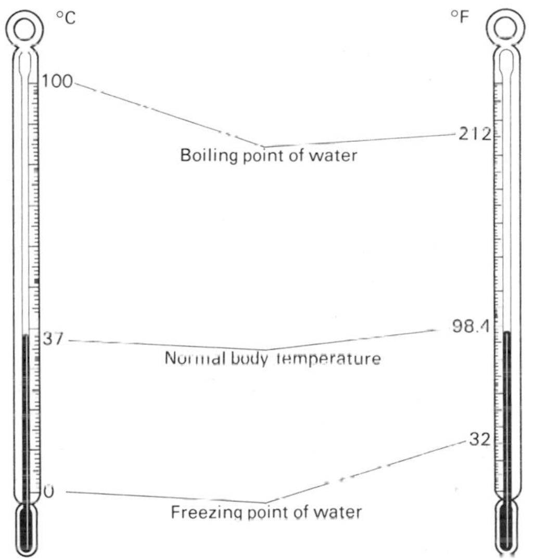

Conduction

If a metal spoon is placed in boiling water, its handle quickly becomes hot. This is because the molecules in the bowl of the spoon start vibrating rapidly as the heat energy from the surrounding water is transferred to them. As they vibrate, neighbouring molecules start to vibrate too, thus transferring the heat energy along the whole length of the spoon.

Heat is conducted at varying rates through different substances.

Good conductors of heat conduct heat rapidly and efficiently, e.g. silver, copper, brass, aluminium, iron.

Poor conductors of heat (heat **insulators**) conduct heat slowly and inefficiently, e.g. glass, plastic, wood, cotton cloth, wool, still air.

Examples of conduction and insulation in food preparation

Ovens Insulated with glass fibre or a similar poor heat conductor to prevent heat loss.

Oven gloves Made of a thick insulating material to prevent heat conduction.

Pans Made of metals which are good conductors of heat. Copper can be welded to the base of a stainless steel pan to conduct heat very rapidly. (See p. 266.)

Pan handles Made of an insulating material, e.g. plastic or wood, to prevent heat conduction.

Wooden spoon Poor conductor, therefore useful in the preparation of hot liquids.

Double-based cake tins Layer of air prevents rapid heat conduction and reduces risk of burning.

Oven-proof glass cooking utensils These are inefficient at conducting heat and may thus affect cooking time and the finished result.

Cool boxes Insulation prevents heat entry into box, therefore useful for transporting frozen foods.

Food Some foods, e.g. meat, are poor conductors of heat and require a long time to cook. Metal skewers placed in a joint, or bones, help to conduct heat to the centre.

Frying, stewing, boiling Heat is mainly transferred by conduction in foods cooked by these methods.

Convection

Liquids and gases are poor conductors of heat but heat can be transferred rapidly through them by convection.

As they are heated, the molecules in a liquid or gas expand and rise, thus allowing molecules from the cooler and heavier part of the liquid or gas to fall and be heated in turn. In this way, **convection currents** are set up, until a constant temperature is reached. Heat energy is actually transferred by the movement of the gas or liquid molecules.

Examples of convection in food preparation

Cooking methods Several cooking methods rely partly on convection for the transfer of heat.

Baking and roasting: movement of air molecules in the oven sets up convection currents.

Boiling, steaming: movement of liquid molecules sets up convection currents.

Foods Semi-liquid/solid mixtures, e.g. sauces, have slow convection currents because they are less fluid. If not stirred whilst heating, they burn at the base of the pan as the heat is not carried away fast enough.

Ovens In most gas and electric ovens, convection currents are set up from the heat source. This produces different zones of heat:

- middle shelf: corresponds to the thermostat setting
- top shelf: hotter than the middle shelf
- bottom shelf: cooler than the middle shelf

Advantage can be taken of this to cook items requiring slightly different cooking temperatures at the same time.

Some electric ovens are **'fan-assisted'**. This means that they have a fan at the back which circulates the hot air evenly. This reduces the effects of convection on the zones of heat.

Radiation

In conduction and convection, heat energy is transferred from one place to another through a **medium**, which may be a gas, liquid, or solid. In radiation, heat energy can pass from one point to another without the aid of a medium (molecules), and passes through space or a vacuum.

This is possible because of the existence of **electromagnetic waves**, of which there are several types, including:

x-rays
light waves
heat rays
microwaves

Heat rays are called **infra-red** rays, and when they come into contact with an object, some of them are **absorbed** and are felt as heat, while others are **reflected**. The space between the object and the source of the heat rays is not heated.

Dull, black surfaces absorb and emit heat rays well, whereas white, shiny surfaces reflect and do not emit them well.

Examples of radiation in food preparation

Grilling Grilling relies partly on radiation to heat the food. Gas grills have radiants made of fire clay. Electric grills have heater elements with radiants or metal reflectors.

Roasting Roasting food on a spit relies partly on radiation.

Infra-red grills Infra-red grills have electrically heated wire elements, enclosed in a silica tube for protection. Food is grilled efficiently and rapidly by this method.

Microwave ovens Food can be cooked by microwaves, which are a form of energy emitted by radiation (see pp. 163–6).

Prevention of radiation

Vacuum flask No heat is conducted across the vacuum and heat rays are reflected off the silvered interior into the liquid.

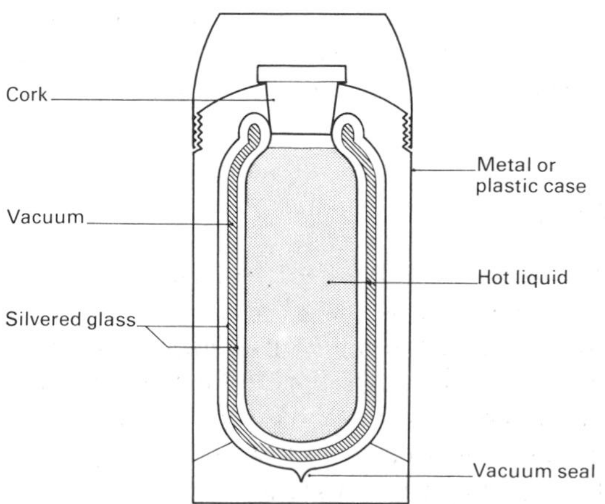

Summary of heat transference in the cooking of food

The different methods of cooking food each rely mainly on one method of heat transfer, although in some cases two or more transfers are involved:

Boiling an egg

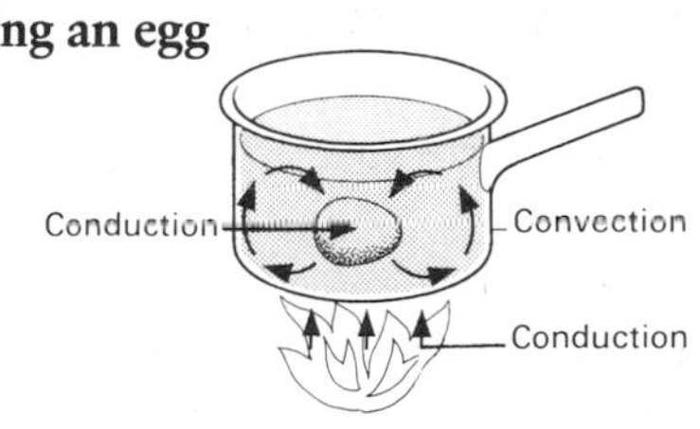

Grilling a chop (bone in)

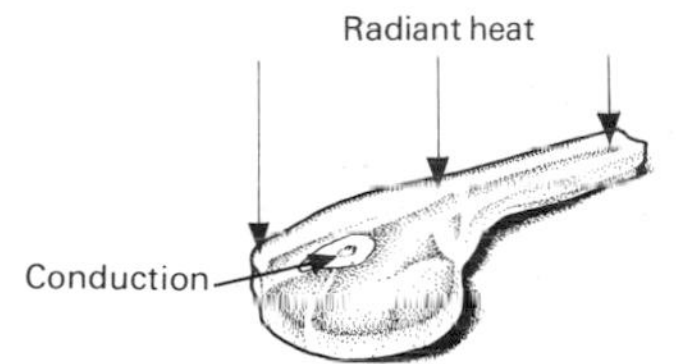

Roasting a rib of beef

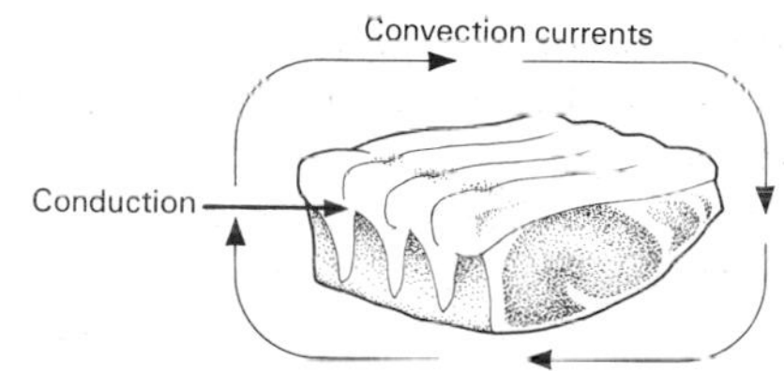

Baking a cake

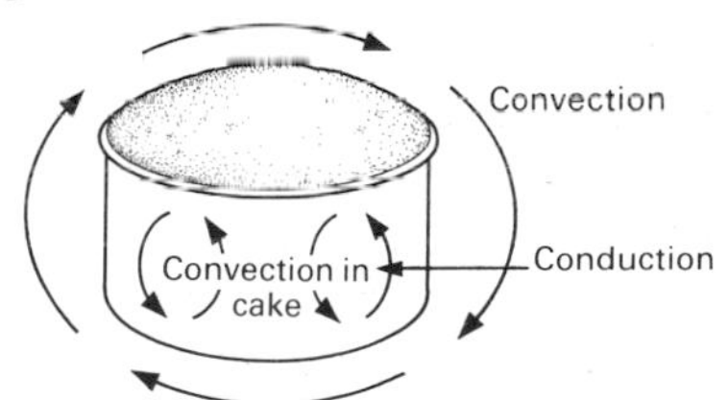

Steaming a pudding

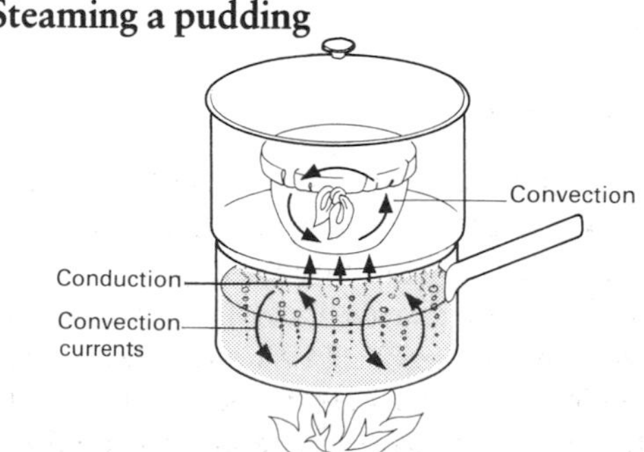

Deep-frying fish

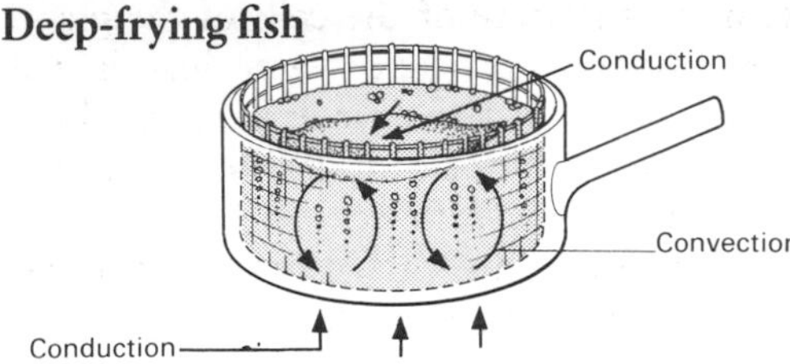

Heat transference in a cooker

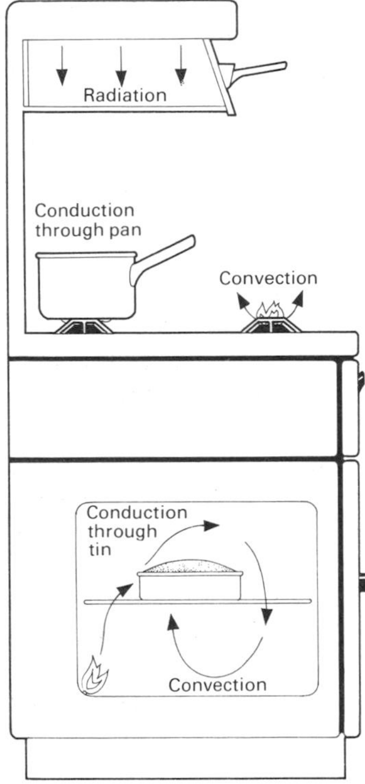

Reasons for cooking food

Many foods can be eaten raw, but the cooking of food is a highly developed art and science, with basic principles underlying the different methods. The main reasons why food is cooked are:

1 To destroy or inactivate pathogenic (harmful) micro-organisms present in the food (see pp. 131–6).
2 To preserve the food from natural and microbiological decay (see pp. 131–7).
3 To destroy natural toxins (poisons) in foods; e.g. red kidney beans must be boiled for at least fifteen minutes to destroy the natural toxin they contain.
4 To aid digestion, e.g. the coagulation of egg protein enables it to be broken down efficiently by gastric enzymes.
5 To make it easier to eat, e.g. cooking meat tenderizes it, thus making it easier to chew and swallow.
6 To make the food more appetizing and attractive, e.g. cooked fish or offal is more appetizing than raw.
7 To enhance the flavour of food, e.g. roasting meat develops extractives which add to the flavour.
8 To give variety in the diet, e.g. potatoes can be fried, boiled, creamed, roasted; chicken can be casseroled, fried, roasted, boiled.
9 To reduce bulk, e.g. green leafy vegetables reduce considerably when cooked so that more can be eaten.
10 To provide hot food in cold climates.
11 Necessary for some cooking processes, e.g. thickening of sauces, dissolving gelatine, preparation of cakes and biscuits.

Revision questions

1 What is heat and how is it produced?
2 How can heat be transferred from one place to another?
3 Name three good and three poor conductors of heat.
4 Name the ways in which conduction is used in the kitchen.
5 How are convection currents set up in liquids?
6 Why is the top of the oven hotter than the bottom, and how can this be used to advantage when baking?
7 Why are fan-assisted ovens different from conventional ovens?
8 How do heat waves heat up objects?
9 How is heat transferred in the following?
a boiling an egg
b baking a cake
c deep-frying fish
10 Give five reasons why food should be cooked.

Food spoilage

Once food has been harvested, gathered, or slaughtered, it starts to deteriorate until eventually it becomes unfit for consumption. This deterioration is known as **decay** and leads to food **spoilage.**

Food spoilage is caused by two main factors:

1 Natural decay within the food itself.
2 Contamination by microscopic forms of life (micro-organisms).

Foods which spoil rapidly are known as **perishable foods** and usually contain relatively large amounts of water and nutrients. Examples: milk, fruit, meat. Processed and cooked foods (e.g. frozen, canned, dried) are also easily susceptible, once thawed, opened, or reconstituted. Foods which contain relatively low amounts of water or high concentrations of salt, acid, or sugar, are less readily affected.

Natural decay

Natural decay in food is the result of:

moisture loss
the action of enzymes

Moisture loss

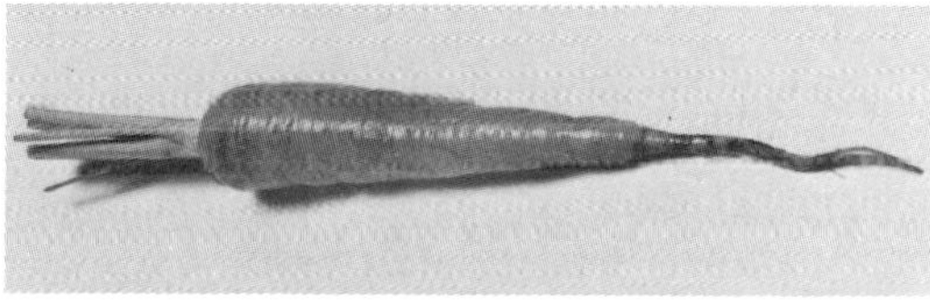

As the carrot dries, it becomes limp and wrinkled.

Moisture loss is most easily demonstrated in vegetables and fruit, which contain large amounts of water. After harvesting they continue to **respire**, i.e. their metabolic functions continue, and this results in loss of moisture through leaves and skins. Before harvesting, such water loss would be replaced from the soil through the roots, to retain the structure of the cells of the plant. After harvest, however, water loss is not replaced, and the vegetable or fruit shrinks in size, becomes limp, and its skin becomes wrinkled and 'leathery'.

Moisture loss also occurs in other foods, e.g. meat, fish, cheese, due to **evaporation** from the surface.

Action of enzymes (see pp. 41–2)

Many enzymes are present in foods, and some remain inactive until a food is harvested or slaughtered. Once activated, such enzymes speed up the process of decay by breaking down the tissues and components of the food in different ways, including:

1 **Oxidation** Oxidase enzymes cause the destruction of certain nutrients, e.g. vitamin C, thiamin, and carotene. (Oxidation also occurs without enzymes – see p. 71.)
2 **Browning** If a food, such as an apple, is cut or bruised, the damaged surface will discolour and turn brown due to the activity of enzymes.
3 **Ripening** Enzymes are involved in the process that causes ripening in certain foods such as fruits and vegetables; e.g. unripe bananas contain starch which is gradually converted to sugars, until the banana becomes very sweet, and its skin colour changes from green to yellow and eventually to dark brown.

Contamination by micro-organisms

Micro-organisms are microscopic plants or animals, many of which are single-celled. Microbiology is the study of such organisms.

The main micro-organisms responsible for the contamination of food are:

bacteria
moulds
yeasts

Each group has many members (species) which are responsible for different forms of contamination. All three groups require a medium in which to grow and reproduce, and food is an ideal medium as it provides nutrients and moisture. Micro-organisms contaminate food by producing waste products or toxins (poisons), or simply make the food inedible by their presence. In some cases, if contaminated food is eaten, it causes illness or **food poisoning**. Micro-organisms which cause food poisoning are called **pathogenic** (harmful) micro-organisms.

Not all micro-organisms are harmful however, and some are used in the food industry to produce foods such as cheese, yogurt, and soy sauce.

Food poisoning and its prevention are discussed on pp. 133–4.

Bacteria

Bacteria are microscopic forms of life – as many as one million individual bacteria can fit onto a pin head. They are single-celled organisms and are found in very many places, including:

- air
- water
- soil
- sewage
- food
- plants
- animals (including man)
- dust

There are many thousands of different species of bacteria, *some* of which are harmful to humans. They can be classified according to their shape:

Spherical bacteria
These are called **cocci**, and they form:

chains called **streptococci** which are the cause of diseases such as scarlet fever and tonsillitis;

pairs called **diplococci** which are the cause of pneumonia;

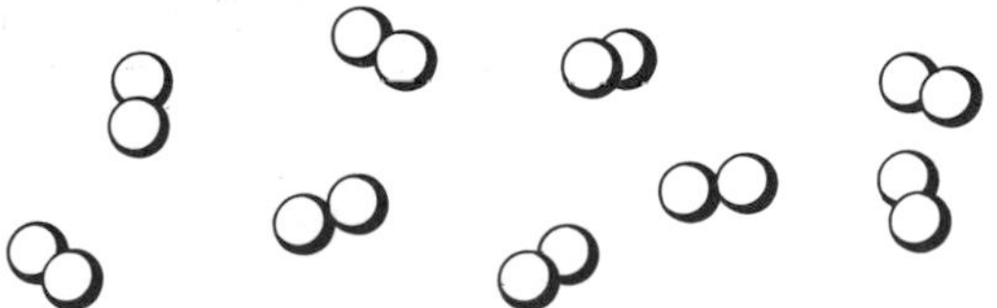

clusters called **staphylococci** which are the cause of boils, septic wounds, and food poisoning.

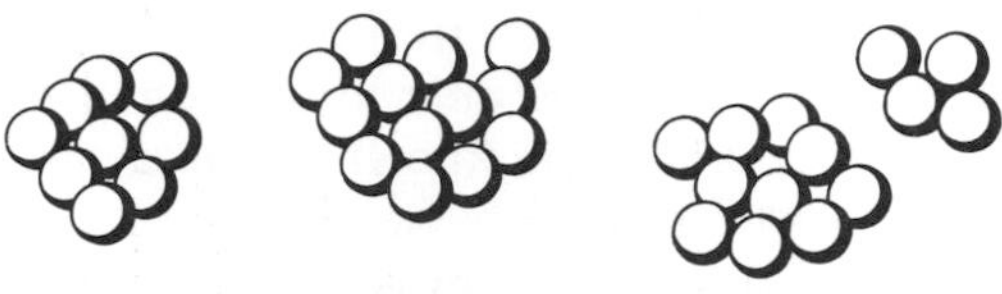

Rod-shaped bacteria
Some are called **bacilli** and are the cause of diseases such as diphtheria, tuberculosis, typhoid, and food poisoning.

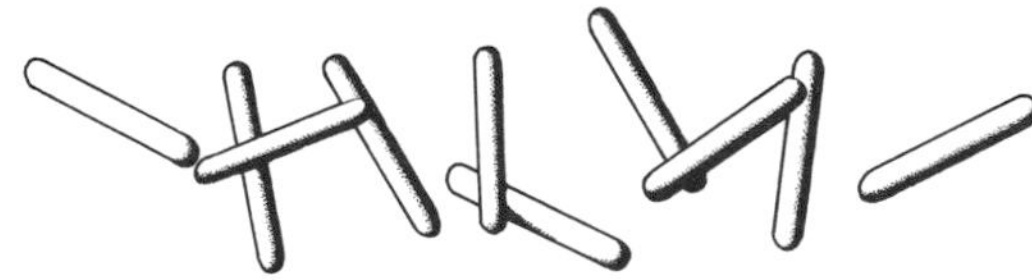

Some are called **clostridia** and cause food poisoning. Some have tiny hair-like projections called 'cilia' to enable them to swim through fluids.

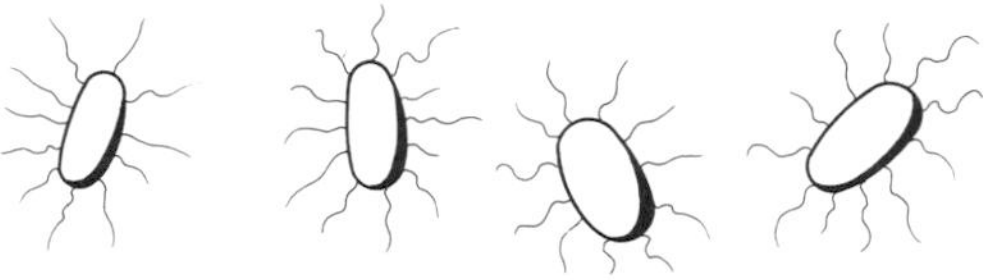

Spiral-shaped bacteria
These can cause diseases such as cholera, syphilis, and infectious jaundice.

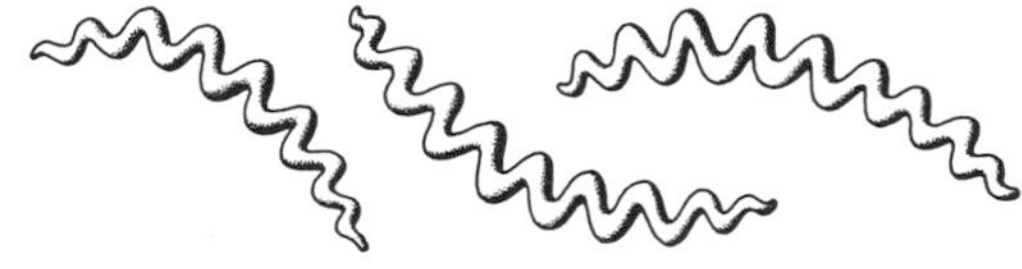

Reproduction of bacteria

Under suitable conditions of temperature, moisture, and food supply, bacteria can reproduce (multiply) very rapidly. They reproduce by dividing into two, and in the space of twelve hours, under the right conditions, a single bacteria cell can give rise to 16,000,000 others simply by dividing in this way:

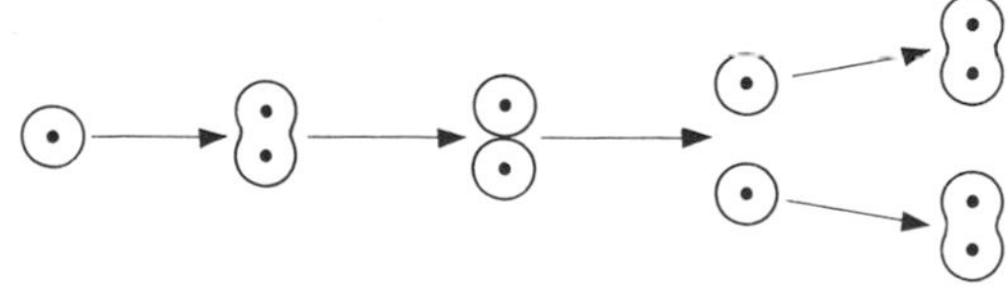

Bacteria type	Name	Illness		Symptoms	Causes	Notes
		Incubation	Duration			
cocci	Staphylococcus aureus	1–6 hrs	1–3 days	severe vomiting diarrhoea exhaustion	nose, skin, cuts, sores; cooked meat, pies, custards, ice cream	Poisoning due to toxins. Heat does not destroy toxin.
bacilli	Salmonella typhimurium	12–48 hrs	7 days	headache, fever vomiting abdominal pain	faeces; sliced cooked meat, poultry, pies, sausages, eggs	Main cause of poisoning in UK. Can be fatal.
clostridia	Clostridium botulinum	12–36 hrs	fatal within 7 days	double vision difficulty with breathing, talking, swallowing	improperly canned food, especially meat, vegetables	Rare, but fatal, in most cases. Exotoxin produced.
clostridia	Clostridium welchii	8–24 hrs	1–2 days	diarrhoea abdominal pain headache	meat, pies, gravy, canned meat; soil	Poisoning due to toxin and bacteria in gut.
bacilli	Salmonella typhi	1–3 weeks	1–2 months	headache tiredness fever, rash haemorrhage	sewage, water, flies; cream cake, watercress, canned meat	Can be fatal. Slow recovery.
bacilli	Bacillus cereus	2–18 hrs	1–3 days	vomiting diarrhoea abdominal pain	faeces; cold meats, gravy, cream, sausages	Poisoning caused by bacteria in body.

When a large number of bacteria are present in one place, they form a **colony**, which is usually visible to the naked eye.

If conditions for division are unfavourable, e.g. if moisture is lacking, then bacteria are able to form **spores** which remain dormant until the right conditions return, when the spore will germinate. Such spores are often very resistant to heat.

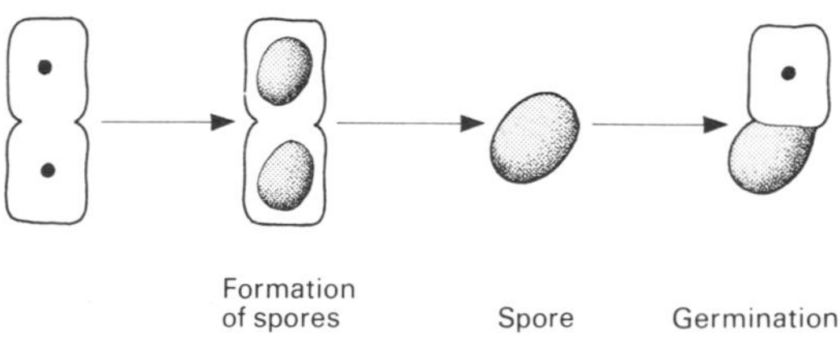

Many bacteria do not require a source of oxygen to grow and multiply. Such bacteria are called **anaerobic bacteria**, and this accounts for their ability to grow in food and intestines, where oxygen supplies are limited. Some bacteria do require oxygen and are called **aerobic bacteria.**

The effect of heat on bacteria

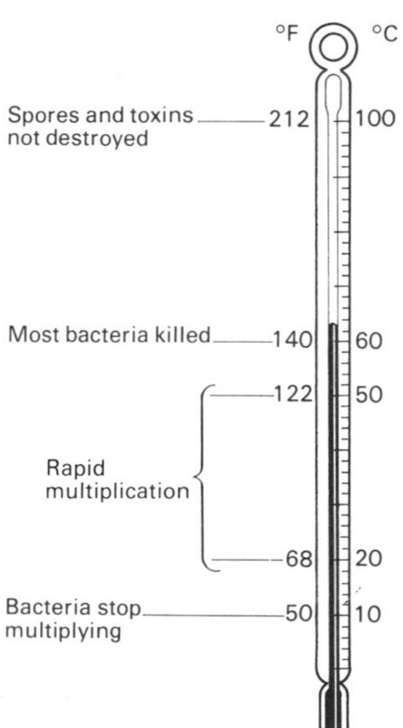

Some bacteria can withstand extremes of temperature, but most are destroyed at temperatures of around 60°C (140°F). Bacteria are able to multiply most rapidly at around 37°C (98·4°F), and this has important implications for the preservation of food by heat (pp. 141–2). At very cold temperatures, most bacteria stop multiplying and become dormant until the temperature conditions become favourable again. This has important implications for the freezing and cold storage of foods and their use (pp. 144–5).

Other effects on the growth of bacteria

Many bacteria are affected by high concentrations of salt, acid, or sugar. These interfere with the normal life processes of the bacteria cells, and either destroy them or prevent reproduction. Such substances are used for food preservation (p. 148). There are, however, some bacteria which thrive in such conditions and may therefore require different treatment to prevent their growth.

Contamination of food by bacteria

As bacteria are so small, it is often difficult to detect their presence in food visually. Also, the flavour, physical appearance, and smell of the food may remain unchanged, so that it is easy to consume contaminated food without realizing it.

However, many species of bacteria cause food poisoning, often with serious outcomes, so it is important to be aware of the causes and prevention of such a situation.

Bacteria can cause food poisoning symptoms in different ways:

1 **Physical presence of bacteria**
If bacteria have had the opportunity to multiply in large numbers in a food, then their physical presence in the intestine may cause irritation and food poisoning symptoms.

2 **Production of waste products (toxins)**
Bacteria, like all living things, have to dispose of waste products which are the result of metabolic processes. These can cause irritation to the intestine and food poisoning symptoms even when only a small number of bacteria are present. The toxins are not destroyed by normal cooking temperatures.

3 **Germination of spores**
The germination of bacterial spores is usually accompanied by the production of highly poisonous substances (exotoxins), only a small amount of which can lead to severe illness or possibly death. In some cases, just one spore can produce sufficient toxin to cause food poisoning.

Food poisoning

Bacteria can be transferred to food by several means, including:

1 Using the same utensils to serve contaminated food and other foods.
2 Careless attention to personal hygiene while handling food, e.g. not washing hands after visiting the toilet, touching nose while preparing food.
3 Leaving skin infections and cuts uncovered while preparing food.
4 Coughing, sneezing, or spitting while preparing food.
5 Incomplete cleansing of food utensils and serving dishes.
6 Pests, e.g. houseflies, cockroaches, beetles, certain moths.
7 Rodents, e.g. rats, mice.
8 Household pets, e.g. dogs, cats, hamsters.
9 Infected or diseased cattle and dairy cows.
10 Contaminated water supply.
11 Soil and dust.

Once bacteria have been transferred to a food, they will grow and multiply under the following conditions:

1 Incomplete thawing and cooking of certain foods, e.g. poultry, pork.
2 Holding cooked foods, e.g. chicken, shellfish, at room temperature before serving.
3 Incomplete or repeated cooking of left-over food (see p. 177).
4 Careless storage of food.

In the UK, food poisoning is a **notifiable disease**, i.e. all cases should be reported by a general practitioner to the Local Health Authority, so that they can inspect food-serving premises and shops to ascertain the cause of the illness and prevent its recurrence.

Quite often, however, the symptoms of food poisoning are relatively mild and may not require medical attention. Such cases are therefore not reported, so it is difficult to ascertain the exact number of cases per year. From the number of cases which are reported, however, it is clear that food poisoning is quite a widespread problem.

Reasons for the increase in the number of cases of food poisoning

1 A greater number of ready-prepared foods are eaten, e.g. meat pies, pasties, partly-cooked breads.
2 More people eat out at restaurants, take-away shops, and hotels. Large-scale catering may result in outbreaks of food poisoning for several of the reasons previously stated.
3 Increases in the import of food, from countries where food hygiene laws may not be strictly enforced.
4 Increases in the import of animal feeds, which may be contaminated and will infect the animal to which they are given.
5 Insufficient training of staff who handle food.

The chart on p. 130 shows the main causes of bacterial food poisoning, and the symptoms.

Moulds

Moulds are tiny plants, which are just visible to the naked eye. They grow on many types of food, especially cheese, bread, and fruit. They require warm moist conditions to grow, but are able to grow at a slower rate in cool places.

Moulds reproduce by means of sporulation. **Spores** are released into the atmosphere and carried in the air. If they land on a suitable food, the spores germinate, and a new mould appears.

Moulds can grow on cheese . . . on fruit . . . and on bread.

There are many types of mould, but among the more common types are:

Pin mould (mucor)

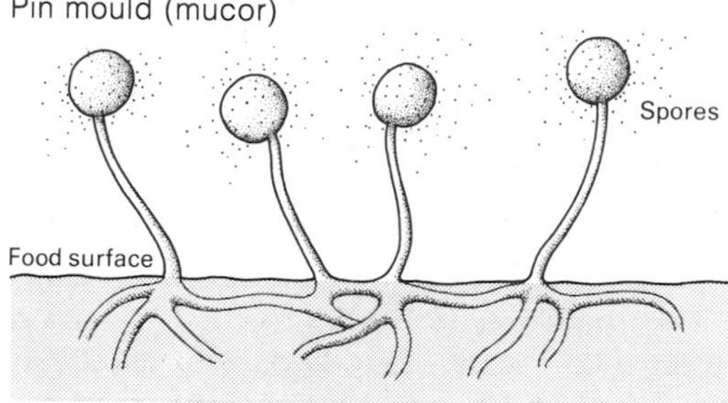

Penicillium

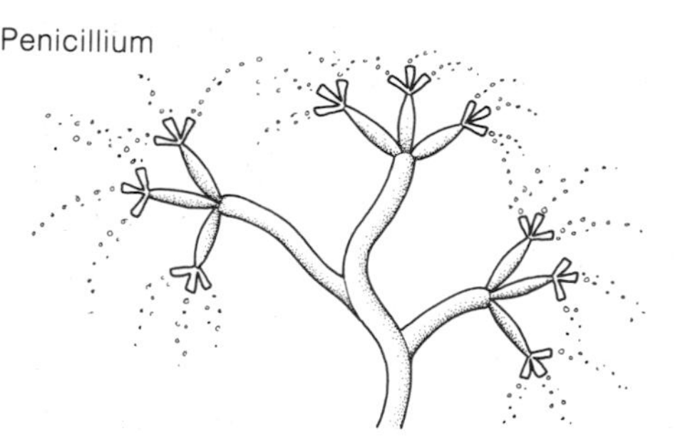

Food that is contaminated with mould often appears to be safe to eat as only the outer part is affected by mould growth. However, recent research has shown that substances produced by the mould which migrate into the food could be harmful to many organs of the body. These substances are called mycotoxins. It is therefore advisable to discard mouldy food completely, rather than just to remove the mouldy part.

Mould growth is prevented by:

- cool, dry storage
- heating to destroy moulds and spores
- acidic conditions

Mould in cheese

Not all moulds are harmful. Specially-produced moulds are added to certain cheeses, e.g. Stilton, Danish Blue, to develop characteristic flavours.

Yeasts

Yeasts are microscopic single-celled plants, which are found in the air and soil, and on the surface of fruits. Some are able to tolerate fairly high acidic, salt and sugar concentrations, and can grow without the presence of oxygen.

Yeast cells reproduce by budding:

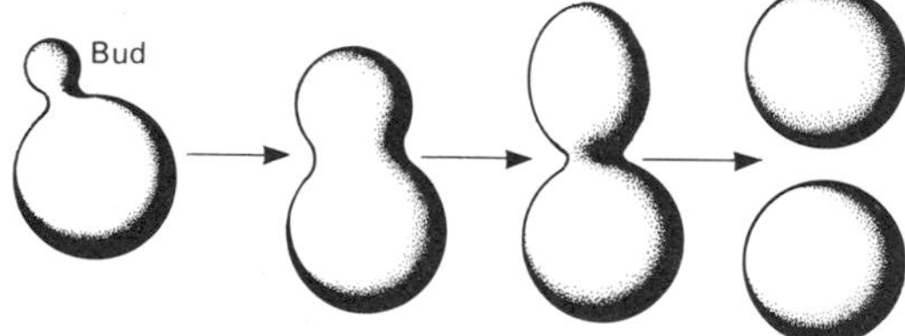

Yeast cell

In order to do this, they must have a supply of water, warmth, and food (see pp. 179–80). The cells remain dormant in very cold conditions, and are killed at temperatures approaching 100°C. Growth is inhibited in the presence of high salt concentrations.

Yeasts can spoil foods such as jam and fruits by fermenting the sugars, to produce alcohol and carbon dioxide gas. The time that this takes will depend on the concentration of sugar in the food and the length of time it is stored. Fruit-flavoured yogurts may also be affected in this way.

Food contamination from other sources

Food can become contaminated by other agents besides micro-organisms, e.g.

chemicals
radiation
pollution

Chemicals

Modern food production often involves the use of chemicals for a variety of purposes, with the aim of obtaining good supplies of high quality food. Such chemicals are used for the following reasons:

1 **Insecticides, pesticides, fungicides,** and **weedkillers** are used to help prevent crops from being attacked by various organisms and plants. They are often applied to the plants well before harvesting and consumption or to a part of the plant that has not yet matured, to prevent harm to the consumer, as many of these chemicals are toxic. However, traces of such substances are left on food and in the soil, and are even found in the air and water supply. This has given rise to concern as it is not entirely clear what becomes of such substances once they are in the body. However, much research has been carried out, and control over the use of such chemicals is enforced to reduce the risk of harm.

2 **Antibiotics** are used for treating cattle, pigs, sheep, and cows, to prevent them from contracting diseases which would affect their health and production capabilities. Careful control over the use of such antibiotics has to be enforced as they may make bacteria become immune to their effect and therefore more likely to affect the animals. Antibiotic traces in food may also cause allergies in some people.

Radiation

The use of nuclear bombs in recent years has led to the release into the atmosphere of radioactive materials, which gradually fall back to earth, and pollute food and water supplies.

This is one of the main reasons for efforts to limit the use of such weapons in tests by different countries.

Pollution

Food may become polluted with chemicals and metals from industrial waste, which is often poured into rivers and the sea, and is ingested by fish and other animals who drink the water. Attempts have been made over the last few years to prevent such pollution, and the situation has improved to some extent. However, there are many areas of the world (including the UK) where the situation still gives rise to concern.

Experiments on food spoilage

NB It is important to observe the rules of hygiene when dealing with bacteria and moulds. The hands should be washed with disinfectant after handling experimental equipment and foods, and the experiments must be carried out in a part of the room where food is not normally prepared, or preferably in a laboratory.

1 Prepare several sterile agar plates with agar-agar broth (as directed by the manufacturer), and leave to set. Wipe swabs of sterile cotton wool over various surfaces and quickly smear over the agar jelly without opening the lid of the plate for too long.

Alternatively, contaminate the plates with some of the following:

cough or sneeze
hands
dirty dishcloth
rubbish bin
sink plug
floor or bottom of a shoe
dust
soil
the air
top of a milk bottle
a house fly

Cover the plates and label. Leave in a warm place for two days. Observe the results, and compare with an unused agar plant. *Destroy plates after use.*

2 Leave a piece of bread in the following conditions:
   a a warm, moist, bread bin
   b a refrigerator
   c a dry warm place.
   Observe and compare the growth of moulds on the bread.
3 Leave some carrots or other root vegetable in a sealed plastic bag at room temperature for four days, and observe the evaporation of water from the vegetable on to the plastic. Note the changes in the vegetable texture and appearance.

Hygienic practices in the handling and preparation of food

The hygienic handling and preparation of food are of great importance in the prevention of food contamination and food poisoning. In large catering establishments and retailing premises, Food Hygiene Regulations have to be obeyed and these are enforced by public health inspectors from the Local Health Authority. These regulations cover all aspects of food handling, including:

manufacture and packaging of food
transport and storage of food
activities and health of food handlers
food preparation premises
sanitary facilities
waste disposal
food preparation practices
food retail premises

If a consumer feels that a particular shop, restaurant, or other food retail outlet is not complying with the regulations, they have the right to report this to the public health inspector, who will investigate and act accordingly. Failure to comply with these regulations can lead to prosecution and closure of premises.

In the home, it is the duty of the person handling the food to ensure that food is prepared as hygienically as possible. This can be achieved by following a few basic rules:

Personal hygiene

1 Before preparing food, tie hair back, wash hands, and scrub nails clean.
2 Always wash the hands after visiting the toilet.
3 Never cough, sneeze, spit, or smoke over the food.
4 Cover up skin infections, cuts, and grazes.
5 Wear a clean apron.
6 Do not lick fingers or spoons and then touch the food with them.

Food purchase

1 Buy food from clean, reputable shops, where the assistants handle the food hygienically, and the food is stored properly.
2 Check that there are no animals in food shops.
3 Check the date stamps on fresh foods.
4 Choose fresh foods wisely (see individual foods for factors affecting choice).
5 Be wary of fresh foods sold on market stalls – they should be covered to protect them from dust and flies.

Food shops must have high standards of hygiene.

Food storage at home

1 Store fresh foods in a cool place. Use them up fairly rapidly, and certainly within the time recommended on the label or pack.
2 Use up old stocks of dried and canned foods before new ones.
3 Cool left-over foods rapidly and eat within twenty-four hours (see p. 177).
4 Keep food protected from flies, pests, and rodents, by the use of muslin cloth, plastic film, or a food net.

Kitchen hygiene

1 Regularly wash and clean work surfaces, the cooker, and the floor.
2 Keep utensils clean and well stored when not in use.
3 Wipe up spills as they occur.
4 Do not allow pets to sit on work surfaces or to eat from utensils and dishes that will be used for humans; some animals carry viruses and bacteria which can be passed on to humans, especially young children whose resistance is not well developed.
5 Rinse out the dishcloth after use and leave to air so that it does not become stagnant. Immerse in diluted bleach or disinfectant regularly.
6 Do not use the dishcloth to wash the floor. Wipe out rubbish bins, and wash pet food dishes with separate cloths kept only for these purposes.
7 Use very hot water and a good detergent for washing dishes, so that all food sediments are removed. Nylon brushes are useful for washing intricate pieces of equipment, e.g. cheese graters, bottle necks.
8 Sterilize infant feeding bottles carefully.
9 Make sure that frozen poultry, pork, cream, and fish are completely thawed before cooking, and then thoroughly cooked to destroy salmonella bacteria which may be present. Incomplete thawing and cooking will provide a suitable temperature for the growth and multiplication of such bacteria, and lead to food poisoning.

Waste disposal

1 Keep dustbins well away from the kitchen, in a cool, shaded position. Protect from flies, cats, and vermin by ensuring that food wastes are wrapped and the lid fits tightly.
2 Disinfect the dustbin regularly, especially in summer. Use a bin liner if possible.
3 Empty kitchen pedal bins every day, and wash out.
4 Keep nappy pails out of the kitchen; leave them in the bathroom.
5 Do not allow the sink waste pipe to become clogged. Disinfect the sink regularly, to kill germs and prevent stagnation.

Revision questions

1 How does food spoilage occur?
2 What are enzymes, and how do they cause food spoilage?
3 How can enzymes be made inactive?
4 How do micro-organisms cause food spoilage?
5 What are pathogenic micro-organisms?
6 Where are bacteria found?
7 How do bacteria multiply, and what conditions do they require for this to take place?
8 How can bacteria be prevented from multiplying in food?
9 How do bacteria cause food poisoning?
10 How are bacteria transferred to food?
11 How do moulds reproduce, and what conditions do they require for growth?
12 What are mycotoxins?
13 In what other ways can food become contaminated?
14 How do Food Hygiene Regulations protect the consumer?
15 How can the housewife ensure that the kitchen and the food that is served are hygienic?

Preservation of food

Food is preserved to prevent natural and microbial decay, by the modification of the conditions which favour enzyme activity and the growth of micro-organisms.

In the past, food was preserved to provide a store of food during winter, when there was no other source of food supply. Today food is preserved for the following reasons:

1 To add variety to the diet, in that foods can be eaten out of season.
2 To make use of food when it is cheap and plentiful and to store it for later use.
3 To vary the diet by preserving food in different ways, e.g. pickling, jam making, whereby a new product is made out of the food.

The aims of preservation

While preventing decay, preservation also aims to retain as many of the qualities of the fresh food as possible, e.g.:

flavour
texture
colour
appearance
nutritional value

Preservation also aims to prevent micro-organisms from contaminating the food once it is preserved, by sealing it from the outside air.

Methods of preservation

Food decay can be prevented by:

1 **Heating** to destroy micro-organisms and enzyme activity.
2 **Removal of moisture** to inhibit microbial growth.
3 **Removal of air** to prevent further entry of micro-organisms.
4 **Reduction of temperature** to inhibit microbial and enzymic activity.
5 **Addition of a chemical preservative** to destroy or inhibit microbial and enzymic activity.

Heat preservation

Most bacteria, yeasts, moulds, and enzymes are destroyed by heating at 100°C (212°F). However, some bacteria and bacterial spores are resistant to such temperatures and higher temperatures are required to destroy them.

Some bacterial toxins are resistant to heat, so that a food which is already contaminated with them may not be made safe to eat by heat treatment.

The main methods of heat treatment are:

sterilization
pasteurization
canning and bottling

Sterilization

At the beginning of the 19th century, a Frenchman, Nicolas Appert, discovered that if food was heated in a sealed container for a period of time at a high temperature, it would remain edible and free from decay for some time, unless the seal was broken. This is because prolonged heating will destroy harmful micro-organisms which are naturally present in the food, and the food will only start to decay when new organisms contaminate it.

Today, sterilization is a commonly used form of heat preservation. Since Appert's early attempts, the process has been greatly improved, so that the flavour and colour of sterilized foods are not so greatly impaired as they used to be. In particular, the ultra heat treatment of milk (see pp. 80–1), which is now in common use, has been one of the major improvements developed from the sterilization process.

Uses of heat sterilization

Milk (see p. 80)
Canned or bottled foods

Effects on nutritive value

Heat-sensitive vitamins thiamin and vitamin C (ascorbic acid) are destroyed to a large extent.

The flavour and colour of milk may be altered considerably (see p. 80).

Pasteurization

Another French scientist, Louis Pasteur, later discovered that less severe heat treatment than that used in sterilization could be effective in destroying pathogenic and souring microbes, without adversely affecting the appearance or flavour of a product.

This process, known as pasteurization, has been successfully developed, and many items are now treated in this way. However, as pasteurization only destroys the harmful microbes, the food will not keep for very long, as other naturally-occurring microbes in the food will begin to cause decay.

Uses of pasteurization
Milk (see p. 80)
Milk products
Fruit juices
Liquid egg for bakery products
Vegetable juices
Beer
Vinegar
Wine

Canning and bottling

Today, canning is one of the most widely used methods of preservation. A huge variety of foods are canned and bottled, providing a safe and convenient method of preserving food.

Both methods rely on heat sterilization to destroy microbes and enzymes and sealing to prevent contamination during storage.

Cans

Modern day cans are made from **steel**, which is coated in a very thin layer of **tin**, and often lacquered to prevent corrosion.

Cans are manufactured in the following way:

1 Strips of the tin-coated steel are cut, and bent to form the body of the tin:

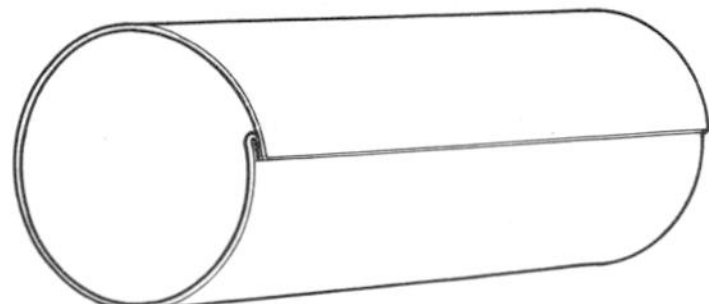

2 An air-tight seam is made which is then soldered:

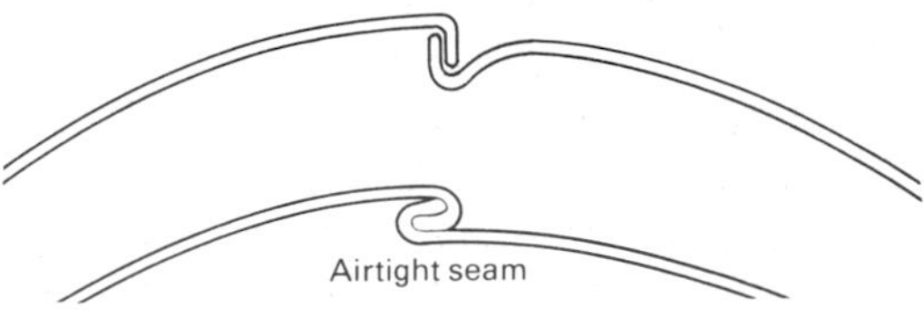

3 The ends of the can are stamped into ridges for strength, and are lined with a rubber solution where they fit over the lip of the can:

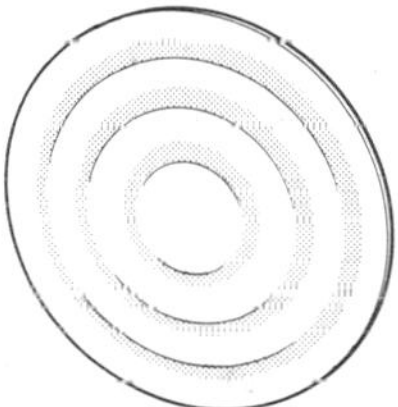

4 One end is then fitted on and sealed and the can is checked for any leaks.
5 The can is then filled with food, any air is removed, and the can is sealed while in a vacuum.
6 The cans are then sterilized in a large **retort**, under pressure, for a carefully calculated period of time. They are then removed and cooled. Most cans are cooled by water.
7 The cans are then labelled and packed.

Cans about to be filled with Heinz baked beans.

Many sizes and shapes of can are produced and some cans are given aluminium ends for easy opening. Aluminium cans are expensive to produce, but they are used for some canned drinks. Some have a ring-pull for easy opening without a can opener.

Uses of canning

Food	Length of time food will keep under normal conditions*
fruit	12 months
milk	12 months
vegetables	2 years
fish (in tomato sauce)	12 months
fish in oil	5 years
meat	up to 5 years

*The food may keep for longer, but should be consumed within this time.

Other foods and products which are canned:
- coffee
- nuts
- sausages
- complete meals (stews, curries, etc.)
- meat pies and puddings
- sponge puddings
- pasta and pulses in sauce
- alcoholic and non-alcoholic beverages
- pâtés
- desserts
- soups
- pet-foods

Using canned foods

Store in a cool, dry place, and rotate the stock so that old cans are used first. Do not buy rusty or 'blown' cans. Rust can weaken the metal and may create a small hole where bacteria can enter and contaminate the food. Blown cans indicate that bacteria are present, as they produce gas which distends the can. Dented tins should also be avoided as these may have tiny punctures in the metal, or damaged seams.

Once opened, canned food should be treated as fresh food and it will deteriorate. Left-overs should be removed from the can and put in a covered container in a cool place.

Bottling

The principles and methods of preservation for bottling food are similar to those used in canning. The glass used must be free from minute cracks which could allow bacteria to enter, and should be heat-proof and strong enough to cope with transport and retail handling.

Glass is heavy and is of course prone to breakage, so bottling is not used as much as canning.

Removal of moisture (dehydration)

Dehydration is a very old method of food preservation and there is evidence that it was used as long ago as 2000 BC.

Micro-organisms are dependent on water for growth and reproduction, and removal of it from their cells relies on the process of **osmosis.** Osmosis is the movement of water from a weak solution to a stronger one, through a **semi-permeable membrane.** When water is removed from food by evaporation, the concentration of sugars and salts in the food becomes stronger. If there are any micro-organisms present in the food, water will pass from their cells (a weak solution) into the stronger solution surrounding them, and this dehydration will destroy them.

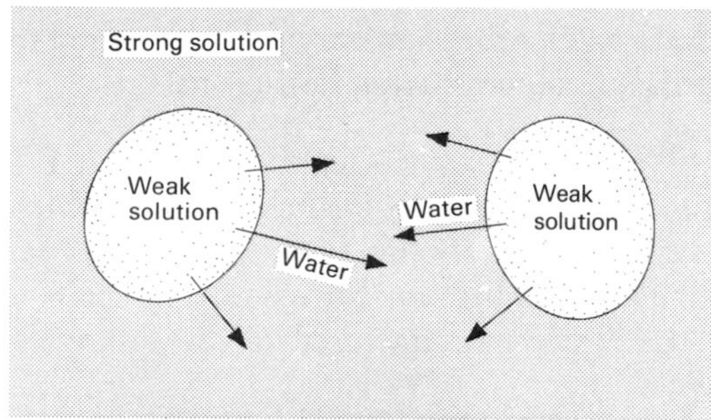

Experiments with osmosis are given on pp. 143–4.

Evaporation of water used to be achieved by leaving food to dry in the heat from the sun, but today it is carried out by passing carefully controlled warm air over food. The food is either placed in trays on rotating drums, or is sprayed through warm air in a tunnel.

Dehydrating solid foods

Food is usually placed on large perforated trays, through which hot air is blown. This is called a **hot air bed**, and is carefully controlled. The product at the end will keep for up to a year quite satisfactorily.

Dehydrating liquid foods

Liquids are usually dried by **spray drying** or **roller drying.**

Spray drying is used for products such as milk and occasionally eggs. A fine spray of liquid is passed into a hot air chamber or tunnel, and the droplets dry almost instantly and drop to the bottom of the chamber. The moisture is removed before it settles. The temperature of the hot air is carefully controlled to prevent coagulation of the protein and alteration of flavour.

Roller drying is used less often as it is a more severe form of treatment and the dried product does not reconstitute so well.

A fairly recent development of dehydration is the use of **accelerated freeze drying.** The food is quick frozen and tiny ice crystals are formed, which are rapidly removed by turning to vapour when the food is heated in a vacuum. There is less damage to the food structure and the water content is extremely low in foods dried by this method. Reconstitution is usually very good. This method is used for coffee, mashed potato, etc.

Uses of dehydration

milk
coffee, tea
fish, meat
vegetables
pulses (peas, beans, lentils)
eggs
soups, instant snacks and meals
herbs

Using dried foods

Dried foods should be stored in a cool, **dry** place. Moisture in the atmosphere may be readily absorbed by some dried foods, e.g. coffee, milk, potato, and this will affect the keeping qualities.

Some dried foods must be packed in foil-lined containers to prevent rancidity (see p. 71) and oxidation from occurring.

Dried foods are very convenient as they are lightweight, take up little storage space, and can be stored for long periods as emergency foods.

Effect on nutritive value and flavour

The heat-sensitive vitamins, thiamin and ascorbic acid, are the most significantly affected, and may be further destroyed when the food is reconstituted and cooked. Freeze-dried foods usually retain slightly more vitamin C than conventionally dried foods.

Flavour and texture changes may be noticeable in many dried foods, and the use of additional flavourings may help to improve this.

Many different kinds of food can be dried.

Experiments to demonstrate the action of osmosis

1 Place a piece of dried fruit (e.g. a prune, apricot, or raisin) in a bowl of water, and another in a bowl of sugar and water, and leave overnight.

It will be observed that the fruit in the plain water will have swollen, and that the other is still shrunken. This is because water has been absorbed in the first fruit due to osmosis, whereas in the second fruit there has been little movement of water as the concentration inside the fruit is similar to the sugar and water solution.

2 Cut radishes into thin slices almost all the way through and place in water (see p. 182). Cut celery into thin strips and repeat.

The cut parts will curl as the cells absorb water by osmosis.

3 Cut some potatoes into chips and soak them in salt and water before frying them.

Some water will leave the potato cells by osmosis, and this will help the chips to remain crisp when they are fried.

4 Sprinkle some fresh strawberries with sugar two to three hours before serving and compare with some others prepared in the same way just before serving.

The first strawberries will become soft. This is because if prepared too far in advance, water leaves the strawberries by osmosis, forming a syrup with the sugar and leaving the fruit without a firm structure.

Removal of air

The removal of air from canned foods has already been discussed. Some foods can be temporarily preserved by **vacuum packaging.** Cold meats, cheese, sausages, fish, etc., can be wrapped in an impermeable plastic film, and the air can be removed under a vacuum. This prevents the entry of micro-organisms until the seal is broken. Such foods are normally stored in a cool place and may have chemical preservatives added to them so that they keep for longer.

Reduction of temperature

When the temperature is reduced, the activities of most micro-organisms are slowed down, until they become **dormant** (inactive), and growth and multiplication cease. Some less resistant types are destroyed at low temperatures.

Once the temperature is raised, growth and multiplication start again, as many of the micro-organisms are not destroyed by cold temperatures.

Some micro-organisms are resistant to cold temperatures, and can continue to multiply and remain active, although probably at a slower rate.

Refrigeration

As long ago as the mid-19th century, attempts were made to chill meat and other foods by packing them with ice, but this did not prove to be very successful. Domestic refrigerators were not available on a large scale in this country until the 1920s, but today most homes have one. More details on refrigerators and how they work are given in Chapter 5, pp. 259–61.

It is only possible to store foods for short periods in domestic refrigerators, which are normally set at 5°C (41°F). This is because at this temperature, microbial activity still takes place, although it is slowed down. Thus food decay will still occur.

However, refrigerators are useful as they enable a few days' supply of fresh foods to be stored, thereby reducing the need to shop every day.

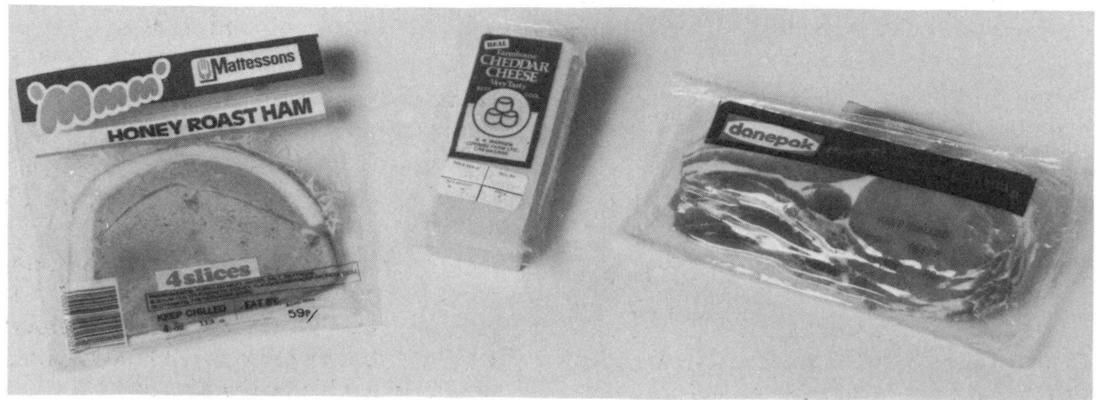

Cheese and cold meats are often vacuum-packed.

The temperatures used in refrigerators are:

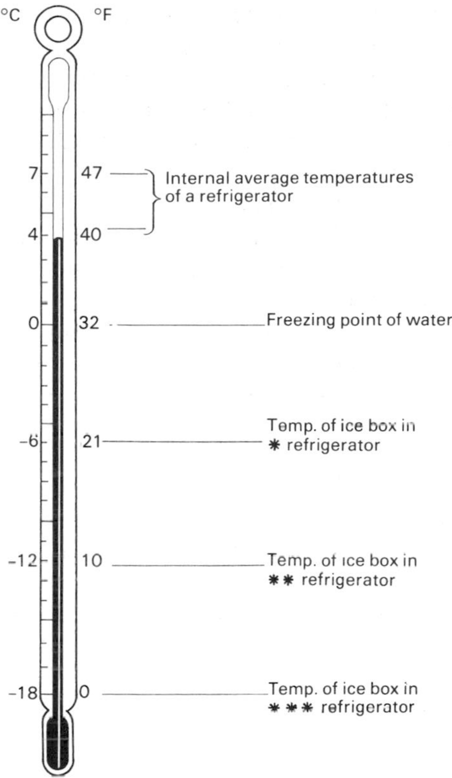

Foods to be kept in a refrigerator should be suitably wrapped before storage (see p. 261), and used up fairly quickly.

Foods which are purchased ready frozen can be stored in the freezer compartment of the refrigerator.

Follow the manufacturer's instructions as to the length of storage time. This is guided by a British Standards Institution Recommendation, made in 1964. According to this recommendation, the following star ratings on a refrigerator indicate the temperature of the freezer compartment and the length of time for which frozen foods can be stored.

Star rating	Temperature	Storage time
*	−6°C (21°F)	up to 1 week
**	−12°C (10°F)	up to 1 month
***	−18°C (0°F)	up to 3 months

Commercially frozen foods normally give this rating on the packet as a guide.

It is *not* possible or safe to attempt to deep-freeze food in a domestic refrigerator, as the temperatures are not low enough.

Many foods that are sold in the shops are held in refrigerated storage during transit or at a warehouse. This is done to preserve the quality of the food before it reaches the consumer. Some foods are stored at cold temperatures in an atmosphere of carbon dioxide. Many micro-organisms produce carbon dioxide as a waste product from their metabolic processes, and the use of this gas retards their growth by reducing the oxygen that they require. Foods which are stored in this way include:

Eggs
If eggs are stored in normal air, carbon dioxide and water vapour are lost through the pores in the shell. This results in the white becoming thinner and deteriorating. In an atmosphere of carbon dioxide gas, this is prevented from happening, and eggs can be stored in a cold atmosphere containing 60% carbon dioxide for up to nine months.

Meat
Beef can be kept in a cold place in an atmosphere of 10–15% carbon dioxide for up to ten weeks.

Some fruits and vegetables
Carbon dioxide is produced by fruits and vegetables during ripening (see p. 131), which occurs after they are harvested. This can be delayed if they are stored in carbon dioxide gas at a temperature of between 0°C (32°F) and 3°C (37°F). This applies to, for example, apples and pears, and root vegetables such as carrots and turnips.

Freezing

The basic principles of refrigeration also apply to freezing, but as the temperatures are much lower in freezing, food can be stored for much longer periods of time.

Deep freezing is the reduction of temperature in a food to a point where not only does microbial activity cease, but the natural decay and deterioration of the food is halted for a considerable length of time.

The temperatures used in freezing are:

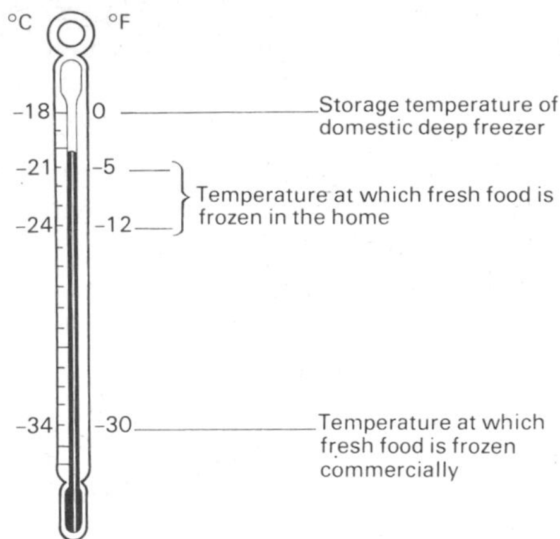

Many foods can be frozen successfully (see pp. 173–6 for more details), and freezer ownership has increased considerably in the last few years in most affluent countries. The advantages of this method of preservation, the types of appliance available, and the methods and rules for freezing foods are discussed on pp. 174–5.

Principles involved in freezing

Most foods contain relatively large amounts of water. When a food is frozen, **ice crystals** are formed in it.

Foods such as fruit and vegetables, which are made up of many cells, can be damaged by the ice crystals, if they are too large. This is because the cells **rupture** if the ice crystal exceeds the size of the cell:

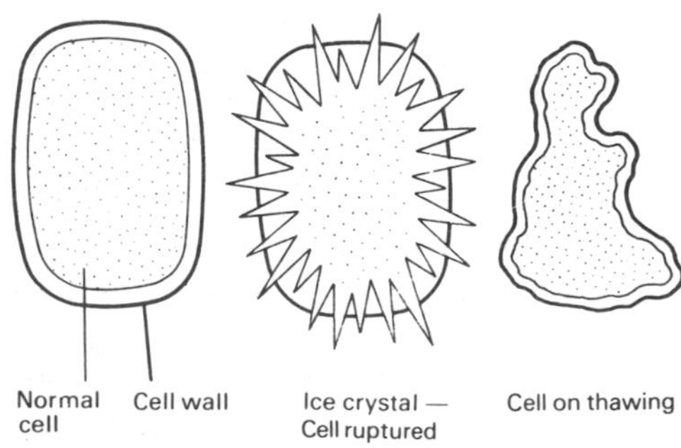

Once the food is thawed, its structure will collapse, releasing most of the liquid of which it is composed, because the cells no longer form the framework of the food.

Large ice crystals are formed in food if it is frozen too slowly. If food is **quick-frozen,** however, the ice crystals are formed rapidly, and are much smaller in size. They remain **within** the cells without rupturing them:

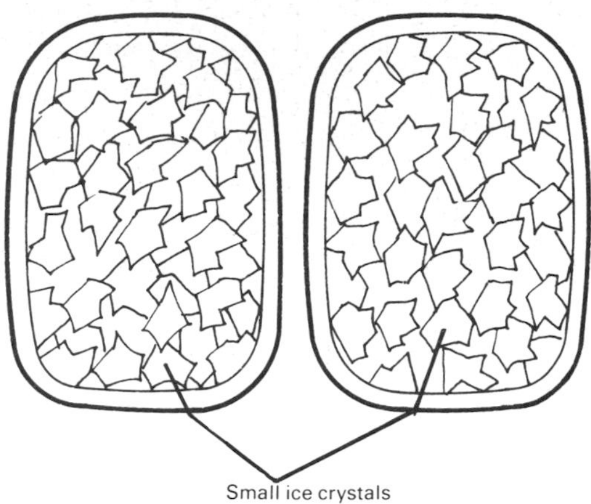

Quick-freezing is defined as the drop in temperature from 0°C (32°F) to −4°C (25°F) in thirty minutes in the **centre** of a pack of food.

Using a home freezer

Most home freezers have a special section where food to be frozen should be placed, to ensure a rapid reduction in temperature, and less risk of structural damage by ice crystals. A switch for **fast-freezing** is used to lower the temperature. This should be operated two to three hours before the food is put in. During this time the temperature will fall to −24°C (−12°F). The recommended amount of food to be frozen at one time will vary according to the freezer, and the manufacturer's instructions for this should be followed. The food should be put separately into the fast-freeze section, and the switch should be left on for twenty-four hours. The close contact of the food with the refrigerated plates will ensure rapid temperature reduction.

Commercial freezing

Food can be quick-frozen in several ways, by:

1 **A blast of very cold air,** which cools the food very rapidly.

Left: A multi-plate freezer.

Right: A freezing tunnel, in which peas are being carried along on a cushion of icy air and frozen individually.

2 **Close contact with refrigerated plates.** The food is passed into a cabinet called a **multi-plate freezer**, and is rapidly frozen to −18°C (0°F).

3 **Immersion in a very cold liquid**, such as brine (salt and water solution) or liquid nitrogen. When liquid nitrogen is used, the process is known as **cryogenic freezing**, and it is used for foods such as strawberries, which do not freeze very well using conventional quick freezing methods. Liquid nitrogen is extremely cold (it boils at −196°C, −320°F), and food placed in or sprayed with it freezes instantaneously, with tiny ice crystals being formed.

The effect of freezing on food

The reduction of temperature does not significantly affect the nutritional value of food, but there may be some destruction of thiamin and vitamin C during the blanching of vegetables.

If meat is frozen too slowly, some of the cells of which it is composed may rupture, and release nutrients into the liquid that drips from the meat when it thaws. In this way there may be losses of protein, thiamin, riboflavin, and nicotinic acid, but these losses are unlikely to affect the nutritional value of the meat to any great extent.

Some flavours become weaker and some become stronger when food is frozen. This has implications for the preparation of cooked foods for the freezer (see p. 175).

Addition of a chemical preservative

Substances (preservatives) can be added to food to inhibit the action of enzymes, and either destroy or inactivate micro-organisms which may contaminate the food.

Preservatives such as vinegar, salt, sugar, and wood smoke have been used for many years for this purpose. Most chemical preservatives work by surrounding the microbial cells with a concentrated solution which draws water out of the cell by osmosis (see p. 142). This renders the cell inactive. Enzyme activity is also affected by the presence of high concentrations of salt, acid, sugar, etc.

The use of chemical preservatives in manufactured foods is strictly controlled by Food Regulations. A permitted list of such chemicals is issued, and no other chemical is allowed to be used. Various stringent safety tests are carried out on preservatives, and the maximum permitted amounts for use in food are determined in the light of these results.

There are many different chemical preservatives in use. Among the more common are:

Antioxidants

These are put into foods for various purposes:

1 To prevent fat rancidity (see p. 71).

2 To prevent destruction of vitamins A and C.
3 To prevent the browning of food by enzymes (see p. 131).

Some foods contain natural antioxidants, e.g. vitamin E is an antioxidant, but these are not usually present in sufficient amounts to be very effective.

Antioxidants are added to the following types of foods:

oils and fats
baked goods containing fat, e.g. cakes and biscuits
apples and pears
dried foods such as milk and meat

Sodium chloride (common salt)

Salt is an effective preservative, and not only prevents food decay, but also adds flavour and nutritional value to the food. Many foods have salt added or are preserved in salt, e.g.:

cheese
sausages
dried fish
canned vegetables (in brine)
bacon

Acids

Some acids are used as preservatives, e.g.:

acetic acid (vinegar)
citric acid
lactic acid
tartaric acid

The acidity of a substance is measured by its pH value (i.e. the number of hydrogen ions in a solution), on a scale of 1 to 14. Substances that have a pH value of 1 to 6 are acidic, 1 being the strongest acid and 6 the weakest; those that have a pH value of 7 (such as water) are neutral; and those that have a pH value of 8 to 14 are alkaline, 8 being the weakest and 14 the strongest alkali.

Acids that are used for preserving, such as vinegar for pickling, are usually fairly strong (about pH 2–3), and are therefore suitable for preserving less acid foods. Some foods are naturally acidic, and can be preserved by other methods, e.g.:

lemon juice	pH 2·4
apples	pH 3·0
rhubarb	pH 3·1
pineapple	pH 3·7
tomatoes	pH 4·2

Most bacteria only grow well at pH 7. Yeasts grow well at pH 4–4·5, and some moulds can grow at pH 2, therefore the strength of an acid used to preserve a food has to be adjusted according to the type of micro-organisms which normally contaminate it.

Sulphur dioxide

Sulphur dioxide is a commonly used preservative for many foods, including:

beer
fruit for jam making
flour for biscuits
fruit juices
pickles
sauces
sausages
soft drinks
tomato purée
dehydrated vegetables

When dissolved in water, sulphur dioxide forms sulphurous acid, which accounts for its preservative action. It also prevents both the oxidation of vitamin C and enzymic browning.

Sugar

Sugar is an effective preservative and adds flavour and energy value to food. It is used to preserve many foods, including:

fruit in jam making (see pp. 232–5.)
canned and bottled fruit
dried fruit (naturally present)

Nitrates and nitrites

These are added to ham, pickled meats, and bacon, to preserve them.

Revision questions

1 Why is food preserved?
2 How does heating preserve food?
3 How should canned, dehydrated, and sterilized food be stored?

4 Describe the following and give examples of foods treated by these processes:
   a sterilization
   b pasteurization
   c canning
5 How does dehydration affect micro-organisms?
6 What are the effects on the nutritive value of food when it is preserved by **a** dehydrating and **b** heating?
7 What chemical preservatives can be added to food?
8 What is osmosis? Why is it important in the chemical preservation of food?
9 What are the principles behind the freezing of food?
10 Why is it necessary to quick-freeze foods?
11 Why are refrigerators used only for the temporary storage of food?

Methods of cooking

The preparation of many foods involves the application of heat (cooking) in a certain way, not only for the reasons stated on p. 130, but also to achieve a particular result.

The selection of cooking method to be used will be influenced by:

1 The particular food to be cooked.
2 The amount of preparation required.
3 The facilities available: fuel, storage, etc.
4 The time available.
5 The needs of the individual being catered for, e.g. state of health, age, etc.
6 Individual preference.

Methods of cooking can be classified according to how heat is applied:

Moist methods: heat applied through the medium of a liquid.

Dry methods: heat applied directly to food.

Frying: heat applied through the medium of fats or oils.

Microwave: heat generated by electromagnetic waves.

Moist methods

Relatively low temperatures are used, which may prolong the cooking time of some foods. The liquid medium may be water, steam, stock, milk, fruit juice, wine, or beer.

Effects on the nutrient content of food

The water-soluble vitamins (B-complex and C) are the most significantly affected by:

1 **Leaching** or diffusion into cooking water, especially in boiling. Some mineral elements may also be affected. As the amount of liquid used increases, more water-soluble nutrients will diffuse out of the food and into the liquid.
2 **Oxidation** Vitamin C is mainly affected. It is destroyed by heat in the presence of oxygen.
3 **Oxidation by enzymes (oxidases)** The presence of oxygen in water encourages the destruction of vitamin C by oxidases. This effect can be reduced by putting food into boiling water, which inactivates the oxidases.
4 **Prolonged cooking and keeping food hot** encourages heat destruction of vitamin C and thiamin.
5 **Preparation prior to cooking** If vegetables are sliced, shredded, or chopped, this increases their surface area, which leads to a greater loss of water-soluble vitamins by leaching and releases more oxidase enzymes. They should therefore be quickly chopped with a sharp knife or torn into pieces just prior to cooking to avoid too much damage to the tissues and the release of enzymes. (See preparation of vegetables, pp. 112–14.)

Starch is softened and made more digestible.

Boiling

Boiling is a common method of cooking, where the liquid (usually water) is heated to boiling point and the heat is then lowered until the liquid is bubbling evenly and rapidly. This is used for rice, pasta, etc.

Simmering Foods that are cooked in hot water but require gentler treatment than boiling to prevent toughening (e.g. fish, meat), or to prevent the food breaking up (e.g. potatoes) should be simmered.

When a liquid is simmering, few bubbles rise to the surface, and the temperature is just below boiling point.

Advantages

1 The transfer of heat by convection is fairly rapid and efficient.
2 Water is readily available.
3 Food is unlikely to burn, though it may disintegrate if overcooked.

Disadvantages

1 Nutrient loss may be high.
2 Soluble matter may be lost into the liquid.
3 Some loss of flavour from meat.

The disadvantages can be partly overcome by serving the cooking water as gravy, sauce, or stock with the meal.

Suitable foods

Most vegetables
Muscular cuts of meat:
lamb: middle neck
beef: brisket (salted), silverside (salted), oxtail
pork: knuckle, ham
Eggs
Pasta, rice, cereals
Fish

Poaching

Poaching is the cooking of food in water at just below the temperature used for simmering, and is therefore a very gentle method of cooking.

The water should only come half way up the food, and the heat should be applied slowly until the right temperature is reached.

Suitable foods

Foods containing protein which would become tough or curdled at higher temperatures, e.g. eggs, fish.

Par-boiling

Par-boiling is the part-cooking of certain foods which are then cooked by another method, e.g. potatoes and parsnips can be par-boiled before being baked (roasted) in fat in the oven.

Par-boiling quickly softens the outside of the food and reduces the amount of time needed for baking.

The food should be placed in boiling water and simmered for five to ten minutes or until the outside is soft. It should then be drained and cooked as desired.

Steaming

Food that is steamed does not come into direct contact with the water, but is cooked in the steam rising from boiling water. Steaming can be carried out in a variety of ways:

1 **Plate method**, e.g. for fish

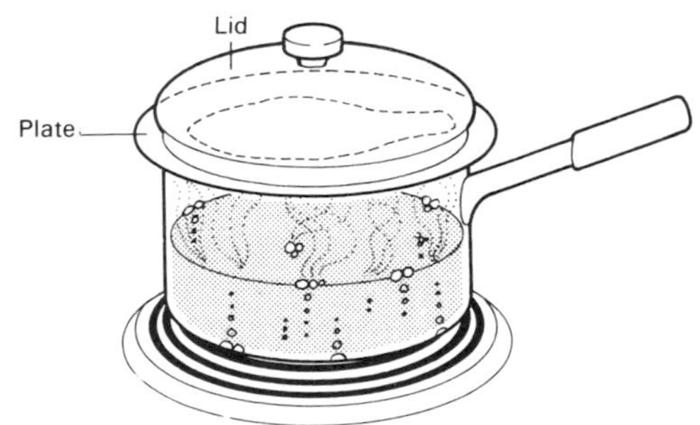

2 **Saucepan method**, e.g. for puddings

3 **Tiered steamer**, e.g. for cooking a whole meal

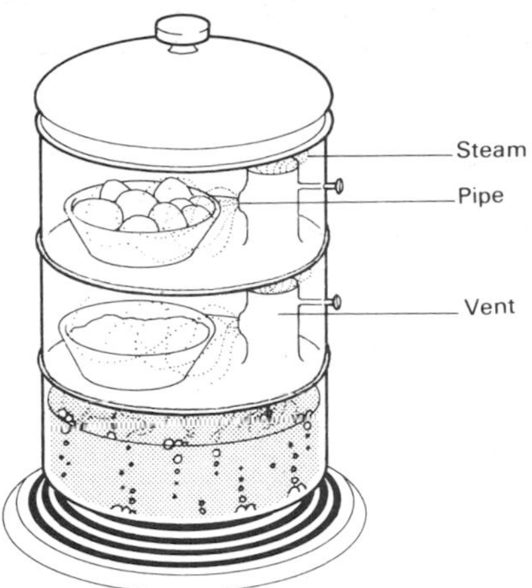

4 **Stepped steamer**, e.g. for puddings

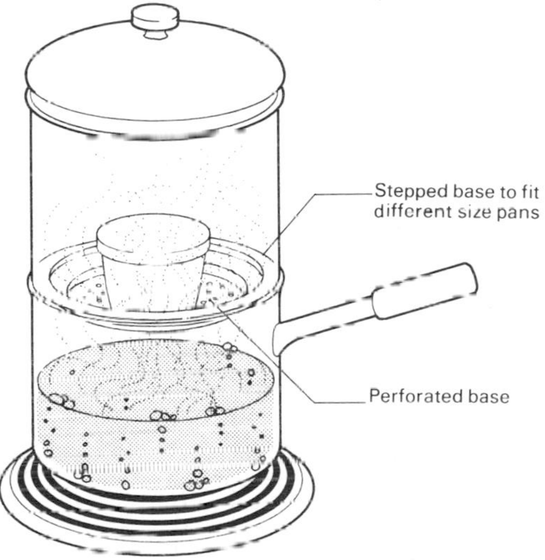

Points to remember when steaming

1 Cover the food with a waterproof lid or wrapping, to prevent condensed water vapour from spoiling the finished result. In the case of steamed puddings, which will rise, a pleat should be made in the covering to allow for this:

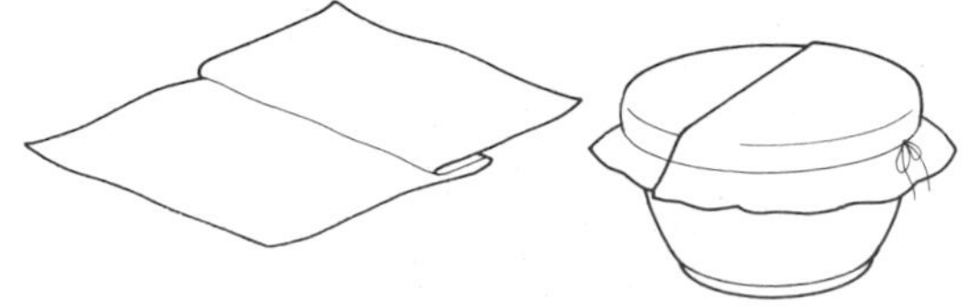

Some puddings basins (plastic) are specially designed to withstand boiling water and have domed lids to allow for the rising of flour mixtures.

2 Keep a kettle of boiling water nearby to replenish the steamer when the water evaporates.
3 Allow water to come to the boil before placing food in the steamer, and ensure that a steady flow of steam is produced.
4 Stand well back when removing the lid of the steamer, to prevent scalding.

Advantages

1 Loss of nutrients by leaching is reduced as the food does not come into direct contact with the water.
2 Food cooked in this way is easy to digest and has a light texture. This is therefore a suitable method to use for convalescent cookery (see pp. 53–5).
3 Little attention is required while the food is cooking, except to replenish the water supply.
4 Food is very unlikely to be overcooked.

Disadvantages

1 Food takes a long time to cook, therefore the heat destruction of vitamin C is more likely to occur.
2 Even with a well-fitting lid, the kitchen is likely to be filled with moisture and should therefore be well ventilated.

Fuel economy

Steaming food is economical on fuel if a small item or whole meal is being prepared in this way. However, food that requires several hours' steaming, e.g. Christmas puddings, may result in minimal fuel economy.

Suitable foods

Puddings: suet, sponge, meat
Fish
Potatoes and other vegetables

Pressure cookery

At normal atmospheric pressure, water boils at 100°C and cannot be raised above this temperature. If the pressure is increased, the water will boil at a higher temperature. This forces steam through food so that it cooks more rapidly. This is the principle on which pressure cooking works.

Types of pressure cooker

Most pressure cookers are made of aluminium, which is thicker than an ordinary pan. It is possible to buy stainless steel pressure cookers, but these tend to be more expensive. All pressure cookers have the following features:

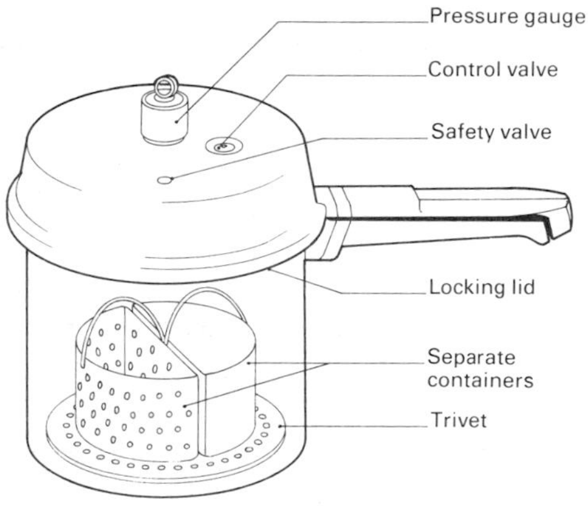

Pressure gauge
This is fitted over the control valve and either has separate weights which allow certain pressures to be built up (see below) or has a central pin which rises as pressure builds up and indicates this by means of marks.

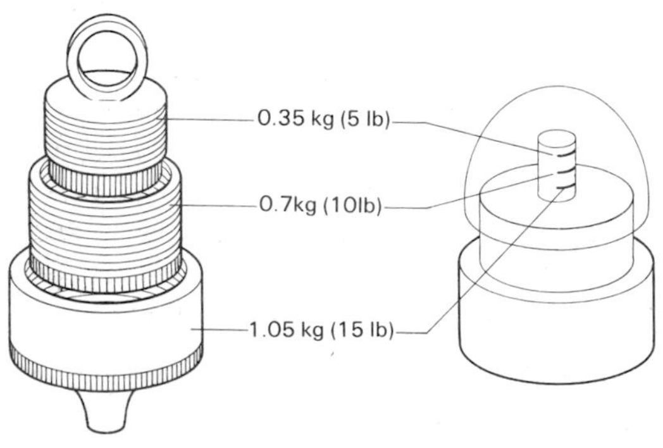

Pressure	**Boiling point of water**
Normal atmospheric plus:	100°C/212°F
Low 0·35 kg/sq cm (5 lb p.s.i.)	107°C/225°F
Medium 0·7 kg/sq cm (10 lb p.s.i.)	112°C/235°F
High 1·05 kg/sq cm (15 lb p.s.i.)	120°C/250°F

Locking lid and rubber seal (gasket)
These ensure that no steam escapes from the rim of the cooker so that pressure will build up inside. The locking lid is also for safety purposes.

Control valve
This allows a small amount of steam to escape to prevent too much pressure building up inside the pan.

Safety valve
Should the pressure become too great inside the cooker (e.g. if the control valve becomes blocked), then it will be released through the safety valve which will either be pushed out or will melt. This should not happen if the cooker is used properly and the control valve is kept clear.

Trivet
This allows food, e.g. chicken, to stand in the steam but not in direct contact with the base of the pan.

Separate containers
These can be used to cook different types of food at the same time, e.g. vegetables.

Pan type

This has a slightly domed lid and can be used to cook most foods, except for large puddings and poultry.

High-domed type

This has a capacity of 6·9 litres ($12\frac{1}{4}$ pints) and can be used for pot-roasting a joint with vegetables or for other large foods.

Automatic type

These have a timer which is set according to how long the food is to be cooked, and releases the steam automatically once cooking is completed. There is also an alarm to indicate that the heat should be turned off.

Points to remember when using a pressure cooker

1 A minimum of 275 ml ($\frac{1}{2}$ pint) water should be used to ensure that sufficient steam builds up inside the cooker.

2 The cooker should be no more than two-thirds full with solid foods (meat, puddings, etc.) and no more than half full with liquids. Exceeding these amounts may result in the control valve becoming blocked.

3 Lock the lid in position and heat the cooker *without* the pressure gauge in position, until the water has boiled and steam is escaping. This ensures that all the air within the cooker is expelled. Any air left inside will affect the cooking temperature and may cause discolouration of some vegetables (e.g. potatoes), due to oxidation.

4 Once a steady jet of steam is coming from the control valve, place the pressure gauge in position and allow pressure to build up to the desired level. A steady hissing sound indicates that pressure has built up.

5 Lower the heat to maintain the desired pressure and cook for the correct time. Timing should commence once the pressure has been reached.

6 When cooking time is completed, turn off the heat and allow the pressure to fall either by leaving the cooker at room temperature or by pouring a gentle stream of cold water over it.

Never attempt to open the lid or remove the pressure gauge before the pressure has fallen to normal.

Examples of cooking time and pressure

Manufacturers usually supply a recipe leaflet with the cooker and their instructions should be followed carefully. The examples below are intended as a guide:

Food	Pressure	Cooking time
Beef casserole	high	20 minutes
Brisket of beef (1 kg/2 lb weight)	high	60 minutes
Steak and kidney pudding	medium	60 minutes
Potatoes	high	5 minutes
Carrots	high	5 minutes
Crème caramel (individual)	high	3 minutes

NB Sponge puddings should be given ten to fifteen minutes cooking time at normal pressure to allow them to rise properly and should then be cooked at medium or low pressure for the stated length of time.

Advantages

1 Economical on fuel.

2 Meals can be prepared quickly.

3 Nutrient loss by leaching is reduced, though heat destruction still occurs.
4 Whole meals can be cooked in one pan.
5 Tough cuts of meat can be cooked quickly and tenderized in the pressure cooker.

Disadvantages

Careful timing is important to prevent foods such as vegetables from being overcooked.

Suitable foods and uses

Jam making, fruit bottling
Stews and casseroles
Vegetables
Meat joints
Puddings
Milk puddings
Soups and stocks

Slow cookers

Slow cookers are operated by electricity and can be used for cooking stews, braises, and other dishes that require long, slow, moist cooking. They can also be used to cook pâtés, soups, fish, and desserts.

There are several types available, but they all have the same basic design. They have a metal or plastic case into which an earthenware or stoneware pot is fitted. The heating element is located under the base or around the sides of the pot. There is no thermostat to control the temperature as very little power is used to operate them (about 55 watts). Food can therefore be left to cook for up to fourteen hours on some models. Some models also have two heat settings. If the cooker has to be left on for longer than originally planned there is usually no adverse effect on the food, unless it is a rice or pasta dish which may become sticky if overcooked.

As the build-up of heat is slow, some models have to be pre-heated for about twenty minutes before food is placed in them. This avoids the risk of food-poisoning bacteria multiplying as the food warms up.

Advantages

1 Once the cooking starts the pot can be left unattended, except for rice dishes which should be stirred occasionally.
2 Little fuel is used.
3 Tough cuts of meat can be tenderized by the moist, slow cooking.
4 Pots that can be lifted out allow a topping (e.g. potato, cheese) to be put on top of the dish, so that it can be grilled.

Disadvantages

1 Pulses and beans may not cook completely at the temperature of the slow cooker, and this may be dangerous if red kidney beans are used as the toxin they contain is only destroyed at boiling temperatures (see p. 115).
2 Meat and poultry may have to be browned in a pan beforehand, although some models have a flameproof pot which can be put on the hob for this purpose.

Stewing

This is a slow method of cooking, which is similar to boiling, but the food is cooked below boiling point. It can be carried out on the hob in a pan with a lid, or in the oven in a covered dish (casserole), on a low heat (Gas 2–3/150–160°C/300–325°F). The liquid in which the food is cooked is normally served with the food.

Advantages

1 Tough cuts of meat can be tenderized by this method (see pp. 95–100).
2 Relatively economical.
3 Nutrient losses are kept to a minimum as the liquid is served with the meal.
4 The flavour is retained as the liquid is served with the meal.

5 Certain fruits, e.g. plums, rhubarb, are improved by this method as the cellulose is softened. The fruit acids help to keep vitamin C and thiamin losses to a minimum.
6 A whole meal can be prepared in one container, which saves time and clearing up.
7 A large variety of stews and casseroles can be prepared.

Disadvantages

1 Stewing is a long, slow method of cooking. The use of an automatic oven is helpful, as a stew can be prepared in advance and left to cook as required.
2 There is little variation in texture and consistency, therefore crisp foods should be served with a stew.

Suitable foods

Beef: flank, chuck steak, oxtail, leg, shin
Lamb: middle neck, breast, liver, kidney
Mutton and veal: breast, neck, kidney, liver
Poultry: chicken
Fruit: plums, rhubarb, apricots, apples

Braising

Braising is a combination of stewing and roasting. Cuts of meat or poultry are placed on a bed of fried vegetables, bacon, and herbs (a **mirepoix**) with sufficient liquid to cover the mirepoix and keep the food moist. A well-fitting lid is placed on the pan to prevent loss of liquid, while the food is cooking in the steam rising from the stock. When the food is tender, it is browned in a hot oven with the lid off.

During cooking, the liquid should simmer, not boil, to prevent toughening the meat.

Advantages

1 A whole meal can be cooked in one pan, which saves time and fuel.
2 Tough cuts of meat can be used.

Disadvantages

Meat may not develop a good colour and may need to be grilled at the end of the cooking time.

Suitable foods

Beef: brisket, flank, topside
Lamb, mutton, or veal: loin, neck, breast
Rabbit
Offal: hearts, liver
Poultry: chicken joints or whole small bird

Revision questions

1 Describe the effect of moist methods of cooking on the nutrients in food.
2 Why is boiling a common method of cooking?
3 What are the disadvantages of boiling?
4 Name five foods suitable for boiling.
5 What is the difference between boiling and simmering?
6 Why is poaching a suitable method of cooking for delicate foods such as fish and eggs?
7 Why are potatoes par-boiled before being roasted in the oven?
8 Why is steaming a suitable method of cooking for people who are suffering from digestive upsets?
9 Why is steaming a useful method of cooking for retaining water-soluble nutrients?
10 What points should be remembered for successfully steaming food?
11 What safety factors should be implemented when steaming food?
12 What are the advantages and disadvantages of steaming food?
13 What is the principle behind pressure cooking?
14 What are the safety features on a pressure cooker?
15 What are the advantages of pressure cooking?
16 Why should all the air be excluded from the pressure cooker before building up the pressure?
17 How do slow cookers work, and what are the advantages of owning one?
18 What are the advantages of stewing, and why is it suitable for cooking tough cuts of meat?
19 What is braising? Name five foods suitable for this method.

Dry methods

Higher temperatures than those used in moist methods of cooking are employed in dry cooking, and this has different effects on the nutritive value and physical appearance of the food.

Effects on the nutrient content of food

All nutrients, except for most of the mineral elements, are affected to some extent, particularly the heat-sensitive vitamins, thiamin and vitamin C.

1 **Fats** At high temperatures, fat molecules decompose into their component glycerol and fatty acid parts, which affects the nutritive value and keeping qualities of the fat (see pp. 70–71).

2 **Proteins** are very sensitive to heat, but their nutritive value is not seriously affected by dry heat, except if they are heated to very high temperatures (e.g. in roasting) for a prolonged time. In this case some amino-acids may be destroyed, and toughening of the protein may reduce digestibility (see p. 14).

3 **Carbohydrates** The effect of heat on starch and sugar has already been described (see p. 20), and there is little effect on nutritive value, except for the increased digestibility of starch in the presence of a liquid.

4 **Non-enzymic browning** (**Maillard reaction**) If a food containing protein and carbohydrate together is dry heated, a reaction occurs between the two. This results in the production of substances which cannot be digested and which therefore cause the loss of a small amount of protein and carbohydrate. Such losses are insignificant, and the substances contribute to the appearance of the cooked product as they are brown in colour. Foods which demonstrate this reaction include bread, roasted nuts, breakfast cereals, and biscuits.

Baking and roasting

Strictly speaking, **baking** is the cooking of foods such as flour mixtures (cakes, pastries, bread, biscuits), and fruits and vegetables (baked apples, potatoes) by convection in the oven, without the addition of fat except to prevent mixtures sticking to cooking vessels, e.g. baking tins, flan cases.

Roasting was traditionally carried out over an open fire, with the meat being rotated on a spit. Nowadays, roasting is generally described as the cooking of meat or vegetables in the oven, basting them with hot fat to prevent drying and to develop colour and flavour.

In either case, account must be taken of the heat variation in an oven due to convection currents (see p. 128). This means that in most types of oven the upper part is the hottest and the lower part the coolest. Items such as cakes, pastries, and bread should not be placed on the floor of the oven as there is insufficient heat to bake these items properly. However, egg custards, fish, fruit and other foods which require slow cooking can be baked at this level of the oven. Fan ovens provide more uniform heating regardless of shelf position, and food on different shelves will brown evenly.

The source of heat in an oven will affect the way in which baking tins should be placed and the evenness of baking.

In a **gas oven**, the source of heat is usually at the back, so that the heat circulates from back to front:

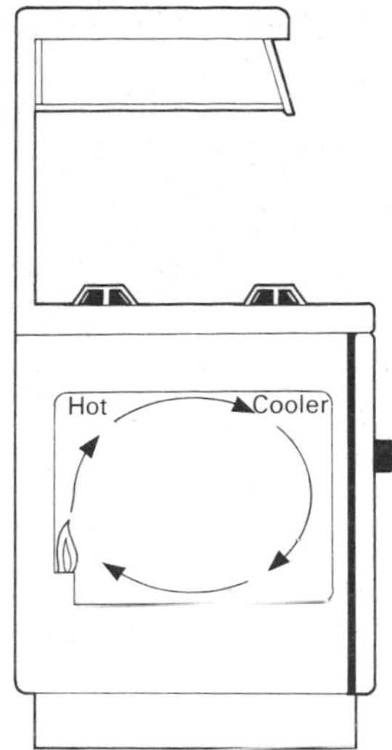

In an **electric oven**, the source of heat is usually at the sides, so that the heat circulates from side to side:

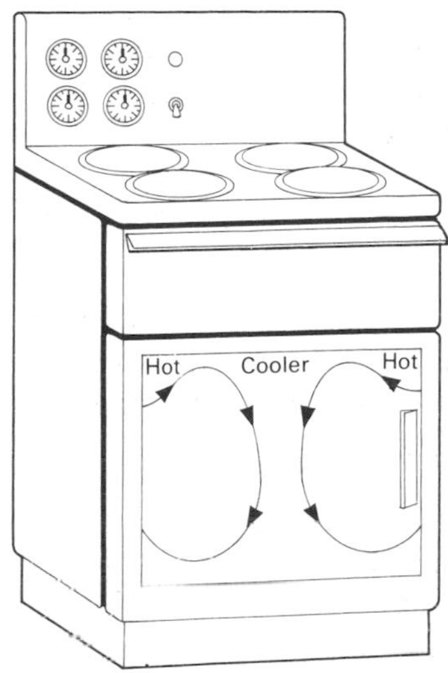

Therefore, the correct way to position food to be cooked in a gas oven is as shown below:

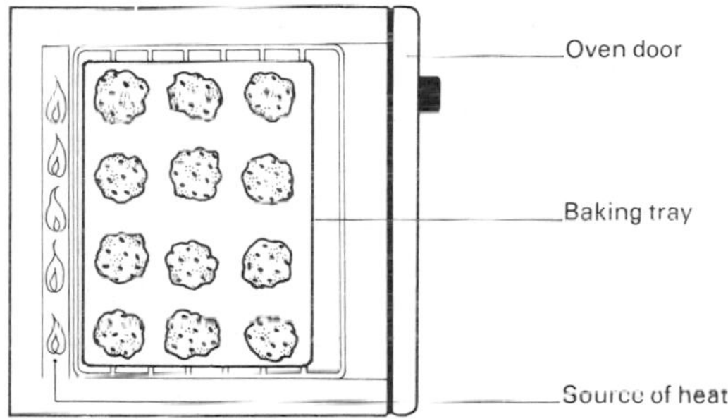

Therefore the correct way to position food to be cooked in an electric oven is as shown below:

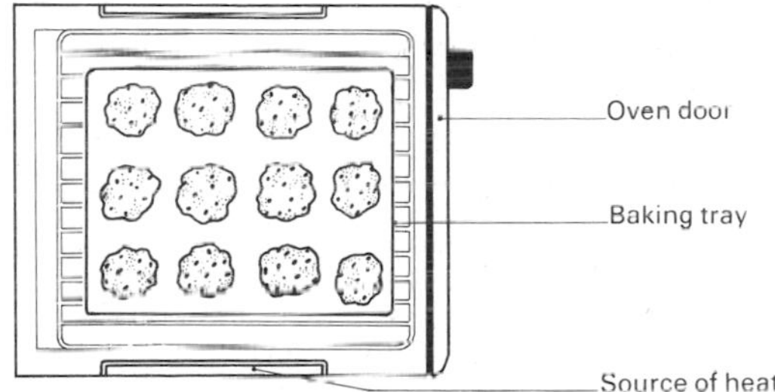

The oven temperature will vary according to what is being baked (see p. 284), and is controlled by the thermostat (see p. 255). If there is a discrepancy between the oven setting and the recommended baking time in a recipe, then it is wise to have the thermostat checked. The use of aluminium foil to line the ceiling of the oven in order to reduce food spattering may affect the evenness of baking, as heat may be reflected on to the food more intensely.

Points to remember when baking

1 Several items can be baked at once to save on fuel, if they require slightly different temperatures. Careful timing will ensure that all the items cook evenly and successfully.
2 The oven should be pre-heated for at least ten minutes before items are placed in it for baking. This is important for cakes, pastries, and bread, where heat is required for raising agents to work efficiently.
3 When the baking time is nearly complete, items can be checked by carefully opening the oven door, without adversely affecting the finished result. The oven door should not, however, be opened too soon or too often, as this will cause a drop in temperature.

Methods of roasting meat

There are four main methods of roasting meat in the oven:

Method A: searing method

The meat is put into a very hot oven (Gas 8–9, 230–240°C, 450–470°F) for the first twenty minutes to sear the outside and develop the flavour and extractives. The heat is then lowered to complete the cooking. This method is only suitable for tender joints of meat, e.g. topside of beef, leg of lamb or pork, and care should be taken not to over-harden the meat.

Method B: meat thermometer

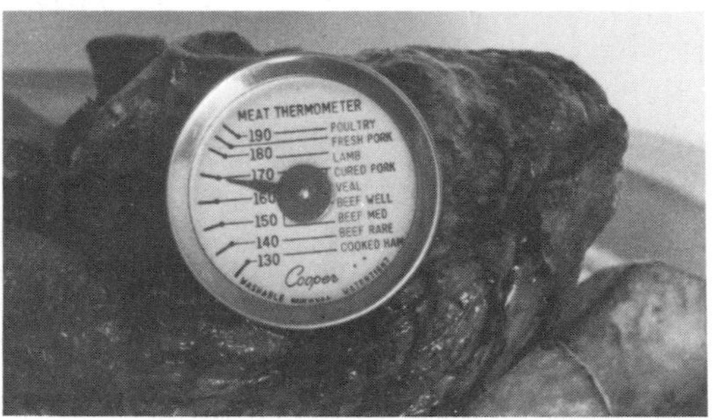

The meat should be cooked at Gas 6–7, 200–225°C (400–425°F). A meat thermometer, which is stuck into the thickest part of the joint, is used and the internal temperature of the joint is registered on the dial. This indicates when the meat is cooked inside and is therefore quite accurate. Any cuts of meat can be cooked by this method.

Different meats have individual temperature readings for when they are cooked:

Beef, well cooked	70°C (160°F)
Lamb and mutton	80°C (175°F)
Pork	85°C (180°F)

Method C: slow roasing

The joint is baked at a cool temperature (Gas 3, 170°C, 325°F) for double the usual time, resulting in a tender joint which does not, however, develop such a full flavour. This method is suitable for cuts such as breast of lamb, belly of pork or brisket of beef.

Method D: cold oven method

The meat is put into a cold oven, set at Gas 7, 220°C (425°F), and the gradual rise in temperature tenderizes the meat and develops the flavour as heating continues. Any cuts of meat can be cooked by this method, but it is particularly suitable for the less tender cuts, e.g. shoulder of lamb, brisket of beef.

Timing the roasting of a joint

It is important to follow the recommended cooking time for a joint of meat to ensure that it is well cooked. This is especially important with poultry and pork joints, which must first have been well thawed out, to prevent the risk of food poisoning.

The chart below indicates how long joints should be cooked according to their weight and the method used to roast them:

Type of meat	Method A	Method D	Method C
Beef: large joints	20 mins per 450 g (1 lb) + 20 mins	Same as for method A in all cases, but allow an extra 20 minutes overall for heating the oven.	30 mins per 450 g (1 lb)
small joints	15 mins per 450 g (1 lb) + 15 mins		25 mins per 450 g (1 lb)
Pork: all joints	35 mins per 450 g (1 lb) + 30 mins		55 mins per 450 g (1 lb)
Veal: large joints	35 mins per 450 g (1 lb) + 30 mins		45 mins per 450 g (1 lb)
small joints	25 mins per 450 g (1 lb) + 25 mins		40 mins per 450 g (1 lb)
Lamb: large joints	25 mins per 450 g (1 lb) + 20 mins		35 mins per 450 g (1 lb)
small joints	15 mins per 450 g (1 lb) + 15 mins		25 mins per 450 g (1 lb)
Stuffed meat	extra 10 mins per 450 g (1 lb)		Allow 20 minutes extra for oven to heat up.
Covered joint	extra 20 mins for any weight		
Poultry	20 mins per 450 g (1 lb) + 20 mins		

Suitable joints for roasting

Beef Fore rib, sirloin, topside, silverside, top rump.
Pork All main cuts can be roasted.
Veal All main cuts can be roasted.
Lamb Best end of neck (Crown roast), loin (whole), saddle, leg, breast, shoulder.

Suitable vegetables for roasting

Potatoes	Turnips
Parsnips	Onions

These should all be par-boiled first.

Advantages of roasting

1 Suitable joints of meat can be tenderized (see p. 98), and their flavour well developed.
2 Little attention is required while the meat is roasting, except to baste the joint.
3 Fuel can be saved if other items are baked in the oven at the same time.

Disadvantages of roasting

1 Moisture loss by evaporation is quite marked and can cause undesirable drying out of a joint.
2 Fat from the meat will spatter at high temperatures and cause the oven to become dirty very easily. Self-cleaning ovens (see pp. 257–8) help to reduce this problem, and the meat can be covered by foil or placed in a roasting bag.
3 Meat may shrink in size quite markedly as a result of moisture loss and protein denaturation.
4 High temperatures may result in toughening of protein and reduced digestibility.

Roasting bricks

Special clay crocks or roasting bricks can be purchased for roasting most types of meat and poultry and for baking fish. The meat is placed in one half of the brick with little or no additional fat added to it, the lid is placed on top, and the brick is put into a cold oven, set at Gas 7–8, 220–230°C (425–450°F). No basting is required, as the joint self-bastes inside the brick and develops extractives and colour on the surface. A substantial volume of juices is also collected, which can

be used for gravy. Oven cleaning is reduced, as the meat is covered. Roasting bricks should be cleaned with hot water and vinegar, as detergent will soak in and taint the food.

Microwave roasting

Meat can also be roasted in a microwave oven (see pp. 164–7).

Pot-roasting

If no oven is available, meat can be pot-roasted, i.e. cooked in a pan with a lid on, over a gentle heat and with a little fat. The meat should be turned occasionally so that it browns on all sides and cooks evenly. Slow cookers and pressure cookers can also be used for pot-roasting.

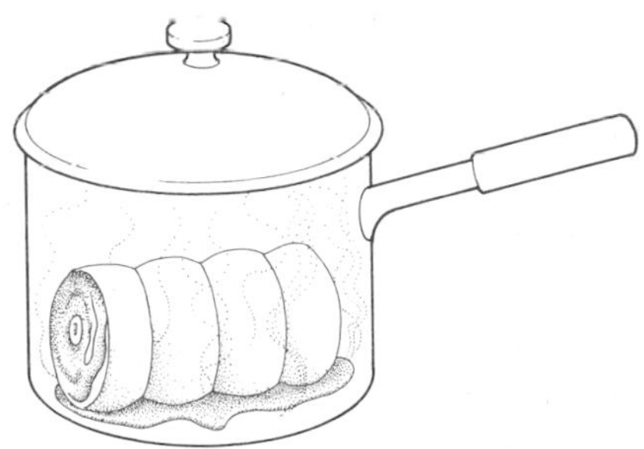

Grilling

Grilling is the cooking of food by radiation under a gas or electric grill (see p. 254). The surface of the food is quickly sealed, and the flavour is well developed. The food must be moistened with fat to prevent it from drying out and turned frequently to ensure even cooking. The food to be grilled should not be more than 2·5–3·5 cm (1–1½″) thick, to allow for heat penetration. The use of skewers or bones in meat joints helps heat penetration by conduction.

Grilling can also be used to brown foods such as cheese, potatoes, sauces, and crumpets, and to toast bread.

Advantages

1 Grilling is a quick method of cooking and is therefore suitable for snack meals, and for time-saving meals.
2 It is a good method of cooking for slimmers because the fat from meat bacon, etc., drains away.

Disadvantages

1 Grilling requires careful timing to prevent overcooking.
2 Meat to be grilled must be tender and will therefore be more expensive.

Suitable foods

Tender meat cuts (see p. 99), e.g. chops (chump, loin), steaks (rump, sirloin), rashers
Cutlets, poultry breasts
Sausages, beefburgers
Offal, e.g. kidney, lamb's liver
Fish fillets
Tomatoes, mushrooms

Revision questions

1 How are the following affected by dry methods of cooking?
  a fats
  b carbohydrates
  c proteins
  d vitamin C
2 What is the Maillard reaction, and how does it occur?
3 What is the difference between baking and roasting?
4 Why should the oven be pre-heated for baking foods such as cakes and bread?
5 Describe the methods of roasting meat.
6 Name two cuts of beef, lamb and pork which are suitable for roasting.
7 Give the roasting times for the following, when using (i) the searing method and (ii) the cold oven method:
  a beef (large joint)
  b pork
  c lamb (small joint)
  d poultry
8 What are the effects of roasting meat on the texture and protein content?
9 How is pot-roasting different from oven roasting?
10 Why must food that is to be grilled be moistened with fat and turned frequently?
11 What are the advantages of grilling?
12 Give four examples of foods that are suitable for grilling.

Frying

Frying is a quick, convenient, and popular method of cooking, which involves high temperatures. Solid fats or oils are used (see pp. 70–74).
There are three types of frying:
  deep frying
  shallow frying
  dry frying

Effect on nutritive value

1 When food is fried, some fat is absorbed (see p. 40) and this increases the fat content of the food and consequently its energy value. This should be taken into account when planning meals.
2 The temperatures are higher than those used in boiling, etc., and this leads to the destruction of heat-sensitive nutrients.

Choice of fat or oil

The fat or oil used in deep frying must be suitable for heating up to 200°C (400°F) without burning. Some fats and oils are especially produced for this purpose (see pp. 70–74). Vegetable oils and lard are suitable. For shallow frying, the temperatures are lower and butter or margarine can also be used.

Deep frying

Deep frying involves the immersion of a food in a pan of hot fat, so that the food is covered by the fat while frying.

A strong, deep pan should be used, with a frying basket, or an electric fryer with a built-in thermostat can be purchased for domestic use.

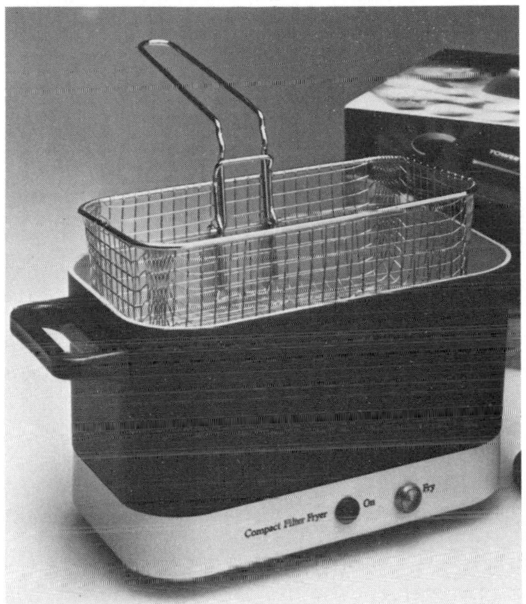

Domestic electric deep-fat fryer.

Preparing food for deep frying

Foods that are to be deep fried, e.g. fish, meat, fruit, should first be coated to prevent over-cooking and the loss of juices from the food, and to prevent the food breaking up and absorbing too much fat. Suitable protective coatings include:

beaten egg
beaten egg and breadcrumbs
beaten egg and seasoned flour
beaten egg and oatmeal
egg, flour, and milk batter

When the food is placed in the hot fat, the egg in the coating coagulates rapidly and thus forms a protective layer around the food, which becomes crisp and golden brown. The food inside continues to cook by conduction and retains its flavour and texture.

Preparing fat for deep frying

Clear, fresh fat or oil should be used. It must as far as possible be free from water and impurities. The presence of moisture in the fat will affect the keeping qualities and will cause the fat to spatter when it becomes hot. Impurities, such as crumbs or flour from previous fryings, will decompose at high temperatures and cause 'off' flavours and odours. They will also affect the keeping qualities of the fat (see p. 71).

Fat should not be heated beyond the required temperature, as decomposition of the fat molecules occurs at high temperatures and this leads to the release of **free fatty acids** which affect the keeping qualities and flavour of the fat. Free fatty acids also reduce the temperature at which the fat will ignite (see pp. 70–71).

The fat should be heated gently to the required temperature, which is indicated by the use of a food or sugar thermometer. The appropriate temperatures for deep frying are shown below:

Food	Temperature of fat	Time
Meat or poultry portions	180–185°C (350–360°F)	Meat: up to 8 minutes Poultry: up to 12 minutes
Doughnuts	180–185°C (350–360°F)	4–5 minutes
Fish fillets	180–185°C (350–360°F)	Up to 6 minutes, if coated with batter. Up to 8 minutes, if coated with egg and breadcrumbs.
Fritters	180°–185°C (350–360°F)	3 minutes
Potato chips	150°C (300°F) then increase to 185°C (360°F)	5 minutes, until soft. Remove chips. Cook at higher temperature for approx. 2 minutes, until crisp and golden.

Important rules for deep frying

1 Do not fill the pan more than half-way with oil or fat, as the oil or fat will rise rapidly when food is placed in it, and could boil over.

2 Lower the food gently into the hot fat. *Do not* drop it in as it will splash and cause burns.

3 Do not overfill the pan, as this will considerably lower the temperature of the fat and affect the finished result.

4 Heat the fat to the required temperature before putting the food in, so that it starts to cook immediately. If the temperature is too low, fat will be absorbed and this will affect the texture and finished result of the food.

5 Do not overheat the fat, as the outside of the food will cook too quickly and the inside will not cook sufficiently. The keeping qualities of the fat will also be reduced (see pp. 70–71).

6 Turn the food over carefully as it is frying to ensure even cooking.

7 Have ready a plate with a piece of absorbent kitchen paper on which to drain the food when it is cooked, and a perforated spoon with which to lift the food out. Cooking tongs can also be used. A frying basket is useful for helping to drain the fat when the food is lifted out.

8 When the food is cooked, turn off the heat and allow the fat to cool before straining it through a piece of muslin to remove impurities.

9 Store the fat in a cool, dry, dark place, to prevent it from becoming rancid due to oxidation (see p. 71). Use a suitable container, e.g. a bottle or can.

Safety rules for deep frying

1 *Never* leave a deep-fat frying pan unattended when cooking.

2 Do not heat the fat beyond the required temperature (see pp. 70–71).

3 Keep the pan handle turned towards the side of the cooker to prevent it being knocked over.

4 If the fat starts to smoke, turn the heat off immediately as this means it is near to its flash point (see pp. 70–71).

If the fat catches fire:

Do not attempt to carry the pan outside. Turn the heat off and smother the flames with either a lid, a thick damp towel, or a flat baking tin.

Do not attempt to extinguish the flames with water, as this will cause the flames to flare up and the burning oil may float on top and spill over.

Do not touch the pan until the fat has cooled down.

Left: The fat has been heated to smoke point.
Right: Adding water to burning fat has disastrous effects.

Suitable foods for deep frying

Scotch eggs, rissoles, fish cakes
Fruit and meat fritters
Doughnuts, choux pastry aigrettes
Small poultry joints
Fish portions
Potato chips and crisps
Onion rings

Shallow frying

Shallow frying involves the cooking of food in a layer of hot fat that comes about half-way up the food. A strong, large, flat frying pan is used.

Heat is conducted from the base of the pan to one surface of the food at a time. This means that the food has to be turned over at regular intervals to ensure even cooking and heat penetration.

Food that is to be shallow fried does not necessarily have to be coated beforehand as the frying can be fairly gentle. Foods with a high moisture content may cause the fat to spatter and a lid or spatter guard can be used to prevent this.

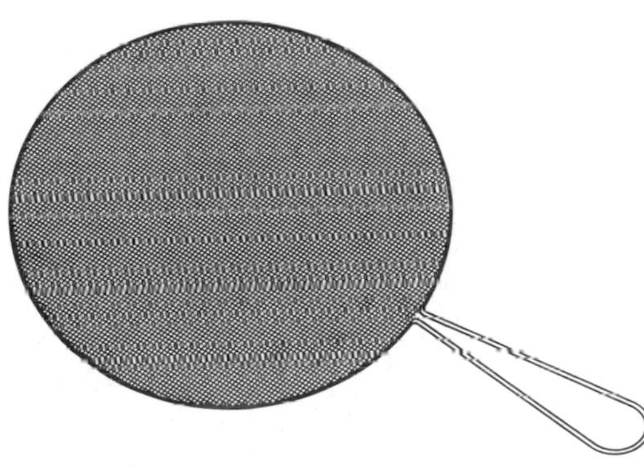

In general, the rules given for deep frying (see pp. 161–2) also apply to shallow frying.

Suitable foods for shallow frying

Tender meat joints, e.g. chops, cutlets
Offal, e.g. liver, kidney
Fish cakes, rissoles, beefburgers
Sausages, bacon rashers
Vegetables
Eggs
Fish, e.g. herrings in oatmeal

Dry frying

Some foods, e.g. bacon and sausages, can be fried without the addition of fat, as they contain sufficient fat to prevent them from sticking to the pan.

It is possible to buy oil sprays, which spray a very thin layer of oil onto the pan for shallow frying. This reduces the energy value of the fried food. Non-stick pans are most suitable for this form of frying, as there is less risk of the food adhering to the pan.

Revision questions

1 Why must some foods which are to be deep fried be coated first? Give three examples of suitable coatings.
2 What causes fat that is used for frying to deteriorate?
3 Why must the frying pan be only half-filled with oil or fat, and why is it important not to overfill it with food when hot?
4 Why is it important to regulate the temperature of the fat carefully when frying?
5 What safety precautions should be followed when frying?
6 Give five examples of foods that are suitable for deep-fat frying and five suitable for shallow frying.

Microwave cookery

During the Second World War, it was discovered that microwaves could pass easily through rain and fog and that they had heating properties. Microwave ovens were developed, and during the 1960s began to be more commonly used in catering establishments. At the present time microwave ovens are becoming increasingly popular as their availability increases and their manufacturing costs decrease.

Electro-magnetic waves

Energy can be emitted in the form of electro-magnetic waves. This process is known as **radiation.** It is the process by which light and heat from the sun reach the earth.

If produced in sufficient intensity, certain waves can cause a rise in temperature in an object with which they make contact. Those which are capable of this include:

heat radiation
infra-red waves
microwaves

Microwaves move at the speed of light and have a very **high frequency**, i.e. they vibrate millions of times a second. If absorbed into an object, the vibrations of the microwaves agitate the molecules within the object, causing friction. If you rub your hands together, the friction makes them become warm. Similarly, the vibration of microwaves within an object will cause a rise in temperature as their energy is converted into heat energy.

Microwaves are either **reflected, transmitted**, or **absorbed** by different materials:

Reflection
Microwaves are reflected from metal, which does not heat up.

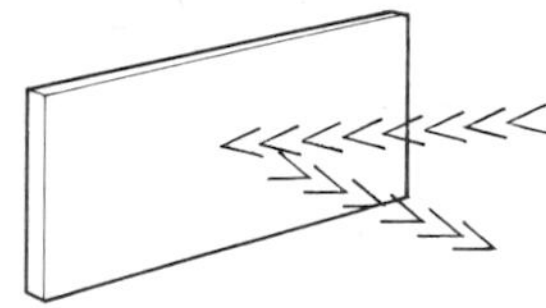

Transmission
Some materials, e.g. paper, china, some plastics, transmit microwaves, but do not heat up.

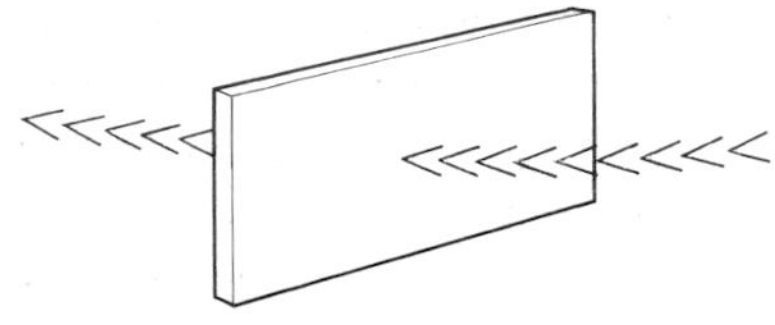

Absorption
Some materials, e.g. food, absorb microwaves and become hot.

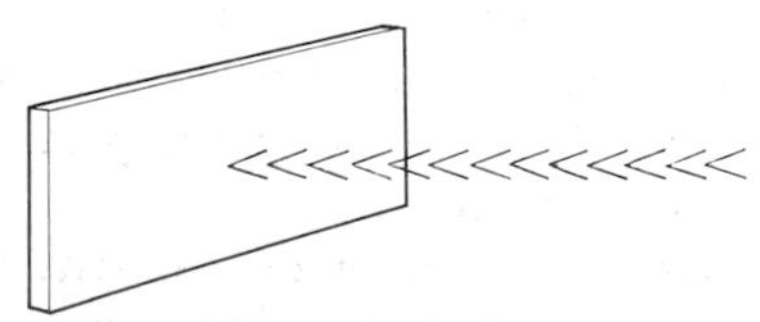

How food is cooked by microwaves

Microwaves are able to penetrate up to five centimetres into food and produce heat rapidly by the agitation of molecules throughout the food. Conventional methods of cooking rely on the much slower conduction of heat from the surface of the food to the interior. Food cooked by microwaves is cooler on the surface than in the interior as the heat radiates from the food out to the cooler surroundings of the microwave cooker, which does not itself heat up.

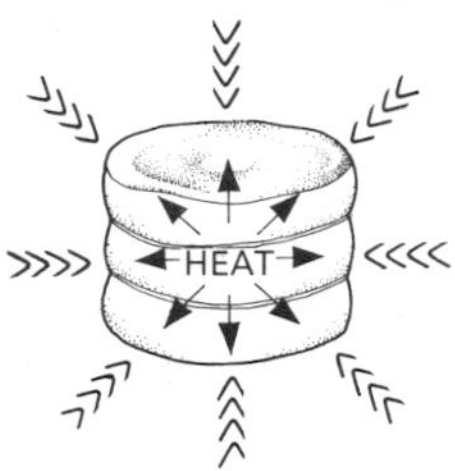

Microwave cookers

Several types of microwave cooker are now available to the consumer, but they all have the same basic design and parts:

Cavity The food is placed in here, on a plate or dish.
Magnetron This is the valve which generates the microwaves.
Guide This determines the length of the waves and guides them into the cavity.
Mode stirrer This distributes the microwave energy evenly in the cavity.
Door The door has a safety seal to prevent leakage of microwaves to the exterior.

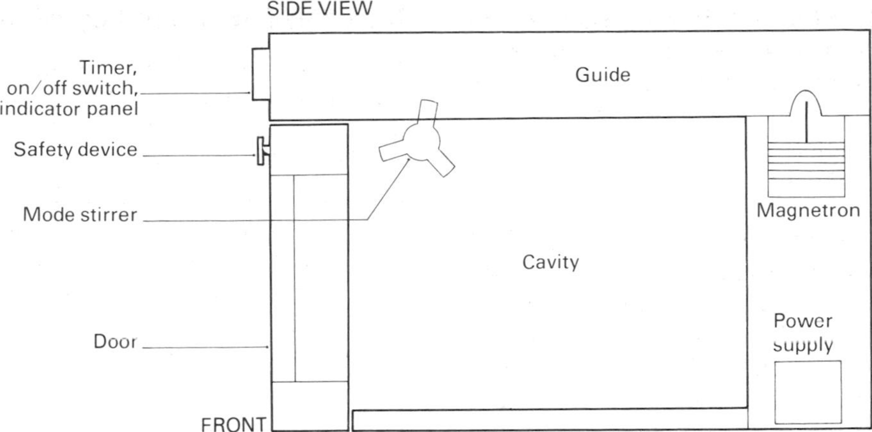

Power supply This converts the mains supply to the required voltage for the correct operation of the magnetron valve.

Safety device This ensures that the microwaves cease to be emitted once the door is opened.

Timer This controls the time during which microwaves are emitted, and switches the cooker off at the end of the set time.

On/off switch This may be in addition to a mains output control switch.

Indicator panel This may include a time chart for different foods as well as operating instructions.

Microwave ovens, unlike conventional ovens, do not heat up, and the only heat produced is that generated within the food.

The instruction leaflet for individual cookers should be carefully studied, but the following rules apply to most models.

Containers for food

Suitable containers:

oven-proof glass	china
ceramics	paper

Some plastic films and containers are also suitable, but not all, as the heat from the food may cause some plastics to distort or melt, particularly when fat or syrup is heated to a temperature above 150°C (300°F).

Polythene pouches, such as those used to hold frozen foods, can be used as long as they are pierced beforehand. Otherwise they may burst during cooking.

The following containers are *not* suitable:

metal foil dishes
dishes with a metal trim

These reflect the microwaves back to the magnetron and cause 'arcing'. This may cause permanent damage to the cooker.

melamine plastic ware

Melamine may scorch and char.

polystyrene containers

These deform and give off a strong odour if heated for too long.

Timing and cooking the food

1 Foods vary in the amount of time they require to be heated up, and this should be taken into account.
2 The greater the volume of food, the longer the time required to cook it as penetration by the microwaves will take longer.
3 If the food is very cold to begin with, it will take longer to cook than if it is at room temperature.
4 Thick portions of food (those more than 3–5 cm thick) take longer to cook as the microwaves lose their power to heat the deeper they penetrate into the food. This may produce uneven cooking in items such as bread and pastries.
5 Light, porous foods absorb microwaves more readily than more compact, moist foods such as meat.
6 The greater the moisture content of the food, the longer the cooking time.

7 Food should be separated, not stacked up in the cooker, as this will affect the penetration of the waves.
8 Foods that are traditionally eaten browned or crusty, e.g. meat, cakes, and bread, may need to be finished off in a conventional oven or grill, as they will not develop these characteristics in a microwave cooker. Special 'browning' plates can be purchased for the microwave oven. These are heated in the cavity, before food such as meat is placed on them. When the food comes into contact with the hot plate, it will brown as in frying or roasting.

Advantages of microwave cooking

1 Food is cooked very quickly. This cuts down on fuel costs, preparation time, and wastage (food is only heated as required).
2 The food heats up but the oven does not. This prevents the kitchen from becoming uncomfortable to work in.
3 It is useful for preparing foods and meals that are required quickly, and for entertaining.
4 There is less heat destruction of nutrients as cooking time is short.
5 Some foods, e.g. vegetables, are improved in colour and flavour as cooking time is shorter.
6 There is less danger of food poisoning as food does not have to be kept warm.
7 Food spills do not burn on the cooker as it does not become hot.
8 The cooker is usually portable (though it is heavy) and can be placed on an ordinary worktop and operated from a normal mains supply.
9 Frozen foods can be defrosted in some models.
10 The food can be cooked on the dish on which it is to be served, which saves washing up.
11 The serving dish or cooking utensil does not become heated by the microwaves, and can therefore be handled. It may only become hot by the conduction of heat from the cooked food.

Disadvantages

1 It is easy to overcook the food, so careful attention must be paid to timing.
2 Food will not become crisp, and may not develop characteristic flavours, colours, or textures.
3 Irregular-shaped foods may affect the cooking time and finished result of foods cooked on the same plate. This may necessitate separate cooking.

Suitable foods

Most foods can be cooked in a microwave cooker. The main exceptions are pastries and some cake mixtures, which need to be baked in a conventional oven (see pp. 194–5).

Safety regulations

Safety regulations on the manufacture and design of microwave cookers operate in several countries, and are being introduced in the UK. Much research into the use of these cookers has been carried out to ensure that there is no possibility of accidental leakage of microwaves while the cooker is in use.

Revision questions

1 What are microwaves and how do they heat food?
2 Why do microwave ovens stay cool when in use?
3 In a microwave oven, what do the following parts do?
a magnetron
b guide
c mode stirrer
d safety device
4 Give three examples of suitable containers to use in a microwave cooker, and give reasons for your answers.
5 What are the advantages and disadvantages of microwave cookery?
6 How do the thickness and temperature of food affect their cooking time in a microwave cooker?
7 Which foods cannot be successfully cooked by microwaves? Give reasons for this.

Freezer cookery

The principles underlying the freezing of foods as a method of preservation are discussed on pp. 145–6.

Home ownership of freezers in affluent countries such as the UK has increased considerably in the last decade, and in 1979 41% of homes in the UK owned a freezer. A large range of commercially frozen foods can now be bought in bulk to store in the home.

Freezer ownership is both convenient and time saving, but freezer management should be carefully studied in order to achieve the best results as economically as possible.

Advantages of owning a freezer

1 Freezing is a simple and effective way of preserving food, and, providing the basic rules are followed, it is a safe method. There is very little effect on the flavour, colour, appearance, and nutritive value of most foods.
2 Whole meals, snacks, and parts of meals can be stored in a freezer for convenient use during the week.
3 It is usually cheaper to buy foods such as meat in bulk, and then to store them in the freezer for long-term use.
4 Home-grown or 'pick-your-own' produce can be frozen at home, which saves you money.

5 Foods can be eaten out of season.
6 Parties and other special occasions can be catered for in advance and the foods stored until they are needed.
7 'Emergency' foods can be stored for unexpected guests or for when the larder is depleted.
8 Freezers are inexpensive to run, if used wisely; on average they use two units of electricity per cubic foot per week.
9 Various sizes of freezer are available to cater for varying needs and family size.
10 Time can be saved on shopping if food is bought in bulk for the freezer.
11 Left-over foods and items such as stock or fruit juice can be frozen for later use, to save wastage.

Disadvantages of owning a freezer

1 The initial cost and outlay for a freezer is high, but by sensible use, this cost can gradually be retrieved.
2 In order to work and run efficiently, a freezer should be well stocked, which means that plans should be made to buy or freeze more food as stocks run down.
3 To prepare a bulk buy or harvest of foods may entail a good deal of work in a short space of time.
4 There may be a tendency to fill the freezer with uneconomic commercially frozen food.
5 A family may find that it is eating more foods such as meat, shellfish, etc., just because they are in the freezer, and this may be uneconomic and unnecessary.
6 Storage space may be limited, so the freezer may have to be housed outside the kitchen and this may be inconvenient.

Types of freezer

There are several types and makes of freezer available, and a study of consumer association reports on these is often a valuable guide to buying one. It is important to evaluate your needs before buying a freezer, based on the following points:

1 How much you can afford to pay.
2 What types of food you are likely to freeze (home-grown or commercially frozen).
3 The number of people in the family, allowing approximately 56·6 litres (2 cubic feet) per person.
4 How much entertaining is catered for.
5 How much floor space is available.
6 Your preference for style.

There are three main types of freezer:

chest freezer
upright freezer
refrigerator/freezer

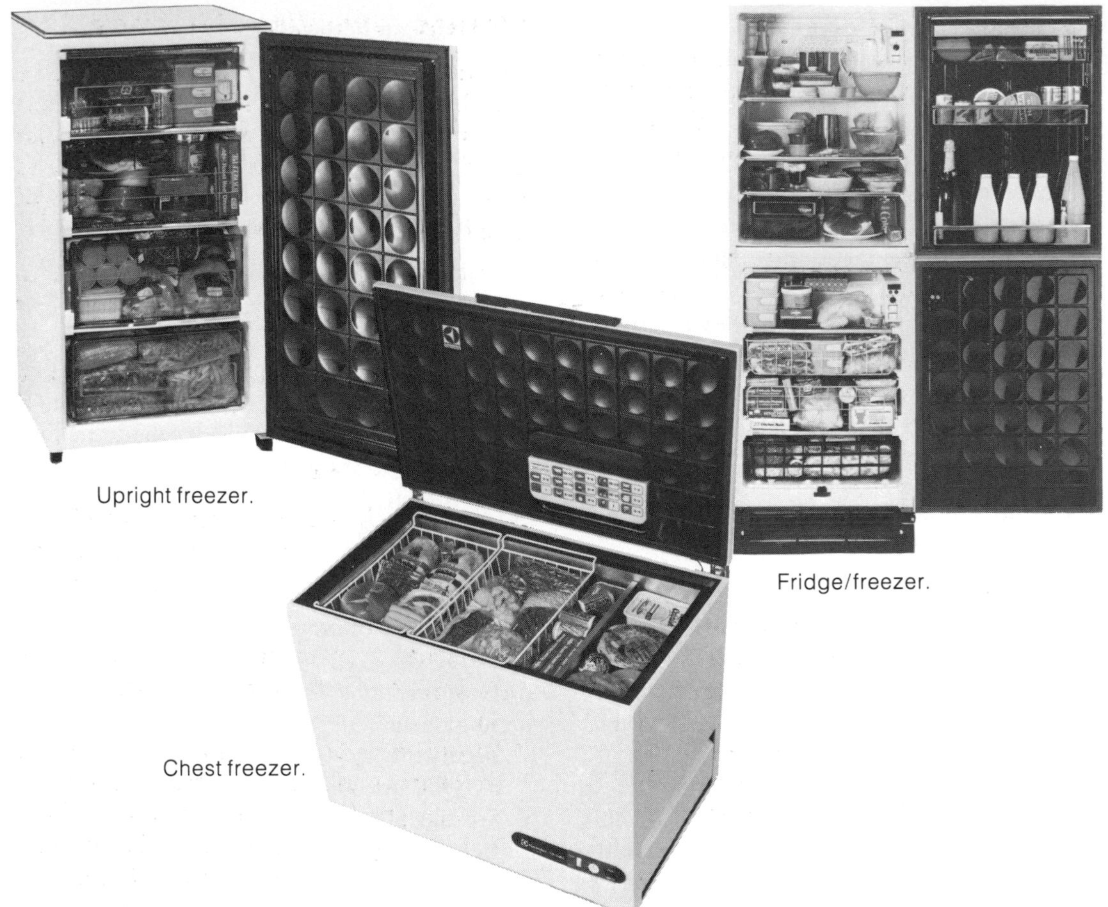

Upright freezer.

Chest freezer.

Fridge/freezer.

Chest freezers

Chest freezers have a top-opening lid, and their sizes range from 141·5 l (5 cu ft) to 509·4 l (18 cu ft). Removable baskets and open trays are sold as extras for this type of freezer, which makes the packing and removal of food much easier. All models stand on the floor, and some which are table-top height can be used as work surfaces.

Advantages

1 Chest freezers are slightly more economical to run, and require defrosting less often.
2 Large, bulky foods, e.g. meat joints, can be easily stored.

Disadvantages

1 It may be difficult to reach the bottom of the freezer or to see the contents at a glance.
2 Chest freezers take up more floor space than other types.

Most models have a separate compartment for fast-freezing food.

Upright freezers

Upright freezers have a front-opening door, and the food is placed on shelves, which are usually adjustable to cope with different foods. Their sizes range from 57 l (2 cu ft) to 113 l (4 cu ft) for small, free-standing models, and from 113 l (4 cu ft) to 572 l (20·2 cu ft) for floor-standing models. The larger types often have two doors, and the lower half can be used for long-term storage.

As upright freezers take up less floor space than chest freezers, the weight they hold is more concentrated on one small area. It is important to check that the floor is strong enough to withstand such constant weight.

Advantages

1 It is easy to pack and unpack the goods from the freezer and to check the contents.
2 Some models have spaces and racks on the inside of the door to hold small items.
3 Little floor space is taken up.

Disadvantages

1 When the door is open, heavy, cold air falls out quickly, so the motor must work more to maintain the temperature.
2 Upright models require defrosting more frequently, and the shelves may become iced up easily, which makes the removal of food difficult.
3 These models are slightly more expensive to run.
4 Bulky foods may be more difficult to store in upright models.

Some models have one or two fast-freeze shelves for quick freezing of foods.

Refrigerator/freezers

Refrigerator/freezers usually consist of two separate cabinets, joined together, with separate doors. Normally, the freezer compartment is below the refrigerator, and it may operate independently or in conjunction with the refrigerator.

These models are particularly useful to single people or small families, and there is a range of sizes available.

The advantages and disadvantages are similar to those for the upright models, although the refrigerator/freezer may be slightly more economical to run.

NB It is often possible to buy second-hand **conservators** from shops or ice cream manufacturers. These are *not* designed to freeze food, only to store foods which are already frozen at −18°C (0°F). They should not be considered if food is to be frozen at home. Appliances that are *are* suitable for freezing food will have the following symbol displayed:

Storage capacities of freezers

The maximum storage capacity of a freezer may be more than the *actual* storage space available, due to the waste of space that arises when uneven-shaped packages are used. The approximate holding capacity of 28·31 (1 cu ft) of freezer space is:

16–20 identical, tub-shaped, 575 ml (1 pint) cartons
or 8 kg (20 lb) poultry or meat
or 35–40 identical, square or rectangular 575 ml (1 pint) cartons

Siting the freezer

In order for the freezer to operate efficiently it must be placed in a suitable position. The following points should be considered when choosing a site:

1 Dampness may damage the motor and the exterior of the freezer, so the site must be dry.
2 Insufficient air circulation will result in inefficient removal of heat from the condenser (see pp. 258–9), so the freezer will not work properly. There must be at least 25 mm (1″) of space around the freezer.
3 A site that is always hot will cause the motor to work overtime to maintain the temperature inside the freezer, so it must be kept in a cool place.

Suitable sites include:
a cool dry kitchen
utility room
a dry garage, conservatory or outhouse
spare living-room or bedroom

Running costs of freezers

Several factors help to determine the running costs of the freezer, including:

1 The size and type of freezer.
2 The number of times the door or lid is opened.
3 The amount of food that is stored in the freezer; if there are large gaps this may increase running costs as the motor will have to operate more frequently to maintain the temperature.

4 How often the freezer is defrosted; if too much ice is allowed to build up the work of the motor will be increased.
5 Where the freezer is kept, and the climate; more electricity will be used in warm weather to maintain the temperature.
6 How often fresh food is frozen; food to be frozen raises the temperature of the freezer and causes the motor to work more often.

Insurance

A full freezer may contain food that is worth a great deal of money, the loss of which would be financially disastrous. It is therefore a wise precaution to insure the contents against power failures, breakdown of the motor, or theft of the contents.

Many insurance companies will insure against such losses, often as part of the house contents insurance, but many do not cover the loss incurred if the freezer is accidentally switched off. It is useful to cover the mains switch with tape or a label to prevent this happening. These insurance policies are usually fairly inexpensive. It may also be possible to insure the freezer itself for repair costs.

Power failure or moving house

In the event of a power failure, the freezer should be left closed, and the food will remain in perfect condition for at least six hours, or longer if the freezer is well packed and full. If the freezer has to go away for repair, it may be possible to hire another from the firm carrying out the work. It is also possible to buy alarms which will sound if the temperature rises in the freezer cabinet, before any damage is done to the food.

If moving house, it is advisable to run down the stocks of food in the freezer for a few weeks in advance so that there is not so much to move on the day. The freezer should be the last item to be put into the van and the first to be removed, so that it can be connected immediately. If the food has to be unpacked, it is possible to buy dry ice to surround the food in a packing box, with newspaper to provide extra insulation. The food should remain frozen for several hours in this way.

Equipment

Apart from packaging materials, little special equipment is required for running a freezer, and many of the items may already be in the home. The following are needed:

a large saucepan for blanching (see p. 174)
a fine wire-mesh blanching basket
a large bowl for cooling blanched foods
a liquid measuring jug
a funnel for filling bags with food
a sharp knife, fork, and draining spoon

Packaging materials and labels

Food that is to be frozen must be well packaged to prevent:

1 **Dehydration and oxidation** Cold air is very drying and if dehydration occurs, oxidation reactions will take place in the food. This will cause foods such as poultry and meat to develop 'freezer burn' (visible greyish, fibrous patches on the surface of the meat), and fats to become rancid (see p. 71).
Many materials will prevent water from evaporating, but not water vapour.
2 **Contamination** by dirt, insects, and moulds.
3 **Transfer** of flavours from one food to another.

A suitable packaging material should have the following qualities:

moisture-vapour-proof
greaseproof
waterproof (for liquids and odours)
odourless and odour-proof
strong and durable
economical of storage space
easy to use
able to withstand very low temperatures

There are three main groups of packaging materials:

sheet wrapping materials
bags
rigid containers

Sheet wrapping materials

This category includes:
- aluminium foil
- polythene sheeting
- freezer paper

Aluminium foil

This is obtainable in rolls of varying widths and lengths. It is fairly expensive to buy, and is often not reusable for the freezer. It is suitable for most foods except those that contain acid (e.g. fruits), and has the advantage of being flexible enough to be moulded around foods of different shapes.

Aluminium foil makes a good outer wrapping for foods, but it is easily punctured. Extra-thick foil can be bought, but is more expensive.

Polythene sheeting

This is also sold in rolls of varying lengths and widths and is used to wrap foods. It needs to be sealed with special freezer tape that does not lose its adhesiveness in cold temperatures.

The thin, self-clinging films that are available are not suitable as outer coverings, but can be used to wrap individual foods that are part of a pack.

Freezer papers

These are strong, moisture-proof papers which are coated on the inside and can be written on on the outside. They have to be sealed with freezer tape.

Bags

This category includes:
- cellophane and paper bags
- polythene bags

Cellophane and paper bags

These tend to be more expensive than polythene bags but are easy to use.

Polythene bags

Polythene is made in different thicknesses or gauges. Ordinary household bags are not usually suitable. For freezing, 120–150 gauge polythene bags should be used, which are specially produced for freezing and are available in a range of sizes.

Polythene bags should be sealed with paper-covered wire ties. They can be re-used providing there are no punctures in the polythene.

Most foods can be stored in these bags, and liquids can be frozen into easy-to-store blocks, by placing the bag in an empty carton, filling it, and freezing it in the carton. Once solid, the bag can be removed and easily stored.

Rigid containers

This category includes:
- plastic or polythene boxes or tubs
- waxed cartons or tubs
- aluminium containers
- ceramic or glass containers

Plastic or polythene boxes or tubs

These are fairly expensive to buy, but have the advantage of being reusable time and time again. They usually have tightly-fitting lids, which make the boxes air-tight.

Square or rectangular shapes take up the least space and are easy to pack into the freezer; round ones are less useful. Empty ice cream and margarine containers can also be used, but these should be made air-tight with freezer tape if necessary.

The food should be cooled before it is placed in these containers, as the hot plastic may release toxic substances, or may 'deform' into a permanent shape.

Waxed cartons or tubs
These are only suitable for cold foods, as the wax coating will melt easily. They are useful for storing small amounts of food.

Aluminium containers
These are available in many shapes and sizes, and can be used for heating the food once it has thawed. Acidic foods should not be frozen in these containers as they will cause corrosion. These containers are reusable, but care should be taken to ensure that they are thoroughly cleaned after use, as food residues can become trapped in the folds of metal at the corners of the dishes.

Ceramic or glass containers
Ceramic casseroles which are able to withstand cold temperatures are available, but they are a waste of space in the freezer and once put in, will be out of use for some time. It is therefore wise to line the casserole with foil, cook the food and freeze it until solid. The frozen block can then be removed and the casserole released for further use. The casserole can be thawed in the casserole dish when required.

Glass jars and bottles which withstand low temperatures can be used, but headspace should be provided to allow for expansion of the food during freezing, otherwise they may shatter. Glass becomes more brittle as the temperature is lowered, so care should be taken when handling glass containers in the freezer.

Labels

It is important to label food packs in the freezer, as they often become unrecognizable once frozen. The date on which the food was frozen should always be marked on the label, to indicate when the food should be used up.

Tie-on or adhesive labels can be bought in different colours, to make identification easier in the freezer. The label should indicate the contents of the food pack, how many servings it contains, and when it was frozen.

Care of the freezer

It is important to take care of a freezer so that it works efficiently and gives value for money.

The outside of the freezer should be kept clean and free from rust, and the hinges of the lid or door may require oiling from time to time.

Defrosting

It is important to defrost the freezer when the frost reaches a thickness of about 1 cm ($\frac{1}{2}''$) inside the cabinet. The manufacturer's instructions should be carefully followed, but as a guide, the following points should be studied:

1 Chest freezers normally require defrosting only once or twice a year; upright freezers require defrosting two or three times a year.
2 Try to defrost the freezer when the food stocks are low.
3 Remove the food, wrap it in newspaper and blankets, and put it in a cold place.
4 Switch off the electricity, leave the freezer open, and place bowls of hot water inside, so that the steam speeds up the melting of the ice.
5 Gently scrape off the ice with a plastic or wooden spatula; *do not* use sharp or pointed tools which could damage the interior walls.
6 Use a towel to catch water at the bottom of the freezer. Some models have a drain plug which can be opened to release the water.
7 When all the ice has been removed, wash the inside with a clean cloth and a solution of bicarbonate of soda and water (1 tablespoon to 4 litres/2 pints water). *Do not* use detergent as this may leave a smell in the freezer which could taint the food.
8 Allow the freezer to dry, then replace the food neatly. It is a good idea at this point to make an inventory of the contents. Do not open the freezer once it has been switched back on until it has reached the required temperature.

Using the freezer

There are several basic rules to follow for the successful use of a freezer. There are also specific rules for the freezing of individual foods, which are usually supplied in recipe books.

Basic rules

1 Freeze only fresh foods.
2 Freeze food when it is at the peak of quality; i.e. when just ripe or ready for eating.
3 Once prepared or harvested, freeze the food quickly to avoid deterioration.
4 Handle and freeze the food hygienically.
5 Use suitable packaging materials and wrap the food properly.
6 Pack food in single or multiple portions according to family size and needs.
7 Remove as much air as possible from the package before freezing, e.g. by sucking out the air through a straw, to prevent oxidation of the food during storage.
8 Label the packs clearly. Keep a record of what has been frozen and when.
9 Chill the food in a refrigerator before freezing so as not to raise the temperature inside the freezer too much.
10 Only freeze food in the quantities recommended by the manufacturer for the capacity of the freezer.
11 Store the food only for the recommended storage time (see pp. 175–6).
12 Aim to use up stocks of food before they come into season again.
13 Do not allow the temperature of the freezer cabinet to rise above −18°C (0°F). A thermometer which can be placed inside the freezer is useful for checking this.
14 Never refreeze foods which have been thawed, unless they have undergone a process of cooking, e.g. thawed meat made into a casserole can be frozen.

Choice of food for freezing

Most foods can be frozen, but some are more suitable than others. The length of time that food can be stored varies, and no food can be frozen indefinitely. Once a food has passed its storage life, i.e. the length of time it can be kept frozen in perfect condition, chemical changes start to affect the flavour, quality, and edibility of the food.

Some foods which are available for most of the year and have a long storage time in a fresh state are not worth freezing, e.g. potatoes.

Some foods react poorly to freezing and are therefore unsuitable. These include:

Vegetables

Lettuce, cucumber, and radish become mushy and discoloured on thawing, as their high water content results in large numbers of ice crystals being formed. These rupture the cells, even if quick-frozen (see p. 146).
Boiled potatoes become 'leathery' when thawed, if frozen whole.
Celery has a high water content and loses its structure on thawing, but it can be used as a cooked vegetable in casseroles, soups, etc.

Fruit

Strawberries tend to become mushy on thawing, due to ice crystals rupturing their cells, but they can be used in fruit salads, flans, soufflés, mousses, etc., as their flavour is not impaired.
Bananas and avocado pears turn black if frozen, due to enzyme activity.
Pears tend to lose their texture if frozen, due to the effect of ice crystals on the cells.

Dairy products

Pasteurized milk (non-homogenized) separates out when frozen.
Cream with less than 40% fat separates (e.g. single cream). Whipping or double cream should be whipped lightly before freezing.
Eggs: whole, fresh eggs crack and become gluey. However, egg white and yolks can be frozen separately.
Hard-boiled eggs become leathery.

Mayonnaise separates.
Cornflour-based soups and stews tend to separate.
Icings (except buttercream) crumble and become soggy.

Preparation of food for freezing

Vegetables

Vegetables should be prepared for freezing as soon as possible after harvest, so it is best not to try and handle too many at one time. Most vegetables have to be **blanched.** After washing, peeling, and cutting, the vegetables are plunged into boiling water for a specific length of time (1), then cooled rapidly in iced water (2). Blanching retards the activity of enzymes in the vegetables which would discolour them and spoil their flavour.

Blanching should be carried out in a large saucepan, and no more than 450 g (1 lb) of prepared vegetables should be blanched at one time, as it is important to bring the water back to boiling point within one minute. Blanching should be timed from the moment the water comes back to the boil. Blanching times for various vegetables are given below:

runner beans	1 minute
broccoli	3 minutes
Brussels sprouts	3 minutes
cauliflower	3 minutes
sweetcorn	5 minutes
peas	1 minute
root vegetables	3 minutes

A blanching basket or large sieve makes the transfer of vegetables from the pan to the iced water easy. The blanching water can be used for about six batches of vegetables. After blanching, the vegetables should be well drained and packed for freezing (3).

Fruit

Fruit for freezing should be just ripe and free from bruises. Not all fruits can be frozen raw as some tend to discolour. These must be frozen in a sugar syrup, e.g. peaches, apricots. Some fruits, e.g. apples, must be blanched to prevent discolouration due to oxidase enzymes.

Fruit can be prepared in three ways:

1 **In syrup** 225 g–450 g ($\frac{1}{2}$–1 lb) sugar to 575 ml (1 pint) water should be used, and the syrup allowed to go cold. 275 ml ($\frac{1}{2}$ pint) syrup should be used for every 450 g (1 lb) fruit. Headspace in the container should be allowed for expansion during freezing.

2 **Loose** Fruits such as strawberries and raspberries can be spread out on shallow trays and frozen open (without a cover) until solid, then packed into a container. In this way, they do not stick together.

3 **In dry sugar** 100 g (4 oz) caster sugar to 450 g (1 lb) fruit should be used. The sugar should be sprinkled over the fruit until it is well coated, then packed into containers.

Dairy produce

It is a waste of space to freeze butter or cheese as they can be stored satisfactorily in a refrigerator, unless you buy them in bulk. Double or whipping cream should be lightly whipped before freezing to prevent separation. It is possible to pipe cream into rosettes on paper and freeze them separately for use on cakes, cold sweets, meringues, etc.

Baked foods

Cakes should be frozen open until solid, then packed away in containers. This particularly applies to cakes that have been decorated with cream or butter icing.

Pastries can be frozen raw, and then cooked

when thawed. It is possible to prepare pies in this way. Batches of raw pastry, or portions of rubbed-in mixtures without liquid, are useful to have in the freezer. Frozen cooked pastry may become soggy when it is thawed. **Bread** should be well wrapped to prevent it from dehydrating. Sliced bread can be toasted while still frozen, but whole loaves should be thawed at room temperature.

Fish

Fish should be frozen as soon as possible after being caught. With the exception of fish sold locally from the port, fresh fish from a shop should not be frozen at home as it deteriorates rapidly and will not be completely fresh.

White fish freeze better than oily fish (see pp. 105–8). Small fish can be frozen whole (after gutting and cleaning), and larger fish can be filleted or cut into steaks.

Meat and poultry

It is often possible to buy whole sides of meat, cut into joints for the freezer. Meat and poultry should be frozen quickly, and it may be better to buy large joints already frozen as the domestic freezer may not freeze them quickly enough.

All joints and poultry should be closely wrapped with all the air removed to prevent freezer burn. Small joints, such as chops and cutlets, can be wrapped individually or separated with small sheets of greaseproof paper for easy separation.

Boned joints save room in the freezer.

Offal

All offal should be very fresh for freezing, and is best packed into tubs or cartons as it tends to be messy when thawing.

Cooked foods

Pre-cooked meals and dishes can be frozen successfully, but it is better not to include potatoes, pasta, or rice as these tend to lose their texture and flavour, unless they are covered with a sauce. It is also a waste of space to freeze these foods as they can be stored well in cupboards and are relatively quick to cook.

Fresh ingredients should be used, and food should be prepared quickly and hygienically, to prevent contamination by micro-organisms. The food should be cooked quickly and for the minimum time necessary, and should then be cooled rapidly before freezing.

Seasoning and the use of spices should be minimal, as their flavours tend to intensify during storage. They can be added afterwards.

Packed lunches

It is possible to freeze ready-made sandwiches and rolls or pies for packed lunches, which saves time during the week. Sandwich fillings must be suitable for freezing. Foods such as tomato, egg, or cucumber should not be included.

Storage times for frozen foods

Different foods will keep for different lengths of time in the freezer, and it is important not to exceed storage times. The following list gives storage times for a variety of frozen foods stored at −18°C (0°F):

vegetables	12 months
fruit	12 months
raw meat	
beef and lamb	12 months
mince and offal	2 months
pork	9 months
unsmoked bacon	6 weeks
sausages	6 weeks
smoked bacon	4 weeks
vacuum-packed rashers	3 months
bacon joints	3 months
poultry	
chicken	12 months
duck	6 months
fish	
white, filleted	8 months
oily	4 months
shellfish	2 months
whipped cream	2 months
hard cheese	3 months
cakes	
fatless	6 months
with fat	4 months

pastry	
cooked	6 months
uncooked	3 months
bread	3 months
soups, sauces	4 months
stews	2 months
meat loaves, pâtés	1 month
ice cream	3 months

Thawing frozen food

Some frozen foods, e.g. vegetables, beefburgers, fish, can be cooked from the frozen state. Foods such as cakes must be thawed in order to be able to cut them.

Some foods *must* be thawed completely before cooking, for safety reasons. This includes meat (especially pork) and poultry, shellfish, and cream. Such foods may harbour bacteria (especially salmonella – see pp. 132–4), and if insufficiently thawed, the temperature in the food will remain warm when it is cooked. This will encourage bacterial growth and reproduction, which may cause food poisoning if the cooked food is kept warm. This is more likely in large volumes of food, such as poultry. Large turkeys should be thawed for at least twenty-four hours in a cool place, and chickens for at least eight hours. There should be no signs of ice when the poultry has been thawed.

Most foods should be thawed at room temperature. This takes several hours for large packs, and must be allowed for when using foods from the freezer.

Once thawed, food *should not be refrozen* as this may lead to microbial growth and food poisoning.

Revision questions

1 What are the advantages of freezing?

2 Describe the types of freezer that are available, and list the advantages and disadvantages of each.

3 What are conservators, and why are they unsuitable for freezing food?

4 Where and how should a freezer be sited?

5 How are the running costs of a freezer affected?

6 In the event of a power failure or moving house, how should the food be handled to keep it in good condition?

7 What are the features of a good packaging material for frozen foods?

8 Name five containers or materials suitable for storing frozen foods.

9 How should a freezer be defrosted?

10 What are the basic rules for freezing foods successfully?

11 Name five foods that are unsuitable for freezing.

12 Why must some foods be blanched before freezing?

13 How should the following be prepared for freezing?
- **a** cakes
- **b** pastries
- **c** bread
- **d** fish
- **e** meat joints

14 How long can the following foods be stored in the freezer?
- **a** cheese
- **b** bread
- **c** meat
- **d** vegetables
- **e** sausages
- **f** whipped cream
- **g** stews

15 Why is it important that poultry, shellfish, and pork are completely thawed before use?

16 How should foods be thawed?

Use of left-over foods

As food is an expensive item in a household budget, it makes sense to use up left-over items of food from one meal to prepare another. It is possible to produce tasty and nutritious meals by adding other ingredients to left-over foods, and by careful preparation.

However, it is necessary to follow some important basic rules to ensure that the left-over food is safe to eat as well as appetizing and nutritious. Left-over foods such as meat and fish can harbour bacteria if stored incorrectly or not cooked thoroughly, and can be a major cause of food poisoning (see pp. 133–4). The re-heating of left-over foods is called **réchauffé** cookery.

Rules for preparing left-over foods

1. Use the left-over food preferably within twenty-four hours and certainly within forty-eight hours.
2. Cool the left-over food as quickly as possible, and store in a covered container in the refrigerator.
3. Reheating should be carried out quickly, so the food should be cut up finely or minced to facilitate heat penetration.
4. Do not recook the food, as this will toughen the protein and make it indigestible. Just reheat it.
5. Cook additional ingredients, e.g. vegetables, before adding them to the food.
6. Never reheat food more than once.
7. During the first cooking, moisture will be lost and should therefore be replaced when reheating, by the addition of a sauce, stock, or gravy.
8. Additional flavouring in the form of herbs, spices or seasoning should be included, as much of the original flavour may be lost in the first cooking.
9. Serve the reheated food immediately it is ready. Do not keep it warm as this will encourage bacterial growth.
10. Heat-sensitive nutrients, e.g. vitamin C, which will have been destroyed in the first cooking, should be replaced, e.g. by adding fruit or vegetables.

Methods of cooking used for réchauffé dishes

Some left-over foods, e.g. fish, some meat and poultry, should be protected from being recooked by one of the following means:

- coating in batter
- covering with a layer of sauce or potato
- coating with egg and breadcrumbs
- covering with pastry

Reheating methods

Frying Meat or fish rissoles and croquettes, fritters, burgers, bubble and squeak (fried vegetables).

Baking Meat pies, fish pies, pastry-covered dishes.

Sauces Fish in cheese sauce, curry sauce, savoury mince sauce.

Suggested uses for different foods

Fish Fish in a sauce, Russian fish pie (in flaky pastry), fish cakes, kedgeree, fish pasties, fish mousse.

Meat Curry, shepherd's pie, rissoles, burgers, fritters, croquettes, pasties, meat loaves.

Bread Bread pudding, queen of puddings, raspings, bread sauce.

Vegetables Bubble and squeak, omelettes, salads, pasties with cheese pastry, croquettes, scones (potato), potato cakes, toppings for shepherd's pie, etc.

Stale cake can be used in puddings or for trifle.

Revision questions

1 Why should left-over foods be used up within twenty-four hours and only be reheated once?

2 Give five rules for the preparation of réchauffé dishes.

3 Why is it important not to recook the left-over food?

4 Suggest a dish that can be made from each of the following:

a 225 g ($\frac{1}{2}$ lb) cooked lamb (cold)

b left-over apple purée

c stale bread

Raising agents

In order to make flour mixtures (e.g. cakes, bread, batters, pastries), rise and have a light, pleasant texture, a **gas** must be introduced before baking.

Gases **expand** when heated, and are capable of raising a mixture in the process. This is the principle upon which **raising agents** work. Raising agents are used to introduce a gas into a mixture.

As a mixture rises, the protein in it coagulates (sets), thus forming with the rest of the ingredients a firm structure containing a **network** of many small holes left by the expanded gas. It is important that the mixture is of the correct consistency, otherwise the gas will expand too vigorously and escape before the mixture has set.

The gases used for this purpose are:
carbon dioxide (CO_2)
air (a mixture of gases)
steam (water in a gaseous state)

Raising agents fall into two main categories:
mechanical raising agents
chemical raising agents

Mechanical raising agents

Air is incorporated into mixtures by various mechanical methods:

Sieving
When flour is sieved, air becomes trapped between its many fine particles.

Creaming
When fat and sugar are creamed together, air becomes trapped in the form of tiny bubbles, which make the mixture appear lighter.

Whisking
Egg white is capable of holding up to seven times its own volume of air, due to the ability of the protein **ovalbumin** to stretch. If beaten too much, the ovalbumin will overstretch and break, releasing air and becoming liquid. **Whole egg and sugar**, if whisked together, will trap a large volume of air. This is the main raising agent for sponges.

Folding and rolling
This is used for flaky pastry. Air is trapped between the layers, and is sealed in. During baking, it expands and the fat melts, leaving a space which is filled with steam and raises the pastry.

Rubbing-in
Some air is trapped as the fat is rubbed into the flour.

Chemical raising agents

Carbon dioxide is incorporated into mixtures by the use of:
- bicarbonate of soda alone
- bicarbonate of soda + an acid
- baking powder (contains bicarbonate of soda and acid)
- yeast (not strictly a chemical method as yeast is a living organism, but for convenience it is included here)

Bicarbonate of soda (an alkali)

Chemical formula: $2NaHCO_3$
When heated, the following reaction occurs:

$$2NaHCO_3 \xrightarrow{\text{heat}} \underset{\text{washing soda}}{Na_2CO_3} + \underset{\text{water}}{H_2O} + \underset{\text{gas}}{CO_2}$$

This results in the production of an unpleasant soda taste and a yellow discolouration of the mixture, both of which are undesirable for most mixtures. Bicarbonate of soda is therefore only used on its own for strong-flavoured mixtures such as gingerbread and parkin.

Bicarbonate of soda + an acid

To counteract the above reaction, a weak acid is usually used with bicarbonate of soda, to neutralize its effect on taste and colour, but not on its gas-producing properties. There are a variety of acids that can be used.

Cream of tartar (potassium hydrogen tartrate)
This is often used and it produces a residue which is colourless and almost tasteless, if used in the proportion:

2 parts acid to 1 part bicarbonate of soda

$$KHC_4H_4O_6 + NaHCO_3 \xrightarrow{\text{heat}} NaKC_4H_4O_6 + H_2O + CO_2$$

cream of tartar 2 parts; 1 part; sodium potassium tartrate

Tartaric acid
This is less often used, but is effective as it produces twenty-five times its own volume of gas if used in equal quantities with bicarbonate of soda. The resulting residue is slightly bitter.

Lactic acid (in sour milk)
This is produced by lactic acid bacteria, but its use is not very accurate as it is not possible to gauge the amount present in milk. It is often used in scone-making.

Citric acid (lemon juice) or *acetic acid* (vinegar)
These are not very accurate as it is difficult to gauge the strength of the acid.

Baking powder

This is produced commercially and usually consists of:

- bicarbonate of soda
- acid sodium pyrophosphate
- acid calcium phosphate
- starch, e.g. rice flour

Rice flour or other starch is added to absorb any moisture from the atmosphere, which would otherwise cause a reaction to occur, with the release of CO_2. This would render the baking powder ineffective.

The quality of baking powder is controlled by law, but it can be made at home. It can be added to plain flour and used instead of self-raising flour.

Self-raising flour is prepared from soft cake flour (see pp. 61–3) and a standard strength raising agent: it is useful for plain cake mixtures. It is *not* suitable for:

- scones – too weak on its own
- rich cakes – too much raising agent
- bread, pastries, biscuits – chemical raising agent not required

Yeast

Yeast is a microscopic living plant (see p. 136) which is found naturally on the skins of some fruits and in the air. It is produced commercially on a large scale for the brewing and baking industries.

Yeast can be obtained for baking in both dried and fresh forms.

Dried yeast consists of tiny pellets or fine granules of yeast, which are pale brown in colour. It will keep for a few months in a cool dry place, but will gradually lose its effectiveness. When added to a liquid, it should be allowed to dissolve for a few seconds before being stirred. Sugar should then be added. Dried yeast is more concentrated than fresh, being approximately twice the strength.

Fresh yeast is available from some bakers' shops. It should be pale brown in colour, with a slight characteristic smell and a crumbly texture. It is compacted into blocks. It must be stored in a cold place, well covered to prevent drying. It can be frozen for long-term storage in small pieces and used from frozen if dissolved in warm water. However, fresh yeast becomes less effective if frozen for more than three months.

Fresh yeast is more sensitive than dried yeast to the effects of osmosis (see p. 139), brought about by mixing it with sugar. It is therefore inadvisable to mix it directly with sugar as suggested in some recipes.

Yeast as a raising agent

When provided with the right conditions, yeast will produce CO_2 gas and alcohol during a series of chemical reactions known as **fermentation.** It is the CO_2 gas which is of importance to the baker.

The correct conditions for fermentation to take place are:

1 A source of food (sugar or flour).
2 The correct temperature. It works best between 25–29°C (77–84°F), and as the temperature increases, the yeast is gradually destroyed. At lower temperatures, yeast activity slows down, until at freezing point it is still alive, but dormant.
3 Moisture.
4 The presence of enzymes in the yeast, including:
Maltase: converts maltose to glucose.
Invertase: converts sucrose to fructose and glucose.
Zymase group: convert glucose and fructose to CO_2 and ethanol (alcohol).

Fermentation is a time-dependent process, and during bread making (see pp. 219–22), the dough is allowed to rise or **prove.** During this time, the yeast cells multiply by budding (see p. 136), and to do so, they require energy, which is obtained by fermentation of the carbohydrate in the dough. The CO_2 gas that results from this raises the dough.

During baking, the dough rises rapidly following the expansion of the CO_2 gas, and as the temperature rises, so the yeast activity increases, until at about 55°C (131°F) it is destroyed. The alcohol also produced is evaporated in the heat. At 70°C (158°F) the dough sets as the gluten (see pp. 66–7) coagulates.

Steam

Steam is produced during baking from the liquid present in a mixture, but it is a slower reaction than that of gas expansion. It is therefore only suitable as a raising agent for mixtures that contain a lot of liquid, e.g. batters, choux pastry, flaky pastry; and the oven temperature must be high in order to raise the liquid rapidly to boiling point.

Water vapour expands to 1,600 times its original volume, and is therefore an effective raising agent.

Stretching capacity of mixtures

In order for a mixture to rise, it must have the ability to **stretch** and hold its shape once risen.

In wheat flour, **gluten** is formed from the proteins present when water is added, and when kneaded, it becomes 'elastic' as a result. This gives flour mixtures the ability to stretch.

Different types of wheat flours produce different amounts of gluten when water is added, and are therefore only suitable for certain mixtures (see pp. 65–6).

Using raising agents

1 Store in a cool, dry place.
2 Use only amounts stated in recipes, e.g.:

Baking powder

Scones: 4–5 tsp to 450 g (1 lb) flour
Suet pastry: 4–5 tsp to 450 g (1 lb) flour
Cakes:
½ fat to flour 4 tsp to 450 g (1 lb) flour
¾ fat to flour 3 tsp to 450 g (1 lb) flour
= fat to flour 2 tsp to 450 g (1 lb) flour

NB tsp = *level* teaspoon.

Bicarbonate of soda

Scones: 1 tsp + 2 tsp cream of tartar to 225 g (½ lb) flour

3 Once the mixture is ready, bake immediately as the reaction will start as soon as moisture comes into contact with the raising agent.
4 Pre-heat the oven to ensure prompt expansion of the gas and setting of the mixture.
5 Sieve the raising agent with the flour to ensure even distribution.

Experiments with raising agents

Mechanical raising agents

1 Air trapped in flour:

Fill two equal-sized glasses with flour and knock them gently to allow settlement. Sieve the contents of one glass twice onto paper and carefully tip back into the glass. Observe the result.

It will be noted that surplus flour is left due to an increase in volume from the trapped air.

2 Air trapped by egg white:

Place one egg white into a grease-free measuring jug. Measure the volume of the egg white. Whisk it until it is foamy and standing in soft peaks. Measure the volume again.

It will be noted that the volume has increased substantially due to trapped air.

3 Air trapped by whole egg and sugar:

Repeat the above experiment using 25 g (1 oz) caster sugar and one egg, and whisk until thick and creamy.

4 Expansion of air:

Partially blow up a balloon and tie the end securely. Place the balloon in a warming cabinet, and leave for 10–15 minutes.

It will be noted that the balloon has enlarged due to the expansion of air inside it, from the heat.

Chemical raising agents

1 Acidity and alkalinity:

a Dissolve a little bicarbonate of soda in water and test with red litmus paper.
b Dissolve a little cream of tartar in the water and test with blue litmus paper.
c Dissolve two parts cream of tartar and one part bicarbonate of soda in water and test with indicator (pH) paper.
d Test some sour milk with pH indicator paper.

The reactions will indicate the following:

a Bicarbonate of soda is an alkali.
b Cream of tartar is an acid.
c Bicarbonate of soda and cream of tartar together neutralize each other.
d Sour milk contains acid.

2 Evolution of CO_2 gas:

a Place $\frac{1}{2}$ tsp bicarbonate of soda in a test tube, add hot water and note the length of the reaction.
b Repeat the above using cold water.
c Repeat using baking powder.
d Repeat using bicarbonate of soda with cream of tartar.

Compare results and relate to the reaction which occurs in the oven.

3 Prepare five batches of scones (for basic recipe see p. 206). Use:

a bicarbonate of soda alone
b self-raising flour
c 1 part bicarbonate of soda and 2 parts cream of tartar
d baking powder
e bicarbonate of soda and sour milk.

Compare the results for taste, appearance, texture, and size.

4 Gas production from yeast:

Dissolve 25 g (1 oz) fresh yeast in 150 ml ($\frac{1}{4}$ pint) tepid water. Divide between five test tubes and have five balloons ready.

Test tube 1: add $\frac{1}{4}$ tsp sugar, place balloon over top and stand in warm place.
Test tube 2: place balloon on top and stand in warm place.
Test tube 3: Add $\frac{1}{4}$ tsp salt, place balloon over top and stand in warm place.
Test tube 4: add $\frac{1}{4}$ tsp sugar, place balloon over top and stand in pan of boiling water.
Test tube 5: add $\frac{1}{4}$ tsp sugar, place balloon over top and stand in refrigerator.

Leave the tubes for fifteen minutes. Observe the results and compare gas production.

Expected results:

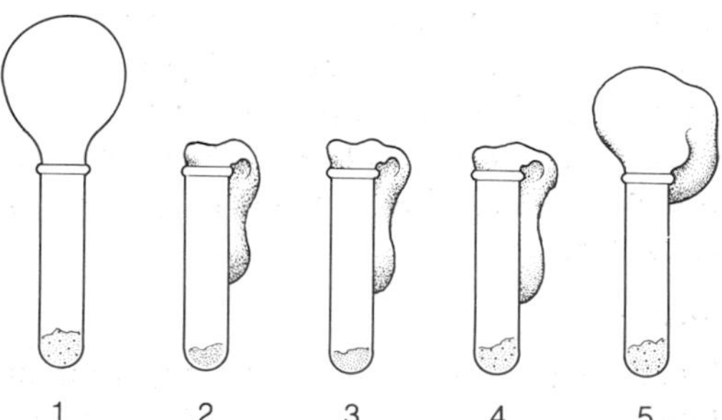

5 **Elasticity of gluten:**
Prepare gluten balls from 50 g (2 oz) of:
a strong plain flour
b ordinary plain flour
c self-raising flour
as described in experiment 1 on p. **70**. Note the size of the gluten balls. Place on a greased baking tray and bake at Gas 7, 220°C (425°F) for fifteen minutes. Observe changes in size and note the colour, structure, smell, and taste of the three samples.

6 **Use of steam:**
Prepare two identical Yorkshire pudding batters. Bake one in a cool oven, starting from cold, and the other in a hot oven which has been pre-heated. Compare your results.

Revision questions

1 What is a raising agent?
2 What is the principle behind the use of raising agents?
3 Why is the consistency of a flour mixture important for particular items?
4 What mechanical methods can be used for raising mixtures?
5 What are the gases used as raising agents?
6 What is bicarbonate of soda, and how does it work?
7 What is baking powder?
8 What is the best raising agent for each of the following?
a scones
b gingerbread
c bread
9 Why must chemical raising agents be sieved with the flour?
10 How should chemical raising agents be stored and used?
11 What is the importance of:
a temperature, moisture and sugar to yeast?
b creaming fat and sugar, sieving flour, beating eggs, and folding in flour in the preparation of a Victoria sandwich?
12 Why should choux pastry and flaky pastry be cooked at a high temperature?

Food presentation

In order for food to be appreciated and enjoyed, the **appetite** must be stimulated before a meal. When this occurs, digestive juices are produced so that the body is ready to receive the food when it is eaten.

Appetite stimulation is influenced by the body senses:
sight
smell
touch
taste
Food preparation should take account of these senses, and food should be attractive, well cooked, appetizing, and well presented.

The appearance of food

The first visual impressions of a meal are important factors in the success and enjoyment of the food. These visual impressions include not only the food itself, but also the way in which it is served and the surroundings in which it is eaten. Colour, design, and decoration are important considerations.

Colour

Food colours
There is a wide variety of natural colours in different foods, and a meal should contain as many variations as possible to make it attractive and interesting. The desire to eat is greatly influenced by colour, and if a food is coloured in an unusual way (e.g. if mashed potato is coloured blue), it will affect the enjoyment of it, even if the taste is the same.

The colours of food can be enhanced by the use of decorations and garnishes. Liquid food colourings should be used in moderation to improve a natural colour rather than hide it.

Colour of surroundings
When planning and serving a meal, it is important to take account of the surroundings in which the meal will be eaten. It is useful to select a colour theme for the table and decorations, and to use serving dishes, serviettes, and other items which blend in with this.

Design and decoration

The first visual impressions of a meal are important, and this applies to the surroundings as well as the food. The table should be neatly arranged, with the appropriate cutlery and decorations. The following points should be considered:

1 The table-cloth, serviettes, etc., should be well laundered and neatly pressed, if made of fabric.

2 The cutlery should be clean, and carefully arranged, so that each course is catered for. Cutlery for the first course should be placed farthest from the serving mat (knives usually on the right), and the cutlery for successive courses are placed in order, towards the mat. Cutlery for sweet courses should be placed above the serving mat.

3 Serviettes should be neatly folded, and placed either on a small plate next to the cutlery, or in a wine glass.

4 Centre table mats for hot serving dishes should be neatly arranged, with the cruet (salt, pepper, mustard, oil, vinegar), and any sauces or relishes that are to be served as accompaniments to the meal.

5 Glasses for wine and water should be placed to the top right hand side of the table mat. A water jug (with ice) should be provided to drink with the meal.

6 Serving spoons and tongs should be neatly arranged in the centre of the table.

7 Table decorations (e.g. flowers, candles, dried grasses, leaves) make the table look attractive, but they should not dominate the table, or be so large that they obscure the vision of the people around the table.

Garnishes and decorations for food

The finishing-off of a dish by garnishing (usually applies to savoury foods) or decoration (usually applies to sweet foods), adds to the visual impact and attractiveness of a meal. The following points should be remembered when garnishing or decorating:

1 Neatness and symmetry are important factors in the overall effect.
2 The garnish or decoration should add colour, flavour, and texture to the dish, and should be edible.
3 The garnish or decoration should enhance the overall effect of the dish, not dominate it.
4 It is usual to serve cooked garnishes with hot foods (but parsley and lemon are also served with hot foods).

Suitable garnishes and their preparation

Tomatoes

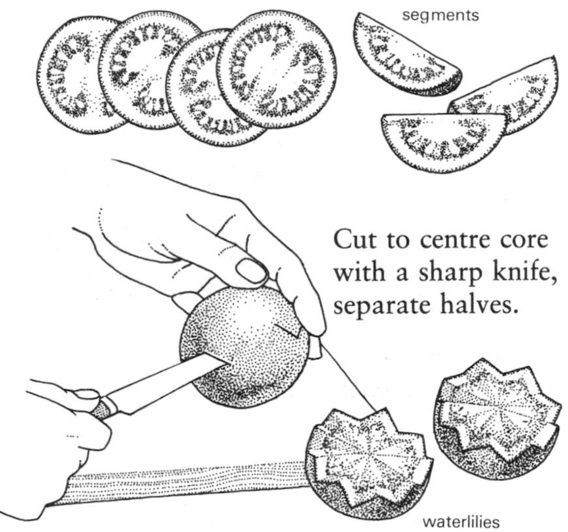

Cut to centre core with a sharp knife, separate halves.

Cucumber

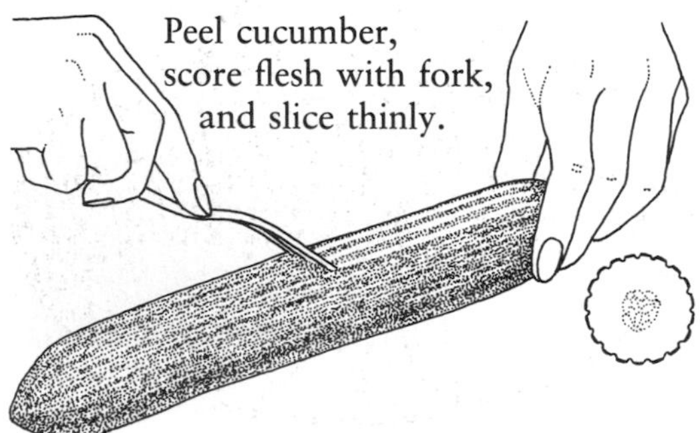

Peel cucumber, score flesh with fork, and slice thinly.

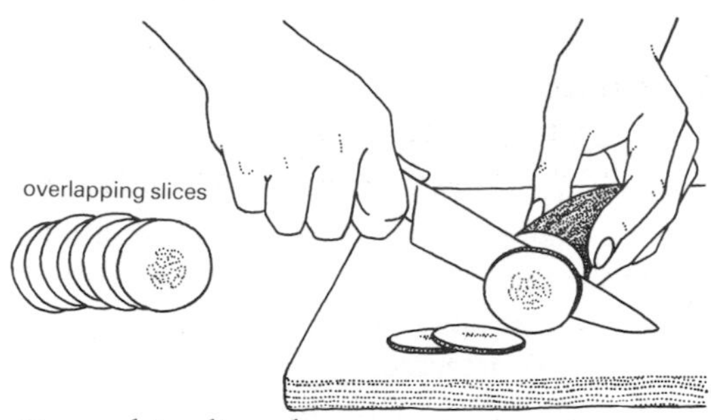

Cut a thin slice almost halfway and twist.

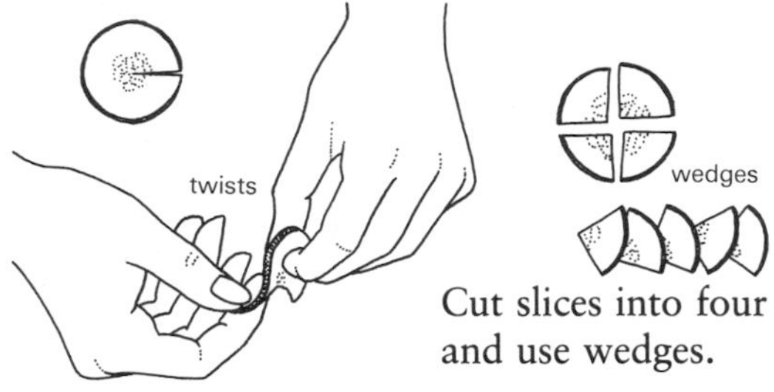

Cut slices into four and use wedges.

The skin can be removed or left on for extra colour.

Parsley

chopped, or in sprigs

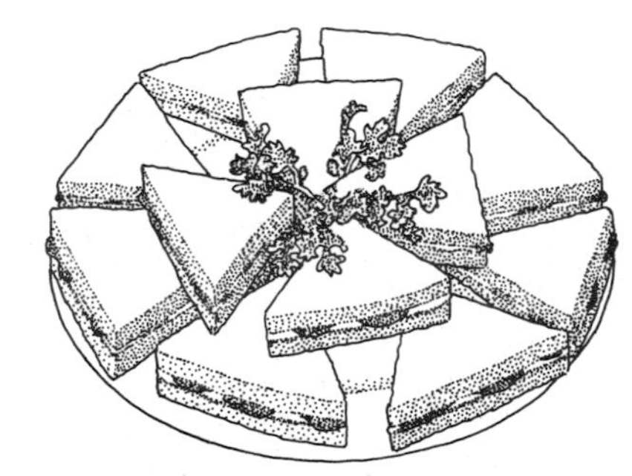

Watercress, cress

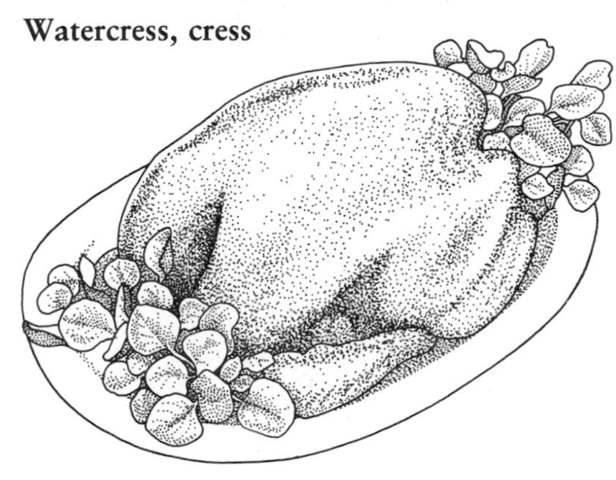

Lettuce

as whole leaves or shredded

Vegetables
diced, grated, strips, or balls
e.g. carrots, mushrooms, beetroot, peppers, celery

Radishes

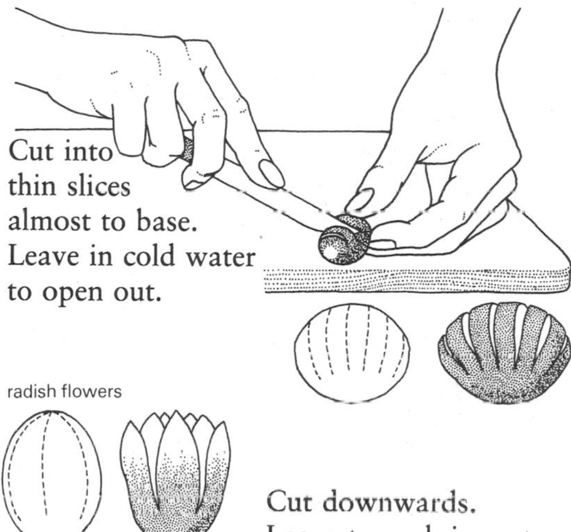

Olives, stuffed olives, gherkins, small onions

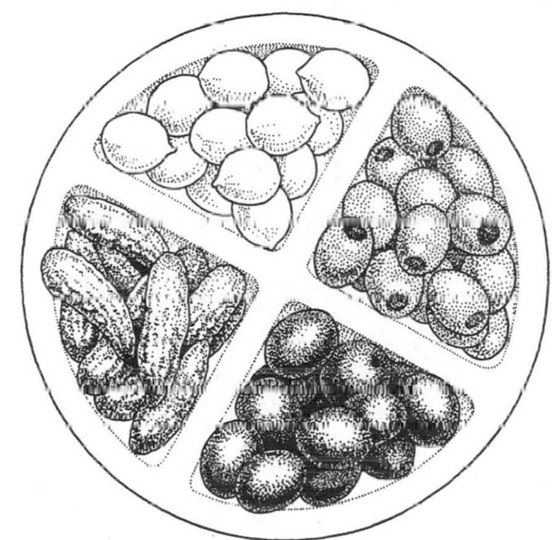

Boiled egg

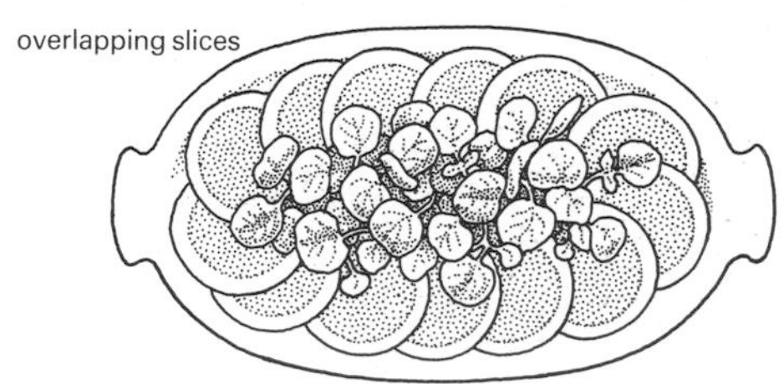

The white (chopped) and yolk (sieved) can also be used separately.

Bread
fried or toasted, and cut into various shapes

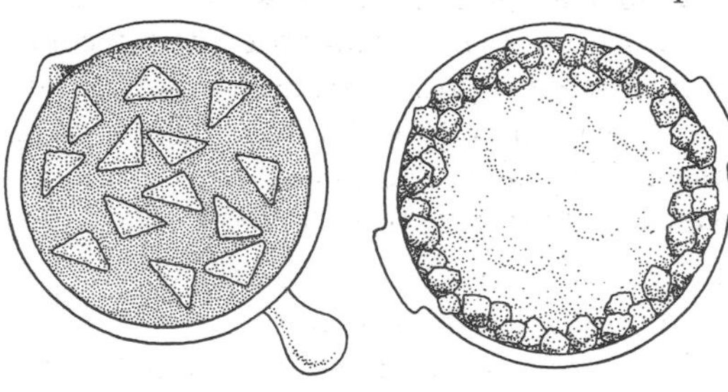

Lemon
Wedges and twists (see instructions for cutting cucumber)

Cheese
grated

Bacon
rashers rolled and grilled

Puff pastry
rolled into crescents and baked

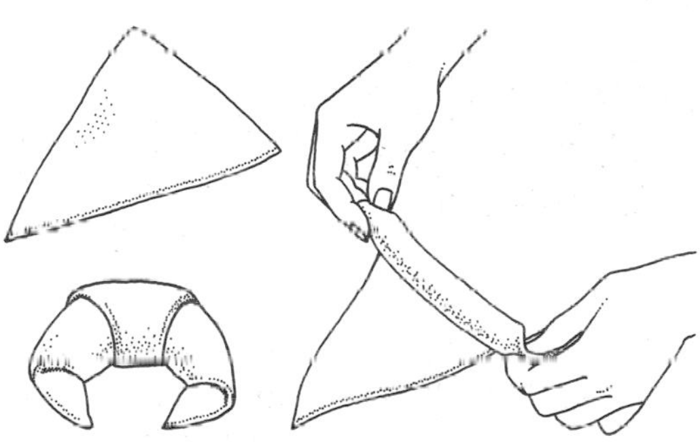

Roll downwards.
Shape into crescents and bake.

Meat frills

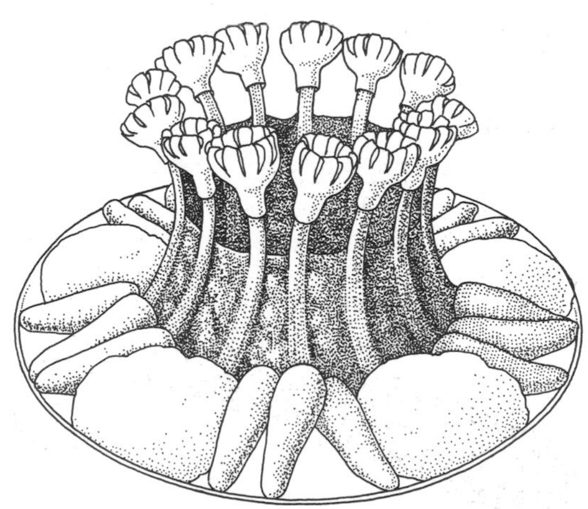

Suitable decorations

Chocolate
grated, flaked, caraque, melted and cut into shapes when cold

Icings
glacé, royal, butter, fondant, etc. (see pp. 204–5), piped in various designs

Marzipan
coloured and made into different shapes, e.g. fruit, flowers, animals, etc.

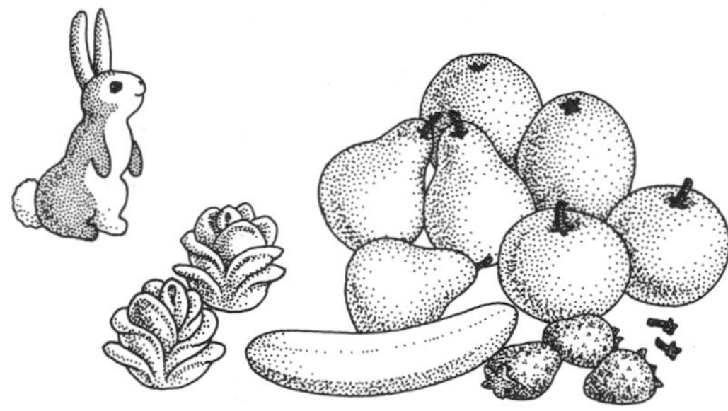

Fruits
fresh, dried, or crystallized

Jelly
chopped or as a glaze

Nuts
chopped, chopped and coloured, flaked, toasted, halved or whole

Sugar
dredged icing or caster sugar, sugar strands, coloured sugar crystals, crushed caramel

Cream
double or whipping cream, whipped and piped

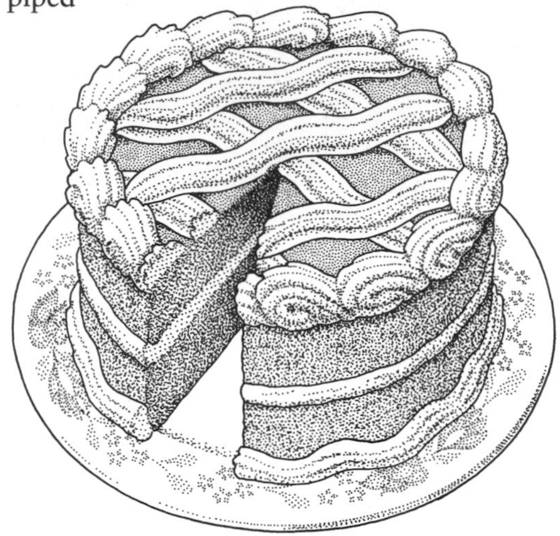

Serving dishes

The dishes in which food is served should be attractive, clean, and hot if they are to contain hot food. If food has splashed on the sides or the lid of the dish, it should be wiped over. Plates should also be clean and if necessary hot.

Sauces should be served in a jug or sauce boat with a saucer underneath, or poured neatly over the food.

Bread and bread rolls can be served in a wicker basket, butter in small 'pats' or curls in a cold dish, and cheese on a cheese board.

Butter pats and curls. Butter must be hard, and pats can be stored in cold water until serving.

Flavour

When food is prepared, its flavour should be checked and adjusted before serving.

Flavours should be subtle, not overpowering, as they can spoil the enjoyment of the meal. Particularly strong flavours such as garlic or curry spices should be carefully used, as guests may find them too strong.

Flavours can be combined to give contrast to the meal, and garnishes or decorations can add flavour to a finished dish as well as making it look attractive.

See pp. 119–20 for further details of the use of herbs and spices.

Texture

The texture of food is an important factor in the enjoyment of a meal, and textures should be varied to avoid monotony, e.g. a meat casserole should have crisp vegetables as accompaniments, with a crunchy sweet to follow.

Heavy, 'stodgy' foods, such as suet puddings, should be served in moderation as they can be rather indigestible in large amounts.

Revision questions

1. How is the appetite affected by the appearance of food?
2. What preparations should be made for the serving of a meal?
3. What points should be remembered when garnishing or decorating food?
4. Give examples of garnishes and decorations for savoury and sweet foods.
5. How should serving dishes and plates be prepared for serving a meal?
6. Why is it important to vary the texture and flavour of a meal?
7. Give an example of a well-balanced meal in respect of colour, flavour, and texture.

Food preparation under examination conditions

Under examination conditions, practical food preparation usually involves carrying out a specific assignment. Within this context, the aim is for a candidate to show:

1. Knowledge and confidence in the use and preparation of different foods for a variety of occasions.
2. Skilful preparation of food using different methods of cooking.
3. Knowledge of the nutritional value of foods and the dietary requirements of different people.
4. Knowledge of how to preserve the nutritional value of food.
5. Awareness of cost and economy and the best use of food for various occasions.
6. Knowledge of and confidence in the use of as many different pieces of kitchen equipment as possible.
7. Hygienic practices in the handling and preparation of food.
8. Ability to present meals of suitable portions in appetizing and attractive ways.

Types of assignment

Some examples of specific practical assignments are given on pp. 191–2, but the types can be grouped under these headings:

Individual requirements

e.g.	convalescent	pregnant woman
	vegetarian	manual worker
	child	anaemic adolescent

Special occasion

e.g.	Christmas	anniversary buffet
	teenage party	picnic
	Guy Fawkes night	child's birthday
	wedding reception	dinner party

Specific foods

e.g. alternatives to meat
convenience foods
economical meals
types of pastry or cake
foods made using a mixer or blender

Choice of practical work

The choice of practical work should be relevant to the assignment and should demonstrate the candidate's abilities. Candidates are often asked to justify their choice of work, and the reasons given should be applicable to the particular situation being catered for.

Occasion	Reasons for choice, in order of priority
Convalescent meal	Nutritional considerations. Portion size in relation to appetite. Stimulating poor appetite. Digestibility and ease of eating meal.
Wedding buffet	Attractiveness, colour, and variety of food. Catering for different tastes. Ease of eating and serving.
Child's lunch	Nutritional considerations and appeal to child. Portion size in relation to age and appetite. Ease of eating.
Anniversary meal	Attractiveness, colour, texture, and complementary flavours. Catering for different tastes. Nutritional balance.
Packed lunch	Nutritional value. Ease of packing to avoid damage to food. Satiety value. Ease of eating with minimum of cutlery.

Methods of cooking

The use of a variety of cooking methods will demonstrate the candidate's knowledge of the use of the cooker and the reactions of different foods under various conditions, and will also add variety to the finished result.

Skills

The use of a variety of skills will demonstrate the candidate's abilities and confidence. These skills include:

pastry making
cake making
meat jointing and preparation
food decoration
soufflé making
yeast cookery
fish preparation
sauce making
garnishing
salad and vegetable preparation
preparation of beverages

Skill in food presentation is also important (see pp. 182–6).

Sensible use of food and economy

Awareness of the cost of food and how to economize are important considerations in food preparation. Skilful cookery does not necessarily require the use of the most expensive foods.

This can be demonstrated by e.g.:

1 Using cheaper cuts of meat, e.g. breast of lamb, belly of pork.
2 Economizing on fuel, e.g. batch baking, or using only the oven or only the top of the cooker.
3 Pressure cooking.
4 Using yogurt instead of cream if possible.
5 Keeping wastage to a minimum.
6 Using up scraps of pastry, etc.

Preparation of food

The following are important whatever the assignment:

1 Tidy, methodical working.
2 Regular clearing of work surface.
3 A high standard of personal hygiene.
4 Hygienic handling of food.
5 Accuracy in weighing and measuring food.
6 Efficiency in the use of time, equipment, etc.
7 Correct use of tools and cooking method.

Plan of work

A timetable or time plan of the work to be carried out during a practical examination is very important as it shows the ability of a candidate to prepare food in a logical order, using time efficiently and fully. Different examination boards have different requirements as to how this should be set out, and the amount of detail required.

An example of a practical assignment, similar to those given in examinations, is set out below. It is intended only as a guide to the requirements of a practical examination.

Sample assignment

With the dietary goals (eat less fat, less sugar, and more fibre) in mind, plan a day's meals for a family of two adults and two school-age children. All four have a packed lunch and eat a main meal in the evening.

When giving reasons for your choice, explain how the meals chosen meet the requirements of the three dietary goals above.

Prepare, cook, and serve the two-course evening meal, including a fresh vegetable or salad. Time allowed for practical: 1 hour 10 minutes.

Chosen meals

Breakfast:
- fresh fruit salad (unsweetened)
- wholemeal toast
  - low fat spread
  - yeast extract or marmalade
- milk or tea to drink

Packed lunch:
- wholemeal bread rolls filled with cottage cheese, tomato, and pickle
- fruit yogurt
- oat crunch bar
- piece of fruit, e.g. satsuma
- fruit juice to drink

Evening meal:
- wholemeal pasta savoury
- coleslaw salad with yogurt dressing
- fresh stawberry sponge flan
- lemonade to drink (home-made)

Reasons for choice

Breakfast

1 The meal is light, as it is summer, but contains a variety of colour, texture, and flavour.
2 The fruits chosen would be in season, and contain vitamin C as well as dietary fibre.
3 Wholemeal toast contains a relatively high amount of fibre in the bran.
4 Low fat spread instead of butter or margarine reduces the fat intake.
5 A reduced-sugar jam or marmalade could be chosen to cut down on sugar intake.
6 Semi-skimmed or skimmed milk could be chosen to reduce fat intake.
7 The fruit salad could be prepared in advance and chilled, to save time in the morning.

Packed lunch

1 Wholemeal rolls contain a relatively high proportion of fibre, and are easy to pack and eat. The fillings are moist, and cottage cheese has a low fat content.
2 Fruit yogurt could be prepared at home by using natural, unsweetened yogurt and adding fruit, thereby reducing sugar and fat intake.
3 Oat crunch bar is filling, and has a good fibre content. It is easy to pack and eat.
4 Fresh fruit provides fibre and vitamin C and is refreshing.
5 Fruit juice can be kept chilled in a vacuum flask, and is refreshing.

Evening meal

1 **Wholemeal pasta savoury:** Wholemeal pasta has a high fibre and low fat content. Skimmed milk and reduced-fat cheese could be used to lower fat content. Vegetables used increase fibre intake.
2 **Coleslaw salad and yogurt dressing:** Ingredients provide vitamin C and fibre. Dressing has a low fat content, compared to salad cream or mayonnaise.
3 **Sponge flan:** Flan has low fat content. Strawberries provide vitamin C and some fibre, and are relatively inexpensive when in season. Wheatmeal flour could be used to increase fibre intake.

4 **Lemonade drink:** Lemons provide vitamin C. Liquid sweetener is used to reduce sugar intake.

Quantities of ingredients for meal

Wholemeal pasta savoury: 225 g (8 oz) wholemeal pasta shells or other shapes, 1 med. onion (finely chopped), 100 g (4 oz) mushrooms (sliced), 2 sticks celery (chopped into small pieces), 40 g ($1\frac{1}{2}$ oz) margarine, 40 g ($1\frac{1}{2}$ oz) flour, 425 ml ($\frac{3}{4}$ pint) skimmed milk, 100 g (4 oz) cheddar cheese (grated), salt and pepper.

Coleslaw salad: 1 med. carrot, $\frac{1}{4}$ white cabbage, 1 small onion, optional ingredients: red or green pepper, chopped apple, peanuts, celery, cucumber, tomato, spring onion, sweetcorn.

Yogurt dressing: small carton low fat natural yogurt, 1 tsp honey (clear), $\frac{1}{4}$ tsp mustard powder, salt and pepper, 1 tbsp finely chopped parsley or fresh mixed herbs, juice of $\frac{1}{2}$ lemon.

Strawberry sponge flan: 50 g (2 oz) wheatmeal flour (plain), 50 g (2 oz) caster sugar, 2 eggs (size 3), 100–175 g (4–6 oz) fresh strawberries, 1 rounded tsp arrowroot, 150 ml ($\frac{1}{4}$ pint) wter.

Fresh lemonade: 2 lemons, 575 ml (1 pint) ice-cold water, liquid sweetener to taste.

Time allowed: 1 hour 10 minutes

Time plan	Order of work
9.30	Light oven: Gas 6, 200°C (400°F) Sponge flan: whisk eggs and sugar until very thick and mixture leaves a trail for 5 seconds. Sieve flour twice and fold in very gently with a metal spoon.
9.40	Pour mixture carefully into greased and lined flan tin. Bake in centre of oven for 15–20 mins. until well risen and spongy to touch.
9.43	Clear up.
9.50	Thoroughly mix ingredients for yogurt dressing. Prepare salad ingredients, chopping them finely and evenly. Dip apple (if used) in lemon juice to prevent oxidation. Combine with dressing, leave to chill.
9.57	Check sponge flan, and remove from oven. Leave for 1 minute before removing from tin.
10.00	Clear up.
10.05	Prepare lemon drink: grate lemon rind finely, squeeze juice. Combine with liquid sweetener and water, chill.
10.10	Wholemeal pasta savoury: boil water and cook pasta for 15–20 mins, until tender. Melt margarine, and gently cook mushrooms, onion and celery until softened. Add flour and cook for 1 minute. Remove from heat, and gradually stir in milk. Reheat, stirring all the time, until boiled and thickened. Stir in $\frac{3}{4}$ of the grated cheese, and season. Put lid on saucepan and leave to one side.
10.20	Fill sponge flan with strawberries, saving 4 of them for the glaze. Sieve or liquidize the 4 strawberries, and mix with the water. Blend with the arrowroot, and heat, stirring constantly until the mixture boils and thickens. Pour carefully over fruit, leave to set.
10.28	Prepare garnishes for pasta savoury.
10.32	Drain pasta, mix with sauce. Pour into heat-proof dish and sprinkle rest of cheese on top. Grill until golden brown, and garnish.
10.37	Serve meal.
10.40	Clear up.

Questions and activities

1 Every year, many people become ill due to food poisoning. Write an account of how you would explain the causes, effects, and prevention of food poisoning to a group of young householders.

2 You have been asked to prepare a midday meal for a ten-year-old child, who is recovering from measles, and has just begun to enjoy a little food again. Suggest a suitable meal, and then list the priorities you would need to consider, under the following headings:
   a presentation of the food
   b hygienic preparation of the food
   c nutritive value of the food
   How could you keep the child amused while in bed?
   How can children be protected against illnesses such as measles?

3 Make a study of the range of cookers available, and using the information that you obtain, suggest suitable cookers for the following situations:
   a a small, single-person bedsitter, with electric power points (13 amp only)
   b a restaurant, selling take-away food such as pies, soup, pasties, as well as sit-down meals, 24 hours a day
   c a caravan, which has the use of calor gas and electricity
   d a large family, living in an area with no gas, but with access to solid fuel, such as logs and coal
   Present your information with detailed reasons for choice, illustrations, etc.

4 You are shortly going away on holiday, and will be travelling by coach and ferry. You will need to take a packed meal to eat on route, and will be carrying your luggage in a rucksack.
   a Make a plan of how you would organize your food, personal belongings, and items required for the journey.
   b What precautions should you take to ensure the security and safety of your home while you are away?
   c If travelling abroad, what precautions might it be necessary to take to prevent illness?

5 Read the following statements, and say in each case whether they are true or false, giving a detailed reason for your answer:
   a Bicarbonate of soda used alone to raise a scone mixture will result in a 'soapy' flavoured, yellow scone.
   b Yeast will multiply and give off CO_2 gas if mixed with warm water and salt.
   c Strong plain flour is the most suitable flour for breadmaking.
   d A Yorkshire pudding mixture will rise quickly in a cool oven.
   e Overwhisked egg white will collapse.

6 The presentation of food has an important influence on its enjoyment.
   a How do food manufacturers try to attract people to buy their products?
   b Make a study of the ways in which traditional dishes from various countries are presented, e.g. the garnishes used, accompaniments.
   c How do our senses work together to enhance the enjoyment of food? Suggest how you could investigate the way the senses work together, and prepare a short experiment to show this. What are your conclusions?

Practical assignments

1 People who live in outlying areas, or who are unable to visit shops very often to buy food and household goods, need to have a good store of food in their home. Investigate the variety of foods that can be stored long-term, and the importance of correct storage conditions. Why are sell-by dates important? From your investigations, prepare, cook, and serve a

variety of dishes or a meal, incorporating foods that could be stored long-term.

2 In Britain, people eat fewer different types of fish than in countries such as Japan and France, and tend to prepare and cook it in limited ways. Investigate the reasons for the increase in the price of fish over the past few years.

Suggest a variety of interesting ways of preparing and cooking two varieties of white, oily, and shellfish, and prepare and serve two of these.

3 You are going to entertain a friend who does not particularly like cooking and has little free time, and who therefore tends to eat a very limited variety of food. Plan an interesting meal to give your friend some ideas on how to cook simple things that do not take long to prepare. Prepare the meal, and say how you would serve it (drink, table arrangement, etc.).

4 Prepare, cook, and serve an interesting selection (e.g. three items) of food that could be used as part of a demonstration to encourage people to follow the dietary goals recommended by nutritionists. Illustrate your work by preparing a display of posters/pictures/written explanations about the importance of healthy eating.

5 Barbeques and eating outdoors are popular today. Make a plan of suitable foods that you would serve at a barbeque, remembering that you would need to have alternative arrangements if the weather should be unsuitable for cooking outside.

Prepare and cook a selection of the items in your plan.

What safety precautions should be taken at a barbeque?

What hygiene precautions should be taken, bearing in mind that most barbeques take place outside in the summer months?

6 Investigate a variety of examples of conduction and insulation in the home, and present your findings in the form of a display. Prepare and cook a selection of items which demonstrate a variety of methods of heat transfer in their preparation.

Energy is an expensive resource. In your practical session, show how heat energy and fuel can be saved.

7 When preparing food and giving meals to babies and young children, what are the important points to remember concerning hygiene, safety, and social training?

What equipment is available to assist parents with preparing and serving food to ensure safety and peaceful mealtimes?

8 **a** Investigate the hygiene precautions that food shops are required to take by law for the safety of their customers.

b How have the following ensured that food is safer to eat?

plastics
sterilization

c What is food adulteration? Investigate examples of this, and find out how the consumer is protected against it.

4/Basic recipes

Using recipes

A basic or foundation recipe is one that has a set of main ingredients used in particular proportions, which are prepared in a certain way. It can be used for more than one dish by varying or adding other ingredients or flavours.

This chapter deals with the main basic recipes on which most dishes are based. It is intended for use as a guide, and other recipe books should be referred to for the many variations that are possible. The proportions of ingredients in each case are tabulated with an explanation of the method of preparation afterwards.

For any recipe, it is important to bear the following points in mind:

1 Ingredients (dry and liquid) must be accurately weighed and measured to achieve the right results.
2 The method of preparation should be carefully followed.
3 Oven temperatures and shelf position for baking recommended by the recipe should be followed.

Measurements

Conversion charts for solid and liquid measurements are given on p. 283.

Both metric and imperial weights and liquid measures are given, and it should be noted that for ease of measurement 25 grammes are taken as being equivalent to 1 ounce. This may result in slightly smaller mixtures in some cases as 25 g is in fact slightly less than 1 ounce (1 oz = 28·35 g).

As the conversion from imperial to metric measurement is not exact, it is important never to mix metric and imperial weights when cooking.

Where eggs are used, the quantities given refer to size 3 eggs.

Abbreviations used:

tsp = teaspoon (5 ml)
dsp = dessertspoon (10 ml)
tbsp = tablespoon (20 ml)

NB All spoon measurements are level.

Many traditional recipes for items such as cakes, pastries, and biscuits, use relatively high proportions of saturated fats and sugar, and frequent consumption of them could be detrimental to health (see pp. 7–10).

It is possible in some cases to adapt a recipe by reducing, omitting, or substituting one ingredient for another, to bring the finished item more in line with dietary goals. In some of the following recipes, suggestions for adapting the recipe are given in a footnote to the traditional recipe.

It should be emphasized that such adaptations may result in a slightly different result e.g. the use of wholemeal flour in a cake may reduce its finished volume.

It should also be remembered that although a particular item may contain a large proportion of fat or sugar in the ingredients, it is the amount and frequency with which it is eaten that affects the daily intake of fat and sugar.

Cakes

Choice and functions of ingredients

Flour

Weak or **soft** flour (see pp. 65–7) is best for cakes as it contains a relatively small amount of gluten-forming proteins. When cakes are baked, the gluten coagulates. This helps to form the structure of the cake, and the lower protein content of weak flours gives the fine, even texture typical of most cakes.
Self-raising flour can be used for plain cakes with the proportion of fat to flour being no more than half. For richer cakes, the amount of baking powder in self-raising flour is too high, so **plain** flour with various amounts of baking powder should be used.

80% extraction flour (see pp. 65–7) can be used, and provides extra fibre, nutrients, colour and flavour. It is possible to buy self-raising flour of this extraction, although cakes made with it may have slightly less volume than those made with white flour, due to the extra fibre.

The starch in flour becomes trapped within the framework produced by the expansion of gas bubbles and gluten during baking, and contributes towards the lightness of the cake.

Fat

Fats are added to cake mixtures:

1 To trap air with sugar during creaming (see p. 199), so that the cake will rise.

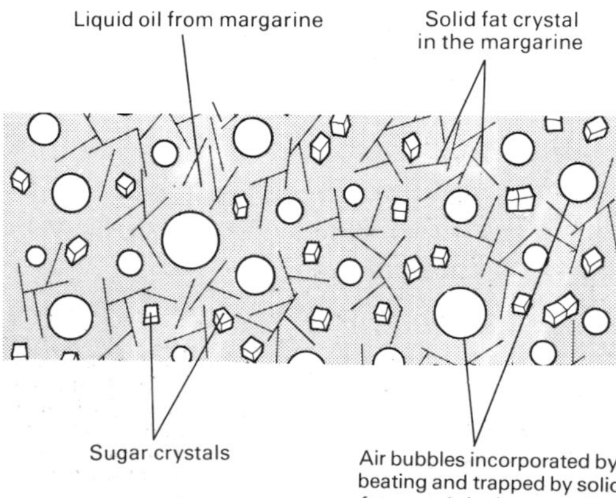

Action of fat and sugar creamed together.

2 To provide 'shortness' to the cake mixture. As fat is insoluble in water, it prevents gluten strands from adhering to each other, thus shortening them. If this did not happen, the baked mixture would be solid and tough due to the gluten strands. The shortening action of the fat results in a tender cake.
3 To add colour and flavour to the mixture.

Margarine is economical and provides colour and flavour. 'Soft' margarine (see pp. 71–4) is specially produced for creaming, but is not very suitable for rubbed-in mixtures as it is too oily.
Butter provides a very good flavour and colour to the mixture. For economy, it can be mixed with margarine or another fat.
White cooking fats (vegetable) do not contribute towards the flavour or colour of the cake mixture, but can be creamed with sugar quite well. They can therefore be used in strongly flavoured mixtures.
Lard is unsuitable for most cake mixtures as it does not cream well and has a distinctive flavour which is not very good for cakes.
Oil can be used for some mixtures where there is an additional raising agent, but it is not possible to trap air during creaming if oil alone is used.

Sugar

Sugar is added to cake mixtures for the following reasons:

1 To add flavour.
2 To help trap air with fat during creaming so that the cake rises.
3 To contribute towards the texture of the cake by dissolving into a syrup and softening the gluten in flour, during baking. If too much sugar is added, the gluten is softened too much and the structure of the cake collapses during baking.
4 To contribute towards the colour of the cake by caramelizing on exposure to the dry heat of the oven (the crust).

Caster sugar is most suitable as it has small crystals which dissolve easily and give a smooth texture to the cake.
Granulated sugar has coarser crystals and therefore has to be creamed more thoroughly

to break these down. It can be used for recipes where the sugar is melted with the fat first.

Soft brown sugar can be used for dark coloured or fruit cakes, and contributes more flavour.

Syrup or treacle can be used with sugar and contribute towards the texture and moistness of the cake.

Eggs

Eggs are added to most cake mixtures for the following reasons:

1 To trap air during whisking with sugar in sponges or beating into creamed mixtures. Eggs are able to hold large volumes of air (see p. 178) which is why they are useful in this respect.
2 To help to set the cake once it has risen during baking, by coagulation of the protein.
3 To add colour and nutritional value to the cake.
4 To **emulsify** the fat in creamed mixtures; the presence of lecithin in egg yolk is responsible for this (see pp. 92 and 226).

When added to creamed mixtures, eggs should be at room temperature, because if they are too cold, they may cause the mixture to 'curdle'. This means that the fat separates from the sugar and eggs when the eggs are added.

Eggs should be fresh. They should be opened into a separate bowl first, to avoid the possibility of spoiling the cake mixture by adding a bad egg to it.

Dry ingredients

Dry ingredients apart from flour, e.g. baking powder, spices, salt, etc., should be sieved into the cake mixture with the flour to ensure even distribution.

Liquid

Liquids apart from egg, e.g. milk, lemon juice, or water, help to raise the cake mixture by the production of steam during baking, but they may also toughen the gluten (see p. 14) and therefore produce a harder texture in the cake.

Flavourings

Flavourings, such as citrus fruit rind, or dried fruit, help to contribute towards the keeping qualities of a cake, by the presence of oil in the former and moisture in the latter.

Dried fruits should be well washed and dried, and large pieces should be chopped to a uniform size. The fruit can be coated with some of the flour to keep the pieces separate and to help prevent it sinking in the mixture.

Flavourings such as coffee powder should be dissolved in water first, to prevent a speckled appearance in the cake.

Addition of egg to creamed fat and sugar.

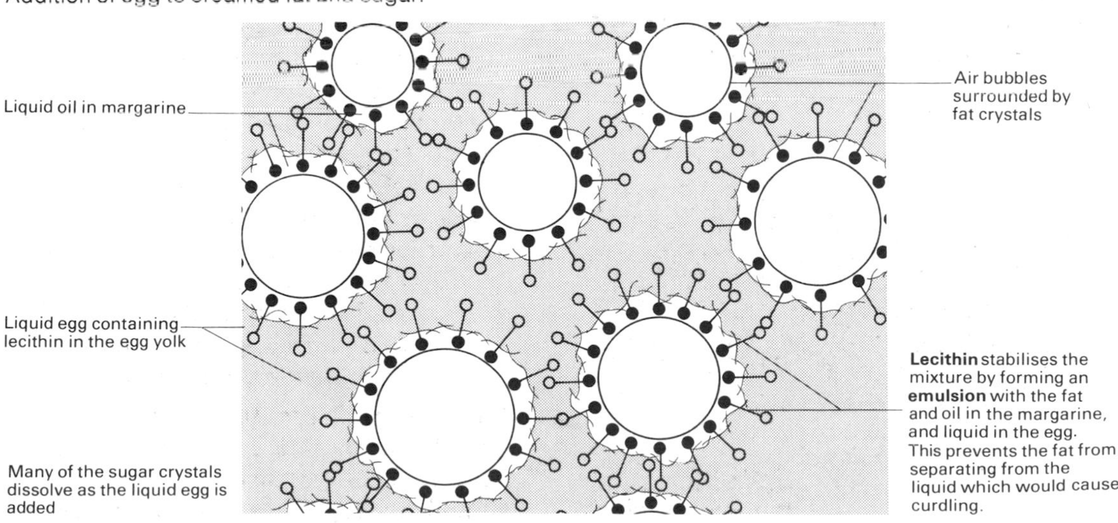

Preparing cakes for baking

Before placing a cake mixture in the appropriate cake tin for baking, the tin should be greased to prevent the cake from sticking. Oil or fresh melted pure fat, such as white vegetable fat, should be used, and applied evenly with a brush in a thin layer on all surfaces with which the cake will come into contact.

It may be necessary to line cake tins for large plain and fruit cakes. Greaseproof paper should be used and must be cut to the right size, neatly arranged in the tin, and greased as well as the tin. Alternatively, non-stick tins can be used.

Small sponge cakes which are cooked in fancy tins should be cooked in a tin that has been greased then dusted with flour or flour and sugar, as it may be difficult to line them.

Before baking, the oven should be pre-heated to the correct temperature, to ensure that the cake will start to rise as soon as it is placed inside.

To line a Swiss roll tin:

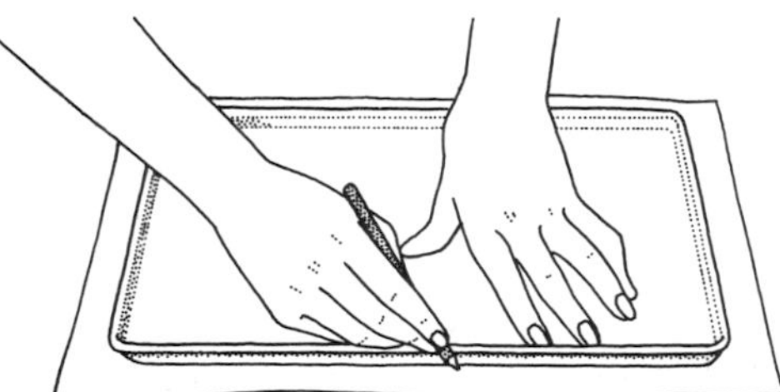

1 Grease the tin. Place it on a sheet of greaseproof paper and draw a pencil line round the base of the tin.

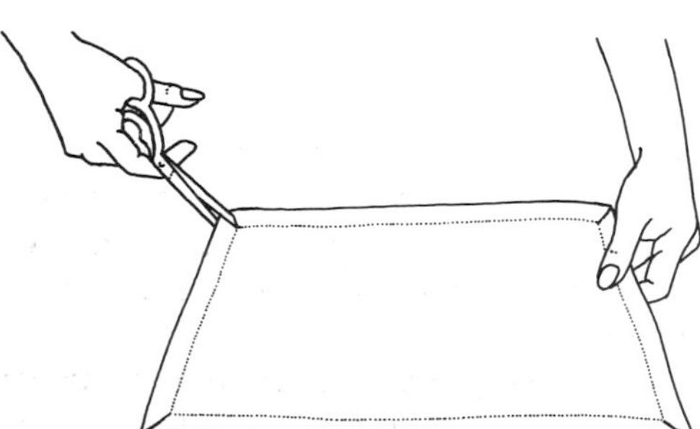

2 Cut the paper about 2 cm (¾″) away from the pencil line. At the corners, make diagonal cuts into the pencil line. Place the paper in the tin and grease.

To line a cake tin (square or round):

1 Grease the tin. Cut out two pieces of greaseproof paper to fit the base of the tin. Place one piece in the base.

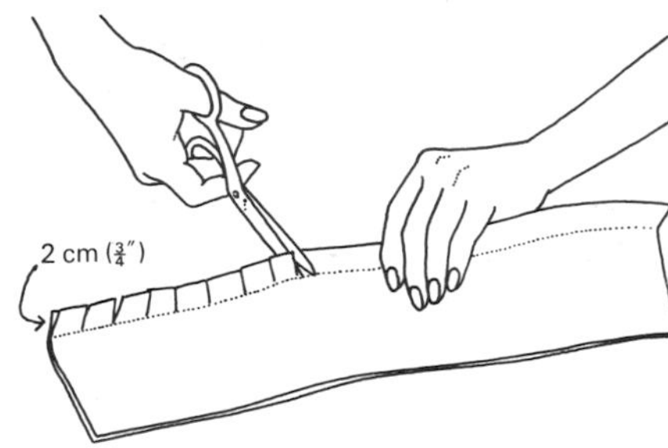

2 Cut out a strip of greaseproof paper (double thickness) to fit round the sides of the tin, plus 5 cm (2″) extra. Turn up about 2 cm (¾″) at the folded edge. Snip at 1 cm intervals.

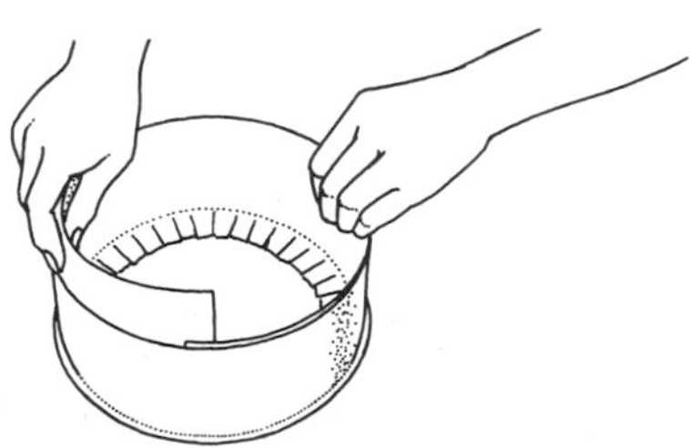

3 Place the paper around the sides of the tin with the folded edge at the bottom. Grease.

4 Place the other base in the tin and grease.

Rubbed-in cakes

225 g (8 oz) SR flour[1]	*Large cakes*	*Small cakes*
100 g (4 oz) fat[2]	Gas 4, 180°C (350°F)	Gas 5, 190°C (375°F)
100 g (4 oz) sugar[3]	for 1 hour, then:	12–15 minutes
1 egg	Gas 2, 150°C (300°F)	
70 ml (2½ fl oz) milk[4].	for ½ hour	

Uses and variations	Oven temperature and cooking time
Small cakes (12–16) **Lemon:** add rind and juice of 1 lemon. No milk. Sprinkle with sugar. **Polka dot:** add 100 g (4 oz) chocolate chips. **Coconut:** add 50 g (2 oz) dessicated coconut. **Chocolate:** add 25 g (1 oz) cocoa, omit 25 g (1 oz) of the flour. **Butterfly cakes:**use plain mixture. Cut out circle from top, fill with buttercream and arrange the 2 halves of the circle as wings on top.	Gas 4, 180°C (350°F) 15–20 minutes middle shelf of oven
Jam buns: add the rind of half a lemon. Use 1 tbsp milk. Mix to a dough, roll into 12 balls. Make a hole in the top of each, fill with jam, brush with water and sugar before baking. **Rock cakes:** add 100 g (4 oz) dried fruit and ¼ tsp mixed spice. Mix to a dry dough. Place in 12 rocky piles on baking sheet.	Gas 5, 190°C (375°F) 15–20 minutes
Large cakes **Coffee:** add 3 tsp coffee powder (dissolved in hot water). Add 50 g (2 oz) chopped nuts. **Fruit:** add 200 g (8 oz) dried fruit, 1 tsp mixed spice, and 1 tbsp marmalade or syrup. **Chocolate:** as for small cakes, plus 1 tbsp syrup.	15 cm (6″) round tin *or* 20 × 10 cm (8 × 4″) shallow tin Gas 4, 180°C (350°F) for 1 hour, then Gas 2, 150°C (300°F) for ½ hour

Method

1. Sieve the flour and baking powder (and spice, cocoa, etc., if used), to ensure even distribution and lightness, by trapping air.
2. Cut up the fat and rub it into the flour with the fingertips, to coat the flour particles with a layer of fat, and thus produce a crumbly texture. The fingertips should be used as they are the coolest part of the hand and prevent the fat melting.
3. Rub in until the mixture resembles breadcrumbs, and there are no large lumps of fat left. Do not over-rub, as the fat will melt and the cake will have a close, heavy texture.
4. Stir in the sugar and other dry ingredients.
5. Beat the eggs until well mixed.
6. Add the egg and other liquid all at once, and mix quickly to ensure a smooth

[1]wholemeal or wheatmeal. [2]polyunsaturated or fat-reduced margarine. [3]reduce to 50 g (2 oz). [4] (semi-)skimmed

texture. Do not over-beat the mixture as this will lead to an uneven texture.

7 The mixture for most recipes should be a soft 'dropping' consistency, i.e. when some mixture is placed in a spoon, and gently tapped against the side of the bowl, it should drop easily.

8 Place the mixture in the appropriate baking tin and bake at the recommended temperature and time, until it is risen, set, an even brown colour, and no bubbling can be heard.

9 Keep for up to three days only, as after this, the cake may dry out. Store in an air-tight tin or plastic container.

Creamed cakes[1]

Plain mixture	Semi-rich mixture	Rich mixture
225 g (8 oz) SR flour	50 g (2 oz) plain flour	100 g (4 oz) SR flour
100 g (4 oz) fat	175 g (6 oz) SR flour	100 g (4 oz) plain flour
100 g (4 oz) sugar	175 g (6 oz) fat	225 g (8 oz) fat
2 eggs	175 g (6 oz) sugar	225 g (8 oz) sugar
40–80 ml (2–4 tbsp) milk	3 eggs	4 eggs
	20–40 ml (1–2 tbsp) milk	20 ml (1 tbsp) milk
Small cakes	*Small cakes*	*Small cakes*
Gas 5, 190°C (375°F)	Gas 4, 180°C (350°F)	Gas 4, 180°C (350°F)
12–15 minutes	20 minutes	20 minutes
Large cakes	*Large cakes*	*Large cakes*
Gas 3, 160°C (325°F)	Gas 3, 160°C (325°F)	Gas 3, 160 °C (325°F)
1¼–1½ hours	1½ hours	1½ hours

Uses and variations	Oven temperature and cooking time
Plain mixture	
Chocolate: use 25 g (1 oz) cocoa, 200 g (7 oz) flour. Add 20 ml (1 tbsp) syrup. **Cherry:** add 100 g (4 oz) glacé cherries (tossed in flour), and half a lemon rind, grated. **Polka dot:** add 100 g (4 oz) chocolate chips.	17·5 cm (7″) round tin *or* 22 × 10 cm (9 × 4″) shallow tin Gas 3, 160°C (325°F) 1¼–1½ hours, middle shelf of oven
Semi-rich mixture	
Coffee: add 15 ml (3 tsp) coffee powder (dissolved in the milk), and 50 g (2 oz) walnuts. **Madeira:** add the grated rind of 1 lemon, and place citron peel on top after 20 minutes baking. **Dundee:** add 350 g (12 oz) dried fruit, the grated rind of 1 lemon, and 50 g (2 oz) ground almonds.	17·5–20 cm (7–8″) round tin Gas 3, 160°C (325°F) 1½ hours, middle shelf of oven
Queen cakes: add 100 g (4 oz) dried fruit. **Cherry, polka dot,** and **chocolate:** as for plain mixture, but omit syrup in chocolate version.	Divide between 24 cake cases. Gas 4, 180°C (350°F) 20 minutes

[1]For each mixture: flour may be wholemeal or wheatmeal; use polyunsaturated margarine; use ⅔ the stated amount of sugar; milk may be (semi-)skimmed.

Uses and variations	Oven temperature and cooking time
Rich mixture **Victoria sandwich:** use half of the mixture, and divide between 2 sandwich tins, 15 cm (6″) in diameter. When cooked, sandwich with jam, and dust with sugar.	Gas 5, 190°C (375°F) 20 minutes, middle shelf of oven
Ginger: add ½ tsp ground ginger, and 50 g (2 oz) crystallized ginger. **Madeira** or **coffee** version can be made from this mixture.	as for plain mixture Bake for 1½–2 hours.

Method

1 Cream the fat and sugar with a wooden spoon until light and fluffy in texture. This will trap air in the form of tiny bubbles, to act as a raising agent.

2 Beat the eggs until well mixed, and add a little at a time to the fat and sugar, beating well at each addition, until the mixture thickens. This will ensure that the fat becomes emulsified by the egg yolk and is prevented from separating out (curdling). Air is also trapped by the eggs at this stage, which is important for the raising of the mixture.

3 Sieve the flour, to trap air, and fold gently into the mixture a little at a time, using a metal spoon. A metal spoon will cause the minimum of disturbance to the air bubbles. It is important not to beat the flour in as this will cause trapped air to be released and reduce the volume of the mixture.

4 Fold the liquid in gently with other ingredients, e.g. fruit, until a soft dropping consistency is reached.

5 Bake at the appropriate temperature and time until well risen, an even brown colour, and set.

Whisked sponges

75 g (3 oz) plain flour[1]
75 g (3 oz) caster sugar
3 eggs

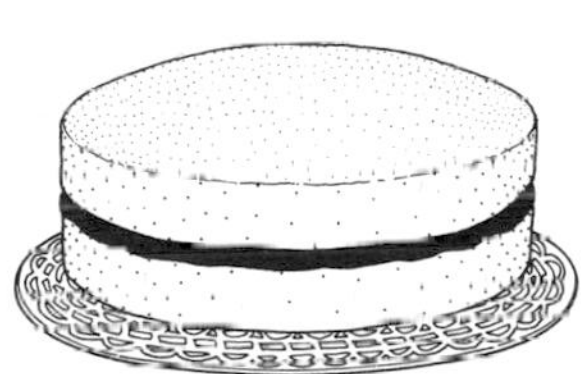

Uses and variations	Oven temperature and cooking time
Plain sponge sandwich: divide mixture between two 15 cm (6″) sandwich tins, and sandwich with jam when baked. **Chocolate:** use 12½ g (½ oz) cocoa powder and 60 g (2½ oz) flour.	Gas 5, 190°C (375°F) 15–20 minutes, middle shelf of oven
Swiss roll: use the same mixture or ⅔ of it for a thinner Swiss roll. Use jam, buttercream, or cream as a filling. When using buttercream or cream, roll the sponge up with a piece of greaseproof paper, leave until cold, then unroll, fill, and reroll.	Gas 6, 200°C (400°F) 12–15 minutes Roll up as soon as possible after baking.

[1]wholemeal or wheatmeal.

Uses and variations

Sponge gateau: use the same mixture, bake in a Swiss roll tin, and cut into three rectangles. Fill with fruit and cream, coat the sides with cream then nuts, chocolate, flaked almonds, or sugar strands.

Fruit sponge flan: use ⅔ of the basic mixture and bake in a flan case. Fill with fruit and coat with a clear glaze.

Oven temperature and cooking time

Bake as for Swiss roll.

Gas 5, 190°C (375°F)
20 minutes, middle shelf of oven.

Method

1 Whisk the eggs and sugar until very thick and creamy. The mixture should have increased in volume at least twice, and should leave a trail that stays visible for at least five seconds when the whisk is removed. This stage is vital to the success of a whisked sponge, as the raising agent for the mixture is the air trapped by the eggs and sugar. The mixture becomes thicker and lighter as the air is trapped, and a greater volume is produced when the eggs have been stored at room temperature.

2 Sieve the flour and cocoa, if used, twice, to make sure it is very light. Gently fold it into the mixture with a metal spoon to cause the minimum disturbance to the air bubbles. If the mixture is beaten at this stage the volume will be lost, and the baked product will be flat and tough.

3 Pour the mixture into the tin, which must be well lined and greased because the mixture contains no fat. Bake as directed. The mixture is cooked when it is well risen and spongy to the touch, and is an even brown colour.

4 **Swiss roll:** once the mixture is baked, it should be removed and prepared immediately as the flexibility of the sponge decreases as it cools.

One-stage cakes

100 g (4 oz) SR flour[1]
100 g (4 oz) soft margarine or whipped cooking fat[2]
100 g (4 oz) caster sugar[3]
2 eggs
½ tbsp milk if required

Uses and variations

Victoria sandwich cake
small cakes
chocolate
coffee
dried fruit
lemon

Method

1 Sieve the flour.

2 Add all the other ingredients and beat until smooth with a wooden spoon, for two minutes.

Soft magarine or whipped cooking fat are used as they are able to incorporate air into the mixture more readily than block margarine. It is important to beat the mixture for two minutes to allow this to happen.

3 Dried fruit should be added after the mixture has been beaten, as it would make the mixture difficult to beat if added at the beginning.

4 Use as required.
Bake small cakes at:
Gas 4, 180°C (350°F) for 15–20 minutes.
Bake Victoria sandwich cakes at:
Gas 5, 190°C (375°F) for 20 minutes.
Bake large cakes (17·5–20 cm (7–8″) tin) at:
Gas 4, 180°C (350°F) for 1 hour, then
Gas 2, 150°C (300°F) for ½ hour.

[1]wholemeal or wheatmeal. [2]polyunsaturated or fat-reduced margarine. [3]use ⅔ the stated amount of sugar.

Melted cake mixtures

Gingerbread:

450 g (1 lb) plain flour[1]
1 tsp salt[2]
1 tsp bicarbonate of soda
1 tbsp ground ginger
175 g (6 oz) fat[3]
225 g (8 oz) brown sugar[4]
175 g (6 oz) treacle
175 g (6 oz) syrup
275 ml (½ pint) milk[5]
1 egg

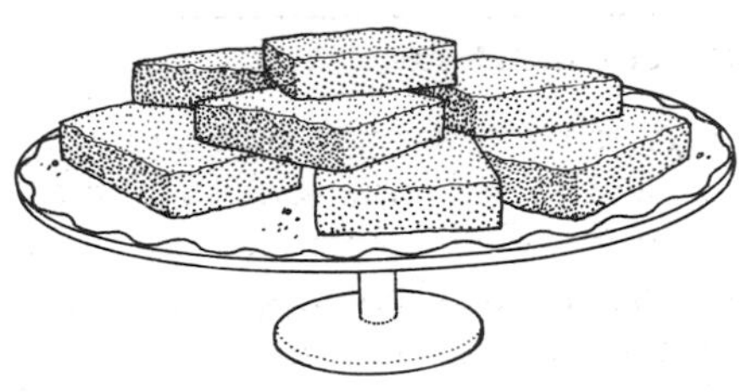

Use a 20 cm (8″) square tin or a Swiss roll tin for half the mixture.
Gas 3, 160°C (325°F)
1½ hours (square tin)
½ hour (Swiss roll tin)

Uses and variations	Oven temperature and cooking time
Orange gingerbread: use 1 tsp ground cinnamon, 1 tbsp ground ginger, and 1 tsp bicarbonate of soda. Add the grated rind and juice of 1 orange and 75 g (3 oz) candied peel. Use 3 eggs, 175 g (6 oz) treacle (*no* syrup), and a little milk.	20 cm (8″) square tin, or a Swiss roll tin for half the mixture Gas 3, 160°C (325°F) 1½ hours (square tin) ½ hour (Swiss roll tin)
Parkin: use 225 g (8 oz) plain flour[1] 100 g (4 oz) fat[3] 100 g (4 oz) sugar[4] 100 g (4 oz) treacle 100 g (4 oz) syrup 225 g (8 oz) medium oatmeal 4 tsp ground ginger 2 tsp ground cinnamon 1 tsp bicarbonate of soda 1 egg 150 ml (¼ pint) milk[5]	22 cm (9″) square tin Gas 4, 180°C (350°F) 1–1¼ hours

Method

1. Sieve the flour, bicarbonate of soda, and spices into a bowl.
2. Melt the fat, sugar, syrup, and treacle in a pan over a gentle heat. Do *not* boil the ingredients as this will affect the flavour and the sugar may burn.
3. Pour the melted mixture into the dry ingredients, and add the beaten egg and milk.
4. Mix quickly to a smooth consistency, add any extra ingredients, and pour into the tin, which should be greased and lined.
   Do not leave the mixture standing before baking, as the bicarbonate of soda will start reacting once the liquid is added, and the carbon dioxide gas will be lost.
5. Bake as directed. The oven temperature is low to avoid the risk of burning, as there is a high sugar content.
6. Remove the cake from the oven when it is well risen, set, and has stopped bubbling.

[1]wholemeal or wheatmeal. [2]omit. [3]polyunsaturated or reduced-fat margarine. [4]use ½ stated amount. [5](semi-)skimmed.

Faults in cake making

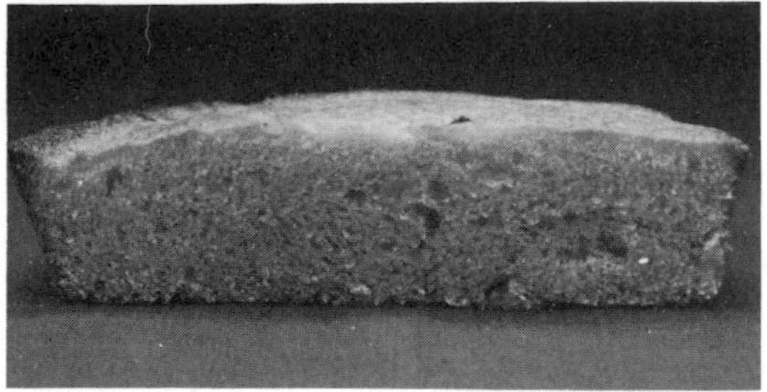

A perfect Victoria sandwich.

Curdling of uncooked cake mixture (see p. 198).

Cause

If the egg is very cold, the fat is cooled by it. Fat globules become surrounded by water from the egg, making emulsification of the fat by the egg yolk very difficult. The mixture will therefore hold less air, which will result in a close textured cake. Curdling may also result if too much egg is added at one time.

Remedy

The addition of a little flour from the mixture may help to absorb some of the water from the egg and enable emulsification of the fat to occur.

Cake has sunk in the middle

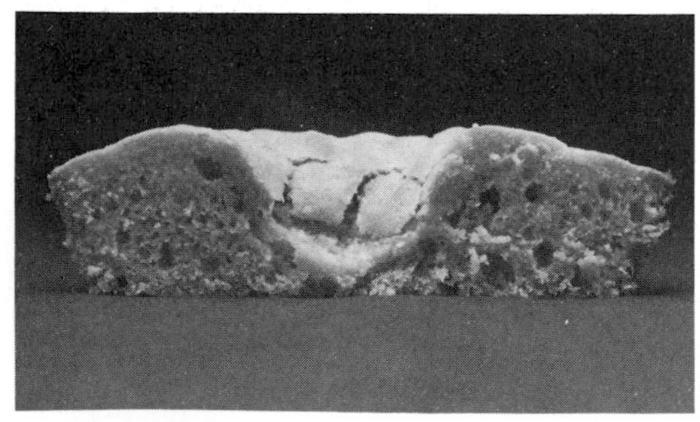

Causes

1 Too much sugar or syrup, causing the gluten to be over-softened so that it collapses.
2 Too much raising agent, causing the gluten to overstretch and collapse.
3 Undercooking, caused by the wrong temperature or cooking time.
4 Opening the oven door before the gluten has set, so that the heavy cold air makes it sink.

Cake has risen to a peak and is cracked

Causes

1 The oven temperature is too high, causing the mixture to rise rapidly to a peak, then overcook.
2 Too much mixture for the size of tin.
3 Placing the cake on too high a shelf in the oven.

Cake has a heavy texture

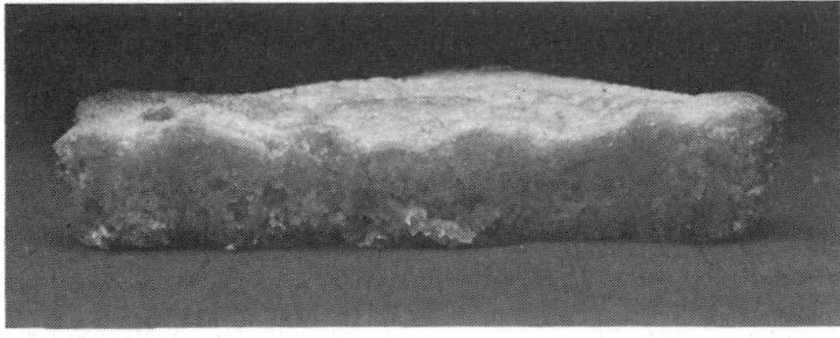

Causes

1 Too much liquid in the mixture.
2 Too little raising agent used, or incorporated during creaming or whisking.
3 The mixture has curdled and does not hold sufficient air.
4 The oven temperature is too low, or the cake has not been cooked for long enough.
5 Overbeating when adding flour, causing loss of air.
6 Overbeating after adding a liquid.

Cake has a coarse, open texture

Causes

1 Too much raising agent has been used, causing large pockets of gas to be produced.
2 The flour has not been mixed in sufficiently.

Cake has risen unevenly

Causes

1 The oven shelf is not level, which may be due to the floor on which it stands.
2 The cake mixture was placed too near the source of heat, which has caused it to rise quickly on one side.

Cake has a hard, sugary crust

Causes

1 The sugar is too coarse for the mixture and does not dissolve in time.
2 Too much sugar has been used.

Cake is badly shaped

Causes

1 The in has been badly lined or filled with the mixture.
2 The mixture is too stiff and does not even out when baked, or is too wet and has spread out too much.

Cake is dry

Causes

1 Too much chemical raising agent has been used.
2 Too little liquid has been used.
3 Cake has been overcooked.

Fruit has sunk in fruit cake

Causes

1 The mixture is too wet and the heavy fruit cannot be held evenly throughout.
2 The fruit is wet and therefore adds too much liquid to the cake.
3 Too much sugar or raising agent has been used, causing the structure to collapse and the fruit to sink.

Experimental work with cakes

1 Prepare a quarter of the basic creaming method *rich* cake mixture and use as follows:

   a Use 100 g (4 oz) sugar instead of 50 g (2 oz). Bake as directed for a Victoria sandwich and observe:
   the length of time taken for the mixture to set
   the appearance of the crust
   the texture of the cake
   the appearance of the cake after 20 minutes in the oven

   b Bake at gas 8, 230°C (450°F) for 15 minutes and observe the crust and inside of the cake.

   c Use all plain flour and compare the finished result with a cake made with all SR flour.

   d Bake as directed, but open the oven door after 10 minutes cooking time and then shut it abruptly. Observe finished result.

   e Add the egg all at once so that the mixture curdles. Beat in the flour with a wooden spoon and observe the volume of the finished cake.

2 Prepare a whisked sponge cake mixture (see p. 197) and use as follows:

   a Use a wooden spoon and beat the flour in after the eggs and sugar have been whisked. Observe the volume of the finished cake, compared to one where the flour has been carefully folded in.

   b Add the flour to the eggs and sugar before whisking and then whisk. Observe the mixture before baking and the volume of the finished result.

   c Whisk the eggs and sugar as directed, then fold in the flour (unsieved) quickly (but not roughly) and bake. Observe the texture of the final baked result.

Cake icings and decorations

Many cakes are enhanced by the addition of an attractively applied icing or other decoration, and celebration cakes are traditionally iced and elaborately decorated to suit the occasion. Some basic recipes are given here for a variety of icings and frostings.

Almond paste (marzipan)

This is applied to rich fruit cakes before they are iced, to act as a barrier between the cake and the icing. It also forms an airtight seal over the cake to prevent it from drying out.

225 g (8 oz) ground almonds
100 g (4 oz) caster sugar
100 g (4 oz) icing sugar
1 egg
few drops almond essence
1 tbsp lemon juice
few drops vanilla essence

Method

1 Sieve the sugars and almonds.
2 Add the flavourings. Gradually add the beaten egg and mix to a smooth paste.
3 Knead until completely smooth.
4 Store temporarily in a plastic bag.

Royal icing

This icing can be poured or spread over a cake to form a smooth coating, or if made slightly stiffer can be used for piping decorations onto the cake.

450 g (1 lb) icing sugar
3 tsp glycerine (for softer icing)
2–3 egg whites
4 tsp lemon juice (for a hard brittle icing)

Method

1 Sieve the icing sugar into a bowl.
2 Whip the egg whites until foamy but not stiff.
3 Gradually add the icing sugar, beating well in between to produce a soft white icing.
4 For pouring over a cake: the icing should coat the back of the spoon and pour slowly but smoothly from the bowl.

For piping: the icing should stand in soft peaks.

Glacé icing

This icing can be used to decorate creamed or rubbed-in cakes or sponges.

225 g (8 oz) icing sugar
1–1½ tbsp water
flavouring
colouring

Method

1 Sieve the icing sugar.
2 Gradually add the water and beat well in between to form a smooth icing of the required consistency.
3 Do not add too much water as it is very rapidly absorbed and will produce too thin an icing.
4 Add colouring drop by drop until the required shade is reached. Add flavouring in the same way.

Butter icing

50 g (2 oz) butter or soft margarine
100 g (4 oz) icing sugar

Method

1 Sieve the icing sugar.
2 Soften the butter or margarine by creaming it in a bowl.
3 Gradually add the icing sugar, beating well to produce a smooth, light icing.
4 Add 1 tsp warm water to soften the icing, or more if required.
5 Colour and flavour as required.
If flavoured with coffee or cocoa, dissolve these in hot water first to avoid a speckled appearance in the finished icing.

Sugar paste

450 g (1 lb) icing sugar
1 tbsp liquid glucose syrup
1 egg white

Method

1 Sieve the icing sugar into a bowl.
2 Mix the egg white and the glucose syrup and gradually work in the icing sugar, beating well in between.
3 When the icing becomes too stiff to mix with a spoon, knead gently with one hand and work in the rest of the sugar until a smooth paste is formed. Roll out to the size required and cover the cake, using the fingers dusted with cornflour to smooth it down.

Chocolate frosting

175 g (6 oz) icing sugar
50 g (2 oz) plain chocolate
2 tbsp hot water
12·5 g (½ oz) butter or margarine
few drops vanilla essence

Method

1 Sieve the icing sugar into a bowl.
2 Put chocolate, water and butter into a pan and warm gently until the chocolate has melted. Beat until smooth and cool slightly.
3 Add the vanilla essence and the icing sugar and beat until smooth.
4 Use at once to coat the cake.

Decorations

The following decorations can be used for small or large cakes:

crystallized violets or fruits
chocolate curls or flakes
small jelly sweets
flaked or chopped almonds
walnuts (shelled)
coarsely grated coconut
angelica
glacé fruits
small silver or gold balls
sugar strands
toasted chopped nuts

Biscuits

Home-made biscuits and cookies are usually easy to make. A few examples of biscuits made by different methods are given here.

Biscuits made by the creaming method

Shrewsbury biscuits

225 g (8 oz) plain flour[1]
100 g (4 oz) fat (butter or margarine)[2]
100 g (4 oz) sugar[3]
1 egg
2 tsp grated lemon rind

Makes 20–24 biscuits

Uses and variations

Vanilla biscuits: omit lemon rind, add a few drops of vanilla essence.
Spiced biscuits: omit lemon rind, add 1 tsp mixed spice and 1 tsp cinnamon.
Walnut and chocolate biscuits: add 50 g (2 oz) finely chopped walnuts. Shape into oblongs. When cooked, dip the ends into melted chocolate.
Fruit biscuits: add 50 g (2 oz) dried fruit (chopped).
Cream biscuits: cut into small squares in pairs and bake separately. Sandwich together with buttercream when cold.
Iced biscuits: cut into fancy shapes and when cold, coat with glacé icing, and decorate with jelly sweets, chocolate, silver balls, etc.
Almond biscuits: use 175 g (6 oz) flour and 50 g (2 oz) ground almonds.
Coconut biscuits: use 175 g (6 oz) flour and 50 g (2 oz) desiccated coconut.

Method

1 Cream the fat and sugar until light and fluffy, to ensure that the biscuits have a light crumbly texture.
2 Add the egg gradually.
3 Stir in the flour and other ingredients to form a fairly stiff dough. Knead until smooth on a floured surface.
4 Roll out to 6 mm ($\frac{1}{4}$") thick, cut out and place on a greased baking tray.
5 Bake at Gas 4, 180°C (350°F) for 15–20 minutes until golden brown.

Piped biscuits

175 g (6 oz) plain flour[1]
225 g (8 oz) fat (butter or margarine)[2]
50 g (2 oz) icing sugar
50 g (2 oz) cornflour
a few drops vanilla essence

Makes 20–24 biscuits

Uses and variations

Butter whirls: pipe into flat whirls and decorate with a small piece of glacé cherry before baking.
Viennese biscuits: pipe the mixture into paper cake cases, leaving a gap in the centre. Bake at Gas 4, 180°C (350°F) for 20–25 minutes. Fill with jam when baked and cold, dust with icing sugar.
Chocolate fingers: pipe into fingers in pairs and bake separately. Sandwich together with buttercream when cold, and dip the ends into melted chocolate.
Nut cookies: pipe into stars and sprinkle with chopped nuts before baking.

Method

1 Cream the fat and icing sugar until smooth and light.
2 Fold in the flour and cornflour and add the vanilla.
3 Pipe on to a greased baking tray using a large star nozzle.
4 Bake at Gas 5, 190°C (375°F) for 10–15 minutes.

[1]wholemeal or wheatmeal [2]polyunsaturated or fat-reduced margarine. [3]use $\frac{1}{2}$ stated amount.

Biscuits made by the melting method

Flapjacks[1]

225 g (8 oz) rolled oats
100 g (4 oz) fat (butter or margarine)[2]
75 g (3 oz) brown sugar[3]
75 g (3 oz) golden syrup

Method

1 Melt the syrup, fat, and sugar over a low heat. Do not boil.
2 Remove from heat and stir in the oats, ensuring that they are well coated.
3 Press the mixture into a greased Swiss roll tin and level out.
4 Bake at Gas 4, 180°C (350°F) for 30 minutes until golden brown and set. The mixture will still be soft at this stage.
5 Mark into 20 fingers and leave for 5 minutes.
6 Gently remove from the tin. The flapjacks will become crisp on cooling.

Ginger nuts

100 g (4 oz) plain flour[4]
50 g (2 oz) fat (butter or margarine)[2]
75 g (3 oz) golden syrup
25 g (1 oz) brown sugar
½ tsp bicarbonate of soda
1 tsp ground ginger

Method

1 Melt the fat, sugar, and syrup in a pan over a low heat. Do not boil.
2 Sieve the dry ingredients and make a well in the centre.
3 Pour in the melted ingredients and mix to a soft dough.
4 Divide into 12 balls and place on a greased baking tray. Flatten slightly with a fork and bake for 15 minutes at Gas 4, 180°C (350°F), until golden brown.
5 The biscuits will become crisp on cooling.

NB It is important to weigh the syrup and other ingredients accurately, as too much will result in the biscuits spreading during baking.

Biscuits made by the rubbing-in method

Shortbread

100 g (4 oz) plain flour[5]
50 g (2 oz) ground rice[6]
100 g (4 oz) butter[7]
50 g (2 oz) caster sugar

Variations

Orange shortbread: add the finely grated rind of 1 orange.
Chocolate shortbread: use 75 g (3 oz) flour and 25 g (1 oz) cocoa.

Method

1 Rub the butter into half of the flour and ground rice, then gradually work in the rest of the flour, sugar, and other ingredients.
2 Knead until the dough is short and smooth.
3 Roll out to 6 mm (¼″) to 12 mm (½″) thick, and cut into individual biscuits or shape into one large shortbread.
4 Bake at Gas 3, 170°C (325°F) for 15–20 minutes for the individual biscuits or 45 minutes for the large shortbread. The shortbread should be a pale golden brown colour, and will become crisp on cooling.

NB Butter is used to give the shortbread its rich flavour. This recipe can also be made by the creaming method.

For a large shortbread, a wooden or special plastic mould can be used into which the dough is pressed before baking, then removed. This gives it a traditional pattern. The mould should be dusted with flour first to make it easy to remove the dough.

Biscuits made by the whisking method

Sponge fingers

Use the recipe for a whisked sponge (see p. 197), and pour a little of the mixture into a greased eclair tin. Bake at Gas 5, 190°C (375°F) for 10–15 minutes until risen and set. Remove the fingers carefully.

---

[1]add dried fruit and nuts to increase fibre content. [2]polyunsaturated or fat-reduced margarine. [3]use ½ stated amount of sugar. [4]wholemeal, or wheatmeal, or use 25 g (1 oz) fine oatmeal and 75 g (3 oz) flour. [5]wholemeal or wheatmeal. [6]wholemeal semolina. [7]polyunsaturated margarine.

Scones

Choice and functions of ingredients

Flour

Soft or weak flour is best for scones as it gives them a light texture.
Self-raising flour can be used, as scones require a chemical raising agent (see below).
Wholemeal flour is suitable if used with a chemical raising agent, and provides fibre as well as extra flavour.

Raising agent

A relatively high proportion of chemical raising agent is used which gives the scones their light texture, but at the same time tends to make them dry. They are therefore best made and eaten on the same day.

Suitable raising agents include:

Baking powder with plain flour, in the proportion:

4–5 tsp to 450 g (1 lb) flour

Too much baking powder will leave an acid tasting residue in the baked scones.

Bicarbonate of soda with cream of tartar (see pp. 175–6), in the proportions:

2 tsp bicarbonate of soda 4 tsp cream of tartar	to 450 g (1 lb) flour

using fresh milk as the liquid.

If sour milk is used, the lactic acid in it can be used to replace half of the cream of tartar, in the following proportions:

2 tsp bicarbonate of soda 2 tsp cream of tartar 275 ml (½ pint) sour milk	to 450 g (1 lb) flour

Fat

Butter or margarine can be used, and the proportion is low:

50 g (2 oz) to 450 g (1 lb) flour

Liquid

Milk is normally used to mix scones, and the proportion is relatively high:

275 ml (½ pint) to 450 g (1 lb) flour

This gives a soft, elastic dough which is able to stretch sufficiently for the raising agent, during baking.

Plain scones

450 g (1 lb) plain flour[1]
4–5 tsp baking powder
275 ml (½ pint) fresh milk[2]
or
450 g (1 lb) self-raising flour[1]
275 g (½ pint) fresh milk[2]
or
450 g (1 lb) plain flour[1]
2 tsp bicarbonate of soda
4 tsp cream of tartar
275 ml (½ pint) fresh milk[2]
or
450 g (1 lb) plain flour[1]
2 tsp bicarbonate of soda
2 tsp cream of tartar
275 ml (½ pint) sour milk[2]
50 g (2 oz) fat[3]
½ tsp salt[4]

Uses and variations

Sweet plain scones: add 50 g (2 oz) sugar.
Cheese scones: add 100 g (4 oz) grated cheese.
Fruit scones: add 100 g (4 oz) dried fruit.
Wholemeal cheese and herb scones: use wholemeal flour, add 100 g (4 oz) grated cheese and 1–2 tsp mixed dried herbs.
Herb scones: add 2 tsp mixed dried herbs. This mixture can be used instead of bread dough as the base of pizzas.

Method

1 Sieve the flour and raising agent, to ensure even distribution.
2 Rub in the fat with the fingertips until it is well mixed.
3 Stir in any other ingredients.
4 Add the liquid all at once, and mix quickly to ensure even distribution, until a soft dough is formed.
5 Knead until smooth, to develop the elasticity of the dough, then roll on a lightly floured surface, to 2 cm (¾″) thick.
6 Cut into rounds or triangles.

 [1]wholemeal or wheatmeal. [2](semi-)skimmed. [3]polyunsaturated margarine. [4]omit.

7 Brush the tops with milk or egg to give a golden colour. Do not brush the sides as this will inhibit the scones from rising.
8 Bake at Gas 8, 230°C (450°F) for 10 minutes at the top of the oven to ensure quick, even rising.

Girdle scones

Girdle scones are cooked on a girdle or solid electric hot plate.
The basic plain scone recipe is used.

Method
1 Heat the girdle or hot plate until moderately hot.
2 Prepare the dough as for the oven-baked scones, but roll them out to 6–12 mm ($\frac{1}{4}$–$\frac{1}{2}$") thick.
3 Place the scones on the girdle or hot plate and cook for 8 minutes on each side.

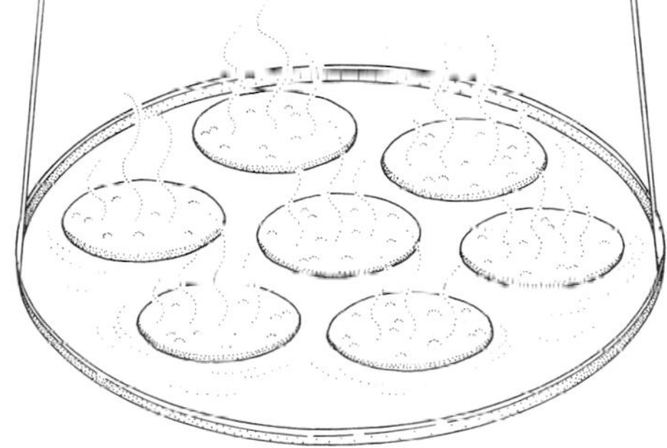

Drop scones

These are prepared as a thick batter and are cooked on a girdle or electric hot plate.

450 g (1 lb) plain flour[1]
3 tsp baking powder
or
450 g (1 lb) SR flour[1]
1 tsp baking powder
100 g (4 oz) caster sugar or golden syrup[2]
100 g (4 oz) fat[2]
2 eggs
scant 575 ml (1 pint) milk[4]

Method
1 Sieve the flour and baking powder.
2 Rub in the fat until well mixed.
3 Stir in the sugar (if used).
4 Add the beaten egg and $\frac{3}{4}$ of the milk (and the syrup if used), mixing gradually to a thick batter. Add more milk if necessary.
5 Lightly grease the girdle or hot plate and heat it until the fat is hazing slightly.
6 Drop tablespoons of the mixture, wide apart, on to the hot plate. Cook until the mixture rises and the bubbles break, then turn over and cook the other side until the scones are golden and spongy.
7 Keep warm in a clean cloth until serving.

Faults in scone making

Perfect scones.

The scones have spread and lost their shape

Causes
1 Too soft a dough due to too much liquid.

[1]wholemeal or wheatmeal. [2]use $\frac{1}{2}$ stated amount. [3]polyunsaturated margarine. [4](semi-)skimmed.

2 Bad kneading, particularly during the second rolling of the dough to use up scraps.
3 Twisting the cutter round when pressing out the shapes from the dough.

The scones are heavy and poorly risen

Causes
1 Insufficient raising agent.
2 Insufficient liquid.
3 Too heavy handling.
4 Oven temperature too cool.
5 Scones baked too low in the oven.

The scones have a rough surface after baking

Causes
1 Bad kneading.
2 Rough handling.

Girdle scones

The scones are unevenly cooked

Cause
Hot plate, girdle, or frying pan is thin or in uneven contact with the heat.

The scones have spread

Cause
Too thin a batter.

Pastries

Choice and functions of ingredients

Flour

With the exception of suet pastry for which self-raising flour may be used, **plain flour** should be used, as baking powder does not produce the correct texture. For shortcrust pastry, **soft** plain flour should be used to give a light, crumbly texture.

For flaky and rough puff pastry, **strong** plain flour is best, as it has a higher protein content, resulting in the formation of more gluten when water is added. This enables the dough to stretch well and to produce flakes during preparation and baking.
Wholemeal or **80% extraction** flour can be used for shortcrust pastry to provide extra dietary fibre, vitamins, colour, and flavour, but it is not suitable for flaky or rough puff pastry as it does not form flakes very well, due to the presence of the bran (see pp. 65–7).

Fat

Fat is used in pastry making to provide 'shortness' as in cake mixtures (see p. 194), except that for pastry, the fat is not mixed as thoroughly with the flour as it is for cakes. This causes the fat to form layers between strands of gluten, so that the pastry is tender and flaky.
Margarine is suitable for pastry making as it gives flavour, colour, and some shortness. Block margarine is best to use as it is easier to rub in; soft magarine tends to be too oily.
Butter is suitable as it gives a good flavour and shortness, but it is more expensive than margarine.
Lard is suitable as it provides very good shortness, but lacks flavour.
White vegetable fats produce similar results to lard.
Oil can be used, but lacks flavour.

A mixture of lard or vegetable fat and margarine or butter are normally used to combine good shortening power with flavour and colour. Any fat used should be cold and firm.

Liquid

Water is used to bind the ingredients together into a dough, except for rich doughs, where egg yolk may be used.

The water should be cold, or chilled in the refrigerator, so that it does not affect the temperature of the fats. Accurate measurement is important so that the correct consistency is produced. The water should be mixed in quickly with a flexible knife until a smooth dough is produced.

Preparing pastry for baking

It is important that all the ingredients and utensils are kept cool while preparing the pastry so that the fats do not melt before baking. If they do melt, the pastry will be difficult to handle, and the fat will not form layers with the gluten strands. When the pastry is baked it will be very fragile and will crumble too readily.

The pastry should be handled lightly to avoid toughening it by developing the gluten. This means that kneading should be gentle, and rolling out should be carried out with short, light strokes.

If possible, allow the pastry to rest in a cool place for about twenty minutes to allow the fat to harden up. This changes the texture of the dough and makes it easier to roll. When rolling out and using, do not stretch the dough, as it will shrink when baked and may affect the holding capacities of flans, tarts, etc.

Bake in a pre-heated oven to ensure that the fat is quickly absorbed by the starch grains, and the water turns to steam to raise the pastry and make it light. If the fat runs out of the dough before it is absorbed, e.g. if the oven temperature is too low to allow absorption to take place, the dough will become tough and dry.

Do not grease baking tins as the fat in the pastry prevents it from sticking.

Shortcrust pastry

$\frac{1}{2}$ fat to flour, e.g.:
225 g (8 oz) flour[1]
50 g (2 oz) lard[2]
50 g (2 oz) margarine[3]
5 tsp (25 ml) water to every
100 g (4 oz) flour

Gas 6, 200°C (400°F)
15–20 minutes for empty flan case

Uses and variations	Oven temperature and cooking time
Cheese pastry: add 50–100 g (2–4 oz) grated Cheddar cheese, and a pinch of cayenne pepper, to a 225 g (8 oz) mixture. Use beaten egg to bind.	Gas 6, 200°C (400°F) The time will vary according to the recipe.
Rich shortcrust: add 25 g (1 oz) caster sugar to a 225 g (8 oz) mixture. Bind with egg yolk and water.	Gas 6, 200°C (400°F) for 15 minutes, then: Gas 4, 180°C (350°F) to avoid burning.
Uses: pies, pasties, flans, tarts, etc.	

[1]wholemeal or wheatmeal. [2]well-chilled polyunsaturated white vegetable fat. [3]well-chilled polyunsaturated margarine.

Method
1 Sieve the flour.
2 Cut up the fats and rub into the flour with the fingertips until the mixture resembles breadcrumbs and is pale yellow in colour. It is important not to over-rub the fats and flour at this stage, as this will produce oily pastry that is difficult to combine with water.
3 Measure the water accurately and add, stirring with a palette knife to form a firm but pliable dough.
4 Knead on a lightly floured surface for a few seconds until smooth.
5 Roll out, using short, light strokes in one direction until the required size is reached. Do not stretch.
6 Lift pastry on a rolling pin to transfer it from the work top to the dish.

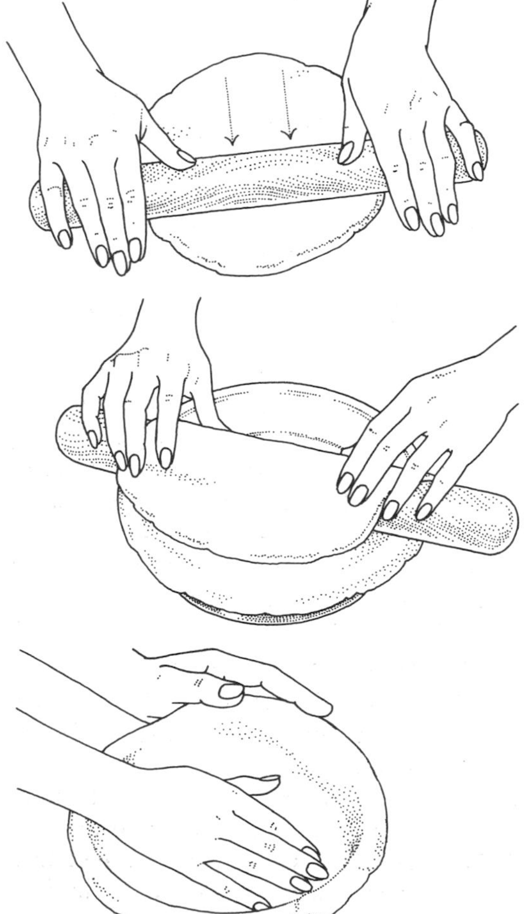

Shortcrust pastry (one-stage method)

150 g (5 oz) fat
(½ lard[2] and ½ block margarine[3]
225 g (8 oz) flour[1]
50 ml (10 tsp) water

Method
1 Place fats, water, and one third of the flour in a bowl and mix thoroughly with a fork for half a minute.
2 Add the rest of the flour and mix to a firm dough.
3 Knead until smooth on a floured board.
4 Chill for 10 minutes, then use as for ordinary shortcrust pastry.

This method has the advantage of quickness in preparation and avoids the problems of over-rubbing, streaking of the fat, or uneven addition of water.

Flaky or rough puff pastry

¾ fat to flour, e.g.:
225 g (8 oz) flour[1]
75 g (3 oz) lard[2]
75 g (3 oz) margarine[3]
½ tsp salt to 450 g (1 lb) flour
20 ml (1 tbsp) water to each 25 g (1 oz) flour

Lemon juice can be added to soften the gluten and form a more elastic dough:
20 ml (4 tsp) per 450 g (1 lb) flour

Cook at Gas 7, 220°C (425°F).
The time will vary according to the recipe.

Uses and variations

cream horns
sausage rolls
eccles cakes
fruit turnovers
pasties
vol-au-vents
pie crusts
cream slices
Russian fish pie

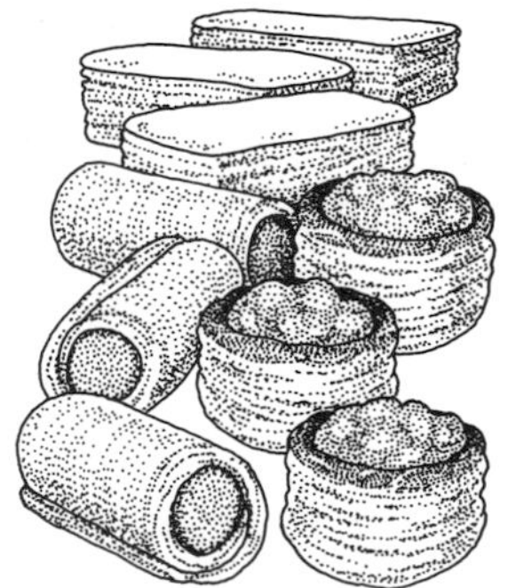

[1]wholemeal or wheatmeal. [2]well-chilled polyunsaturated white vegetable fat. [3]well-chilled polyunsaturated margarine.

Method for flaky pastry

1 Mix the two fats together on a plate so that they are evenly distributed in the pastry.

2 Shape the fat into a block and divide into four equal pieces:

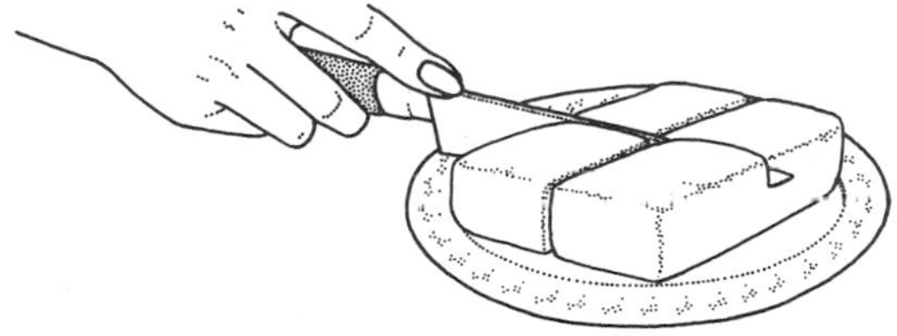

3 Sieve the flour and salt, and rub in one quarter of the fat until it is evenly distributed.

4 Add the liquid all at once and mix to a soft, elastic dough. The dough is of this consistency due to the high proportion of water and gluten, and will enable the pastry to stretch and flake during baking. The lemon juice helps to develop the gluten and to form a more elastic dough.

5 Roll the pastry to a rectangle, three times as long as it is wide. Mark into three squares.

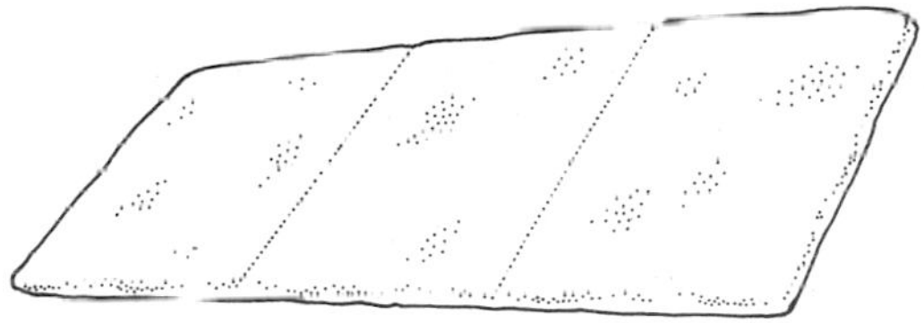

6 Divide the next quarter of fat equally on to the top two thirds of the rectangle:

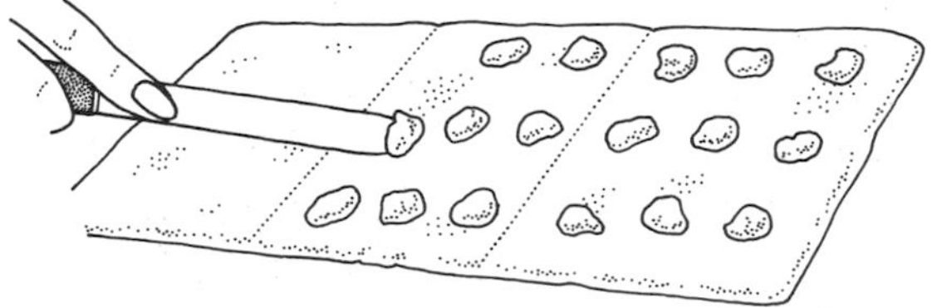

7 Fold the bottom third to the middle, and the top third to the bottom:

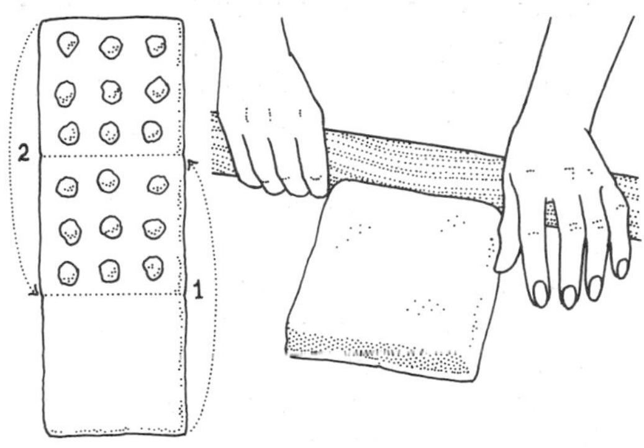

8 Seal the edges, and place in the refrigerator for at least five minutes to harden the fat. Give the pastry a quarter turn:

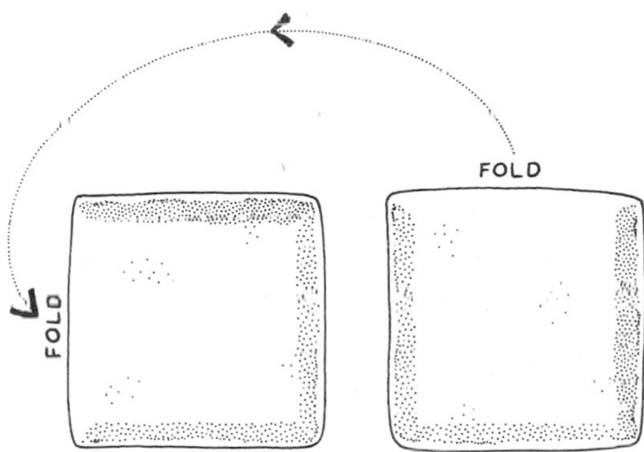

9 Roll out to a rectangle and repeat the division of fat, folding, resting, and rolling with the last two quarters of fat (three times in all). Then repeat the rolling, folding, and sealing one more time without fat. Leave the pastry to rest for ten minutes and use as required.

Method for rough puff pastry

1 Follow the directions for flaky pastry down to rubbing one quarter of the fat into the flour (no. 3).
2 Cut up the remaining fat into small pieces and stir into the rubbed-in mixture.
3 Add the water all at once and mix to a dough that will be lumpy due to the fat.

4 Roll into a rectangle as for flaky pastry, and roll and fold without extra fat four times in all, resting the dough in between, as for flaky pastry:

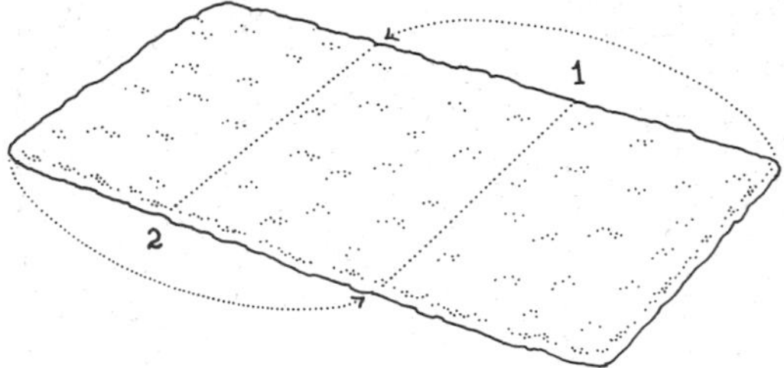

It is important for both flaky and rough puff pastry that the fat is cold and hard, so that it does not melt during the preparation. Once in the oven, the fat melts and is immediately absorbed by the starch in the flour. The steam produced from the water causes the pastry to puff up, thus separating the layers, which set to a crisp texture because of the flour and water mixture.

Choux pastry

62½ g (2½ oz) plain flour[1]
50 g (2 oz) fat[2]
150 ml (¼ pint) water
2 eggs

Uses and variations

chocolate eclairs
profiteroles, choux buns

Cheese aigrettes: add 50 g (2 oz) parmesan cheese, fry mixture in small amounts in hot fat, dust with more cheese. Serve hot.

Method

1 Place the fat and water in a pan and bring to the boil. Remove from the heat.
2 Add the flour immediately and beat until the mixture forms a ball and leaves the side of the pan. The water should be at boiling point when the flour is added, so that the starch absorbs the water and is softened and cooked. Strong flour produces more gluten when the liquid is added. This makes the dough more elastic and enables it to rise well during baking.
3 Leave the mixture to cool slightly, and gradually add the beaten eggs, a little at a time, until well mixed. The egg yolk will emulsify the fat at this stage.
4 Place the mixture in a piping bag and shape according to the recipe.
5 The pastry should be baked at a relatively high temperature initially, in order for the steam from the water to raise the mixture. The oven temperature is then lowered to allow the mixture to set without burning. Cook for 10 minutes at Gas 6, 200°C (400°F) then for 20 minutes at Gas 4, 180°C (350°F) on the top shelf of the oven. The oven door should remain closed during baking as opening it will cause heat to be lost and the dough will collapse before it has set.
6 Any uncooked dough can be removed after baking, and the eclairs etc. should be split open to release the steam which would make the pastry lose its crispness.

Suet pastry

½ fat to flour, e.g.:
450 g (1 lb) plain or SR flour[1]
225 g (½ lb) shredded suet[3]
2 tsp salt[4]
275 ml (½ pint) liquid (usually water)

Uses and variations

steamed puddings, e.g. roly-poly
steamed meat puddings, e.g. steak and kidney
baked jam puddings

Oven temperature and cooking time will vary according to the recipe used.

Method

1 Sieve the flour and salt.
2 Stir in the shredded suet. If fresh suet is used, it should be coated in a little flour and coarsely grated.
3 Mix thoroughly.
4 Add the water and mix to a soft, pliable dough.
5 Knead lightly and roll to the required thickness and shape.

[1]wholemeal or wheatmeal. [2]polyunsaturated or fat-reduced margarine. [3]vegetable 'suet' now available. [4]use ¼ stated amount.

Faults in pastry making

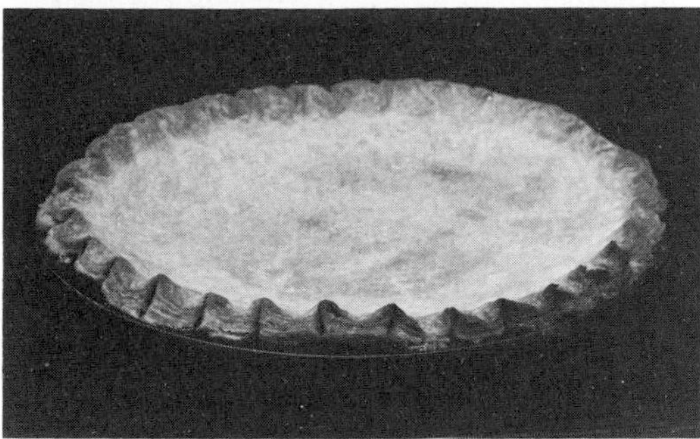

Perfect shortcrust pastry.

Pastry is hard and tough

Causes

1 The ingredients were too warm.
2 Over-kneading and heavy handling.
3 Incorrect proportion of ingredients, e.g. too much water in shortcrust pastry, too little water in flaky pastry, or too much flour.
4 Oven temperature too cool.

Pastry is blistered

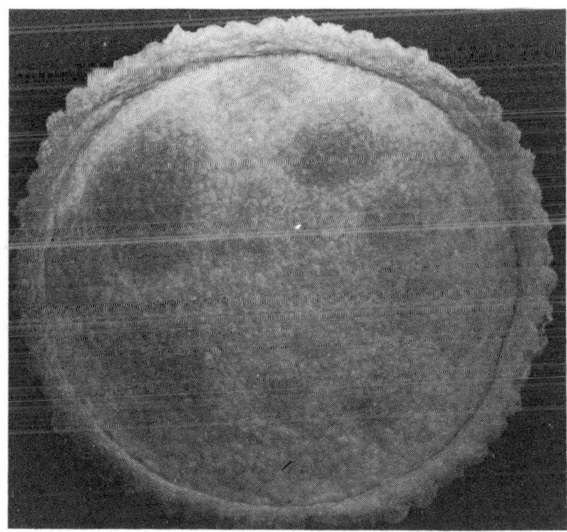

Causes

1 Uneven addition of water.
2 Oven set at too high a temperature.
3 Fats insufficiently and unevenly rubbed in to the flour.

Pastry is soggy in a pie

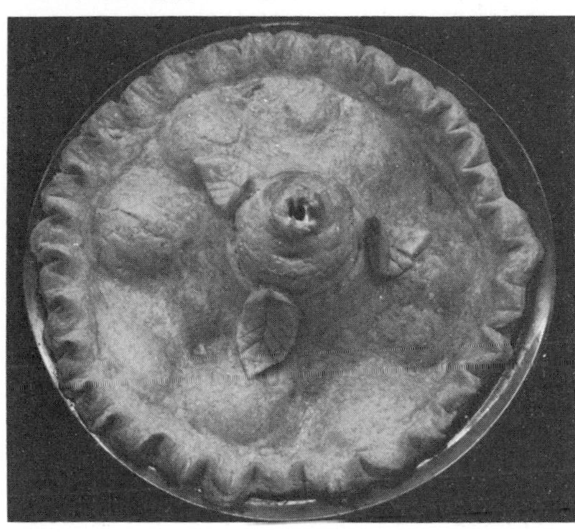

Cause

Steam not allowed to escape during cooking.

Pastry is fragile and crumbly when cooked

Causes:

1 Too much fat.
2 Over-rubbing the fat into the flour.
3 Too little water.

Pastry has shrunk during cooking

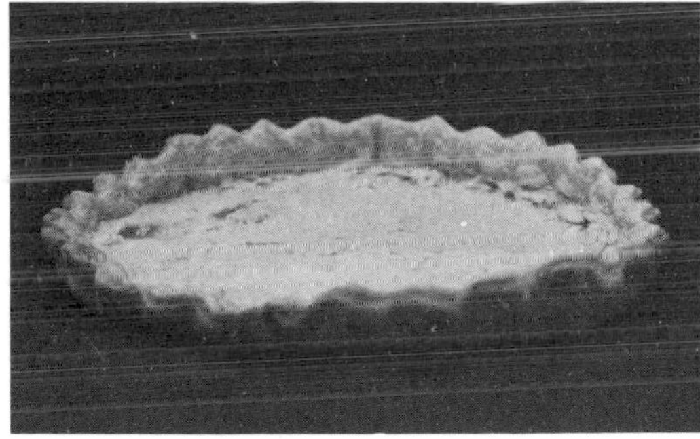

Cause

The pastry has been stretched during preparation and rolling.

Flaky or rough puff pastry

Perfect flaky pastry.

Pastry has not flaked well

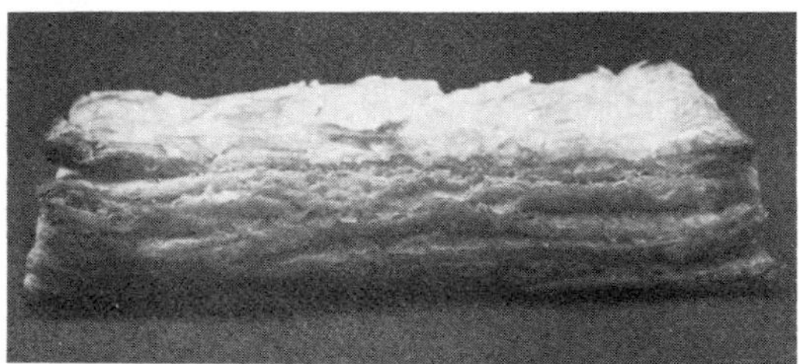

Causes

1 Oven temperature too cool, so fat has melted and run out of the pastry before being absorbed by the starch. Steam has not been produced quickly enough.
2 Mixture was too dry.
3 Pastry has been rolled and folded unevenly with uneven addition of fat.
4 Fat has melted during preparation and the pastry has not had sufficient time to rest in a cool place.

Pastry has risen unevenly

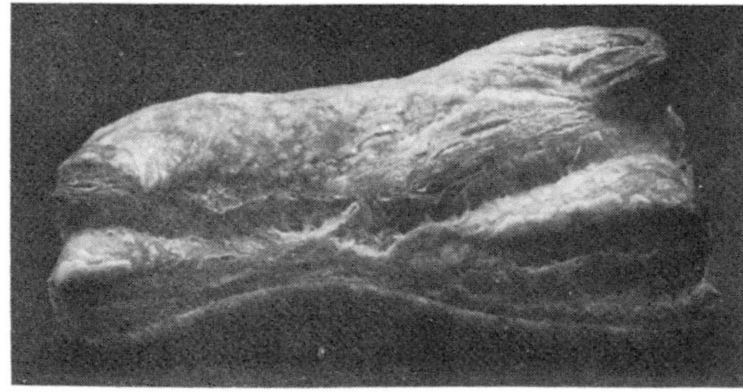

Causes

1 Fat has been added unevenly.
2 Pastry has been rolled and folded unevenly.
3 Pastry was tilted in oven.

Choux pastry

Perfect choux pastry.

Pastry has not risen well

Causes:

1 Insufficient cooking time, therefore the steam has escaped and the pastry collapsed before it had set.
2 Incorrect oven temperature.
3 Insufficient beating.

Puddings and sweets

There are many recipes for puddings and sweets, and it is not possible to list them all here. However it is possible to classify them according to the main types. 'Pudding' usually refers to a hot food, and 'sweets' are usually cold.

Puddings

Milk puddings

These are made with cereal grains or pasta:
Whole or large grains, e.g. rice, barley, large tapioca (see p. 69).
Medium or crushed grains, e.g. sago, seed tapioca (see p. 69), semolina, macaroni, flaked rice
Powdered grain, e.g. cornflour, arrowroot (see p. 69), ground rice.

Proportions

575 ml (1 pint) milk[1]
50 g (2 oz) cereal or pasta
25 g (1 oz) sugar[2]

Variations
Add:
cinnamon, lemon rind, nutmeg, or egg yolk.
Serve with:
stewed or fresh fruit, jam, or syrup.

Milk and egg puddings

Egg custard

Proportions

275 ml (½ pint) milk
1 egg
1 tbsp caster sugar
vanilla essence
grated nutmeg for top

Variations
crème caramel
Queen of puddings
bread and butter pudding

Puddings made by the rubbing-in method

Fruit crumbles

225 g (8 oz) plain flour[3]
100 g (4 oz) margarine or butter[4]
50 g (2 oz) sugar[5]

Variations
apple
plum
rhubarb
blackberry and apple
raspberry
apricot

Steamed puddings

Use the basic cake recipe (p. 197), cover with foil or a lid and steam for 1½–2 hours.

Variations
chocolate
date
jam
syrup
chocolate and pear

Suet puddings

175 g (6 oz) plain flour[3]
1½ tsp baking powder
75 g (3 oz) shredded suet[6]
50 g (2 oz) sugar
150 ml (¼ pint) milk[1]

Variations
Use 75 g (3 oz) flour
and 75 g (3 oz) breadcrumbs
Add:
75 g (3 oz) dates *or*
2 tbsp jam or syrup *or*
75 g (3 oz) currants *or*
2 tbsp marmalade

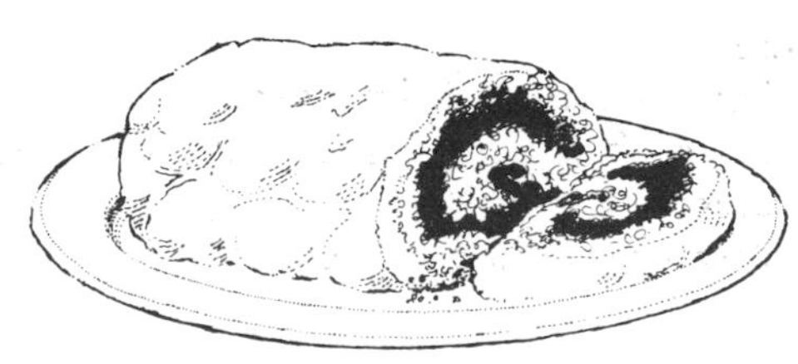

[1](semi-)skimmed. [2]liquid or granular sweetener, used according to instructions on packet. [3]wholemeal or wheatmeal. [4]polyunsaturated margarine. [5]use ½ stated amount. [6]vegetable 'suet' now available.

Suet pastry

Roly-poly pudding

175 g (6 oz) suet pastry (p. 214)
3 tbsp jam[1]

Roll pastry to an oblong, spread with jam and roll up. Wrap in foil and steam for two hours.

Variations
Use mincemeat
or syrup mixed with breadcrumbs

Puddings made by the creaming method

Use cake mixtures (see pp. 199–200) according to recipe and bake or steam.

Variations
chocolate
dried fruit
syrup
lemon
pears and chocolate
pineapple upside-down pudding
Eve's pudding

Puddings made with pastry

Shortcrust
fruit pies and tarts (hot or cold)
flans (hot or cold)
Bakewell tart (hot or cold)
lemon meringue pie (hot or cold)
apple dumplings
custard tart (hot or cold)

Flaky or rough puff
fruit and cream layers
apple turnovers

Puddings made with batters

fruit fritters (hot or cold)
pancakes and crepes

Puddings made with fruit

stewed fresh fruit
stewed dried fruit
baked apples

Cold sweets

Frozen

ice creams
sorbets

Set with gelatine

jellies
milk jellies
whips (a whisked jelly)
mousses and soufflés
cheesecakes

Whisking method

sponge gateaux
fruit sponge flans

Set with cornflour starch

blancmange
fruit fools

Set with egg protein

egg custard
crème caramel

Fruit

fresh fruit salad
fruit creams

Miscellaneous

trifle
summer pudding (bread slices soaked with a mixture of soft fruits)
profiteroles (choux pastry)

[1]use sugar-reduced jam or unsweetened fruit puree e.g. apple.

Yeast mixtures

Choice and functions of ingredients

Flour

Strong, plain flour from spring wheat, e.g. Canadian wheat, which has a high gluten content (see p. 65), is most suitable for yeast mixtures as it produces a strong, 'elastic' dough, The elasticity of the gluten enables yeast doughs to stretch and hold CO_2 gas in small pockets, as it is produced by the yeast during fermentation (see p. 180).

During fermentation, sugars naturally present in the flour (including maltose which is the result of amylase enzymes in the flour acting on the starch and breaking it down into disaccharides) are converted to glucose, and this is fermented by the yeast to CO_2 gas and alcohol.

During baking, the gluten coagulates and the starch gelatinizes with the water. Together these result in a rigid loaf, containing a network of gas pockets. The starch on the outside is changed to dextrin (see p. 19) and the sugars in the flour caramelize, making the crust brown.

Wholemeal flour is suitable for bread making, and provides extra dietary fibre, B vitamins, and flavour.

Self-raising flour is not suitable because of the baking powder it contains.

Yeast

The choice, use, and function of yeast in baking is discussed on pp. 179–80. Yeast should be fresh and in good condition, so that its activity is sufficient to raise the dough.

Liquid

The liquid should be accurately measured and should be at blood heat (i.e. warm to the touch) to activate the yeast to ferment. Hot water will destroy the yeast and cold water will slow down its activity.

Salt

Salt is added to influence the rate of fermentation, strengthen the gluten, and improve the flavour of bread.

Fat

Fat may be added to improve the keeping qualities of the dough and add colour and flavour.

Bread mixture

450 g (1 lb) strong plain flour[1]
12½ g (½ oz) fresh yeast
or 1 rounded tsp dried yeast
2 tsp salt[2]
1 tsp sugar[3]
275 ml (½ pint) warm water

Gas 8, 230°C (450°F)
15–20 minutes for rolls
40 minutes for loaf

Bun mixture

225 g (8 oz) strong plain flour[1]
12½ g (½ oz) fresh yeast
or 1 rounded tsp dried yeast
½ tsp salt
25 g (1 oz) sugar[3]
25 g (1 oz) fat[4]
1 egg
scant 150 ml (¼ pint) warm milk[5]
½ tsp mixed spice (optional)

Gas 7, 220°C (425°F)
20–25 minutes

[1]wholemeal or wheatmeal. [2]use ½ stated amount. [3]omit. [4]polyunsaturated or fat-reduced margarine. [5](semi-)skimmed.

Uses and variations	Oven temperature and cooking time
Wholemeal bread: use 100% extraction flour. **Brown bread**: use wheatmeal flour or 50% wholemeal and 50% white flour. **Milk bread**: add 25 g (1 oz) fat, and use milk instead of water.	Gas 8, 230°C (450°F) 20 minutes for rolls 40 minutes for a loaf
Fruit buns: to bun mixture, add 50 g (2 oz) currants or other dried fruit and $\frac{1}{4}$ tsp mixed spice. Glaze with sugar and milk after baking. **Chelsea buns**: roll the dough to an oblong, and brush with 50 g (2 oz) melted butter. Sprinkle with 50 g (2 oz) sugar and fruit. Roll up, cut into equal pieces, and bake close together in a round sandwich tin.	Gas 7, 220°C (425°F) 20–25 minutes

Method

Bread making (traditional method)

All ingredients and utensils should be warm to assist the fermentation.

1 Dissolve the yeast in some of the liquid and add 1 tsp sugar. Leave it to stand in a warm place for ten minutes. This activates the yeast and starts the fermentation process.
2 Sieve the flour and salt. Rub in the fat if used.
3 Add the yeast liquid and the rest of the liquid all at once.
4 Mix quickly to a soft dough, which is elastic and pliable.
5 Knead the dough vigorously either by hand or in an electric mixer using a dough hook. Kneading ensures thorough distribution of the yeast in the dough so that it is in contact with the natural sugars in the flour. It also helps to develop the gluten so that it is capable of stretching during fermentation.

6 Cover the dough with a damp cloth to prevent the formation of a skin, and leave it to rise or 'prove' in a warm place for one to two hours. During this time the process of fermentation takes place, and the reactions involved are summarized below:

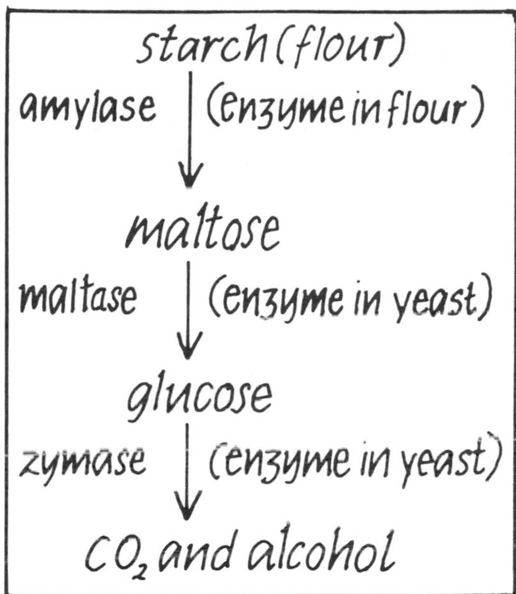

The temperature inside the dough should be about 25°C (77°F) for this to work efficiently.

7 'Knock back' the dough by kneading it again, to bring the yeast into contact with more of the flour.

8 Shape the dough into loaves or rolls. Place in the appropriate greased tin and leave to rise again for 40 minutes so that more CO_2 gas is produced.

9 Bake according to directions, until risen, set, golden brown in colour, and hollow-sounding when tapped with the finger.

Bread making (quicker method)

It is possible to shorten the period of time required for making bread by the traditional method, by subjecting the dough to very intensive kneading in the first stage, for a longer period of time, shaping it into rolls or loaves, and then allowing it to rise for half an hour before baking. This method is often used in bakeries where large mixers provide the means for the thorough kneading.

The Chorleywood process

This quicker method of bread making was developed at the British Baking Industries Research Association at Chorleywood, and became known as the Chorleywood process. In this method, extra yeast and water are used, and ascorbic acid (vitamin C) is added as a dough improver. Fat is also added.

Almost any type of flour can be used and even weak flour will produce good bread, as the shorter fermentation time results in a smaller loss of protein than in the traditional method. Strict temperature control is also less critical as the rapid fermentation reactions cause the dough temperature to rise.

The bread can be made and baked within two hours. This is a time saving of 60% compared to the traditional method, and is therefore useful to large bakeries. Bread made by this method also has better keeping qualities.

For making bread at home, vitamin C tablets, which are obtainable from chemists, can be added to the yeast liquid before it is added to the flour. The dough should be kneaded for five minutes, then shaped and left to rise before baking.

Left: Mixing the dough . . .

Above: . . . and taking the bread out of the oven.

Changes during the baking of bread

1 The dough first rises quickly, as the CO_2 gas expands in the heat.
2 Yeast activity increases at first, but gradually decreases as the temperature of the dough increases.
3 At 54°C (130°F) the yeast is killed and fermentation stops.
4 The water is absorbed by the starch granules in the flour. They swell and gelatinize, and support the structure of the loaf.
5 The gluten starts to coagulate at 73°C (165°F), and continues to do so until baking is complete.
6 Water, carbon dioxide, and alcohol escape from the dough during baking
7 Dextrin is formed on the outside of the loaf due to the reaction between the starch and the heat and steam. The sugars are converted to caramel which gives a brown colour to the crust.

Faults in breadmaking

A perfect loaf.

Loaf is small and dense

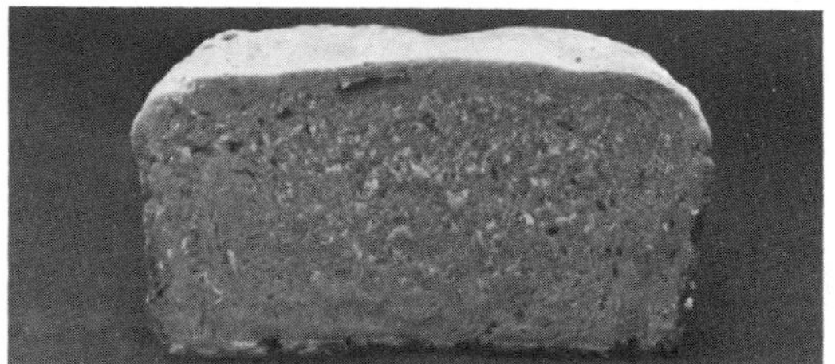

Causes

1 Insufficient fermentation.
2 Insufficient liquid resulting in a dough which is too stiff to allow expansion.
3 Inactive yeast, which has not produced enough CO_2 gas.

Loaf has not risen well, and is hard and coarse in texture

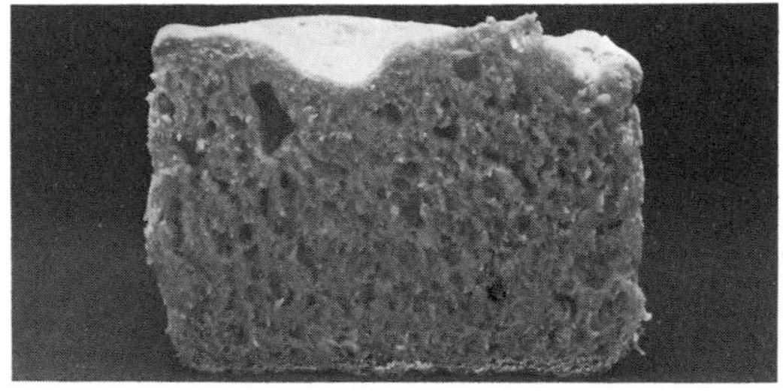

Causes

1 The dough has been overfermented, resulting in a breakdown of the gas pockets in the dough, due to the increase in pressure from the CO_2 gas. This causes gas pockets to break down and release gas and to form large, uneven holes in the texture of the baked dough.
2 Yeast has been killed before the loaf is baked.

Traditional bread roll and loaf shapes

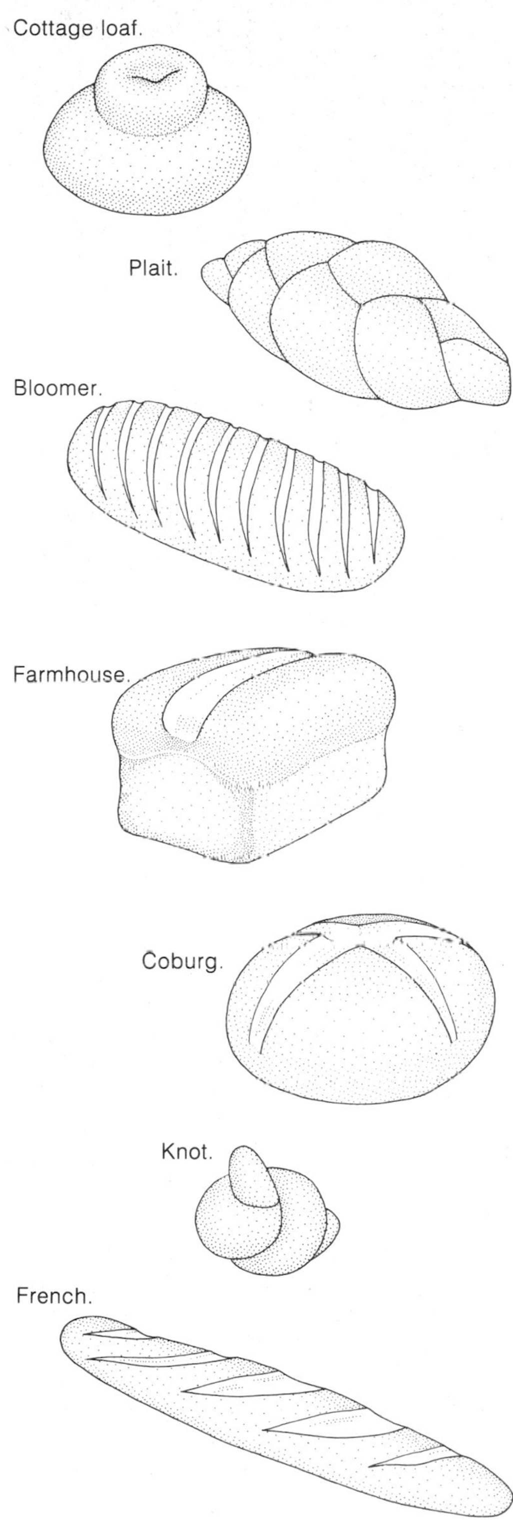

Sauces

A sauce is a thickened, flavoured liquid which can be added to a food or dish for any of the following reasons:

1 To enhance the flavour of the food which it accompanies.
2 To provide a contrasting flavour to an otherwise mildly-flavoured food, e.g. cheese sauce with cauliflower.
3 To provide a contrasting texture to particular solid foods, e.g. poultry or fish.
4 To bind ingredients together for dishes such as fish cakes or croquettes.
5 To add colour to a dish, e.g. jam sauce with a steamed sponge pudding.
6 To contribute to the nutritional value of a dish.
7 To reduce the richness of some foods, e.g. orange sauce with roast duck, apple sauce with roast pork.
8 To add interest and variety to a meal.

Sauces should be carefully flavoured and should be tasted before serving, so that adjustments can be made.

A sauce can be served as:

a coating for vegetables, meat, or fish
part of a meal, e.g. a casserole of meat
an accompaniment to a meal, e.g. cranberry sauce with roast turkey, mint sauce with roast lamb

Consistencies of sauces

The consistency of a sauce will vary according to how it will be served with the food (see above). Sauces can be classified into three main consistencies:

pouring
coating
binding (panada)

A **pouring** sauce, at boiling point, should just glaze the back of a wooden spoon, and should flow freely when poured.
A **coating** sauce, at boiling point, should coat the back of a wooden spoon, and should be used as soon as it is ready, to ensure even coating over the food.

A **binding** sauce or **panada** should be thick enough to bind dry ingredients together, so that they can be handled easily to be formed into rissoles, cakes, etc.

All sauces should be free from lumps and should not be overcooked, as this may spoil their flavour.

Thickenings

Sauces may be thickened by:

- **starch**, in flour, cornflour, arrowroot, etc.
- **protein**, from eggs
- **emulsification** of oil and water
- **puréed** vegetables or fruits

Sauces thickened by starch

Starch is the main polysaccharide produced by plants (see pp. 19–20), and is present in plant foods in the form of tiny granules. The size and shape of these are peculiar to the species of plant from which they come.

If starch is mixed with cold water, it will not dissolve. However, on heating to 60°C (140°F), water is absorbed by the granules, and they begin to swell. As the temperature increases, so does the swelling, until at 85°C (185°F), the granules will have swollen to five times their original size, and the liquid will be thickened. If heating continues, some of the granules will rupture, releasing starch which will form a **gel** with the water. On cooling, the gel will set, and the sauce will become solid.

It is important that sauces of this type have the liquid **blended** with the starch component before cooking, to prevent the formation of lumps of starch granules, which will not cook properly and will cause the sauce to have an uneven texture. During cooking, the sauce should be stirred continually, to ensure even heating of the liquid, and smoothness in the finished result. If the sauce is not stirred, the convection currents in the liquid (see p. 128) will not be sufficient to circulate the liquid, and it will cook at the base of the pan and result in a lumpy texture.

Roux sauces

Plain white sauce

Pouring consistency
12·5 g (½ oz) flour
12·5 g (½ oz) fat
275 ml (½ pint) liquid

Coating consistency
25 g (1 oz) flour
25 g (1 oz) fat
275 ml (½ pint) liquid

Panada
25 g (1 oz) flour
25 g (1 oz) fat
150 ml (¼ pint) liquid

The liquid can be milk, stock, or vegetable liquor.

Uses and variations

Cheese sauce: use all milk (may be skimmed) for the liquid. Add 75 g (3 oz) grated cheddar cheese (may be fat reduced), cayenne pepper, and ¼ tsp. mustard.
Mushroom sauce: use all milk (skimmed can be used). Add 50 g (2 oz) sliced mushrooms, either fried or poached in milk, salt and pepper.
Onion sauce: use all milk. Add finely chopped, cooked onion.
Parsley sauce: use all milk. Add 1 rounded tbsp finely chopped parsley.

Brown sauce

Pouring consistency

12·5 g (½ oz) flour
12·5 g (½ oz) fat
275 ml (½ pint) stock
1 small carrot
1 small onion
salt and pepper
½ tsp yeast or meat extract

Roux sauce (one-stage method)

Ingredients for each of the three consistencies are in the same proportions as for roux sauces made by the traditional method.

Method

1 Place all ingredients in a saucepan.
2 Heat gently, stirring all the time until the mixture boils.
3 Continue cooking for three minutes until thick and glossy.

This method is quicker than the traditional one, and avoids the risk of overheating the fat and flour at the roux stage.

Method

1 Melt the fat in a pan and add the flour. Stir until well mixed and heat gently for one minute. During this time, the starch granules will begin to soften and the starch will start to cook. The fat and flour mixture form the 'roux'.
2 Remove from the heat. Gradually add the liquid, stirring well at each addition, to form a smooth paste. If the liquid is added too quickly, lumps will form which will be difficult to remove.
3 When all the liquid has been added, return to the heat, and, stirring all the time, bring to the boil and cook for two mintues. The sauce must be stirred to prevent the formation of lumps.
4 Remove from the heat and add the seasoning and other ingredients. If cheese is used, add it as soon as the sauce is cooked so that it melts. Do not return it to the heat as the protein in the cheese may overcook and become stringy in texture.

For the brown sauce:

1 Fry the vegetables in the fat until brown, add the flour and continue as above.
2 When the sauce has boiled, allow it to simmer for 15–20 minutes, then strain it before serving.

Both sauces should have the following qualities:

smoothness
a good colour

In addition, the white sauce should be glossy in appearance.

Cornflour sauces

Pouring consistency
275 ml (½ pint) liquid
(milk, water, or fruit juice)
1 rounded tbsp cornflour
25 g (1 oz) sugar
flavouring

Variations

Chocolate sauce: add 1 tbsp cocoa powder and ¼ tsp instant coffee (optional). Blend with the cornflour and milk; *or* melt 50 g (2 oz) chocolate in the milk.
Lemon sauce: use the grated rind and juice of 1 lemon, and reduce the liquid accordingly. Stir in the lemon juice when the sauce has been cooked.
Butterscotch sauce: use water, and dissolve 100 g (4 oz) brown sugar with 25 g (1 oz) butter in 150 ml (¼ pint) of it. Add the grated rind of 1 lemon and boil for 5 minutes. Blend the cornflour with the rest of the water, and mix with the rest of the liquid. Thicken as normal over a medium heat.

Method

1 Blend the cornflour gradually with the liquid to a smooth paste. Add the rest of the liquid.
2 Heat gently, stirring all the time, until the sauce has boiled and thickened. Continue heating for two minutes to ensure thorough cooking of the starch.
3 Cornflour sauces remain opaque when cooked and are therefore not suitable as glazes over fruit.

Arrowroot sauces

Arrowroot can be used in place of cornflour. It becomes clear when cooked, and can therefore be used for glazing. It should be used in the proportions of:

150 ml (¼ pint) liquid, e.g. fruit juice
2 tsps arrowroot

Variations

Jam sauce: use 150 ml ($\frac{1}{4}$ pint) water, 2 tbsp jam, and 1–2 tsp lemon juice.
Syrup sauce: use 150 ml ($\frac{1}{4}$ pint) water, 2 tbsp syrup, 2 tsp lemon juice.

Sauces thickened by the coagulation of protein

The coagulation of protein by heat is discussed on p. 14. Eggs are normally used to thicken sauces in this way, and as egg white coagulates at a lower temperature than the yolk, it is better to use the yolk alone to prevent spoiling the sauce by overcooking the white.

If the yolk is used as an additional thickener for sauces that contain starch, it should be added after the other ingredients have been cooked and cooled to below boiling point, but not less than the coagulation temperature of the yolk (70°C, 158°F). If the temperature is too high, the protein will coagulate rapidly and cause it to harden and spoil the texture of the sauce.

If the yolk or whole egg is used as the only thickener, as in egg custard, it should be well mixed with the liquid, cooked gently (e.g. over a pan of boiling water) to prevent overcooking, and cooled rapidly as soon as it has thickened to stop the coagulation.

Egg custard sauce

275 ml ($\frac{1}{2}$ pint) milk
1 whole egg *or* 2 egg yolks
1 tbsp sugar
few drops vanilla essence

Method

1. Thoroughly mix the egg and milk.
2. Add the sugar.
3. Pour into a double saucepan or mixing bowl over a pan of boiling water.
4. Cook, stirring all the time, until the egg coagulates and the sauce coats the back of the spoon.
5. Remove from the heat, stir in the vanilla essence, and cool quickly to stop the coagulation. Serve immediately.

Sauces thickened by the emulsification of fat

If oil and water are thoroughly mixed, they become dispersed in each other and form an **emulsion**. After standing for a while, the emulsion will separate and the oil will float on top of the water. In order to prevent this separation, the emulsion must be stabilized by the addition of an **emulsifier**. Egg yolk contains a substance called **lecithin** (see p. 94) which acts as an emulsifier, and is added to mayonnaise to prevent the separation of the oil and water (in the vinegar).

When the emulsion is stabilized by the lecithin, it thickens. The thickness can be adjusted by the amount of vinegar added to the mayonnaise. The oil must be added slowly and thoroughly mixed with the egg yolk to prevent it from separating out.

Mayonnaise

150 ml ($\frac{1}{4}$ pint) oil
2 tbsp vinegar or lemon juice
1 egg yolk
$\frac{1}{4}$ tsp dry mustard
$\frac{1}{4}$ tsp salt
1 tsp caster sugar
pepper

Method

1. Beat the dry ingredients into the egg yolk in a small basin, to help the lecithin to stabilize the emulsion.
2. Add the oil drop by drop, beating thoroughly in between.
3. Continue adding the oil until the mixture starts to thicken, then add the vinegar, drop by drop.
4. Add the oil and vinegar until the mayonnaise is the consistency of lightly whipped double cream.
5. Adjust the seasoning.

It is possible to make mayonnaise in the liquidizer of an electric mixer, and the oil can be added in a slow trickle, while the machine is running.

Sauces thickened by a purée

Cooked or raw fruit or vegetables can be puréed to produce a smooth sauce, by rubbing them through a nylon sieve or processing them in a liquidizer.

Fruit which is subject to enzymic browning (see p. 131) should first be cooked or mixed with an acid (e.g. lemon juice), to inactivate the oxidase enzymes which cause the browning when the fruit is cut.

Apple sauce

450 g (1 lb) cooking apples
2 tbsp water
25 g (1 oz) butter
sugar to taste

Method

1 Peel, core, and slice the apples.
2 Stew the apples in the water and butter until soft.
3 Purée and add sugar to taste.
4 Serve with roast pork.

Tomato sauce

1 onion
1 carrot
25 g (1 oz) fat
1 tbsp cornflour
1 medium can plum tomatoes
seasoning

Method

1 Slice the onion and carrot, and fry in the fat until soft.
2 Add the tomatoes and juice from the can.
3 Mix the cornflour with 2 tbsp water and add to the pan.
4 Simmer for 30 minutes, then purée.
5 Season to taste.

Batters

Batters are a mixture of flour (usually plain), liquid (milk or water), and egg.
They vary in consistency according to their use in a recipe.

Thin batter

100 g (4 oz) plain flour[1]
$\frac{1}{4}$ tsp salt
275 ml ($\frac{1}{2}$ pint) liquid[2]
1 egg

Uses:
toad-in-the-hole
Yorkshire pudding
pancakes

Coating batter

100 g (4 oz) plain flour
$\frac{1}{4}$ tsp salt
150 ml ($\frac{1}{4}$ pint) liquid
1 egg

Uses:
deep fried fish, poultry joints

Fritter batter

50 g (2 oz) plain flour
pinch of salt
3 tbsp water
1 egg white
2 tsp vegetable oil

Uses:
banana, apple, pineapple fritters
corned beef, sausage fritters

Method

1 Sieve the flour and salt. Make a well in the centre.
2 Add the egg and a little liquid and gradually work in the flour.
3 Add more liquid and mix to a smooth batter. Add the rest of the liquid and beat for five minutes.
4 During beating, some air is incorporated into the mixture, and this has a limited action as a raising agent during cooking.

[1]wholemeal or wheatmeal. [2]skimmed milk.

The main raising agent is steam, which is produced during cooking from the large volume of water in the mixture. In order for this to be effective the cooking temperature must be high so that the water vaporizes rapidly.

5 Use the mixture according to the recipe. Some recipes suggest leaving the mixture to stand for a while, but this is not essential.
6 If food is to be coated with the batter, it must be dry to ensure good adhesion when the batter is applied.
7 If the coated food is to be deep fried, the fat should be at the right temperature. If it is too hot, the batter will cook rapidly, leaving the inside partly cooked or raw. If the fat is too cool, the starch will absorb it, and the food will be heavy and oily.

Salads

A salad is usually a mixture of raw vegetables and fruits, but cooked and pickled foods can also be included.

Salads can be served as:

1 A starter to a meal.
2 An accompaniment to a main course of meat, poultry, fish, etc.
3 A complete main course, including meat, fish, poultry, cheese, egg, or pulses and nuts for protein.
4 A filling for sandwiches and rolls in packed meals.

Salads are nutritionally important because:

1 Vitamins and minerals which are easily lost in cooking are preserved.
2 Fibre is provided by many raw fruits and vegetables, and also by pulses if used.
3 Salads provide bulk to the diet and are useful in energy-reduced diets, as most raw fruits and vegetables have low energy values.
4 Water is provided by raw fruits and vegetables.

Points to remember when preparing salads

1 Ingredients used should be crisp, fresh, well cleaned, and refreshing.
2 The ingredients should be prepared just before consumption to preserve their freshness and crispness.
3 A variety of colours, flavours, and textures should be included to make the salad interesting to eat.
4 The ingredients should be attractively and neatly served with the minimum of handling.
5 The salad should be easy to serve and eat.
6 A dressing should be served as an accompaniment or included in the salad.

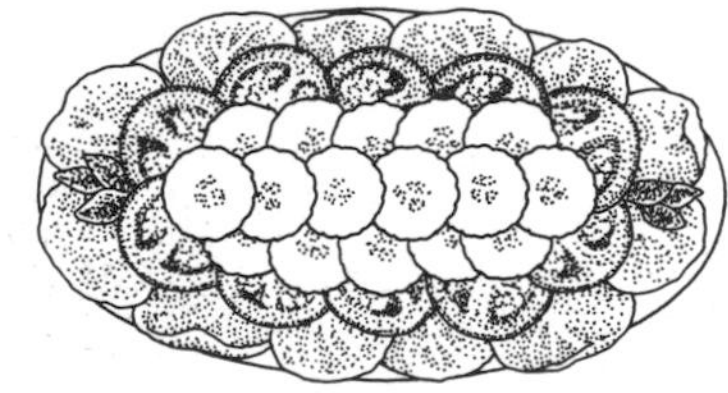

Suitable salad ingredients: preparation

Raw vegetables

lettuce	Discard outer damaged leaves. Wash well, dry. Shred or tear leaves or leave whole.
watercress	Discard damaged leaves and thick stalks. Wash well and inspect thoroughly for insects.
mustard and cress	Wash while still in punnet. Cut in bunches, using the stalks.
cucumber	Wash the skin if it is to be left on. Slice thinly.
spring onion	Remove roots and outer skin. Wash well. Cut tops off.
tomato	Choose firm tomatoes. Wash well, or remove skin by placing in boiling water for ½ minute, then peeling off skin. Slice or segment the tomato.
radish	Remove stalks and roots and wash well.
celery	Trim off leaves and root ends. Scrub each stalk well and slice.
pepper (capsicum)	Wash well. Cut in half, lengthways, and remove core, seeds, and pith. Slice or dice.
chicory	Discard damaged leaves. Wash, halve lengthways or slice.
carrot	Use young carrots. Wash well, serve whole if small or grate.
cabbage	Use firm white cabbage. Shred finely and wash well.
cauliflower	Use the head, broken into very small florets.
mushrooms	Wash, peel if necessary, and slice thinly.

Cooked vegetables

beetroot	Wash well, boil until soft with skin on, cool. Remove skin, slice or dice, and serve in vinegar or on its own.
potato	Diced in potato salad or hot, new potatoes with mint and butter.
carrots	Diced in potato salad.

Beans

red kidney beans	Soak overnight in cold water, then boil for *at least* 20 minutes until soft.
haricot beans butter beans	} As above.
broad beans	Wash and boil gently for 15 minutes until soft.
French beans runner beans	} Boil until soft and serve with a dressing.

Herbs

Fresh herbs can be sprinkled over salads or mixed into dressings to give extra flavour and interest.

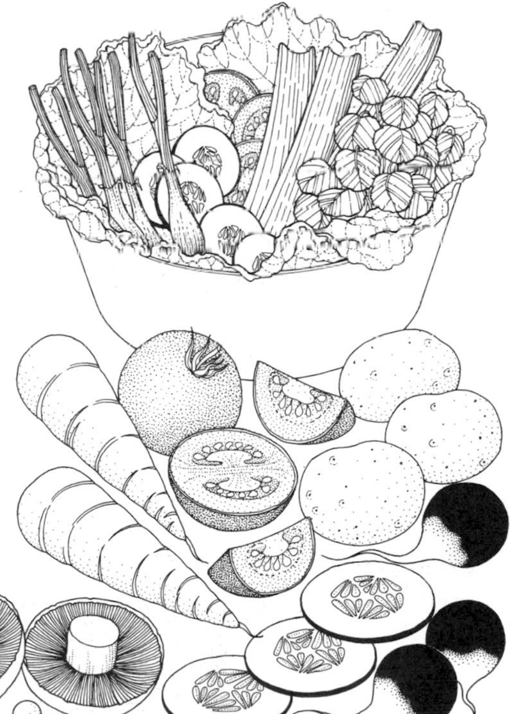

Fresh fruits

apple	Leave skin on. Slice and core, sprinkle with lemon juice to prevent browning.
banana	Sprinkle with lemon juice.
grapes	De-seed.
citrus fruits	Remove segments, discarding pips and pith.
pineapple	Remove hard core.

Nuts

almonds	Use blanched, flaked or toasted almonds.

walnuts
peanuts
cashew nuts
hazel nuts
Brazil nuts

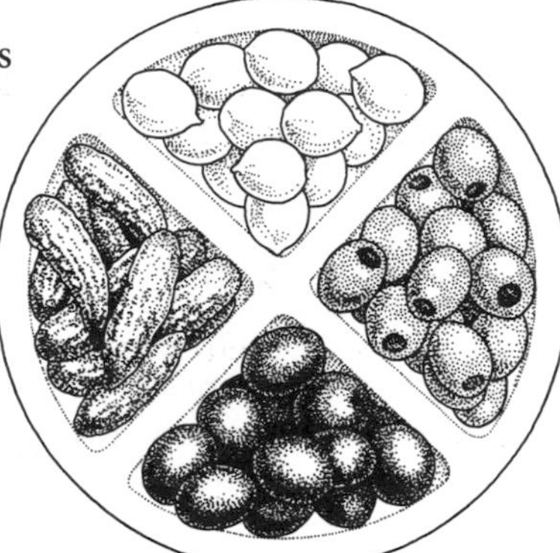

Pickles

olives
walnuts
gherkins
capers
onions
chutneys

Garnishes for salads

Sieved hard-boiled egg yolk
grated cheese
nuts
chopped, fresh herbs

Salad dressings

Salad dressings can be served separately, or combined with the salad ingredients.
They are added to salads to:

1 Provide extra flavour.
2 Moisten the salad.
3 Aid chewing and swallowing the salad vegetables.

If the dressing is to be combined with the salad ingredients, it should be added just before serving, as soaking the ingredients will soften the leaves of salad vegetables and the vinegar acid will cause staining.

Oil and vinegar dressing (French dressing)

6 tbsp oil (e.g. corn oil, olive oil)
2 tbsp vinegar or lemon juice
¼ tsp each of dry mustard, sugar, salt, and pepper

Vinaigrette dressing

Add finely chopped spring onion and parsley to the above recipe.

Method for both
Place all the ingredients in a small, screw-topped jar and shake vigorously until the oil is emulsified and the mixture is cloudy. Use immediately as the oil will separate fairly soon afterwards.

Salad cream

1 yolk from a hard-boiled egg
1 tbsp oil
¼ tsp made mustard
2 tbsp cream or evaporated milk
2 tsp vinegar
1 tsp Worcester sauce
seasoning

Method
1 Sieve the egg yolk, and work gradually into the seasonings, vinegar, and oil.
2 Whip the cream and fold in last.

Yogurt dressing

small carton plain yogurt
¼ tsp sugar
seasoning and mustard to taste

Method
1 Combine all ingredients thoroughly.
2 Chopped chives, parsley, onions, etc. can be added.

Mayonnaise

See p. 226.

Soups and stocks

Soups

Soups are included in meals for the following reasons:

1 As appetizers.
2 To provide hot food in cold weather.
3 To provide flavour and variety.

On their own, soups do not contribute greatly to the nutritional value of the diet because of their high water content, but if eaten with other foods, e.g. bread, their value will be increased.

Types of soup

Soups are normally based on one main ingredient, e.g. a vegetable, meat, or pulses, and can vary in consistency as follows:

Thick soups

These can be either puréed, or thickened by starch or egg protein.
Puréed: these are usually sieved or liquidized and may be further thickened by starch.
Thickened by starch or protein: these may have little solid ingredients in them, e.g. vegetable pieces.

Both types of thick soups can have cream added, and are normally served in cold weather as a substantial part of a meal.

Clear soups

These usually consist of a well-flavoured clear stock, served with a garnish, such as thin strips of carrot.
Broths are a variation of clear soups and usually contain small pieces of meat or poultry, with rice, pasta, or oats.

Mixed soups

These usually contain a mixture of ingredients, e.g. meat and vegetables, with perhaps pasta or rice included as well.

Preparing soups

A well-prepared soup should have the following qualities:

a good flavour and colour
non greasy
well seasoned
finely chopped ingredients that are easy to fit onto a spoon.
no lumps, if it is a smooth soup.

For each 575 ml (1 pint) of water or stock, a soup should have:

450 g (1 lb) vegetables
or 225 g ($\frac{1}{2}$ lb) meat or poultry
or 100 g (4 oz) pulses (soaked)

It is important not to overcook the soup as this may spoil its flavour. If stock is used as the liquid, it should be fresh and well flavoured.

Serving soups

Soups can be served with any of the following:

croutons of toast or fried bread
bread rolls or sticks
grated cheese
slices of bread with grilled cheese on top
chopped fresh parsley
strips of carrot or celery

Usually 150 ml ($\frac{1}{4}$ pint) of soup per person is sufficient to serve.

Stocks

A stock is a well-flavoured liquid which is obtained by simmering a food in water for some time in order to extract flavour from it.

Stocks have little food value on their own, and are mainly used as the bases of soups, sauces, and gravies.

Types of food suitable for stock making

1 Vegetables and vegetable liquid, except for green vegetables which can be bitter.
2 Bones from meat, fish, and poultry.
3 Meat, poultry, and giblets.
4 Bones and scraps of white fish.

Rules for making stock

1 The ingredients must be fresh and clean.
2 The ingredients should be cut up so that all the flavour can be extracted, and fat should be removed.
3 The ingredients should be covered with cold water, brought slowly to the boil, and simmered for 2–3 hours. To concentrate the flavour, the lid should be removed to allow water to evaporate.
4 The stock should be skimmed to remove fat and other ingredients which produce a foam on the surface.
5 The stock should be strained as soon as it is ready, and cooled quickly and stored in a cold place.
6 Use the stock as soon as possible. It will keep for up to three days if stored in a cool place.
7 Do not use the stock more than once. Warm stock is an ideal breeding ground for bacteria.

Stock which is made from bones usually sets to a jelly due to the conversion of collagen to gelatine (see p. 97), but it has little food value as there is only a small amount of protein present.

Stock cubes or powders can be used in place of home-made stock and are quick and convenient to use.

Home preservation of fruit and vegetables

Preservation of fruit

The two main methods of fruit preservation in the home (apart from freezing) are:

jam or marmalade making
bottling

Fruit can be preserved for many months in this way, and eaten out of season.

Jam making

Jam is prepared by boiling fruit with a sugar solution until it forms a 'gel' which sets on cooling.

In order for a gel to form, the jam should contain:

pectin
acid
sugar

and it is important that these are present in the right concentrations.

Pectin

Pectin is a polysaccharide (see p. 20), and during jam making, its molecules form a three-dimensional network (which is the framework of the gel) with the water, sugar, and solid matter from the fruit.

Pectin will not form a satisfactory gel until the pH (see p. 148) of the mixture is about 3·5 (acidic). It is found in the cell walls of fruits and vegetables. The amount present depends on the type of fruit and its age. Unripe fruit contains more acid and pectin (which is released during the stewing of the fruit), whereas over-ripe fruit contains pectin which has been converted into a form which is unable to form a gel.

Acid

Acid is needed to extract the pectin from the fruit during stewing, and fruits which have a high pectin content are normally acidic. Acid is also required to improve the colour and flavour of the jam, and to prevent the sugar from forming crystals during storage.

Sugar

Sugar is added as a preservative (see pp. 147–8), and to form the gel. It must be accurately measured, as too much will cause crystallization of the sugar, and too little will prevent proper setting and will encourage fermentation to take place. The sugar should be about 60% of the total finished weight of the jam.

Preserving sugar is specially made for this purpose and is composed of large crystals which are purer than ordinary granulated sugar, and consequently cause less scum to form during boiling. Granulated sugar is an acceptable alternative, however, and is cheaper to buy.

Choice of fruit

The fruit used for jam making should be:

- slightly under-ripe
- free from blemishes and mould growth
- clean

Fruits rich in pectin
cooking apples
damsons
gooseberries
bitter oranges
lemons
blackcurrants
redcurrants

Fruits with a good pectin content
blackberries
plums
apricots
raspberries

Fruits with a poor pectin content
strawberries
cherries
pears

In order to make a successful jam from fruits with a poor pectin content, other fruits that are rich in pectin can be added, or a commercially prepared pectin concentrate can be used.

Proportions of ingredients required

Fruits with a rich pectin content

575 g (1¼ lb) sugar	Expected yield of jam:
450 g (1 lb) fruit	950 g (just over 2 lb)
425 ml (¾ pint) water	

Fruits with a good pectin content

450 g (1 lb) sugar	Expected yield of jam:
450 g (1 lb) fruit	750 g (just under 1¾ lb)
150 ml (¼ pint) water	

Fruits with a poor pectin content

350 g (12 oz) sugar	Expected yield of jam:
450 g (1 lb) fruit	575 g (1¼ lb)
20 ml (1 tbsp) lemon juice	
No water	

Expected yields of jam

The total amount of added sugar in the finished jam should be about 60%. In order to work out how much jam should be produced (the yield), the following calculation should be used:

$$\frac{\text{amount of sugar} \times 10}{6} = \text{yield of finished jam}$$

Equipment required for jam making

Pan A large, thick-based pan should be used, to allow space for the boiling mixture to rise, and to prevent the jam from burning on the base. Special preserving pans are most suitable, and they normally have a large handle and lip for easy pouring.

Wooden spoon, with a long handle, for easy stirring.

Measuring jug A heat-proof jug should be used for transferring the jam to the jars.

Jars Empty, used jars are suitable, providing that they have no cracks or chips in them. They must be well cleaned, and warmed in the oven before use, so that they do not crack when the hot jam is put into them.

Jam jar covers can be bought in different sizes, and consist of:

1 Small waxed circles of paper, which are placed, waxed side down, on to the hot jam. The wax melts, and forms an airtight seal over the jam, to prevent mould growth.
2 Larger cellophane circles which fit over the neck of the jar, and are kept in place with a rubber band. They are placed over the jar while the jam is hot, and on cooling, they shrink to form a second seal over the jam.

Equipment to test for setting A sugar thermometer, a cold plate or saucer, or both.

Labels Self-adhesive labels are best, and should indicate the contents of the jar and the date of preparation.

Method

1 Wash the fruit, and remove bruised or over-ripe pieces. Dry it.
2 Prepare the fruit:
remove stalks and leaves,
remove stones or cores,
chop the fruit as required.
The stones of plums, apricots, etc., can be included when the fruit is being stewed as they usually have some pectin in and around them. They should be removed at the end of the stewing process.
3 Grease the preserving pan with margarine or butter, to prevent the fruit from sticking and to reduce the amount of scum produced when the jam is boiled.
4 Add the water (if included) to the fruit and simmer until the fruit is very tender. This stage is important, as the pectin is extracted from the fruit with the help of the acid which is either added or is present in the fruit.
Fruits that are rich in pectin have water added to soften them properly, and it also prevents the jam from setting too hard due to the high pectin content.
Fruits which have a good pectin content have water added to soften them, and it should all evaporate at this stage.
Fruits that have a poor pectin content have lemon juice added to assist the extraction of the pectin that is present.
The amount of time required for stewing at this stage will vary:
Soft fruits (raspberries, strawberries, etc) will require up to 20 minutes.
Apricots, plums, and similar fruit will require up to 30 minutes.
Hard fruits with tough skins (blackcurrants, oranges, etc.) will require between 40 minutes and 3 hours.
5 After stewing the fruit, test it for pectin. Cool some of the fruit and juice for a few minutes, in a glass. Add three parts methylated spirit to one part of the fruit liquid, and leave for one minute. Gently pour this into another glass, and observe its consistency.
A high pectin content is indicated by the liquid forming one large clot with the methylated spirit.
A medium pectin content is indicated by the liquid forming several smaller, firm clots with the methylated spirit.
A poor pectin content is indicated by the liquid forming small, thin clots with the methylated spirit.
6 If the pectin content is poor, the fruit may be stewed for longer, and retested, or fruit with a high pectin content can be added, but it must have been stewed separately first.
7 Whilst the fruit is stewing, wash the jars well and warm them in the oven so that they are completely dry and ready to take the hot jam.
8 Add the sugar all at once. It can be prewarmed in the oven to make it dissolve more quickly. Stir it over a gentle heat until dissolved.

If the sugar is added before the fruit has been sufficiently stewed and softened, it will cause the skins to become tough.

9 Bring the mixture to the boil quickly, and stir it occasionally. Boil rapidly to reach setting point quickly, and thus prevent the spoilage of flavour and colour by overcooking.

Remove any scum that appears on the surface with a draining spoon.

When testing the jam for setting point, remove the pan from the heat to prevent overcooking, which will result in a hard jam.

To test for setting point:

Temperature When jam is at setting point, it should reach 105°C (221°F). This can be checked with a sugar thermometer, which should be kept in a pan of boiling water, so that it is ready to take a reading.

Wrinkle test Have ready a cold plate or saucer. Place a little of the jam on it and leave to cool. Push the jam with the finger; if it wrinkles, the jam has reached setting point.

Flake test Dip a clean, dry, wooden spoon into the jam. Allow it to cool slightly, then let the jam run gently over the side of the spoon. If it comes off in wide flakes it is ready; if it pours off in a thin trickle, it needs more boiling.

10 When set, pour into the hot jars, fill to the top, seal and cover while still hot, and leave the jam to cool and set at room temperature. Label when cool, wiping the jars if necessary.

Qualities of a good jam

Well-made jam should have the following qualities:

a good flavour
a bright colour
a clear appearance
evenly distributed fruit
a firm, but easy-to-spread texture.

Storage of jam

Jam should be stored in a cool, dry, dark place. Screw-on lids can be used as an extra seal. If the jam is stored in warm, moist conditions, the growth of moulds will be encouraged.

Faults in jam making

Jam has crystallized

Causes

1 Insufficient boiling of jam.
2 Overcooking of jam.
3 Too much sugar used.
4 Insufficient acid in the mixture.

Jam has mould growing on top

Causes

1 Incorrect storage.
2 Poor quality or over-ripe fruit was used.
3 Insufficient sugar used.
4 Incorrect filling of jar and sealing, resulting in a layer of air at the surface of the jam.

Jam has fermented

Causes

1 Insufficient boiling of jam, so that it does not set properly.
2 Insufficient sugar used.
3 Poor quality fruit used.

Jam has not set

Cause

Insufficient pectin or acid.

The jam may need reboiling, or the addition of more acid or commercial pectin. Reboiling should be carried out with care to avoid spoiling the flavour of the jam.

Fruit is tough

Causes

1 Insufficient stewing.
2 Sugar added too soon.

Jelly making

Jellies are made from the same ingredients as jam, but they are prepared in a slightly different way, to produce a well-flavoured and coloured jelly that is clear and contains little solid matter from the fruit.

Method

1 Wash and dry the fruit.
2 Prepare the fruit, but do not remove stones, skins, or cores.
3 Stew the fruit as for making jam, using the same proportions of water for the various types of fruit.
4 Mash the fruit to a pulp.
5 Use a jelly bag or a double piece of muslin, and place in position over an upturned stool.

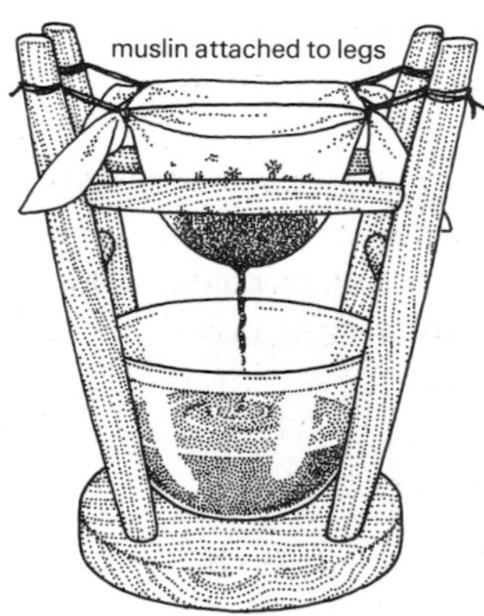

6 Pour the fruit pulp into the bag and leave it for at least three hours to drip into a clean bowl. Do not squeeze the bag as this will result in a cloudy jelly.
7 Test the juice for its pectin content, then add the sugar:
   Rich pectin content
   allow 575 g (1¼ lb) sugar
   to 575 ml (1 pint) fruit juice
   Good pectin content
   allow 450 g (1 lb) sugar
   to 575 ml (1 pint) fruit juice
   Poor pectin content
   allow 350 g (12 oz) sugar
   to 575 ml (1 pint) fruit juice
8 Boil the jelly as for the jam and remove any scum that forms. Test for the setting point in the same way as for jam.
9 Pour into jars, seal and label.

Marmalade making

Marmalade making is similar to jam making in most respects, except that in the first stage of extracting the pectin from the fruit, a longer stewing time and more water are required.

450 g (1 lb) fruit
1150 ml (2 pints) water
900 g (2 lb) sugar

Suitable fruits

lemons
limes
oranges – Seville oranges are best for flavour
grapefruit
tangerines

Oranges, grapefruits, and tangerines usually require additional acid from lemons or limes (citric acid), so that they form a proper gel.

Preparation of the fruit

The skins of the citrus fruit should be shredded coarsely or finely, depending on the required texture of the finished result, and the pith and pips should be separated and placed in a muslin bag which can be removed after stewing the fruit.

The skins must be stewed until very tender, otherwise they will spoil the finished result.

Bottling

The principles behind bottling as a method of preservation are discussed on pp. 141–2. For home preservation, it is recommended that bottling is used for fruits only, as the temperatures required for vegetable bottling are very high.

For bottling to be successful, the following are required:

good quality fruit
securely sealed and sound containers
proper and thorough heat treatment

Fruit

Fruit for bottling should be ripe (except for gooseberries which should be slightly under-ripe), so that it has the best colour and flavour. It should not be soft, however, as the heat treatment will cause overripe fruit to disintegrate.

Most fruits are suitable for bottling and their preparation is discussed later.

Containers

Containers for bottling should be made of heat-proof glass, which is free from cracks, flaws, and chips, and is very clean. Special jars for this purpose can be bought in different sizes.

The containers are sealed with rubber rings which are fitted on to the rim with a screwed- or clipped-on lid, while the contents are still hot. On cooling, the fruit and syrup will shrink, preventing air from being drawn in, and causing a vacuum to be produced.

The rubber seals should be used only once, but the containers and lids can be re-used many times.

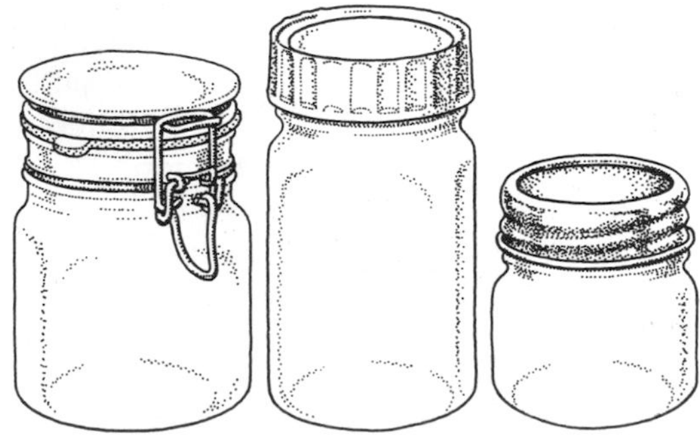

Heat treatment

Heat treatment can be carried out in:

the oven
a water bath on the hob
a pressure cooker

Oven treatment

This is a simple and satisfactory method of bottling. The containers with their contents packed with syrup or without (depending on the fruit) should be placed in the middle of the oven, with a 5 cm (2″) space between them. The lids should be placed loosely on top.

The oven should be pre-heated and the containers heated at gas 2, 150°C (300°F) for 30 minutes to 1 hour 40 minutes, depending on the type of fruit.

Water bath treatment

A large water bath is required for this method, and the containers holding the fruit and syrup should be placed in the warm water until almost covered (with the lids on, but not tight).

The water should then be heated until it is simmering (i.e. just below boiling point) for 25 minutes to an hour.

Pressure cooker treatment

The cooker must be large enough to accommodate the containers. They should be heated in boiling water first, with their contents, for one minute.

Put on the lids, and stand the containers on the trivet, not touching each other. Add 850 ml ($1\frac{1}{2}$ pints) water, and bring it to the boil. When steam is coming from the control valve, fit on the pressure gauge and heat gently to 0·35 kg/sq cm (5 p.s.i.) for one to five minutes, depending on the fruit.

Allow to depressurize slowly. Tighten the lids and leave to cool.

Preparation of the fruit

The fruit should be cleaned, and damaged or over-ripe pieces removed.

Fruit such as plums can be left whole or else halved and the stones removed.

Fruit such as apples and pears should be peeled and cored, and sliced or quartered. It is advisable to immerse them in salt water to prevent enzymic browning, but they should be rinsed before bottling.

The fruit should be carefully packed into the containers, to waste as little space as possible, but the fruit should not be squashed as this will bruise it.

It is better to bottle fruit in syrup, as in water alone, the fruit tends to lose its colour and flavour.

Syrup

225 g (8 oz) sugar
575 ml (1 pint) water

Dissolve the sugar in half the water over a gentle heat, then add the rest of the water. The syrup may be added boiling or cold.

The containers should be filled to the top (except for pressure-cooker treated fruit, where the syrup should be added to within 2·5 cm (1″) of the top), and tapped gently to expel any air in the jar.

NB After heat treatment, the lids should be tightly screwed or clipped onto the jar to form the seal, before the contents cool down.

Times for bottling different fruits

Fruit	Oven method	Water bath method	Pressure cooker
soft berries	45–60 mins	35 mins	1 min
damsons rhubarb	50–70 mins	40 mins	1 min
apricots plums	60–80 mins	50 mins	1 min
pears	70–90 mins	70 mins	5 mins
tomatoes	80–100 mins	80 min	5 mins

Pickling

Vegetables, some fruits, nuts, and hard-boiled eggs can be preserved by pickling. The principles behind pickling as a method of preservation are discussed on p. 148.

Preparation of foods for pickling

Vegetables should be immersed in a salt solution (brine) or sprinkled with salt for a few hours before pickling, to inhibit the growth of bacteria and to extract some of the water they contain by osmosis so that the finished result is crisp.

Brine

100 g (4 oz) salt
1150 ml (2 pints) water

NB Beetroot should not be treated with salt.

Vinegar

Vinegar used for pickling should contain at least 5% acetic acid.
Malt vinegar (brown) has a good flavour.
Distilled vinegar (white) has a weaker flavour, but is suitable for paler vegetables.
Spiced vinegar can be bought or home made. The spices add to the flavour and tanginess of the pickled food.

Spiced vinegar

575 ml (1 pint) vinegar
4 tsp pickling spice (cloves, peppercorns, dried chilli peppers, cinnamon, ginger, etc.)

This can be heated to just under boiling point for two hours, strained and cooled, or the spice can be added to the vinegar and left to infuse for two months.

Jars

Any jar can be used, as long as it is free from cracks and chips. The lid should have a waxed or plastic interior. Metal lids will corrode with the acid in the vinegar.

The food should be loosely packed into the jar, to within 2·5 cm (1″) of the top. The vinegar should then be poured into the jar to cover the food completely. Any air bubbles should be allowed to rise to the top.

The jar should be tightly sealed, and the pickled food left for at least two months before consumption to allow the flavour and crispness to develop. The only exception is cabbage, which should be eaten after two weeks as it softens if stored for longer.

Chutney making

Chutneys are a mixture of fruit, vegetables, spices, vinegar, and sugar, which are cooked until they reach the consistency of jam, but do not actually form a gel.

Chutneys originate from India, and there are many variations. The main proportions are:

450 g (1 lb) fresh fruit, e.g. tomato, mango, peach, apple, marrow, gooseberry, etc.
225 g ($\frac{1}{2}$ lb) dried fruit, e.g. sultanas, currants, raisins, dates, etc.
225 g ($\frac{1}{2}$ lb) onions or shallots
225 g ($\frac{1}{2}$ lb) sugar
275 ml ($\frac{1}{2}$ pint) vinegar
1–2 tbsp spices, e.g. cayenne, paprika, turmeric, cardamon, allspice, ginger, etc.

The fruit can be under-ripe, and chutneys are a useful way of using up gluts of under-ripe tomatoes, etc.

Method

1 Mince or finely chop the fruit and onions (the dried fruit can be left whole), and stew gently in a large pan until soft.
2 Add the rest of the ingredients and cook gently until the consistency of the chutney is thick and pulpy.
3 Pour into hot jars, and seal as for jam making.

Beverages

It is important to serve drinks (beverages) with meals, and throughout the day, as a means of supplying water in the diet, and to add variety and interest.

Coffee

Instant coffee in the form of a powder or granules is very popular today, particularly as it tends to be cheaper than ground coffee (made from fresh roasted coffee beans).

Ground coffee has more flavour, but it should be bought in small quantities as it loses its flavour when stored. Keeping coffee in the refrigerator helps to keep it fresh for longer.

Preparation

Generally, the proportions to use are:

575 ml (1 pint) water
4 tbsp (level) ground coffee

Percolator method

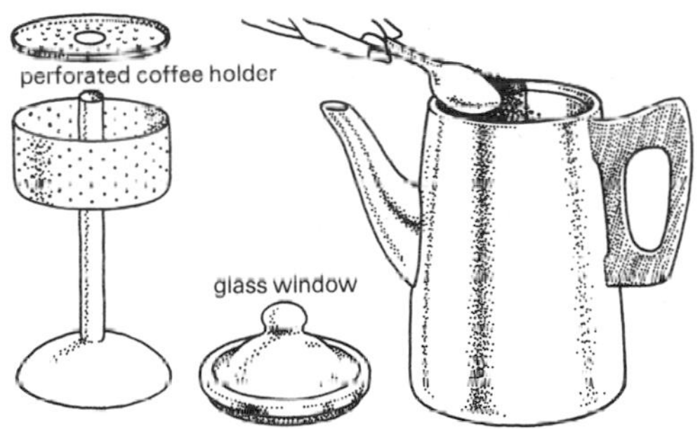

1 Put the coffee into the perforated holder. It should come only half way up to allow the coffee to swell and the water to percolate through it.
2 Measure the water into the pot, then place the coffee holder in the pot.
3 Heat slowly on a gas or electric hob, until the coffee can be seen percolating gently through the glass window in the lid.
4 Continue percolating until the coffee is a rich brown colour (about ten minutes).
5 Remove the coffee holder and serve.
6 Do not reboil as this tends to spoil the flavour of the coffee.

Jug method

1 Rinse out the coffee jug with boiling water, and add the measured coffee.
2 Add boiling water and allow the coffee to infuse for three to five minutes, stirring occasionally.
3 Leave to stand for a minute to allow the coffee to settle.
4 Pour carefully from the jug.
5 A special coffee filter may be used. These may already be folded; if not, fold as shown, place the filter in the holder, and the coffee in the filter. Pour the boiling water slowly over the coffee.

Coffee should be served with either hot milk or cream, and brown sugar.

Tea

Tea is a very popular beverage in the UK. The strength at which it is made is a matter of personal taste.

Generally, the proportions to use are:

1 tsp (level) of tea per person plus 1 extra
150 ml ($\frac{1}{4}$ pint) water per person

When preparing tea, the pot should be rinsed with boiling water before the tea is added. Boiling water should be poured onto the tea and it should be left to infuse for three to five minutes.

Strain the tea when serving. Serve with white sugar or sugar lumps and cold milk.

Lemon tea

Lemon tea is served with sugar and wedges of lemon.

Cold drinks

Cold drinks are easy to make and are refreshing to drink, particularly when made with fresh fruit. Some suggestions are given below.

Milk shakes

Use ice-cold milk or cold milk and natural yogurt, and mix with:
  fruit purée, e.g. strawberry, banana
  fruit syrup (available in bottles)
Milk shakes can be prepared in an electric liquidizer or whisked by hand.
Suggested flavours:
  banana
  strawberry
  coffee
  chocolate
Sweeten to taste.
Serve with:
  chopped nuts
  whole pieces of fruit
  grated chocolate
  ice cream

Lemon drink

the finely grated rind and juice of 2 lemons
575 ml (1 pint) ice-cold water
sugar to taste

Fresh fruit juice

Squeeze the juice from any citrus fruit and sweeten to taste if required.
A combination of juices adds variety, e.g.:
  grapefruit and orange
  lemon and orange

To serve fruit drinks

1 Dip the rim of the glass in egg white or water and then in sugar before filling.
2 Cut a thin slice of lemon or orange and slit it half way, then arrange it on the glass rim.
3 Place fresh mint leaves on the surface of the drink.
4 Serve with ice cubes.

All drinks should be served on a tray, with additional items such as sugar and cream in separate containers.

5/The kitchen

Kitchen planning

Modern houses tend to have smaller kitchens than older houses do, yet today more labour-saving equipment is available to put into them. The kitchen is a working room, and in order for it to be easy and efficient to work in, it must be well planned. Besides its main function as a place where food is stored and prepared for meals, the kitchen is also used for laundering and cleaning, hobbies, and very often entertaining and eating in.

The equipment and kitchen units should be positioned in a logical order so that they form a continuous working area to suit the sequence and stages of the main activities carried out in the kitchen. For meal preparation, this sequence would be as follows:

food storage → preparation → cooking → serving → clearing up

The kitchen should be designed in such a way that time and energy are not wasted by moving from one area to another, and that excessive bending and stretching in order to use equipment are avoided.

Kitchens often contain a dining area, and some have a separate utility room for laundering, although this is not very common.

The following kitchen plans are examples of different working layouts. The most efficient layouts are based on a U, L, or parallel lines plan.

L–shaped kitchen.

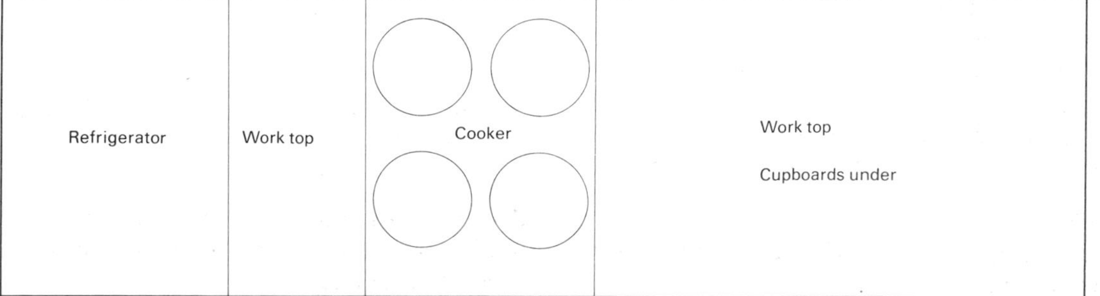

U-shaped kitchen.

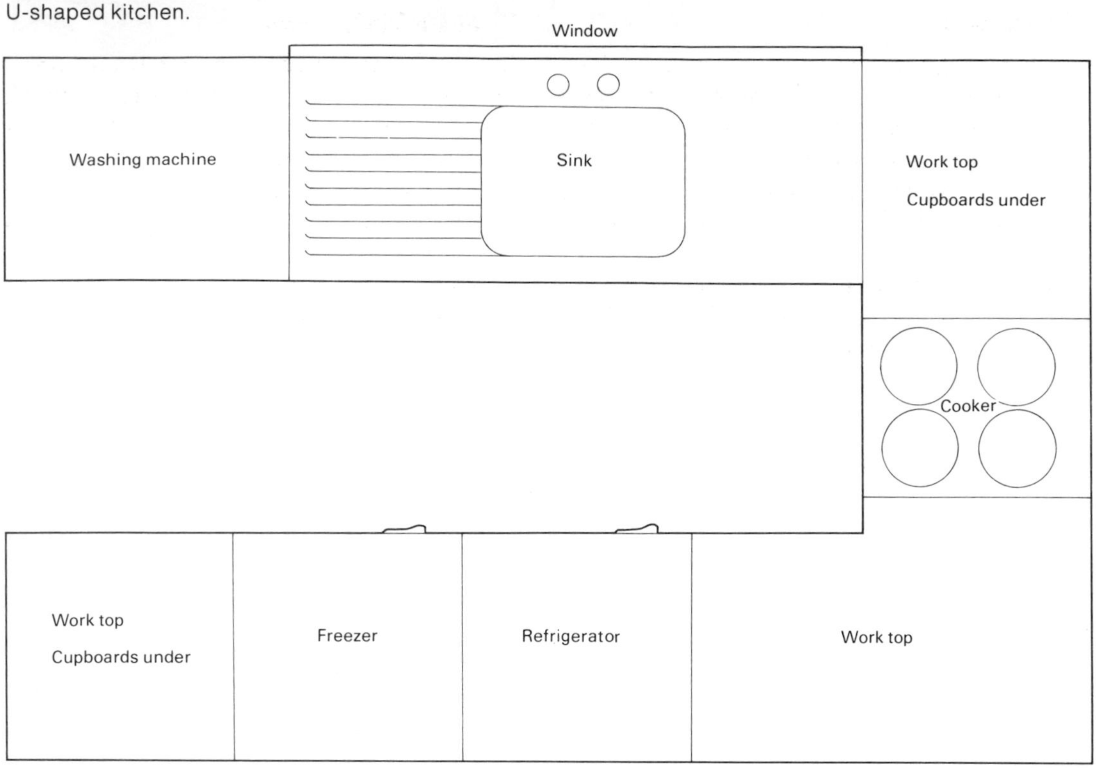

Window

Washing machine

Sink

Work top

Cupboards under

Cooker

Work top

Cupboards under

Freezer

Refrigerator

Work top

Parallel lines kitchen.

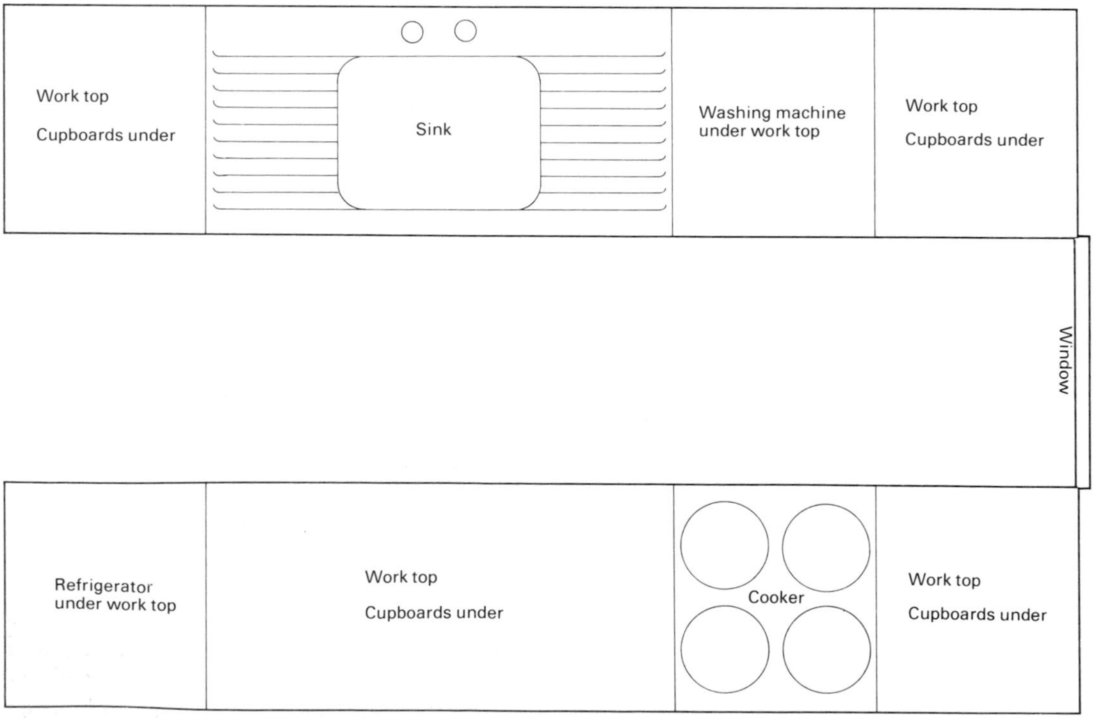

Work top

Cupboards under

Sink

Washing machine under work top

Work top

Cupboards under

Window

Refrigerator under work top

Work top

Cupboards under

Cooker

Work top

Cupboards under

Kitchen units

A wide range of self-assembly and ready-made kitchen units can be purchased, in a variety of styles, materials, and colours. They may be made from:

- solid wood, e.g. pine, oak, beech
- plastic-veneered (outer covering) chipboard

Usually the interior and shelves are made of plastic-veneered chipboard which is easy to clean and reduces the price of the complete unit.

Types of kitchen unit

Base units are fixed to the walls and floor, and usually have a work top fitted on them. They include drawer units as well as cupboards. Some have rectractable work tops to provide an extra work area. Wire baskets can be fitted into cupboards on hinges so that extra storage space is available. Waste bins can be fitted to a cupboard door so that they open when the door is opened and can be shut away when not in use.

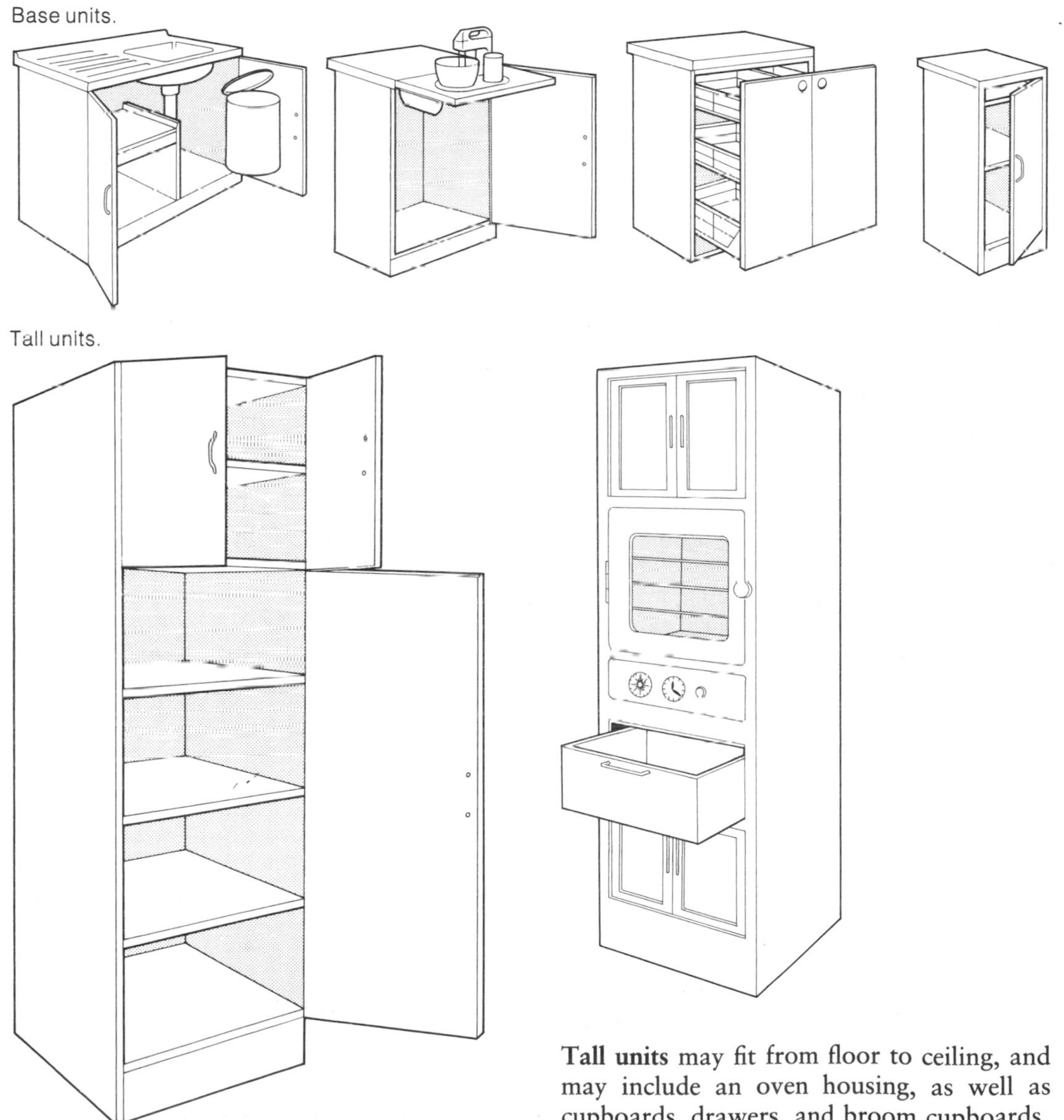

Tall units may fit from floor to ceiling, and may include an oven housing, as well as cupboards, drawers, and broom cupboards.

Peninsular units are base units that do not adjoin a wall, but jut out into the kitchen. They are often used to form a barrier between the kitchen and dining area, and have cupboards on both sides.

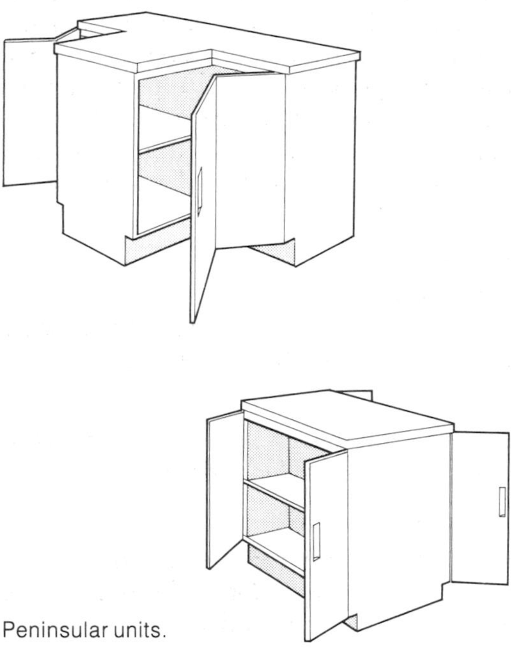

Peninsular units.

Wall units provide useful extra space, and can be fitted along the walls and into the corners. They should be of a suitable height so that the user can reach comfortably into them without danger of pulling something down on to themself. The cupboard doors should not be too wide so that they do not obstruct the worktop when opened. Some cupboards have sliding doors.

Wall units.

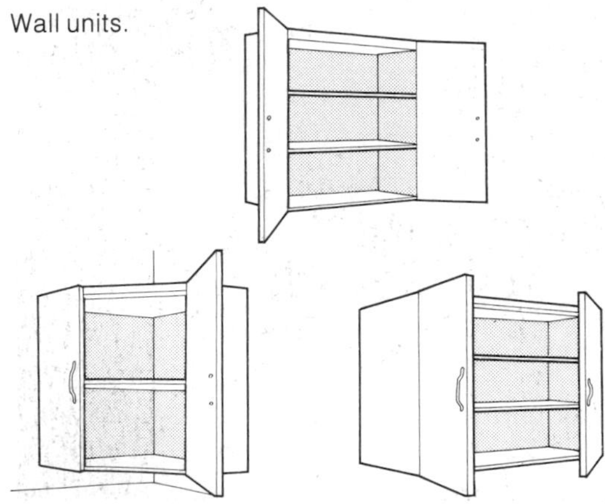

Island units are completely separate base units, which usually stand in the centre of a large kitchen, with a hob or sink unit in the work top. They may house cupboards all the way round or shelves at either end.

Island unit.

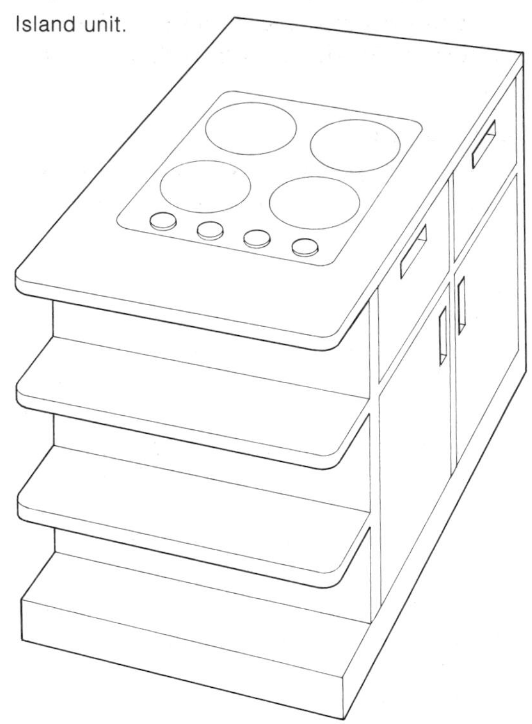

Work tops are usually made of plastic, either melamine or formica sheet, covering a thickness of chipboard. They are often made with a rolled edge, which is comfortable to work against. Cooker hobs can be fitted into the worktop, as can sink units, chopping boards, heat-resistant sections for standing pans on, and special shallow sinks for washing vegetables.

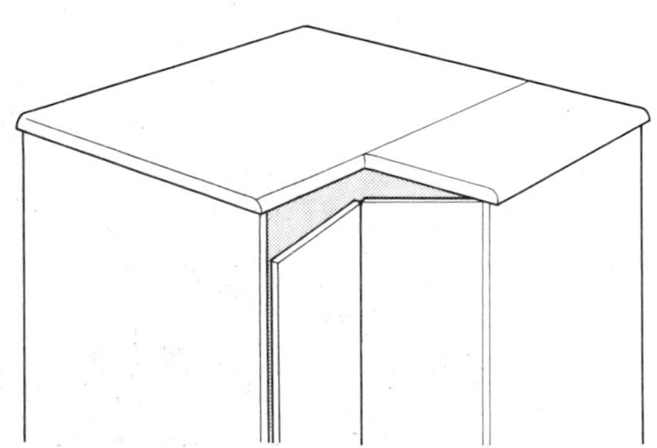

Storage space

Storage space is required in the kitchen for food, utensils, serving dishes, small equipment, and large equipment. The kitchen units should ideally be laid out to give sufficient storage space for all these items in the area of the kitchen where they are most used.

Food storage

Food can be divided into four main groups according to how it should be stored:

Dry foods
(flour, sugar, coffee, tea, rice, biscuits, canned foods)
These should be stored in a dry cupboard, at 12°C (54°F) or above. Dampness due to condensation or leakage will encourage mould growth and rancidity and will reduce the shelf life of such foods considerably.

A cupboard above the refrigerator (which gives out heat) or with a hot water pipe running through it will provide a suitably dry atmosphere. Wall units are often suitable for this purpose and can be fitted with adjustable shelves and racks for holding small packets and jars.

Semi-perishable foods
(bread, vegetables, fruit)
These require storage at 6–12°C (43–54°F), in a well-ventilated cupboard that has a relatively high humidity (moisture content in the air). This is to help prevent vegetables from wilting and deteriorating, but the humidity must be controlled by good ventilation to discourage mould growth.

Traditionally, walk-in larders or pantries were used for such storage, but today these are a rare inclusion in the kitchen. Many kitchen units have ventilation grids, or a backless cupboard that can be placed against an air brick on the external wall of the house. Such cupboards are best positioned on a north-facing wall of the house which will be cooler.

Perishable foods
(eggs, cheese, milk, meat, fish)
These should be kept at temperatures below 6°C (43°F), i.e. in the refrigerator.

Ready-frozen foods
These should be kept in either the ice box of a refrigerator or a domestic freezer.

The sink area

Much of the work carried out in the kitchen occurs in this area, and it can be used to store a variety of items, including:

cleaning materials
household chemicals
kitchen linen (tea-towels, cloths, etc.)
pans
cutlery
vegetable racks
waste bin

Cleaning materials and household chemicals should be stored in a high cupboard if there are young children in the home as they are a potential danger if stored in a cupboard under the sink (see p. 275).

Cutlery is best stored in a drawer, and sectioned cutlery trays help to keep it neat. Sharp-bladed knives should be stored with the blade pointing downwards, or in a special knife rack.

Pans can be stored in cupboards, on racks, or on shelves, but they should not be placed too high as they could fall on to the person trying to reach them. The same applies to other heavy equipment and glass articles such as mixing bowls.

The **waste bin** can be fitted to the inside of the sink cupboard door so that it opens when the door is opened. It is best to have the waste bin in the sink area for easy disposal of rubbish. Bin liners help to keep the bin clean and make it easier to dispose of rubbish. Large waste bins are not advisable in the kitchen as they tend not to be emptied until they are full. By this time the waste at the bottom will have started to harbour bacteria and this is unhygienic.

The **washing machine** is often placed in the sink area so that it can be plumbed in to the sink pipes and the waste water can escape through the sink drainage.

Electrical items, e.g. mixers, should be kept in a dry place, and are usually more accessible if kept covered on a work top.

Large equipment

Refrigerators and freezers can be put under work surfaces, or on top of one another if the freezer is an upright type. They must, however, have some ventilation around them to allow heat from the motors to escape.

Washing machines Front-loading automatic washing machines can be kept under a work top and plumbed in to the water supply, to avoid having to move them. Twin-tub machines can also be kept underneath work tops. Top-loading automatic machines require easy access and therefore need to stand under a removable work top or on their own. Automatic machines must be near to drainage.

Tumble driers can be placed on top of certain washing machines, and need some form of vent at the back to allow the moist air to escape.

Cookers can either be free standing, or can be fitted into kitchen units with the hob in the work surface and the oven in the wall or a special unit. If the hob and oven are separate there are often problems with removing them should the owner decide to move house. If the cooker has an extractor hood fitted above, it should be placed near to an outside wall to allow extracted air to be ducted out. There should be a work top either side of the cooker to form a continuous sequence in the food preparation area.

Ventilation

Ventilation is necessary in a kitchen to extract from the air steam, odours, and grease which would otherwise spoil decorations and travel to other parts of the house.

Open windows are the simplest form of ventilation, but they cause draughts and a loss of heat. A variety of air extractors and ventilators are available for use all over the house, but for the kitchen, a cooker hood and/or window or wall extractor fan are the most suitable.

Cooker hoods

Cooker hoods either extract or recirculate air, and must have an external outlet if the air is to be completely removed. Some hoods filter the air, remove the odours, then recirculate it. They are normally placed directly above the cooker.

The hood works by drawing air in with a fan and passing it through a filter. Air from the cooker enters a grid underneath the hood and grease particles are trapped by a washable aluminium mesh panel. Hoods which recirculate the air have a carbon or charcoal filter to absorb odours, and this has to be replaced every year or eighteen months according to use.

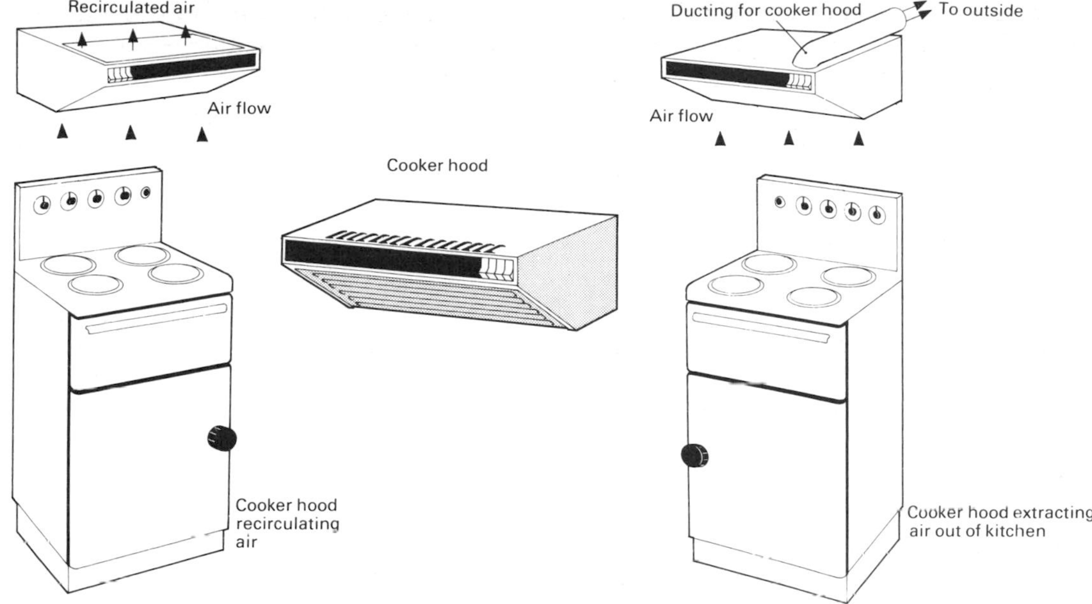

Extractor fans

Extractor fans are usually fitted in windows or outside walls, with suitable ducting to the outside. An electric motor draws in air by the fan and takes it to the outside. Some types can be reversed to blow fresh air into the room. On the outside, a shutter is fitted to prevent draughts from entering the room when the fan is not in use.

The fan should be placed near the ceiling, but away from hobs and cookers, as it may affect gas burners. The fan unit should be cleaned periodically to remove any fluff or grease that collects in it.

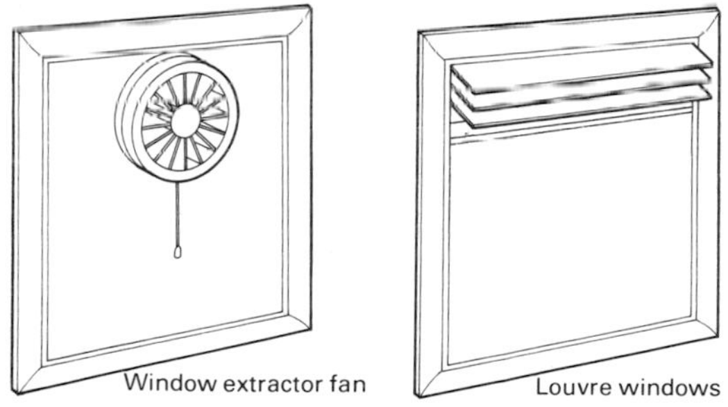

Windows

Louvre windows provide good ventilation as an alternatve to ordinary windows, and can be opened at various angles without creating excessive draughts.

Lighting

It is important that a kitchen has sufficient light to make working in it a safe and comfortable task.

Windows should be well placed and large enough to provide adequate daylight, as well as ventilation.

Fluorescent lighting provides bright, direct lighting. The bulbs are in the form of tubes which are fitted close to the ceiling.

Ordinary light bulbs should be of at least 100 watts strength to give adequate light, and can be fitted with a glass globe cover that does not shade any of the light. Small strip lights can be fitted under wall cupboards to shine directly on to work surfaces, thus providing light where it is most needed.

Decoration

A wide range of wall coverings, paints, and materials are suitable for use in the kitchen. Colour is, of course, a matter of personal choice, but colours which create an impression of coolness, e.g. cream, pale blue, green, yellow, and white, are often used as the kitchen is inclined to become hot.

Ideally, decorations used in a kitchen should be easy to clean and should not absorb grease or odours which would spoil their appearance.

Suitable wall coverings include:
vinyl (plastic) coated wall papers
ceramic glazed tiles
washable vinyl emulsion paint

Flooring

Kitchen floors should have the following characteristics:

easy to clean
non-slip
no loose parts or edges that someone could trip over
relatively warm to the feet
non-absorbent to grease and liquids.

Loose mats and a highly polished finish should be avoided as they may easily result in falls. The flooring should be well fitted and firmly held down.

Suitable flooring materials include:
vinyl tiles or sheet flooring
ceramic tiles
quarry tiles

Vinyl flooring is probably best as it is relatively warm to the feet, is easy to fit into the kitchen, and is not so hard as quarry or ceramic tiles. It can be purchased in a wide variety of colours and designs, and the more expensive brands are usually shrink-resistant and do not wear out for many years.

Carpeting in a kitchen is not advisable as it is difficult to keep clean, and absorbs stains very easily. Carpet tiles and industrial hard-wearing carpeting can be used, but may also be prone to staining.

Curtains

Curtains around a kitchen window are prone to absorbing odours and grease and must therefore be washed regularly. They should not be able to reach the cooker as this is a fire hazard, and should not hang over the window sill into the sink area where they will get wet.

Roller blinds are a suitable alternative to curtains as they can be kept out of the way during the day time. They can be made of either plastic material or specially stiffened fabric. Their main disadvantage is that they may be subject to mould growth if they become damp as they roll up tightly with little air space around them.

Venetian blinds can be used but they tend to become greasy and dusty and are laborious to clean.

Electric sockets

Electric socket outlets are normally placed on the wall above work tops in a kitchen, for the convenient use of mixers and other equipment. As so many labour-saving devices for the kitchen are electrical, it is best to have a minimum of five socket outlets in different places in the kitchen.

Cleaning the kitchen

As the main function of the kitchen is food preparation, it is important that it should be kept clean and hygienic. Most of the modern materials used in a kitchen are easy to clean and there are many products available to make cleaning an easy task. It is a good idea to get into a routine with cleaning, so that there is never a build-up of dirt which would be difficult to remove. The following routines should therefore be followed:

Every day

1 Wipe over work surfaces and cooker hob after use.
2 Sweep up any dry crumbs, dust, etc., from the floor.
3 Wipe up any spillages.
4 Wipe down the sink and draining-board.
5 Empty the waste bin and rinse it out.

Every week

1 Sweep and wash floor.
2 Wipe top and fronts of units.
3 Wash all surfaces and walls thoroughly.
4 Clean oven if required.

Every few weeks

1 Wipe out and tidy unit cupboards and drawers.
2 Move oven and other large equipment and clean behind them.
3 Defrost the fridge (see pp. 260–1).

Revision questions

1 What are the main functions of a kitchen?
2 Describe the sequence of work involved in preparing food.
3 Why is it important that a kitchen layout should be well planned?
4 What fittings are usually included in:
   a base units
   b tall units
   c island units?
5 How should the following be stored?
   a dry foods
   b semi-perishable foods
   c perishable foods
   d frozen foods
6 How should the following be stored?
   a cleaning materials
   b cutlery
   c sharp knives
   d waste bins
   e pans
   f refrigerators and freezers
   g washing machines
   h tumble driers
7 Why is it necessary to ventilate a kitchen?
8 Describe how cooker hoods and extractor fans work.
9 What are louvre windows?
10 Why is good lighting important in a kitchen?
11 What colours are particularly suitable for a kitchen and why?
12 Suggest two wall coverings suitable for a kitchen.
13 What features should a kitchen floor have?
14 Which type of flooring is most suitable for a kitchen?
15 What are the disadvantages of having curtains or a roller blind at a kitchen window?
16 How many electric sockets should a kitchen have and where should they be placed?
17 What cleaning processes should be carried out in a kitchen on a daily and a weekly basis?

Materials used in the home

Kitchen equipment and other household items are made from a variety of materials, including:

plastics
glass
wood
ceramics
metals

Plastics

Plastics were invented at the end of the nineteenth century. Their production was rapidly developed in the 1920s, and now many different types of plastic are made for a wide variety of purposes.

All plastics are made from three raw materials:

oil
coal
cellulose

The amounts used, and the addition of other ingredients, account for the differences between the various plastics.

General properties of plastics

1 Generally strong, particularly nylon. Many stretch, and some will split.
2 Good insulators of electricity.
3 They do not corrode or decay.
4 They have good resistance to most chemicals.
5 They are non toxic and can be used to wrap and hold food.
6 They are waterproof and generally greaseproof.
7 Most expand with heat and eventually melt.
8 Some are very hard and will withstand scratching.
9 Some are good insulators of heat.
10 They can be moulded into shapes and made into sheets and films.
11 They are relatively cheap to produce in large quantities.

There are two main groups of plastics:

thermoplastics
thermosetting plastics

Plastics in the kitchen.

Thermoplastics include many different types of plastic, each with specific uses, e.g.:

Polythene Packaging films, squeeze bottles, buckets, brushes, wire and cable insulation, containers for food.
Polypropylene Transparent wrapping films, pipes, bottles.
Polyvinylchloride (PVC) Material for aprons, rainwear, household chemical bottles.
Nylon (polyamide) Spun into fibres for fabrics, parts of machines, brushes, ropes.
Polytetrafluoroethylene (PTFE) Non-stick coating for pans and baking tins (known as 'Teflon').

Thermosetting plastics include:

Phenolics Saucepan handles, switches, formica for work tops.
Melamine Bottle tops, cups, saucers, plates.
Polyester Material, threads, chairs, sinks.
Polyurethane Hardwearing floors, sponges, paints.

Glass

Glass has a wide variety of uses, both decorative and functional. The raw material used to make it is **silica dioxide** which is found in sand and naturally as quartz. Some types of glass also have lime or metals such as lead added.

General properties of glass

1 Hard, but brittle, and will crack and break under stress.
2 Transparent, therefore useful for storage.
3 Poor conductor of heat.
4 Good insulator of electricity.
5 Non toxic.

Glass with special properties:

Heat-resistant glass is mainly used for cooking utensils. It withstands heat from liquids or ovens. Some types can withstand direct heat from a flame or electric hot plate.
Toughened glass can withstand quite severe shocks and impacts without breaking, and will only break into small pieces. Can be used for interior glass doors.

Uses

Lead crystal glass Glasses, vases, ornaments, decanters.
Soda lime glass Most other purposes, including: vacuum flasks, bottles, bowls, windows, light bulbs, cooker doors and panels, mirrors, tumblers, and glasses.

Wood

General properties of wood

1 Good insulator of heat.
2 Resists most chemicals.
3 Has high strength.
4 Shrinks as it dries out.
5 Attacked by insects and fungi unless specially treated.
6 May absorb strong flavours and odours.
7 May stain.

Uses

chopping and bread boards
pot stands
spoons, spatulas
kitchen units
draining boards (old fashioned)
salad and serving bowls
packing crates for foods

Ceramics

These include china and pottery. They have been used in the home for many years, especially in food preparation.

General properties of ceramics

1 Resistant to most chemical substances.
2 Can withstand very high temperatures but may crack if subjected to sudden extremes of temperature.
3 Poor conductors of heat.
4 Washable due to the glazes they are finished with.
5 Can be formed into a wide variety of shapes.

Uses

crockery: plates, cups, jugs, etc.
casserole dishes
serving dishes
clay bricks for roasting
tiles

Metals

There are many types of metal. Their cost and usage depends on how widely they are found in the earth and how easily they can be extracted.

Types

platinum, gold, silver } very expensive
aluminium
lead
iron
zinc
tin
copper
brass

Steel and stainless steel

There are different types of **steel**, and they are all **alloys** (i.e. mixtures) of iron and carbon, plus other metals such as manganese, silicon, tungsten, or nickel. The different types have special properties to fit them for particular uses.

Stainless steel is composed of 0·3% carbon, 18% chromium, 8% nickel, and 73·7% iron. It resists stains and corrosion because it has a protective layer of chromium oxide on the surface of the steel.

General properties of metals

1 Can be made into different shapes, some more easily than others.
2 Very good conductors of electricity.
3 Some are very strong.

Metals in the kitchen.

4 Some corrode when they come into contact with moisture, acids, or other chemicals.
5 Very good conductors of heat.
6 Can be sharpened to produce a cutting edge.

Uses

Stainless steel Sinks, work surfaces, cutlery, pans, baking tins, bowls, serving dishes, cook's knives, scissors, kettles, taps, screws, parts of cookers, refrigerators and other large pieces of equipment.
Steel Casings of washing machines, cookers, refrigerators, freezers. Steel can be coated with enamel, PVC, or paint.
Copper Bases of pans, bowls, jelly moulds, kettles, etc. Used less often today due to cost.
Aluminium Pans, baking tins, cutlery (light, cheap, and abundant).
Cast iron Casseroles, pans; usually coated with enamel (very heavy, rusts easily).

Revision questions

1 What are the raw materials used to make plastics?
2 What are the general properties of plastics?
3 Name the two main groups of plastics and give three examples of each with their uses.
4 What is the raw material used to make glass?
5 What are the general properties of glass?
6 Why is heat-resistant glass useful in the kitchen?
7 What are the general properties of wood?
8 What are the main uses of wood in the kitchen?
9 What are the general properties of ceramics?
10 Why are ceramics useful in the kitchen?
11 What are the general properties of metals?
12 What are the the following used for in the kitchen?
  a stainless steel
  b aluminium
  c cast iron

Cookers

The cooker is probably the most important piece of equipment in the kitchen. There are many types available to choose from, with a range of features and controls.

The most popular fuels used to heat the cooker are gas and electricity, although solid fuel cookers or ranges are still used in many homes. Microwave cookers (see pp. 163–6) are a relatively new development in food preparation and are becoming increasingly popular.

Cookers are a combination of three units:
the hob
the grill
the oven

These are available either as one complete free-standing unit or as separate units which can be housed in work tops and kitchen walls.

Cookers may also have one or more of the following features:
spit-roaster
griddle
automatic timer
self-cleaning oven lining
time clock and oven timer
glass window in oven door
storage space for baking tins
oven light
double oven
warming drawer for plates

Cookers are generally made of steel with a vitreous enamel finish, which is available in a variety of colours as well as white.

The hob

Most hobs have four hotplates or burners, and the hob is the most frequently used part of the cooker.

Electric hobs

The hotplates are usually 17·5 cm in diameter or sometimes 15 cm. The most familiar type of hotplate is the **radiant ring**, which consists of an electrical element enclosed in a spiral tube which glows red when heated.

Some have a dual circuit which enables the whole ring or just the centre part to be heated to conserve energy if only small pans are used.

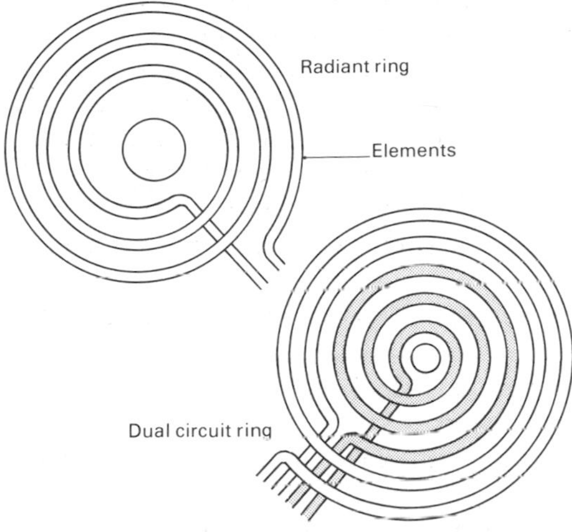

Some hobs have **disc rings** which are a continental design, and are flat discs with an indentation in the centre. The element is housed under the disc. The discs do not glow red when heated, and are easier to clean than radiant rings.

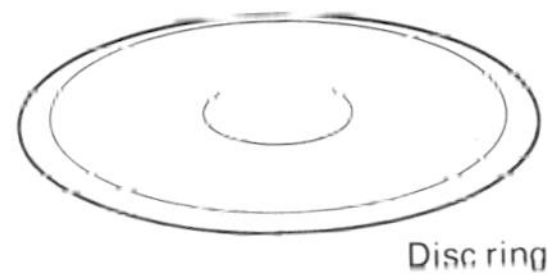

A recent development in electric hobs are **ceramic hobs**, where the elements are housed underneath a flat, ceramic top in insulated bowls. The heated areas are marked on the surface, which can be easily cleaned after use with a special non-abrasive cream which also conditions the ceramic surface.

Electric hobs are controlled by separate dials on a panel and food can be simmered easily by turning the dial to its lowest setting. However, a reduction in temperature is not instant as the plate has to cool down first. Heat will be wasted when the plate is switched off, as it takes time to cool down, but careful use can limit this wastage.

A new concept of heating by light, known as **halogen heat**, was launched in 1983. In these ceramic hobs, special tungsten halogen light filaments are housed. The heat they emit is directed upwards by a special insulated reflector placed beneath each filament. 80% of the heat passes through the ceramic surface, but the area around each set of filaments stays relatively cool. There are up to six power settings, to enable food to be cooked slowly or rapidly. The heat control is similar to gas, that is, it is more or less instant, thus saving energy and helping to prevent spillages. Halogen hobs are available as separate units or as part of a freestanding cooker.

Gas hobs

Gas burners give direct heat which is instantly controlled and can be seen. Some cookers have burners of different sizes for large pans or for simmering. Most gas cookers are now lit by electric spark ignition, either from an ordinary electrical plug socket or battery, or by a spark from a piezo electric system that contains a crystal. The spark can be produced at the touch of a button, or automatically when the burner is switched on. Some burners have a re-ignition device fitted which will ignite the gas automatically should the flame go out.

Most gas and electric hobs are fitted with trays to catch any spillages and make them easy to clean. On electric cookers, it may be possible to lift up the whole hob, and on gas cookers, removable spill trays around each burner are often fitted.

The grill

Electric grills

Most electric cookers have grills under the hob, and some have eye-level grills. The grill usually extends to the width of the cooker to enable it to take several pieces of food at one time. The grill pan can be placed at different distances from the elements and often has a food grid which can be reversed to give different heights within the grill pan itself. Many cookers have additional elements in the grill section, so that it can be used as a separate oven if required.

Gas grills

Gas grills are often at eye level but some are under the hob. The grill may be one of two types:
Conventional, where the burners heat one or two grill frets, which then glow and radiate heat on to the food below.
Surface combustion Instead of grill frets, this type has a gauze or plate, and the gas burns over the whole surface, ensuring a very even heat even at low settings.

On both gas and electric grills, the grill pan is usually self supporting, so that when it is pulled out, it will stay level and both hands are left free to attend to the food being grilled. Some cookers have a roasting spit and kebab attachments which give a wider scope for cooking.

Eye-level roasting spit attachment on a gas cooker. A self-supporting grill can also be fitted here.

The oven

Ovens are heated chambers, made of steel and insulated on the outside with glass fibre and an outer casing of steel. The lining of the oven is either coated with enamel or with a self-cleaning layer which vaporizes splashes of grease as they fall on to it. Usually the door and floor lining are not lined with self-cleaning material.

Electric ovens

Electric ovens do not require vents for the escape of fumes, just a small vent to allow steam to escape. This means that the oven is virtually enclosed and therefore heats up quickly and efficiently, maintaining a steady temperature.

There are three main types of electric oven:

convection oven
radiant/convection oven
fan oven

Convection ovens have the heating elements on both sides behind side panels which are removable.
Radiant/convection ovens have uncovered elements in the top and/or bottom of the oven.
Fan ovens (see p. 128) have a fan at the back which circulates the heat and results in more even cooking on all shelves.

Electric ovens are designed to heat from 100–270°C (200–525°F) and on most models it is possible to tell when the oven has reached the temperature at which it has been set by a light on the cooker panel which goes out when the required temperature has been reached.

Many types have an interior glass door through which items being cooked can be observed without letting out heat and spoiling the results.

Gas ovens

Gas ovens made in the UK are heated directly by a burner at the back of the oven. The heat rises and circulates, creating zones of heat (see p. 128). These zones of heat can be used to advantage by cooking foods requiring slightly different oven temperatures on the appropriate shelves at the same time, thus saving fuel.

Continental gas ovens are often heated indirectly by flames below the base of the oven, the heat entering the oven at various points. The heat is therefore even, and food can be cooked on any shelf with similar results.

Most modern gas ovens are lit by electric ignition, and they all have a **flame failure device** to stop the flow of gas should the flames go out. A vent is required for the escape of products of combustion.

Temperature control

Both gas and electric ovens are controlled by a device called a **thermostat.** In an electric oven, this consists of a **bi-metal** strip which contains two different metals (usually brass and invar – a special alloy of iron) which when heated expand and contract at different rates. The bi-metal strip therefore bends when heated, thus breaking a circuit and cutting off the supply of electricity to the oven. The oven cools down and the bi-metal strip straightens, reconnecting the circuit and thus heating the oven up again. In this way the temperature is controlled, and different temperatures can be obtained by adjusting the point at which the circuit is broken. Thermostats like this are also used in hot plates of electric cookers, irons, washing machine heaters, boilers, etc.

Electric oven thermostat.

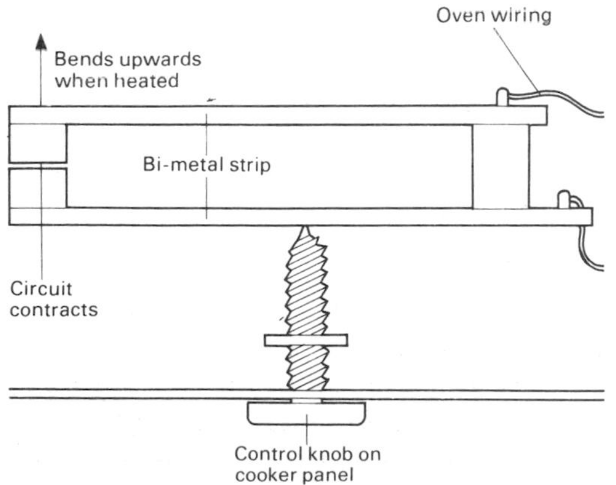

In modern gas cookers, **liquid expansion** thermostats are used, where the heat is controlled by the expansion (when heated) of an oil-based liquid housed inside a **sensing phial.** The gas valve is connected to the control tap via a pin, and the valve controls the flow of gas to the oven. When the oven burner is on, the liquid inside the sensing phial expands, forcing the bellows to open. This causes the gas valve to move down and gradually reduces the amount of gas flowing to the burner in the oven. As the temperature cools down, the liquid contracts, the bellows close, and the gas valve moves up to allow more gas to flow to the burner to heat up the oven again.

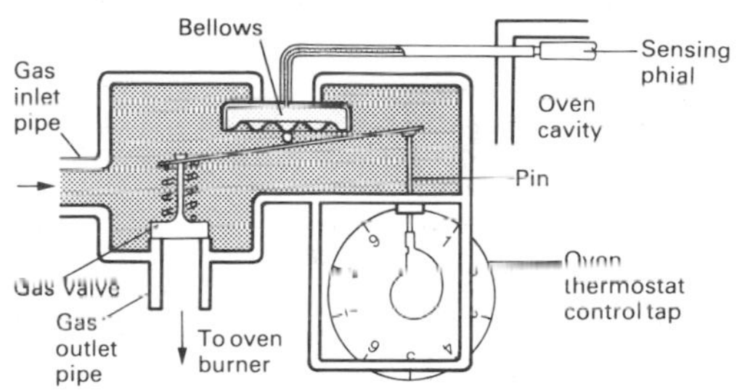

Automatic cooking

Most modern cookers (both gas and electric) are fitted with controls which enable the cooker to be switched on and off automatically. The most obvious advantage of this is that meals can be prepared and then left to cook without the oven having to be switched on manually. A person who is out all day can therefore leave a meal to cook on its own.

Automatic cooking is no different from the ordinary use of the oven except that food is cooked from a cold start, instead of being placed in a pre-heated oven. Most foods cook well in this way. Whole meals can be cooked in ovens where the heat is zoned (see p. 156), e.g.:

top shelf: meat joint
jacket potatoes
middle shelf: braised carrots
braised celery
bottom shelf: egg custard
stewed rhubarb

Gas cookers normally have a safety device which cuts off the gas supply should the oven fail to light at the predetermined time.

There are a few basic rules which should be followed when using an automatic oven:

1 Usually the cooker is designed to heat up very quickly, so there is no need to allow extra cooking time, except for dishes that normally require less than thirty minutes.
2 Always set the timer to turn off the oven when the cooking is completed, to avoid overcooking the food.
3 If a complete meal is being cooked, the total cooking time should be that required by the slowest cooking dish. It is possible to extend the cooking time of certain dishes to fit in with slow cooking ones, e.g. by baking a large pie with a joint of meat or leaving potatoes large if they are to be roasted with a large joint of meat.
4 Avoid using foods which would separate on standing before cooking, e.g. meringue or egg mixtures.
5 Vegetables, e.g. potatoes, which discolour when exposed to air should be parboiled, basted in fat, or cooked in their skins.
6 Cover all foods which are cooked in liquids with a lid or aluminium foil, to prevent them drying out.
7 Avoid overfilling dishes as they may boil over and spoil others beneath.
8 Cover strong-smelling foods.
9 Set the oven temperature to that required by the main dish, and arrange the others accordingly.
10 Foods which are prone to spoilage by bacteria, e.g. poultry, meat, fish, and milk, should not be left in the oven for too long before cooking as the oven will be at room temperature and may encourage bacterial growth. A maximum of two hours in hot weather is advisable. For the same reason, food should not be placed in a warm oven. It is best to chill the foods in a refrigerator before placing them in the oven to reduce the risk of food spoilage.

Solid fuel cookers

Solid fuel cookers or ranges may use coal, coke, or wood as fuel. The fuel is put into a **hopper** with an air supply, and it is then combusted in the **grate** or **fire box**. Fumes are removed via the **flue**, which is usually at the back of the cooker.

The hob

Heat travels by conduction to the hot-plates and the temperature of these can be raised by increasing the air supply to the fuel through an adjustable air control. Heavy insulating

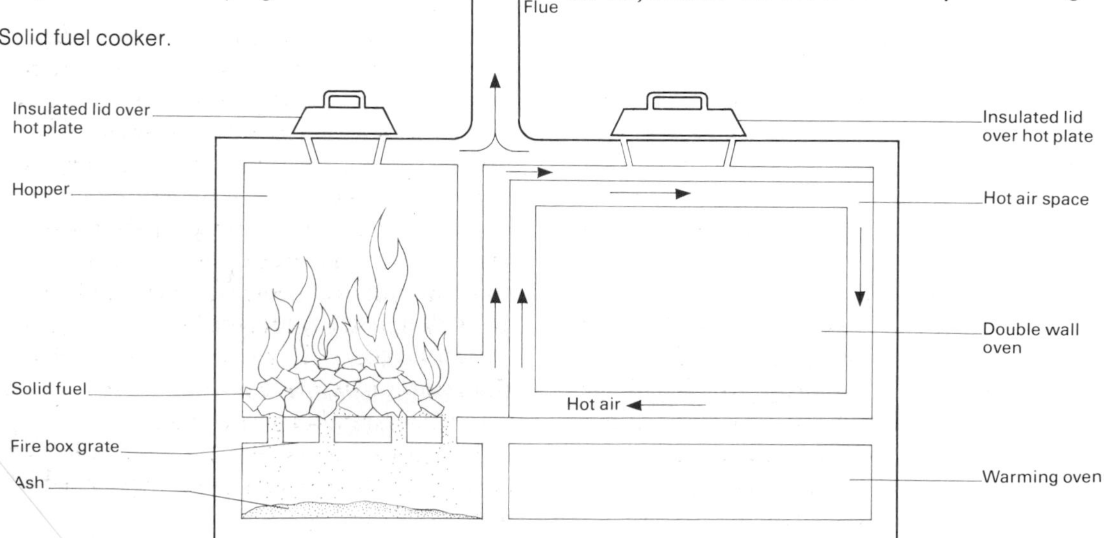

Solid fuel cooker.

lids cover the hotplates when they are not in use. It is necessary to use heavy-based flat pans to make good contact with the hot-plate.

The oven

The oven is different to those found in gas and electric cookers in that the heat is provided from around the outer surface instead of inside.

There are two main types of solid fuel oven:

1 **Single wall** These are heated by **conduction** from the fire box by iron plates connected to and surrounding it.
2 **Double wall** These have an air space between the inner and outer iron walls allowing heat to circulate by **convection**, after the heat has been conducted to the outer wall.

Some models have a thermostatic control, but using these ovens requires practice as it is more difficult to control the temperature of these than that of gas or electric ovens.

Solid fuel cookers often heat the domestic water supply as well, and may need to be kept alight all the time, which means that the cooker will need regular refuelling, but the kitchen will always be warm.

Food cooked in a solid fuel oven does not usually shrink or dry out as much as it does in gas or electric cookers.

Combination cookers

It is possible to buy cookers that combine two or more different ways of heating food within the same piece of equipment. For example, the combination of normal convection (see p. 128) and **fan assisted** heating enables food to be cooked more efficiently. Energy is saved, as lower temperatures are used, but it does mean that a different temperature chart for cooking foods has to be used to achieve satisfactory results. There are also cookers which combine conventional oven heating with microwave cooking in the same appliance. Such cookers can be used to heat foods to a certain temperature quickly using the microwave, and then allowing the conventional oven to complete the browning, tenderizing, or setting of the food.

Choosing a cooker

Cookers are relatively expensive items and before buying one, several factors should be considered:

1 The size in relation to the family's needs and space in the kitchen.
2 The cost in relation to the budget and usage of the cooker.
3 Features that are required, e.g. automatic timing, self-cleaning oven lining.
4 Type of fuel required and facilities available in the home for it.
5 Good design features, e.g. for easy cleaning, operation, and support of pans on the hob.

Cookers should be connected by an expert, and electric cookers must be connected to a 30 amp electricity supply as they draw a heavy current from the mains. Gas cookers must be fitted well to prevent leaks, and can be fitted with an extension pipe to enable them to be moved for cleaning purposes.

It is sensible to have a work top either side of the cooker to enable pans and serving dishes to be placed nearby when cooking.

Cleaning the cooker

The cooker hob should always be wiped over after it has been used, and the oven cleaned every week or so, depending on its usage. The hob should be cleaned with a non-abrasive cleaner, to prevent scratching the enamelled surface.

The oven can be cleaned with a special caustic foam or cream, but care should be taken as this may burn the skin and affect metal and plastic surfaces. Self-cleaning oven linings should only be wiped with a damp cloth to remove the ash left over from food which has been burnt off them.

The grill can usually be dismantled on most cookers to clean away grease which may splash and spit on to it.

Many cookers have glass panels which

should be carefully cleaned to prevent scratching. Ceramic hobs must be cleaned with a special powder or cream designed to clean and condition the surface.

Revision questions

1 What are the three main parts of a cooker and what are their features?

2 What additional features can a cooker have, and what are the advantages of these?

3 What is
a a radiant ring
b a dual circuit ring?

4 What are the advantages of a ceramic hob?

5 What are the two main types of gas grill?

6 What are:
a convection ovens
b radiant and convection ovens
c fan ovens?

7 How can the zones of heat in an oven be used to advantage?

8 Why is a vent necessary in a gas oven?

9 What is a thermostat, and how does it work in **a** a gas oven and **b** an electric oven?

10 What are the advantages of automatic cooking?

11 What are the general rules that should be followed when using an automatic cooker?

12 How does a solid fuel oven differ from electric and gas ovens?

13 What factors should influence the choice of cooker?

14 How should **a** the oven and **b** the hob be cleaned?

Refrigerators

The importance of refrigeration in food storage and the prevention of food poisoning has already been discussed (see pp. 143–4).

Refrigerators work on the following principle: When a liquid evaporates, it absorbs heat. The liquid used in a refrigerator (the **refrigerant**) flows round tubes at the back of the unit, absorbing heat from the interior of the refrigerator and thus cooling it down. The heat that is absorbed vaporizes the refrigerant and it is then turned back into a liquid to start the process over again.

Types of refrigerator

There are two types of refrigerator:
the compression type
the absorption type

The compression type is the most common. It can only be operated by electricity. The ice box is surrounded by a coiled metal tube containing the refrigerant liquid. The heat absorbed from the inside of the refrigerator evaporates the refrigerant, forming a vapour. An electric motor pumps the vapour round to the compressor, where it is condensed back into a liquid. The liquid is cooled by circulation through pipes at the back of the fridge, and it then returns to the evaporator (the ice box) and the whole process starts again. The temperature inside the refrigerator can be adjusted by a thermostat control.

Compression refrigerator.

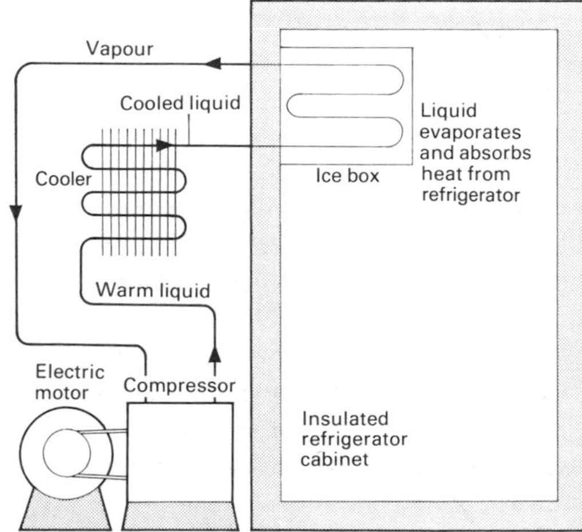

Absorption refrigerator.

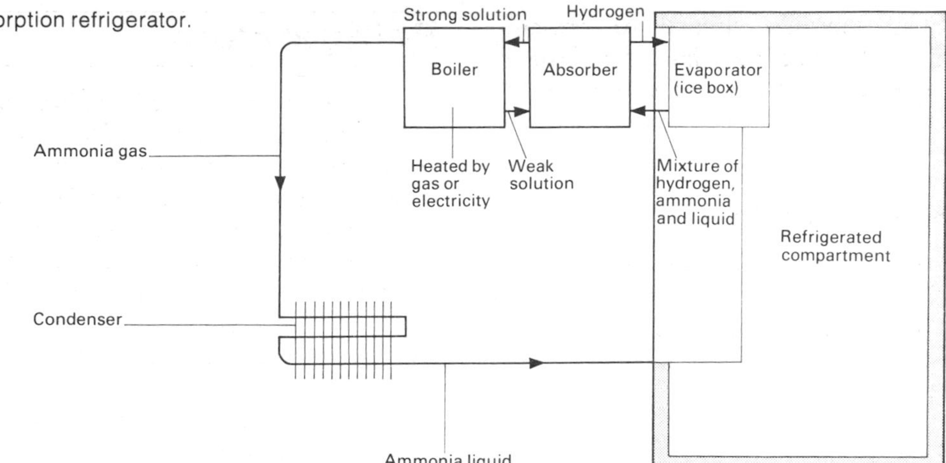

The absorption type is less commonly used. It operates silently, by the application of a small amount of heat, usually gas or a small electric heater.

The refrigerant is ammonia in water and its circulation is assisted by hydrogen gas. The refrigerant is heated by the gas flame or electric motor and the ammonia vapour which is given off passes to the condenser where it becomes liquid. It then passes into the evaporator (the ice box) where there is hydrogen gas. The ammonia evaporates by taking heat from the ice box, thus making it cold. The ammonia-hydrogen mixture is heavier than the hydrogen and falls back into the absorber where the ammonia dissolves in water again and the hydrogen returns to the evaporator. This is a continuous process.

Temperature distribution

Domestic refrigerators are designed to keep the temperature inside below 7°C (45°F). The temperature varies in different areas of the cabinet. The evaporator (ice box) is the coldest, and is normally marked with a star rating (see p. 145) to indicate the length of time that frozen food may be stored in it. It is *not* designed to freeze food, only to store it once frozen.

The door shelves are the warmest part of the cabinet. The diagram on p. 260 shows the zones of temperature within a refrigerator and the types of food that should be stored in each zone.

Choosing a refrigerator

When deciding on which type and size of refrigerator to buy, the following points should be considered:

1 Size and capacity according to need.
2 Storage arrangements inside the refrigerator.
3 Space available in the kitchen.
4 Star rating for frozen food compartment.
5 Workmanship on the refrigerator and its finish.
6 Additional features, e.g. automatic defrosting.

Many people find that a fridge/freezer (see p. 169) suits their requirements for cold storage without taking up excessive space in the kitchen.

Care of a refrigerator

Defrosting

Moisture is drawn from the air and food inside a refrigerator, and it freezes on the surface of the ice box. If this layer of ice exceeds 6 mm ($\frac{1}{4}$") in thickness, it will lower the efficiency of the refrigerator and should be removed by defrosting. Refrigerators can be defrosted in one of three ways:

Manual defrosting

The refrigerator should be switched off, and the food removed and kept in a cool place. The water collected from the melting ice is collected in a tray underneath the ice box,

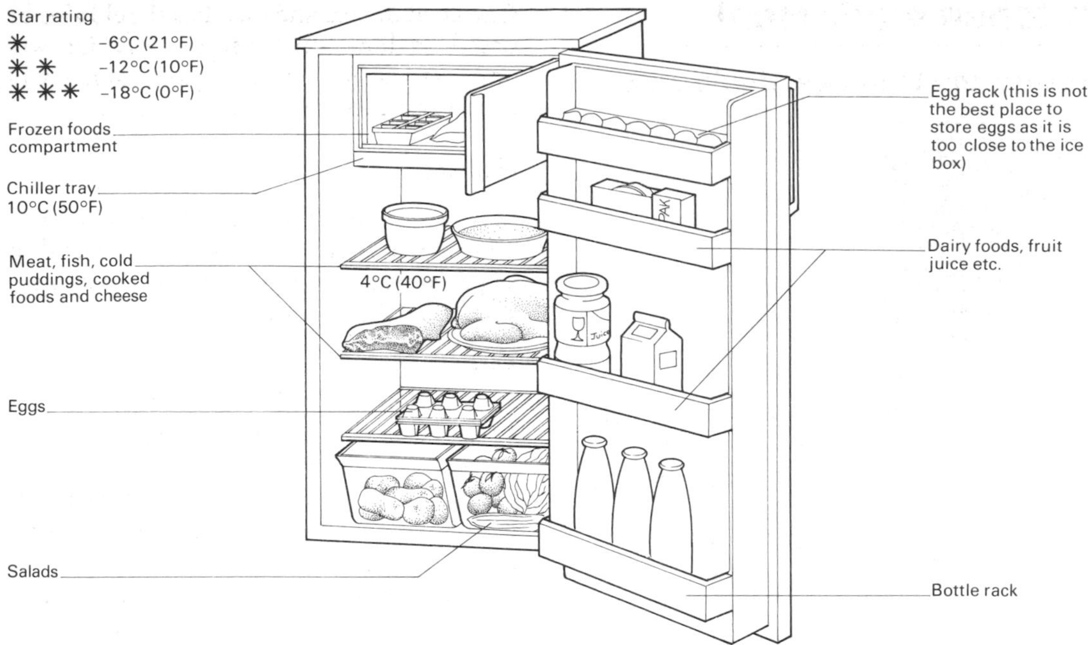

Temperature variation and compartments in a refrigerator.

and is removed. Once all the ice has gone, the cabinet should be washed out with a solution of bicarbonate of soda in water (1 tablespoon to 575 ml or 1 pint), which will not leave a smell. Once dry, the refrigerator can be refilled and reconnected.

Push button defrosting
Some makes have a button which when pressed stops the refrigeration process and allows the ice to melt. When this has occurred, the refrigeration process starts up again.

Automatic defrosting
Some makes defrost automatically when the ice reaches a certain thickness, so that there is no need to check this, and food need not be removed.

It is important that the refrigerator should be kept clean and hygienic inside at all times.

Storing food in a refrigerator

It is advisable to wrap food before placing it in the refrigerator for the following reasons:

1 Food loses moisture as it cools down and therefore unwrapped food will dry out.

2 Some foods absorb odours while others give off odours, and this can spoil the flavour of the food.

Some foods, e.g. meat and fish, should not be wrapped in plastic in the refrigerator as they tend to discolour and develop off flavours and odours without a layer of air surrounding them. Such foods should be stored in a glass or ceramic dish.

Freezers

The choice, care, and use of freezers is discussed on pp. 167–8.

Revision questions

1 What is the principle on which refrigerators work?
2 How do **a** compression refrigerators and **b** absorption refrigerators work?
3 How and where should different foods be stored in the refrigerator?
4 What factors should influence the choice of refrigerator?
5 Why is it necessary to defrost a refrigerator?
6 How should a refrigerator be defrosted?

Kitchen equipment

Mixers and blenders (liquidizers)

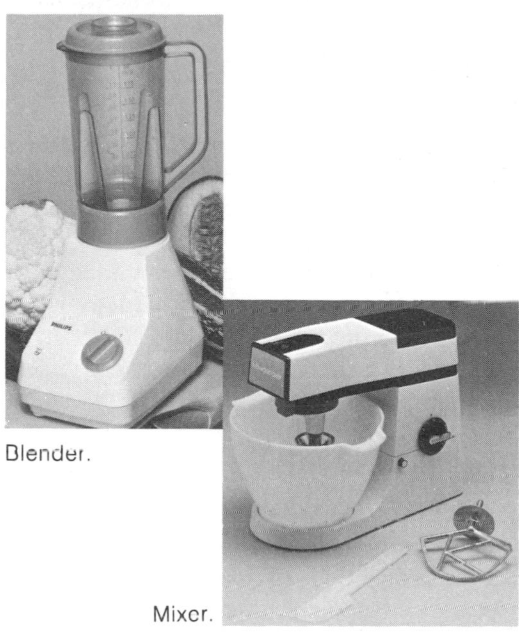

Blender.

Mixer.

Food mixers and blenders have become common additions to the kitchen, and their main value is that they save **time** and **labour**. Instead of human energy being used, electricity is substituted and the machine does the job more quickly and often more efficiently. The fact that many people have less time to spend in preparing food than they did in the past has contributed to the demand for these types of appliance.

A satisfactory and efficient machine should have the following features:

1 It should have the power and capacity to do a range of jobs; e.g. a blender should be able to make a small quantity of mayonnaise as well as blend a large portion of soup; a mincer should be able to mince raw meat as well as cooked meat.
2 It should be easy to keep clean. This is particularly true of mincers and blenders which often take far longer to clean than to use.
3 It should be made of a suitable and durable material.
4 It should be easy to fit on attachments and to use.

Choice of mixers and blenders should also be based on how much use the machine will have, its cost, and the amounts of food it will be expected to cope with each time.

Mixers

Mixers are available as small hand-held models which can be attached to a stand or large, free-standing models which are fitted with a bowl and stand.

Uses

Hand-held models These are very useful for whisking mixtures over the heat, creaming and mashing vegetables in a pan, and whisking and beating ingredients in different containers. They can be moved easily to any part of the kitchen.

Many can have a small blender attached to them, and some fit on to a stand with a bowl so that they can operate without being held. A well-designed hand mixer should be relatively light and comfortable to hold, and the switches should be easy to use. Hand-held mixers often have a wall mounting to keep them tidy when not in use.

Free-standing models These are powerful, large capacity mixers, which operate by the rotation of the beaters on a disc which also rotates, thus thoroughly mixing and incorporating ingredients in the bowl.

Such mixers can have a variety of attachments, including:

1 **Dough hook**, to mix bread doughs and develop the gluten in the flour in a short time.
2 **Blender** (see p. 262).
3 **Electric can-opener**, which usually opens cans of any shape without leaving a jagged edge.
4 **Mincer**, for mincing raw and cooked meats, vegetables for chutney making, cheese, nuts, etc.
5 **Sausage maker**, which is attached to the mincer and produces sausages from meat and other ingredients.
6 **Coffee grinder**, for grinding roasted coffee beans.

7 **Potato peeler**, for fast peeling of up to 1·5 kg (3 lb) of potatoes.
8 **Juice extractor**, for use with citrus fruits.
9 **Slicer and shredder**, for use with carrots, cabbage, onions, beetroot, cucumber, cheese, chocolate, apples, potatoes, etc.
10 **Cream maker** Home-made cream can be made from unsalted butter and milk and becomes thick when processed through the machine.
11 **Bean slicer**, which slices beans finely and can also be used to shred citrus peel for marmalade making.
12 **Sieve**, which is used to remove the stones from fruit for jam making and to purée fruits and vegetables.

Attachments are usually expensive, so their purchase should meet definite and regular requirements. The bowl of the mixer should be deep enough to hold the ingredients without causing them to be thrown out at the top of the bowl.

Blenders (liquidizers)

A well-designed blender should have the following features:
- handle
- pouring lip for liquids
- base which is easy to fix and remove
- strong but transparent goblet that will withstand heat from liquids
- capacity to blend dry as well as liquid ingredients

Glass goblets are preferable to plastic ones as the latter tend to become scratched and therefore unhygienic after they have been used several times.

Blenders can be used for a variety of purposes, including:
- soup making
- puréed fruit and vegetables
- batters
- baby food preparation
- chopping nuts, herbs, breadcrumbs
- grinding sugar into caster or icing sugar
- fruit and milk drinks
- mayonnaise and salad dressings

When using a blender for hot liquids, care should be taken not to overfill the goblet. The liquid rises up rapidly when the blades start to rotate, and if overfull, some of it could come out at the top and cause scalding.

General care of mixers and blenders

1 Do not run the machine for longer than necessary as this may overheat the motor.
2 Do not exceed the recommended capacity of the machine.
3 Clean thoroughly after use, taking care when dealing with sharp blades, wires, and the motor.
4 When not in use, store in a dry place, covered to keep dust off.

Food processors

Food processors are a recent development in electrical appliances. These machines carry out a wide range of jobs, using only one piece of equipment, and they do so very rapidly. These jobs include:
- finely chopping vegetables and herbs
- chipping potatoes
- finely slicing vegetables and fruit
- finely chopping meat, cheese, boiled eggs
- chopping fat into flour for pastry
- making breadcrumbs
- grinding whole wheat
- shredding vegetables
- peeling vegetables
- grating vegetables and cheese
- puréeing food

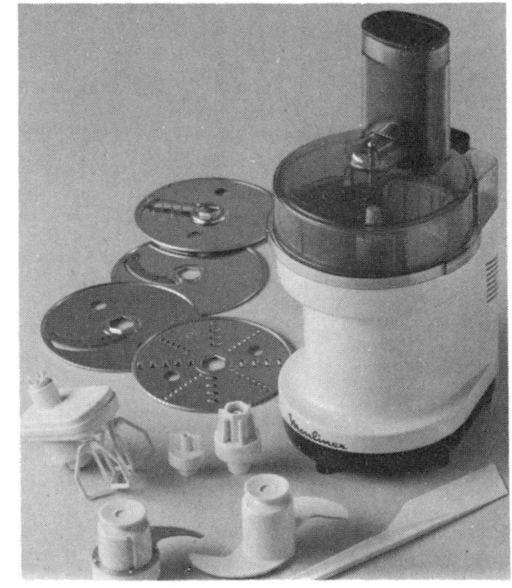

When choosing a food processor, the following features should be looked for:

1 Ease of cleaning.
2 Safety features, e.g. no blade movement until the lid is on.
3 Capacity.
4 Durability.

It is important to assess just how much use would be made of such a machine as they are expensive to buy, but they do save time and labour and often produce a better result than could be achieved by hand.

Dishwashers

Automatic dishwashers save time and energy. The dishes and other items have to be stacked into the machine. They are then thoroughly washed, rinsed, and dried automatically. Instead of three or four washing-up sessions a day, the entire day's load can be washed in one go at night. The wash is very hygienic as high water temperatures are used (60–65°C/140–149°F) and the special detergent used contains a germicide chemical. The drying temperature is usually about 74°C (135°F) which enforces this hygienic process.

Dishwashers work on the following general programme:

1 **Pre-wash** in cold water to remove large food residues.
2 **Main wash** The water is gradually heated to avoid putting stress on delicate items such as glass. The water is agitated around the items while the detergent is added, automatically.
3 **Two short rinses,** which dispose of food residues and detergent.
4 **Final hot rinse** with a liquid rinse aid to break down the surface tension of the water, to leave the items very clean.
5 **Drying** This is either carried out by an electric heater or heat left by the other processes.

Depending on the type of machine, the whole cycle takes from twenty to ninety minutes. Usually the machines are plumbed in to separate taps. They can alternatively be fitted to the sink taps each time, but this is less convenient. Models which have a hot water intake (i.e. the water does not have to be heated first) save heating bills and time.

The sizes range from a four-place setting capacity to a fourteen-place setting capacity for the needs of a large family. Most models are free standing, but some smaller ones can be fitted to a wall.

The detergents used often have a water softener added and some contain enzymes to break down protein and starch stains.

Most items can be washed except for:
hand-painted porcelain
lead crystal glassware
old cutlery with handles fixed by glue that is not heat-resistant
narrow necked vessels

Sink units

Types

Most modern sinks are made from stainless steel which is easy to keep clean, and is strong and hygienic.

Sinks may also be made from fibreglass, fireclay, enamel, or nylon. The draining-board may be separate or may form one whole unit with the sink. Separate draining-boards are less hygienic as they may harbour bacteria in the joins between them and the sink.

Sinks are often positioned by a window where they provide a source of fresh air and an outlet for steam.

The sink should be kept clean by the regular use of a non-scratch cleaning fluid which will remove grease at the same time.

Care of the sink

Avoid putting scraps of food, hot fat, or tea leaves down the sink as these may cause a blockage. If a blockage does occur, the following procedure should be adopted:

1 Pour boiling water, and, if the source of the problem is fat, washing soda, into the sink.
2 Gently put a soft wire down the plug hole to try to remove the blockage.
3 Use a special suction tool to try to shift the blockage.

4 Place a bucket underneath the U-bend under the sink. Undo the inspection screw and examine carefully.

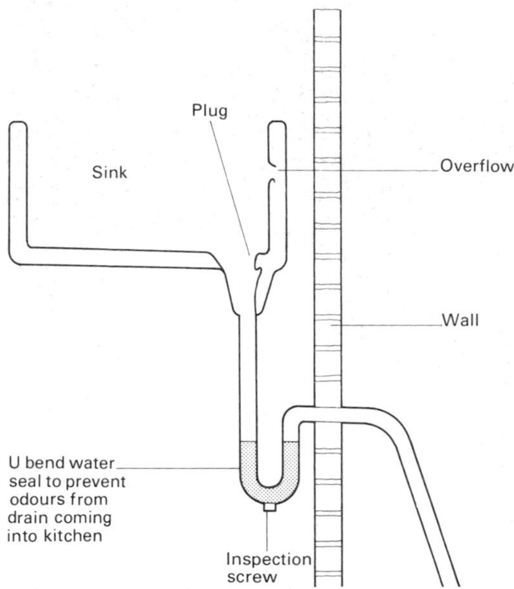

If this fails to remove the blockage, it is best to seek the advice of a plumber.

Once the sink has been unblocked, hot water should be flushed down to remove any debris. It is hygienic practice to pour bleach or disinfectant down the sink on a regular basis to destroy bacteria which may be harboured in the waste pipe.

Waste disposal units

These can be fitted to the sink and work by grinding up food waste so that it can be washed down the drain. They are operated by an electric motor. Care should be taken to avoid dropping small items of cutlery into the unit as these may damage the blades.

Heated food trays and servers

Occasionally it is necessary to keep food hot for someone who is going to be late for a meal, or to keep part of a meal hot for second helpings. Although nutritionally this may not be the best idea, it solves the problem of cooking an extra meal.

Heated food trays and servers can be used for this purpose and they are usually electrical.

Heated food trays have tops made from either metal, toughened glass, or a ceramic finish. The base and feet are insulated so that the tray can be put on to the table. The tray had a tubular element beneath the top which heats it to between 80–85°C (176–185°F) on some models and 110–140°C (230–284°F) on others.

Food servers range from specially heated dishes and portable table cabinets to free-standing cabinets and trolleys. The top may either be a flat surface or have fitted food containers with lids. Some have an unheated cabinet below the heated top for storing plates and cutlery.

Both types of appliance operate from an ordinary socket outlet, which should be disconnected before cleaning.

As with all electrical appliances, when purchasing, check that it carries a BEAB label (see p. 274).

Electric food server.

Pans

Pans are relatively expensive but necessary items in a kitchen. It is advisable to buy the best that you can afford as they will last for many years.

Types

The following types of pan are a suitable range for use in the kitchen:

milk saucepan, with a lip for easy pouring
frying pan
vegetable saucepans – three sizes
egg poacher
pressure cooker

Pans can be made from the following metals:

stainless steel
aluminium
enamelled iron or steel

They can also be made from special heat-tolerant glass.

Stainless steel is a very solid metal and will not chip or flake. It is strong, durable, resistant to rust, little affected by chemical reactions so that it does not stain, and it does not impart a metallic taste to food. It is not a very efficient conductor of heat, so the base of pans made from it is usually composed of three layers, the outer and inner ones being stainless steel and the middle layer being a highly conductive metal to speed up the heating process. Metals such as copper can be welded on to the base of the pan as an alternative to help it heat quickly, but this does increase the price.

Once stainless steel heats up, it holds the heat well so that the hob burner or hot-plate can be turned right down to keep the contents cooking evenly without wasting fuel.

Aluminium is cheaper to produce than stainless steel but is not so strong and is prone to discolouration from certain foods. It is lighter to hold.

Enamelled steel or iron can be made into attractive coloured pans. They conduct heat quite rapidly, but are inclined to discolour and chip after a period of usage.

Aluminium and stainless steel pans can be lined with a non-stick coating of polytetrafluoroethylene (PTFE) which is a plastic that melts at a high temperature and resists food deposits becoming stuck to the surface. PTFE-lined pans should be used carefully. Wooden or plastic spoons, not metal, should be used to avoid scratching the surface. They should be washed in hot water with detergents. Scouring pads and cleansers should not be used.

All pans should have the following features:

1 A relatively thick base and sides for strength and durability.
2 A stable design that will not tip over easily.
3 Handles made of an insulating maerial.
4 A lid that fits well and is easy to remove.
5 A flat base that has good contact with the hot plate.
6 Well-fitting handles that do not become loose.

Electric kettles

Many homes use an electric kettle for boiling water. Non-electric kettles are also available for use on gas or electric hobs.

When buying an electric kettle the following features should be looked for:

1 **Automatic switch-off button** This is useful as it prevents the water from boiling away if you forget to turn the kettle off. It saves wear on the element, prevents the kitchen from filling with steam, and saves electricity if all the water is used.
2 **Safety cut-out device** If the kettle is not automatic, it may have a device to turn off the electricity should the water boil away.
3 The **flex connector** should hold the flex firmly and securely. A frayed flex is very dangerous.
4 The **handle** should be easy to grip, comfortable to hold, and well balanced when the kettle is full. It should not become hot and must be securely fixed.
5 The **lid** should fit well and securely, and be easy to remove and put on, without coming out when the kettle is tipped. The knob on it should be easy to grip without causing the knuckles to be caught underneath the handle, thus causing burns.
6 The **base** must be firm and steady on the work surface.
7 The **spout** should pour well and the steam should be directed away from the hand of the pourer.

Capacity

Various sizes can be purchased, and the electrical rating of the kettle will affect the amount of water it will boil in a certain time. As a guide:

A 2·4 Kw kettle boils 1·5 litres (3 pints) of water in 4–4·5 minutes.

A 3 Kw kettle boils the same amount in 3–3·5 minutes.

Use

The water must cover the element otherwise it will be damaged. The electric plug must be switched off before the kettle is disconnected. It should be placed out of the reach of children.

Jug kettles

Various brands of jug kettle are available. They are made of a special heat-resistant plastic, and have the capacity to boil as little as a cupful of water or up to 1·5 litres (3 pints), because of their tall shape. This saves energy and is useful for single people. When buying a jug kettle, the same features as for an ordinary kettle should be considered.

Kitchen scales

Accuracy in weighing out ingredients is fundamental to good results in food preparation. A variety of scales are available and it is worth buying a good brand to be sure of accuracy and durability.

The following features should be looked for when buying scales:

1 Easy-to-read dial in metric as well as imperial measurements.
2 Good capacity to take joints of meat and vegetables, as well as dry ingredients.
3 Scale pan which is easy to clean and remove.
4 Compact shape that is easy to store.
5 Hard-wearing and sturdy case.
6 Accurate measuring that can be adjusted if necessary.

Types of scale pan

There are two main types of scale:

balance scales
spring balance scales

Balance scales have a pan to which ingredients are added at one end and a platform on the other to which weights are added until the two balance and are level. These are usually very accurate.

Spring balance scales.

Spring balance scales are less accurate and are prone to become faulty relatively easily. The scale holds a spring and as ingredients are put into the pan the spring depresses, indicating the weight by revolving a needle on the dial at the front of the scale. Some types have a bowl into which ingredients are weighed and mixed, and the scale needle can be set back to 0 to add further ingredients, which is a useful feature. Some types can be stored on the wall.

Diet scales are a special type of spring balance scale. They are useful for weighing small quantities such as 5 g or $\frac{1}{2}$ oz. There is more room on the dial to show the markings, so it is easier to weigh accurately.

Use and care of scales

1 Never drop food into them, especially spring balance scales.
2 Never store spring balance scales with a weight in the pan as this will strain the spring.
3 Clean carefully after use.
4 Weigh out on a flat, firm surface.

Cutlery

Many homes have two sets of cutlery, one for everyday use and another for special meals. In both cases, the following features of good design should be looked for when purchasing a set:

1 Strong handles.
2 Well-balanced handles for ease of holding and using.
3 A good cutting edge on knives.
4 A good standard of finish.
5 Well-proportioned prongs on forks and bowls of spoons.
6 Easy-care design that can be cleaned without difficulty and will not retain food deposits in the pattern of the metal.

Cutlery is usually made from either stainless steel, or electro-plated nickel silver (EPNS). It is also possible to buy solid silver and bronze-plated cutlery but these are very expensive.

Stainless steel cutlery is durable and strong and will not discolour. It can be made into a variety of designs to suit most tastes, for everyday use or special meals.

EPNS This type of cutlery is normally kept for special meals, and after continual use, the silver plating may wear off. The silver tends to discolour as it reacts with some foods, but this can be removed by using a special silver cleaner. EPNS cutlery should be treated with care to avoid damaging the silver plating and is best stored neatly in a special cutlery canteen.

Range of cutlery normally purchased

table knives
knives for side plates (smaller)
table forks
fish knives (look for those that can be used by right- and left-handed people)
fish forks
table spoons (for serving)
dessert spoons
soup spoons
teaspoons
coffee spoons
dessert forks

Kitchen knives

It is necessary to have a variety of kitchen knives for different purposes, and it is best to buy a good brand with the following features:

1 A strong, easy-to-grip handle.
2 A well made blade that can be resharpened and retains its sharpness well.
3 A rigid blade that does not bend when cutting (except palette knives which should be flexible).

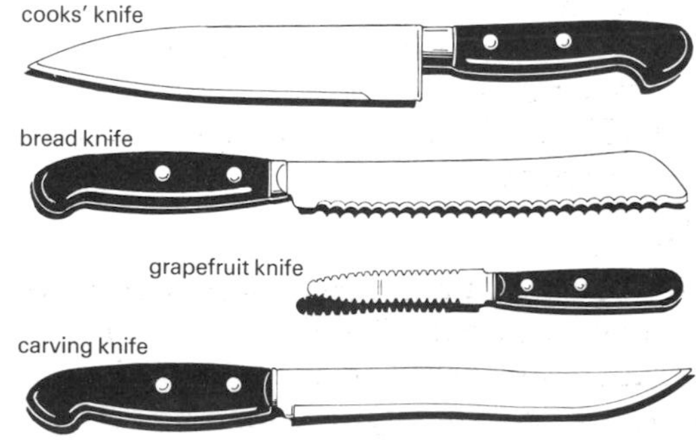

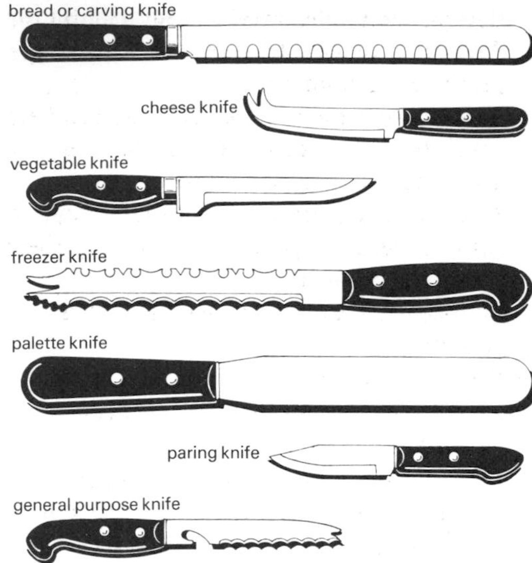

Serrated knives have fine sharp points running along the blade which remain sharp for a long time. They are useful for slicing fruit and vegetables finely.

All sharp knives should be stored with the blades pointing downwards in a drawer or in a special rack. They should be used on a chopping board, cutting away from the body.

Food wrappings and kitchen papers

In addition to the wrapping materials that are used for freezing foods (see pp. 170–82), there are others that are commonly used in the kitchen, including:

Greaseproof paper

This is resistant to grease and is used for:

- lining cake tins
- wrapping foods for packed lunches
- covering puddings that are to be steamed
- covering meat joints in the oven
- tracing decorations on to cakes

It is available in sheets, bags or rolls.

Baking parchment

This is specially made with a non-stick surface that can be used for:

- piping bags
- baking meringues
- separating meat joints for freezing

Waxed paper

This has a layer of wax on both sides and can be used for:

- separating meat joints in the freezer
- wrapping packed lunches
- sealing home-made jam

Rice paper

This is an edible paper that can be used to bake items such as macaroons that stick to a baking sheet and cannot be removed easily. The rice paper can be eaten with the macaroon.

Plastic cling film

This is a useful wrapping as it clings easily to itself and most other surfaces forming a seal over food. It is particularly useful for storing left-over foods in the refrigerator so that they do not dry out, and can also be used to wrap packed lunches. It is not a suitable wrapping on its own in the freezer as it is easily torn and may not form a completely protective layer over the food.

Aluminium foil

In addition to its use in freezing, aluminium foil may be used for:

- covering casseroles or roasting meat
- lining casseroles containing food that will be frozen
- wrapping foods, e.g. corn on the cob, potatoes to be baked in the oven
- covering foods that are to be steamed
- wrapping foods for refrigerator storage

It is a good conductor of heat, and is light, strong, and easy to wrap around dishes.

Revision questions

1. What is the main advantage of owning an electric mixer and blender?
2. What are the features of a well-designed and efficient mixer or blender?
3. What are the uses of hand-held mixers?
4. What attachments can be obtained for free-standing mixers and what are their advantages?
5. How should mixers, blenders, and food processors be looked after?

6 What are blenders used for?
7 What are food processors and what are they used for?
8 What is the main advantage of owning a dishwasher?
9 How do dishwashers clean items and why is the whole process hygienic?
10 What items should not be placed in a dish-washer?
11 Why are heated food trays useful?
12 What types of pans are useful to have in the kitchen?
13 What metals are used for pans and why?
14 What are the features of a well-designed pan?
15 What are the features of a well-designed electric kettle?
16 How should an electric kettle be used so that it is safe and lasts a long time?
17 What are the two main types of kitchen scales and how do they work?
18 How should scales be used so that they remain accurate?
19 What are the features of well-designed cutlery?
20 What are the features of good kitchen knives?
21 List three kitchen wrapping materials and say what they are each used for.

Consumer protection

A wide variety of goods and services are available to consumers today, and in order to protect them from unfair trading, poor service, bad workmanship, and unsafe goods, a number of Acts of Parliament and Codes of Practice have been established to cover most aspects of trade and business.

Consumers need to be aware of their rights under the law, and should find out how they can seek compensation or advice when necessary. In order to get the best value for money when buying goods or services, the following guidelines should be followed:

1 Find out about the goods or service in detail before buying, and compare different types and makes for quality, value, design, after-sales service, and suitability.
2 Ask for a demonstration of use for large pieces of equipment.
3 Read instructions and information leaflets carefully and thoroughly, particularly guarantees and servicing details.
4 Ask various people who have bought a similar item or paid for a service their opinions about it.
5 Consult consumer magazines such as *Which*.
6 Keep all receipts and sales agreements for large pieces of equipment and services.
7 Do not let yourself be pressurized into buying goods or paying for a service that you have not had time to consider.

Whenever a person buys goods or a service, they enter into a contract with the seller. The contract gives both parties rights and obligations, which are covered by law, and also Codes of Practice which are followed by many trade associations. Several Consumers' Associations also exist to monitor the interests of consumers and to deal with complaints.

In the UK people are protected by two types of law:

criminal law
civil law

Criminal law aims to prevent behaviour that would be harmful to the community as a whole, e.g. fraud or dangerous acts such as selling unfit food or unsafe appliances. People who break the law in this way are prosecuted and can be fined or imprisoned accordingly.

Civil law is mainly concerned with people's obligations to one another, as in a contract between a customer and a shopkeeper. If a consumer feels he or she has been wrongly treated, then they may enforce their rights under the law and take the matter to court.

Both criminal and civil law can be statutory, i.e. contained in Acts of Parliament. The following Acts must be upheld by manufacturers, shops, services, and other bodies who sell to the public. They cover most goods and services.

Sale of Goods Act, 1979

Once the seller has entered into a contract with a consumer, he has three obligations which must be fulfilled:

1 The goods sold must be of a merchantable quality, i.e. fit for the purpose for which they were intended.
2 The goods must perform in the way that the seller has told the customer they will.
3 The goods must fit the description which is given of them.

If any of these requirements are broken, then the customer is entitled to claim compensation or a refund, and should complain directly to the seller, not the manufacturer. This does not apply, however, if the customer knows that the goods are faulty, damaged, or second quality before he buys them, or if he ignores the seller's advice about the use of the goods. Sellers are not allowed to refuse to refund money if the goods they sell are faulty under this law, but they can offer to replace or repair the goods. Consumers are not obliged to accept a credit note from the seller if they want their money back.

The act also covers second-hand goods, and those that are reduced in price in a sale, unless the customer knows that they are faulty in some way. However, if faulty goods break down as a result of some other fault, then they can be taken back to the trader.

Manufacturers, and mail order firms are also covered by this act.

Shop traders are not obliged to sell an article if they do not wish to. They are also not obliged to give receipts, and are not allowed to refuse refunds on goods without a receipt.

Consumer Safety Act 1978

Goods have to be labelled with warning symbols, instructions for use, and ingredients lists for the benefit of the consumer. The Act includes strict regulations regarding the safety of cooking utensils, children's nightwear, etc.

Food and Drugs Act 1955

It is a criminal offence to sell unfit food, or to mislead the public about the nature, substance, nutritional value, or quality of food. This Act also includes regulations about food hygiene, and covers all places where food is sold, manufactured, packed, processed, or stored.

Food labelling regulations are also included in this Act and require the contents, ingredients, and name and address of the manufacturer to be printed on the label.

The Act also covers the composition of food and any additives or contaminants associated with it.

The Prices Act 1974

This act requires that prices for goods should be displayed, and that all items of food and drink (except where sold by counter service) should be priced.

Certain foods that are sold by weight, e.g. meat, cheese, must have their unit price (e.g. per pound) displayed.

Restaurants, take-away food shops, public houses, and bars must display a price list.

The Trade Descriptions Act 1968 and 1972

It is an offence for a trader to falsely describe either by word, writing, or drawing, any goods he is selling. This also covers services (e.g. insurance, holidays).

The Weights and Measures Acts 1963 and 1979

It is an offence to sell food items without the quantity of the goods being indicated on the package. Not all foods have to be labelled, e.g. 1 pint milk bottles do not have to state the contents. Most pre-packed food items have to be sold in prescribed metric quantities, e.g. flour is only sold in quantities of 125 g, 250 g, 500 g, or 1000 g.

These are just some of the Acts of Parliament that are enforced to protect the consumer with special reference to food. There are many more Acts and regulations for all aspects of buying goods and services.

How to complain

If consumers feel or have evidence to prove that a trader has broken any of these Acts, or if goods have to be returned to the trader for any reason, it is important that they should be aware of their rights under the law.

Several organizations exist to help the consumer with such matters, should complaining to a trader not prove successful. These include:

Citizens' Advice Bureaux
Local Council Consumer Advice Centres
Local Trading Standards Departments (sometimes called Consumer Protection or Weights and Measures Departments)
Local Council Environment Health Departments

On a national scale there are the following:

The Department of Trade
The Ministry of Agriculture, Fisheries, and Food
The Department of Health and Social Security
The Lord Chancellor's Office

The latter departments would only be called in to help if the local authorities were unable to obtain a satisfactory settlement or if the case was a serious one.

The Office of Fair Trading, which was set up under the 1973 Fair Trading Act, protects consumers' and traders' interests by:

1 Publishing information to help people to know their rights.
2 Encouraging trade organizations to issue Codes of Practice to raise standards of service and deal with complaints.
3 Monitoring traders and checking up on those who break the law.
4 Controlling practices which are not in the interests of consumers or other traders, e.g. monopolies (where one trader supplies and controls a product or service so that no one else can compete with him).
5 Licensing firms which give credit or hire out goods to consumers.

The Office does not deal with individual cases of consumer complaints, or disputes with traders.

There are also public consumer and consultative councils, some of which deal with specific goods and services, e.g. gas and electricity. These include:

Electricity Consultative Council
Gas Consumers' Council
Consumers' Association (who produce magazines and reports on a variety of goods and services)
National Consumer Council
National Federation of Consumer Groups

The Design Council also aids the consumer by examining products and looking for goods which are well made, practical, and pleasant to look at. Suitable goods are given a symbol:

Revision questions

1 What guidelines should consumers follow in order to get the best value for money from goods and services?
2 What is the difference between civil and criminal law?
3 What are the three main principles of the Sale of Goods Act?
4 If a consumer takes back faulty goods to a trader under this law, what is he obliged to do for the customer?
5 What is the Consumer Safety Act and why is it enforced?
6 What areas of food retail does the Food and Drugs Act cover?
7 What does the Prices Act enforce?
8 What does the Trades Descriptions Act enforce?
9 How does the Weights and Measures Act affect the retail of food?
10 Which local organizations exist to help consumers with individual problems?
11 Which national organizations exist to protect and help all consumers and traders?
12 What are Codes of Practice?
13 What is the work of the Design Council?

Kitchen safety

Every year, thousands of accidents occur in the home, and the kitchen is one of the main areas of potential danger. In many cases, accidents can be prevented and only happen because insufficient attention is paid to safety precautions. This does not mean that people should be constantly on guard, but that living safely should become a habit.

The following lists of dangers and safety precautions are grouped according to areas of potential danger in the kitchen, and many of them are a matter of common sense.

Food preparation

Danger	Precaution
knives	Keep sharp, but use on a chopping board, cutting away from the body. Store away from the reach of children with sharp blades pointing downwards.
cooker	Fit a pan guard around the hob to stop children pulling pans down. Always use oven gloves to remove items from the oven. Turn off hotplates and burners after use.
frying	Never overfill pan with fat. Never leave pan unguarded. Heat to required temperature and no higher. Keep pan handle turned inwards. Keep a lid nearby in case fat ignites. Turn off the heat after use.
steaming	Keep face away from pan when removing lid. Do not allow pan to boil dry.
clothing	Keep sleeves rolled up, scarves, ties, etc. tucked in, tie hair back out of the way of flames or electric mixers. Avoid wearing high-heeled or loosely-fitting shoes which may cause a fall.

Floor

Danger	Precaution
spillages	Wipe up immediately to prevent slipping over.
surface	Do not polish the surface too highly. Do not put loose mats on a polished surface. Ensure that there are no curled edges or broken tiles which could be tripped over.

Electrical equipment

Danger	Precaution
wiring	Check that plugs are wired correctly, that there are no bare wires exposed anywhere along the length of flex, and that the flex is not frayed. Check that there is no undue strain on the wire. Keep wires well out of the reach of children, and where they will not be tripped over. Check that the fuse is the correct size for the piece of equipment being used.
plugs	Check that these are not broken and do not have screws missing.

Wiring a plug.

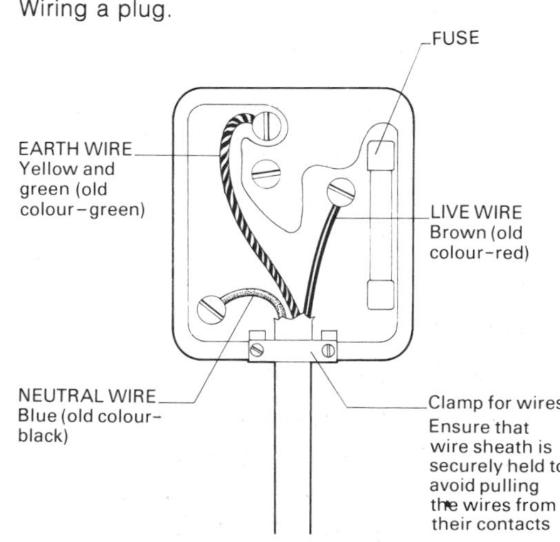

plugs	Do not touch with wet hands. Switch off socket before removing plug to avoid getting a shock from the pins as they are pulled out.
sockets	Cover when not in use to prevent children from putting items into the pin holes. Do not overload by running several items from an adapter plug.
equipment	Buy reliable makes that are covered by a British Standard or other safety check (see p. 274). Use according to instructions. Have equipment serviced regularly. Store in a dry place with the wiring neatly placed to avoid bending it.

Other equipment

Danger	Precaution
storage	Avoid storing heavy items in high cupboards or on high shelves where they may be difficult to retrieve. Avoid stacking equipment where it may fall down. Check that cupboards are securely fixed to the walls. Store sharp or bladed equipment safely. Use a specially designed kitchen stool or other stable chair to stand on to remove items from high cupboards.

Miscellaneous

Danger	Precaution
tea-towels	Do not hang over cooker to dry.
curtains	Keep away from flames.
movement	Never run in a kitchen. Avoid walking around with heavy, hot, or sharp items. Avoid reaching over cooker, and keep face away from steam and hot air from the oven.
cleaning materials	Store out of reach of children. Do not put these into empty soft drink bottles where they may be drunk by mistake. Never mix lavatory powder cleaners with bleach as this causes a dangerous reaction. Wear rubber gloves when using caustic solutions.
fires	Put a guard around all fires, especially where there are children around. Do not dry clothes around fires.
table-cloths	Avoid using these when there are toddlers around who may pull on them and cause items on the table to fall off.

Safety symbols

In order to protect consumers from unsafe goods, various boards and councils have been established to set and maintain standards of safety for goods produced within their jurisdiction. In many cases, manufacturers have to submit their products for testing if they are to be alllowed to sell them to the public. Goods which meet such requirements are sold bearing a symbol of approval from the board which governs those particular goods. These symbols include:

British Standards Institution

The Kitemark This appears on many items which comply with the British Standards Institution codes of practice.

The Safety Mark
This appears only on goods which comply with the British Standards for safety, e.g. gas appliances, light fittings.

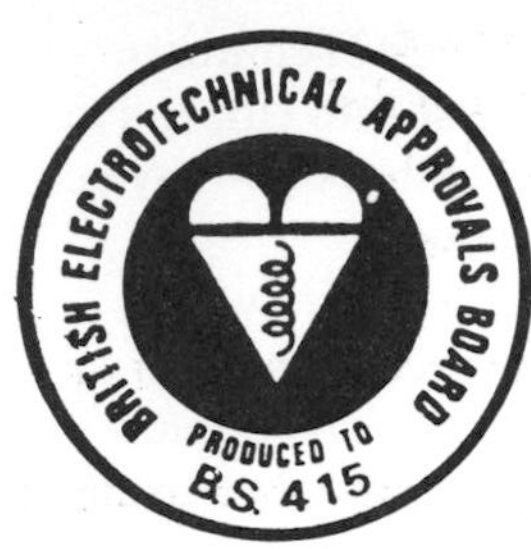

The British Electrotechnical Approvals Board sign appears on most domestic electrical appliances, and it is an assurance that the product is safe.

Furniture Safety Under the Consumer Safety Act, this symbol must appear on new furniture (upholstered) if it is not resistant to lighted cigarettes, matches or both. The label must be permanent.

National Inspection Council for Electrical Installation Contracting Reliable electrical contractors may display this label and they are regularly inspected to protect the consumer against faulty, unsafe, or defective workmanship.

British Gas This appears on products which have passed British Gas standards for performance, reliability, and fitness for purpose.

Many homes now have domestic fire extinguishers in the kitchen or fire blankets which are simple to operate and effective in use. They should be regularly checked. It is important to follow the manufacturer's instructions for using extinguishers, and it is important to remember that water-operated ones must not be used on electrical or chemical fires.

First aid

If an accident occurs in the home or anywhere else, it is important to know what to do to treat the injured person before expert medical help arrives. The following instructions cover the most common causes of injury. It is very useful for anyone to follow a first aid course, such as those run by the St. John's Ambulance Brigade.

Heavy bleeding

1 Lie patient down, raise injured part to reduce blood flow.
2 Press a clean pad on to wound and maintain pressure for ten minutes, until clot forms.
3 Remove loose dirt but do not probe wound.
4 Apply a clean dressing firmly to wound. If anything is lodged in it, put a dressing around it.

Broken bones

a Open fracture (bone is protruding through skin)
b Closed fracture (no open wound; may be internal damage to organs)
c Dislocation (one or more bones pulled out of a joint)

1 Do not move the patient.
2 Make them comfortable.
3 Cover open wounds.
4 Immobilize the injured part with a splint.
5 Bandage it for support.
6 If possible, raise the injured part to prevent swelling and pain.
7 Loosen clothing, cover patient with blanket.
8 Do not give patient anything to eat or drink.

Burns and scalds

1 Cool the whole area with cold water to kill the pain and reduce risk of blistering.
2 Do not remove clothing that has been burnt.
3 Remove clothing that has been soaked in a corrosive chemical (protect own hands first).
4 Remove jewellery if possible as the area may swell.
5 Cover the area with a clean cloth to reduce the risk of infection.
6 Lie patient down and keep them warm. Badly burned patients may be given sips of water.
7 Protect blisters, do not burst them.
8 If clothing catches fire, throw patient to the floor and smother flames with a rug or blanket.

Choking

1 A series of sharp blows between the shoulder blades may dislodge the obstruction. Try to suspend the person over a chair so that the head is lower than the chest.
2 If this does not work, try to hook out the obstruction with a finger.
3 Small children should be turned upside down and hit on the back.

Electric shock

1 If possible switch off the power supply. Do not touch the patient until this is done.
2 If this is not possible, push the patient away from the appliance with a wooden handle or stick.
3 Look for signs of the patient not breathing, and if necessary apply artificial respiration (see p. 276).

Poisoning

The following can all cause poisoning:

acids	lavatory cleaner
ammonia	metal polish
bleach	oven cleaner
carbolic soap	paint thinner
carpet cleaner	paraffin
caustic soda	petrol
detergents	rust remover
polish	shoe polish
grease remover	washing soda

1 Telephone for ambulance.
2 Do not induce vomiting.
3 Dilute the poison by giving tepid milk or water in sips.
4 Wipe face and lips gently with cloth or sponge.
5 Do not pour water into the mouth of an unconscious patient as this may choke them.

If pills have been swallowed, try to make the patient vomit by putting fingers into their throat. Do not give salt water or anything else to make them vomit.

Shock

Shock is a medical term used to describe the effect on the body of a large loss of blood or other body fluid following severe bleeding, burning, heart failure, persistent vomiting or diarrhoea, or an emergency operation. The symptoms of shock are:

cold, clammy skin, heavy sweating
faintness, blurred vision
nausea, vomiting
confusion, anxiety
thirst
shallow breathing, may be rapid
rapid, weak pulse

This is a serious situation and should be treated immediately.

1 Lie patient down with feet raised and head on one side.
2 Try to stop the cause of loss of blood or fluid.
3 Call for medical help.
4 Loosen tight clothing. Do not move unnecessarily.
5 Cover patient with a blanket.
6 Do not give anything to drink.

NB In all cases of injury medical advice should be sought when first aid has been administered.

Artificial respiration

If someone has stopped breathing it is important to give them artificial respiration until medical help arrives in order to save their life. The brain suffers damage if it is without oxygen for more than three minutes and death will follow soon after.

What to do:

1 Check the patient's breathing. If it has stopped:

2 Clear his mouth by removing false teeth, dirt, or any other object.

3 Bend his head back with one hand and push his jaw upwards with the other to lift the tongue away from the back of the throat.

4 Squeeze the nostrils together, place your mouth over the patient's mouth, and blow gently. Watch for the chest to rise.

5 Let the chest fall (take your mouth away) then repeat about fifteen times a minute, continuing until the patient starts to breathe again or until help arrives.

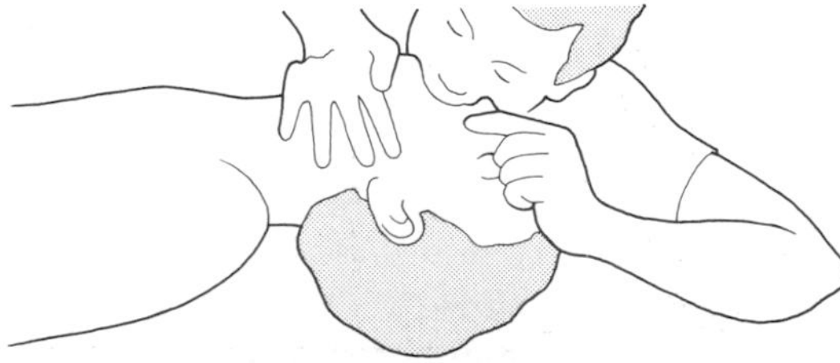

6 Place the patient in the recovery position, with his head to one side in case he vomits, and one arm underneath him to prevent him rolling on to his back.

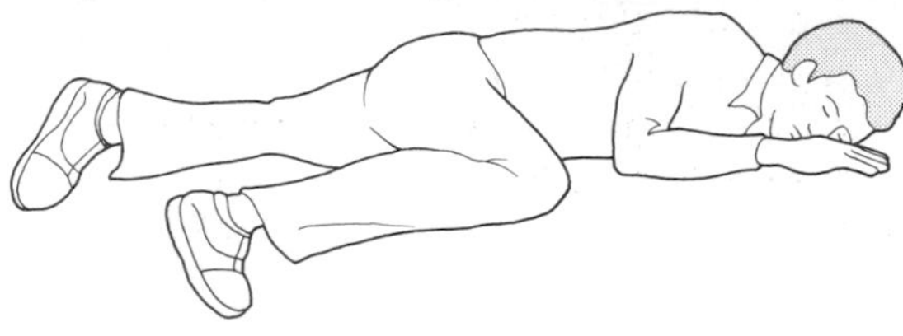

7 If the heart has stopped, it will need to be massaged. Press on the lower half of the breast bone using the heel of one hand and the other on top. Press about once a second five times, then apply artificial respiration again. Repeat until the heart starts beating and breathing is continuous.

First aid kit

A first aid kit should always be kept in the home, to treat both minor and more serious injuries. It should be kept well equipped with the following:

- adhesive plasters (various sizes) for minor cuts and grazes
- prepared wound dressings
- sterilized cotton wool
- gauze bandages in a roll
- triangular bandages for slings
- crepe bandage
- safety pins
- tweezers
- scissors
- roll of surgical tape
- antiseptic solution to clean wounds
- antiseptic cream

A domestic **fire extinguisher** can be kept in a kitchen on the wall in case of fire, and a fire blanket is also a useful addition. A reliable make that complies to British Standards should be purchased.

A fire extinguisher can be kept on the kitchen wall.

Revision questions

1 Study the diagram below and list all the dangers which are apparent in the kitchen illustrated:

2 What should you do if:
a the wires from a plug become frayed?
b the fuse in a plug 'blows' and the piece of equipment fails to work?

3 What are the wiring colours for
a the earth wire in a plug
b the neutral wire in a plug
c the live wire in a plug?

4 What does the British Standards Institution do to protect consumers?

5 What first aid should be applied for the following injuries?
a a deep cut to the arm
b a suspected broken leg
c a scalded hand
d an electric shock
e poisoning from swallowing bleach
f swallowing pills

6 What should a first aid kit contain?

Questions and activities

1 You are moving into the basement flat in a fairly old house. The kitchen is a rather small, square-shaped room, with one window above the sink, one outside door (solid wood) and one inside door. There is only one wall cupboard and a sink unit, both of which need replacing. You are going to decorate and put some more work top space and cupboards into the kitchen, but have only a limited amount of money to spend.

a What would be your priorities when choosing the decorating materials and colour for the kitchen? Give reasons.

b How could you save money when buying kitchen units?

c Draw a plan of your kitchen, showing where you would store the following items:
(Give reasons for your answers.)
cooker
refrigerator
pans
food (dry ingredients)
cutlery
tea towels in use
rubbish bin

d What would be your priorities when choosing flooring for the kitchen? Give reasons.

2 Select three items of kitchen equipment (e.g. something electrical, a saucepan, a knife), study each carefully, and list the following features of each:

a safety features (e.g. guards, insulated handles)

b ease of use (e.g. shape of handle, removal of lid)

c ease of cleaning

Be critical when listing these features, and say how you think they could be improved.

3 What action would you take in the following situations, and how would the law support you?

a You buy a new saucepan, and on first using it, the handle becomes dangerously loose.

b You buy a take-away meal, and notice while you are waiting that there are cats in the kitchen, and food scraps on the floor. The people preparing and serving the food are also wearing rather dirty overalls.

c You buy a packet of biscuits, the label on which states that the packet contains 25 biscuits. You count them, and discover that there are only 23 biscuits in the packet.

4 It is often stated that the kitchen is the most dangerous room in the house. Write an account of the positive ways in which family safety can be ensured in the kitchen.

5 List the reasons why the following materials are suitable for the uses given:

a polythene – made into food containers for the freezer

b wood – made into spoons

c china – made into a flan dish

d stainless steel – made into a sink unit

e heat resistant glass – made into saucepans

f plastics for babies' and children's toys.

Culinary terms

There are many words and expressions used in cookery which refer to a particular process, dish, or method of preparation. The following list gives some of the more commonly used culinary terms.

Aerate
To incorporate air into a mixture (see p. 178).

Au gratin
A food with a browned surface, usually obtained by covering with a sauce (which may contain cheese), sprinkling with breadcrumbs, then grilling.

Bain-marie
A vessel that contains hot water into which other dishes containing sauces, etc., are placed to keep hot without drying out. Also used for cooking foods gently in the oven, e.g. pâtés, egg custards.

Bake blind
To bake a pastry case without a filling. The pastry is normally weighted down with foil or greaseproof paper and baking beans to retain its shape:

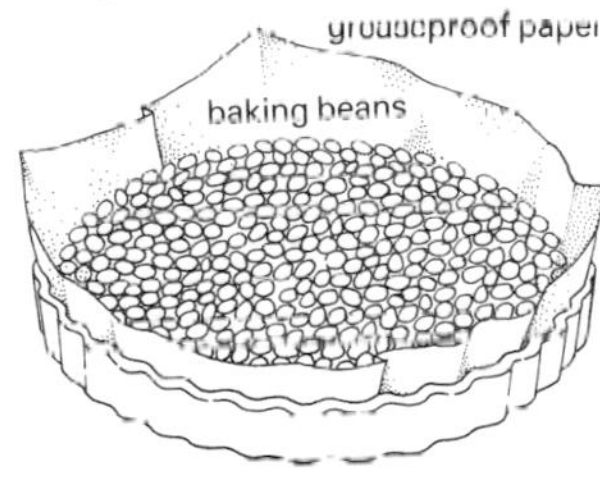

Barbecue
To cook food in the open on a spit or grill over burning charcoal.

Bard
To cover meat, poultry, or game with thin strips of bacon or fat to prevent drying out whilst roasting.

Baste
To spoon fat and juices from the roasting tin over a joint of meat whilst it is being cooked to prevent drying out.

Beat
To incorporate air into a mixture by using a spoon or fork.

Bechamel
A basic white sauce.

Bind
To thicken a sauce or soup with eggs and cream.
May also be used to describe combining ingredients together with an egg for dishes such as rissoles or fish cakes.

Blanch
- a To prepare fruit and vegetables for freezing by placing in boiling water for a set time to inhibit enzyme activity.
- b To put food into cold water and bring to the boil to reduce a strong flavour, to make white, or to reduce saltiness or bitterness.
- c To loosen skins of e.g. tomatoes or nuts for easy removal.

Blanquette
A white stew, usually of poultry, lamb, or veal.

Blend
To combine starch, e.g. in arrowroot or cornflower, with a little liquid and mix to a smooth paste before adding the rest of the liquid.

Bonne femme
A dish cooked simply with a garnish of fresh vegetables or herbs.

Bouillon
A clear soup or stock made with meat or poultry.

Bouquet garni
A mixture of fresh herbs, including thyme, tarragon, sage, and rosemary, tied up in a piece of muslin and added to soups, stews, or stock for flavour; removed after cooking.

Brine
A strong solution of salt and water used for pickling and preservation.

Broil
The American word for grilling.

Buffet
A table on which a variety of cold dishes (sweet and savoury) are served for people to help themselves. Sometimes hot dishes are also served.

Caramelize
To boil a sugar and water syrup to approximately 190°C (380°F) until it changes to a golden brown colour. It then sets when removed from heat and is used for puddings (crème caramel) or for decoration of sweets, e.g. crème brulée.

Carbonnade
A stew made with beef and onions and cooked in beer.

Chasseur
To cook meat or poultry in white wine and mushrooms, e.g. chicken chasseur.

Chaudfroid
A jellied white sauce used to coat cold cooked meat and poultry.

Clarify
To make clear, e.g. by straining through muslin. Clarified butter is made by heating butter gently, and carefully straining off the clear butter on the surface.

Coat
To cover food with a layer of thick liquid, e.g. beaten egg, batter, or egg and breadcrumbs, to protect it when cooking.

Coating sauce
A sauce that will coat the back of a wooden spoon.

Court bouillon
A liquid in which fish is cooked, consisting of water, root vegetables, and wine or vinegar.

Cream
To beat fat and sugar together in order to incorporate air as a raising agent, in cakes and similar mixtures.

Creole
A dish with a rice garnish, peppers and tomatoes.

Croquette
A mixture of meat, eggs, or vegetables coated in egg and breadcrumbs, then fried.

Croutes
Fingers, rounds, or squares of fried bread used as a base for some dishes.

Croutons
Cubes or triangles of toast or fried bread used as a garnish for soups, or dishes with a sauce.

Dice
Small cubes of vegetables or meat.

Dredge
To sprinkle with a powder, e.g. sugar, flour, seasoning.

Dripping
The fat that runs off a roasted joint of meat and may also contain some of the juices.

Emulsion
A mixture of fat and liquid which is prevented from separating out by the presence of another ingredient, e.g. oil and vinegar are emulsified by lecithin in egg yolk.

Entrée
A complete dish, e.g. meat with a vegetable garnish.

Forcemeat
A stuffing that is used for meat, poultry, or vegetables.

Florentine
a A dish containing spinach.
b A biscuit containing fruit and nuts with a chocolate coating.

Garnish
A brightly coloured, edible trimming to a savoury dish (see p. 183).

Girdle
A thick round iron plate with a handle used on top of the cooker to bake girdle scones or Scotch pancakes.

Glacé
a A type of icing (see p. 205).
b Fruit dipped in boiled syrup.

Glaze

a A thin coating of egg yolk or white, or milk, that is brushed onto pastries or scones before baking to give a golden, shiny surface.

b A sugar, jam, or jelly coating brushed onto baked dishes to give a sticky or sweet surface.

Hors d'oeuvres
Small items of food, usually cold, served before a meal to stimulate the appetite.

Infuse
To extract the flavour of e.g. herbs, citrus peel, or spices, by steeping in a hot liquid, and straining to remove the solid matter.

Julienne
Vegetables cut into tiny, neat strips about the size of matchsticks, and used for vegetable dishes or as a garnish.

Jus
Gravy or reduced stock.

Knead
To blend together thoroughly ingredients in a dough, and to distribute yeast evenly throughout a bread dough. The hands are used for this process in two ways:

a Light kneading (for pastry, biscuits, etc.)

b Heavy kneading (for bread)

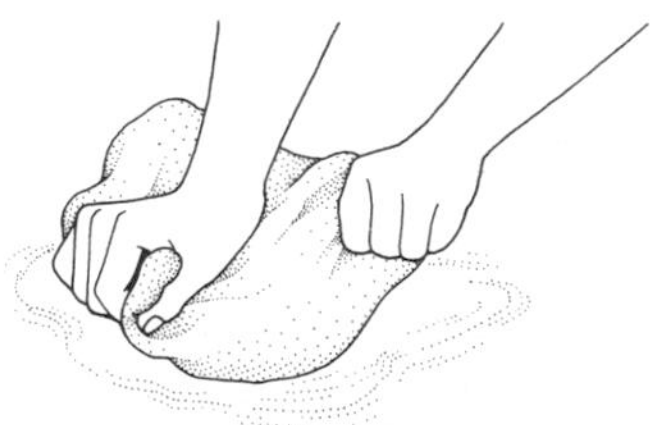

Larding
To thread strips of bacon fat into the surface of a meat joint before roasting. A special larding needle is used.

Liaison
A binding or thickening for sauces, stews, or gravies, e.g. starch, egg yolk, butter, cream.

Macedoine
A mixture of vegetables cut into large dice which may be combined with a white sauce. May also refer to fruit.

Maître d'hôtel butter
Butter mixed with chopped fresh parsley, lemon juice, and seasoning, and cut into small pats to serve with grilled meat or fish.

Marinade
To cover raw meat or fish with a liquid containing wine, oil, vinegar, vegetables, herbs, and spices for several hours before cooking in order to tenderize the muscle fibres. The liquid may or may not be used to cook the meat or fish.

Mirepoix
A mixture of diced vegetables, herbs, and bacon used as the base for braising meat (see p. 152).

Mocha
Indicates that coffee has been used as a flavouring.

Mornay, à la
Vegetables, fish, eggs, etc., coated in a cheese sauce and grilled.

Niçoise
A fish or vegetable dish garnished with tomatoes, garlic, olives, and anchovies.

Panada
A thick roux sauce used to thicken croquettes, stuffings, etc.

Par-boil
To boil until partly cooked (see p. 150).

Petits fours
Small fancy pastries, cakes, and biscuits.

Pilaff
A dish of rice cooked in stock until all the liquid is absorbed.

Pit
To remove the stone of a fruit, e.g. a cherry.

Ragout
A stew made with equal-sized pieces of meat which are first fried, then cooked in stock.

Ramekin
A small oven-proof dish used for individual savoury dishes.

Raspings
Very fine breadcrumbs made from dried bread and used for au gratin dishes, etc.

Ratatouille
A dish of mixed vegetables (tomatoes, aubergines, courgettes) cooked to a soft consistency in oil.

Réchauffé
Reheated cooked food (see p. 177).

Reduce
To evaporate water in a liquid and therefore reduce its volume.

Render
To melt down fat in the oven to obtain fat without meat juices or tissue.

Rissole
A mixture of cooked meat, or fish and vegetable, e.g. potato, bound together and fried.

Roux
A sauce made by cooking equal quantities of fat and flour together, then adding a liquid and heating until thickened (see pp. 224–5).

Sauté
To toss food in a small amount of fat over a low heat, in a pan with the lid on, until the fat is absorbed.

Scald
To heat a liquid to just below boiling point.

Shortening
Any fat used to make cakes, pastries or biscuits.

Simmer
To cook food at just below boiling point so that only a few bubbles rise to the surface occasionally.

Stock
A liquid in which bones, meat, or vegetables have been boiled for some time, which contains some of the flavour and extractives and can be used for soups, stews, etc.

Vinaigrette
A dressing for salads made with oil, vinegar, and spices.

Whisk
To beat air into a mixture rapidly by means of a hand-operated whisk or fork, or an electric whisk.

Zest
The thin outer skin of citrus fruits which contains well-flavoured oils. Used for cakes, sauces, etc.

Weights

It is difficult and impractical to convert imperial weights into metric weights exactly, therefore 25 g is used as equivalent to 1 oz (exact conversion: 1 oz = 28·35 g). As this conversion is slightly less than the imperial measurements, it is necessary to adjust the quantities of ingredients used above 100 g, by rounding them up to the nearest 25 g, as shown in the chart below.

Imperial oz	**Metric** g	
	practical conversion	exact conversion
1	25	28·35
2	50	56·70
3	75	85·05
4 (¼ lb)	100	113·40
5	150	141·75
6	175	170·10
7	200	198·45
8 (½ lb)	225	226·80
9	250	255·15
10	275	283·50
11	300	311·85
12 (¾ lb)	350	340·19
13	375	368·54
14	400	396·89
15	425	425·24
16 (1 lb)	450	453·59

Liquid measures

As with weights, exact conversions from fluid ounces to millilitres are impractical, therefore the following equivalents are used:

Imperial fl oz	**Metric** ml	
	practical conversion	exact conversion
1	25	28·41
2	50	56·83
3	75	85·24
4	100	113·65
5 (¼ pint)	150	142·07
10 (½ pint)	275	284·13
15 (¾ pint)	425	426·20
20 (1 pint)	575	568·26

Oven temperatures

	Uses	**Gas**	**°C**	**°F**
very cool	warming plates	¼	110	225
	keeping food hot	½	120	250
cool	egg custard milk puddings	1	140	275
cool	rich fruit cakes braising	2	150	300
moderate	shortbread meat loaves stews, casseroles	3	160	325
moderate	gingerbread fish	4	180	350
fairly hot	Victoria sandwich rubbed-in cakes	5	190	375
fairly hot	choux pastry Swiss roll baked soufflés	6	200	400
hot	roasting flaky pastry batters	7	220	425
very hot	bread scones	8	230	450
very hot	small puff pastry items browning of foods	9	240	475

Useful addresses for further information

British Food Information Service
301–344 Market Towers
New Covent Garden Market
London
SW8 5NQ

British Standards Institution
2 Park Street
London
W1A 2BS

Consumers' Association
14 Buckingham Street
London
WC2N 6DS

Food Research Institute
Agricultural Research Council
Colney Lane
Norwich
NR4 7UA

Health Education Authority
Hamilton House
Mabledon Place
London
WC1H 9TX

British Egg Information Service
Bury House
125–128 Cromwell Road
London
SW7 4ET

Canned Food Information Centre
22 Greencoat Place
London
SW1P 1EG

Flour Advisory Bureau
21 Arlington Street
London
SE1A 1RN

British Meat
P O Box 44
Winter Hill House
Snowden Drive
Milton Keynes
MK6 1AX

National Dairy Council
5–7 John Princes Street
London
W1M 0AP

Fresh Fruit and Vegetable Education Service
Bury House
126–128 Cromwell Road
London
SW7 4EJ

Sea Fish Industry Authority
Sea Fisheries House
10 Young Street
Edinburgh
EH2 4JQ

Vegetarian Society of the UK
Parkdale
Dunham Road
Altrincham
Cheshire
WA14 4Q9

The London Food Commission
88 Old Street
London
EC1V 9AR

Index